Best Practices in Logistic Regression

Best Practices in
Logistic Regression

Jason W. Osborne
University of Louisville

Los Angeles | London | New Delhi
Singapore | Washington DC

Los Angeles | London | New Delhi
Singapore | Washington DC

FOR INFORMATION:

SAGE Publications, Inc.
2455 Teller Road
Thousand Oaks, California 91320
E-mail: order@sagepub.com

SAGE Publications Ltd.
1 Oliver's Yard
55 City Road
London EC1Y 1SP
United Kingdom

SAGE Publications India Pvt. Ltd.
B 1/I 1 Mohan Cooperative Industrial Area
Mathura Road, New Delhi 110 044
India

SAGE Publications Asia-Pacific Pte. Ltd.
3 Church Street
#10-04 Samsung Hub
Singapore 049483

Acquisitions Editor: Vicki Knight
Assistant Editor: Katie Guarino
Editorial Assistant: Jessica Miller
Production Editor: Stephanie Palermini
Copy Editor: Amy Rosenstein
Typesetter: C&M Digitals (P) Ltd.
Proofreader: Sally Jaskold
Indexer: Michael Ferreira
Cover Designer: Anupama Krishnan
Marketing Manager: Nicole Elliott

Printed in the United States of America

Library of Congress Cataloging-in-Publication Data

Osborne, Jason W., author.

Best practices in logistic regression / Jason W. Osborne, University of Louisville.

pages cm
Includes bibliographical references and index.

ISBN 978-1-4522-4479-2 (pbk. : acid-free paper)
ISBN 978-1-4833-1209-5 (web PDF) 1. Logistic regression analysis. I. Title.

QA278.2.O83 2015
519.5'36—dc23   2013037122

This book is printed on acid-free paper.

SFI label applies to text stock

14 15 16 17 18 10 9 8 7 6 5 4 3 2 1

Brief Contents

Detailed Contents

Preface

"Just what exactly is it that you are graphing? What is the Y axis?"

Twenty years ago I finished my master's degree in social psychology and took a position at a nearby community college. I needed a break before pursuing my Ph.D. Another member of the psychology faculty there at Niagara County Community College, Sue Bland, was also working with faculty from the University of Buffalo Department of Epidemiology on some projects. Knowing I was very much into research and statistics, she encouraged me to talk with them about completing my doctorate there. One conversation let to another, and I ended up not too long after taking graduate courses in epidemiology and also working as a statistician in the Department of Family Medicine at Buffalo. I enjoyed working with the researchers there and also enjoyed learning a whole new area of statistical methods. Although I had taken countless graduate statistics courses in the social sciences, I am not sure I had ever heard of logistic regression, survival analysis, or even an odds ratio until that point. I eventually chose to finish my doctorate in educational psychology, but I worked with the family medicine researchers for several years and after that, I did a good deal of consulting with scholars in nursing and other areas of health sciences.

In 1998, I took my first faculty position in educational psychology at the University of Oklahoma and found myself concerned that nobody else in any area of social sciences I talked with seemed to have heard of logistic regression. Of course, it was not surprising, as I had not either until I stepped outside the silo of psychology. But what a tragedy! I had long been fascinated by the beauty and power of ordinary least squares regression, and having the sister technique of logistic regression made me feel as though I could take on almost any research problem the world had to throw at me—especially when those techniques were combined with multilevel modeling.

So when appropriate, I used logistic regression, but often found the results baffled my social science audiences—whether journal readers or conference attendees. In particular, one gentleman in an educational research conference asked the question I started this preface with. My colleague Meg Blanchard and I were presenting a logistic regression interaction effect exploring whether teachers became more likely to incorporate particular teaching techniques in their practice, and I had not done a good job communicating some of the nuances of logistic regression to the audience. What frustrated me then was my inability to articulate exactly what it was that I was graphing. Of course it was an interaction effect, and the metric was logit. But that meant nothing to the audience, and although I knew a good deal about logistic regression, I was unable to articulate anything satisfactory.

One of the things I always tell my doctoral students is that they do not really know something, and are not really ready to present their research, until they can explain it clearly to a nontechnical audience. I always think of my parents, now 71, who are very well educated and smart but not trained in statistics. I feel as though I am ready to publish or present an idea if I can explain it to them in a way that they will understand the basic concepts (and outcomes, if applicable). I had failed this test, and I do not like failing tests. This book on logistic regression thus became the next challenge I wanted to tackle. I wanted to present logistic regression in a way that would make it accessible to advanced students, seasoned researchers, and anyone else who might be open to the majesty of this quirky technique. My goal was to present logistic regression conceptually, with minimal formulae or mathematics, with pedagogical examples that carried throughout the book, and in a manner that also proposed and demonstrated some best practices along the way. After 20 years of fiddling with logistic regression, my goal with this book was to challenge myself to make it accessible—and indispensable—to my colleagues in the social sciences, as it had become for me.

And thus, this book presents logistic regression how I wish I had learned it—in a logical sequence that slowly builds from simple conceptual understanding to more complex (and more exciting) applications, like polytomous dependent variables, curvilinear effects, and interactions. In each chapter, my goal was to present one or two examples using real data from different disciplines (usually one from the social sciences and one from the medical sciences) to mentor readers in how to interpret output from common statistical software (SPSS, SAS),[1] and even how to write up results from

---

[1]Perhaps examples using R software will make it into the next edition!

select analyses accurately and concisely for publication. Almost every chapter has activities that readers can explore to enhance mastery, as well as results that I obtained from performing these activities, so readers can check their results against mine.[2] Thus, whether students or researchers are working individually or using this book as a text in a class, my goal was to provide the scaffolding and support necessary for them to explore logistic regression in (what I hope is) a stimulating, engaging, and pedagogically useful way.

Finally, be sure to visit the book's website (www.sagepub.com/osbornebplr), where you can download data sets that allow you to enhance your expertise with logistic regression. I am also eager to hear from readers, so do not hesitate to contact me via e-mail at jason@jwosborne.com.

Happy regressing!

---

[2]My wife would like me at this point to remind readers that I am not *always* right, even when doing statistical analyses. Fair enough. But a whole class of my smart doctoral students also replicated the results I present in most chapters, so odds are the results might be helpful to readers. It is good to have someone at home to keep one humble, I am told.

Acknowledgments

My family is always a part of my writing, whether they desire to be or not. My parents have been stalwart and enthusiastic supporters throughout my career, from the seemingly endless years of graduate school through the present. Their 20-plus years of support are the *sine qua non* of my career to this point. Thank you, Mom and Dad, for all the support through the ups and downs, for believing in me when even I had trouble believing in myself, for celebrating the milestones with me, for everything.

My wife has always managed to appear interested and enthusiastic when I rambled on about whatever nerdy topic was fascinating me at any particular moment. Thank you, Sherri, for everything.

My children, Collin, Andrew, and Olivia (in order of appearance), continually inspire me to try to make the world a little better place in whatever way I am able. My hope is that someday they will benefit from someone somewhere doing slightly better science through using best practices in quantitative methods. Thanks to each one of you for everything.

I also need to thank Dr. LaShauna Dean-Nganga for assistance in a few aspects of this book, including assistance in putting together some of the graphs from Chapter 10. Thanks are also due to my students from Old Dominion University (Blake Bent, Nathan Bjornberg, Robert Carlisle, Katelyn Cavenaugh, Gabrielle D'Lima, Jennifer Giblin, Chris Herbert, Kellie Kennedy, Robert Milletich, Elaine Murphy, Gina Polychronopolis, and Julia Zaharieva) who allowed me to pilot-test the book as I taught their class. They frequently gave insightful feedback and suggestions, and made this book a better product in too many ways to count.

Special thanks go to the reviewers who gave valuable feedback at all stages of the development of this book, from proposal to final draft. Reviewers are the cornerstone on which scholarly research depends and yet are routinely underappreciated. So thank you to: Yang Cao, University of North Carolina at Charlotte; Wing Yi Chan, Ph.D., Georgia State University; Robert T. Greenbaum, John Glenn School of Public Affairs, xxii ◆ BEST PRACTICES IN LOGISTIC REGRESSION

The Ohio State University; Professor David Han, University of Texas at San Antonio; Ting Jiang, Metropolitan State University of Denver; Michael Howell-Moroney, University of Alabama at Birmingham; Shanta Pandey, Washington University in St. Louis; Dr. Chuck W. Peek, Department of Sociology and Criminology & Law, University of Florida; Daniel Pontzer, Department of Criminology and Criminal Justice, University of North Florida; P. Neal Ritchey, University of Cincinnati; Daoqin Tong, University of Arizona; Frank B. Underwood, University of Evansville; Denna L. Wheeler, Oklahoma State University Center for Health Sciences; and Yoosik Youm, Yonsei University, South Korea. I appreciate the many hours each of you spent reading my work, and this book is markedly better specifically because of those efforts.

Thanks finally to all the folks at SAGE who have been such a pleasure to work with for the past eight years, especially Vicki Knight. Although they clearly have questionable taste in repeatedly allowing me to propose and publish books with them, they have allowed me to be myself and to have a good deal of fun writing these three books. I look forward to the next one.

About the Author

Jason W. Osborne, Ph.D., is Professor and Department Chair in the Department of Educational and Counseling Psychology, Counseling, and College Student Personnel in the College of Education and Human Development at the University of Louisville, in Louisville, Kentucky. This is his third book on best practices in statistical research methods, and he is author of more than 60 peer-reviewed journal articles. Aside from statistics and research methods, he has research interests related to identification with academics and motivation to achieve and stereotype threat. His research has been cited more than 5,100 times, according to citation analytics. He is the proud father of three children, none of whom show any overt passion for statistics (yet!).

1

A CONCEPTUAL INTRODUCTION TO BIVARIATE LOGISTIC REGRESSION

So you want to research something really interesting?

Let's say you want to research something interesting and important, like why students drop out of school before completing their degree, why people choose to use illicit drugs, what predicts whether an individual will die from a particular cause, whether a citizen will vote, or whether a consumer will purchase a particular type of product.

How would you do it? To be sure, researchers have been examining these types of outcomes for as long as curious people have been using scientific methods. But if they are not using logistic or probit regression (or similar procedure), odds[1] are they are not getting the most from their data.

Throughout the book, I will use simple, intuitive examples from a range of disciplines to demonstrate important aspects of logistic regression. In addition, example data sets will be available on the book's website so that readers can further enrich their logistic regression experience!

What is logistic regression, the oddly named and often underappreciated type of regression that many researchers in the social sciences have rarely, if ever, heard of? Decades ago, I took statistics courses from people

---

[1]Pun completely intended.

who I think were (or still are) some of the smartest and best teachers and scholars of statistics I have ever met. Despite having taken courses in regression models, ANOVA, multivariate statistics, hierarchical linear modeling, structural equation modeling, and psychometrics, I found that logistic regression was not covered in psychology and many social sciences disciplines back then. Indeed, many of the classic, beloved textbooks I used as a graduate student and as an assistant professor (such as the fabulous texts on regression by Pedhazur and Cohen and Cohen, and the excellent multivariate text by Tabachnick and Fidel) failed to cover the issue back then.[2] Today most texts covering regression at the graduate level give at least a cursory introduction to the topic, and the latest revisions of the classic texts I mention above now also introduce readers to the topic.

In fact, had I not by quirk of fate ended up working as a statistician and research associate in a medical school for several years, taking epidemiology courses and working with health science researchers, I would probably not have been exposed to logistic regression in any meaningful way. Logistic regression, I discovered, is widely used outside the particular niche of the social sciences I was trained in. Researchers in the health sciences (medicine, health care, nursing, epidemiology, etc.) have been using logistic (and probit) regression and other precursors for a very long time. Unfortunately, because it is a quirky creature, researchers often avoid, misuse, or misinterpret the results of these analyses, even in top, peer-reviewed journals where logistic regression is common (Davies, Crombie, & Tavakoli, 1998; Holcomb, Chaiworapongsa, Luke, & Burgdorf, 2001).

So why do we need a whole book dedicated to the exciting world of logistic regression when most texts cover the topic? It is a creature separate and unique unto itself, complex and maddening and amazingly valuable—when done right. Just as many books focus on analysis of regression (ANOVA), ordinary least squares (OLS) regression, factor analysis, multivariate statistics, structural equation modeling, hierarchical linear modeling, and the like, my years of experience using and teaching logistic regression to budding young social scientists leaves me believing this is a book that needs to be written. Logistic regression is different enough from OLS regression to warrant its own treatise. As you will see in coming chapters, while there are conceptual and procedural similarities between logistic and

---

[2]Of course, that was a long time ago. We calculated statistics by scratching on clay tablets with styli by candlelight and walked uphill, in the snow, both ways to get to class. Well, the second part at least is true. It was Buffalo back before climate change . . . everything was covered with snow year-round and everything was, indeed, uphill no matter what direction you were going. Or so it seemed with the wind. But I digress. The point is that it was just a really long time ago.

OLS regression, and to other procedures such as discriminant function analysis (DFA), the mathematics "under the hood" are different, the types of questions one can answer with logistic regression are a bit different, and there are interesting peculiarities in how one should interpret the results.

In other words, it is not the case that logistic regression is just multiple regression with a binary dependent variable. Well, yes, it is that, on the surface, and conceptually. But it is much more. The more I use it, and the more I teach it, and the more I try to dig into what exactly those numbers mean and how to interpret them, the more I have discovered that this stuff can be seriously confusing, and complex, interesting, and powerful. And really fun.

To be clear, it is in no way just multiple (OLS) regression with a binary outcome. My goal in this book is to explore the fun things researchers can do with logistic regression, to explicate and simplify the confounding complexities of understanding what logistic regression is, and to provide evidence-based guidance as to what I think are best practices in performing logistic regression.

WHAT IS ORDINARY LEAST SQUARES REGRESSION AND ♦ HOW IS LOGISTIC REGRESSION DIFFERENT?

We will get into the mathematics of how logistic regression works in subsequent chapters. Right now, there are a few conceptual similarities and differences that we can address to orient the reader who is not deeply familiar with the two types of analyses. First, let's remember that OLS regression—what we will often call linear regression or multiple regression—is a solid and very useful statistical technique that I have frequently used since the late 1980s. This contrasting is in no way attempting to set up logistic regression as superior to OLS regression (and certainly not vice versa). Just like I cannot say a hammer is a favored tool over a drill, I cannot give preference to one regression technique over another. They both serve different purposes, and they both belong in a hallowed place inside the researcher's toolbox.

The primary conceptual difference between OLS and logistic regression is that in logistic regression, the types of questions we ask involve a dichotomous (or categorical) dependent variable (DV), such as whether a student received a diploma or not. In OLS regression, the DVs are assumed to be continuous in nature.[3] Dichotomous DVs are an egregious

---

[3]Although, in practice, measurement in OLS regression is not always strictly continuous (or even interval).

violation of the assumptions of OLS regression and therefore not appropriate. Without logistic regression, a researcher with a binary or categorical outcome is left in a bit of a pickle. How is one to study the predictors of illness if in fact we cannot actually model how variables predict an illness?

Over the years, I have seen kludgy attempts such as using *t*-tests (or ANOVA) to explore where groups differ on multiple variables in an attempt to build theory or understanding. For example, one could look at differences between people who contract a disease and those who do not across variables such as age, race/ethnicity, education, body mass index (BMI), smoking and drinking habits, participation in various activities, and so on. Perhaps we would see a significant difference between the two groups in BMI and number of drinks per week on average. Does that mean we can assume that those variables might be causally related to having this illness? Definitely not, and further, it might also be the case that neither of these variables is really predictive of the illness at all. Being overweight and drinking a certain number of drinks might be related to living in a certain segment of society, which may in turn be related to health habits such as eating fresh fruits and vegetables (or not) and exercising, and stress levels, and commute times, and exposure to workplace toxins, which might in fact be related to the actual causes of the illness.

No disrespect to all those going before me who have done this exact type of analysis—historically, there were few other viable options (in addition, prior to large-scale statistical computing, logistic regression was probably too complex to be performed by the majority of researchers). But let's think for a minute about this process. There are many drawbacks to the approach I just mentioned. One issue is that researchers can have issues with power if they adjust for Type I error rates that multiple univariate analyses require (or worse, they might fail to do so). In addition, using this group-differences approach, researchers cannot take into account how variables of interest covary. This issue is similar to performing an array of simple correlations rather than a multiple regression. To be sure, you can glean some insight into the various relationships among variables, but at the end of the day, it is difficult to figure out which variables are the *strongest* or most important predictors of a phenomenon unless you model them in a multiple regression (or path analysis or structural equation modeling) type of environment.

Perhaps more troubling (to my mind) is the fact that this analytic strategy prevents the examination of interactions, which are often the most interesting findings we can come across. Let us imagine that we find sex differences[4] between those who graduate and those who do not, and differences in household income between those who graduate and those who do not. That might be interesting, but what if in reality there is an interaction between the sex of the student and family income in predicting graduation or dropout rates? What if boys are much more likely than girls to drop out in more affluent families, and girls are more likely to drop out in more impoverished families? That finding might have important policy and practice implications, but we are unable to test for that sort of interaction using the method of analysis described above. Logistic regression (like OLS regression) models variables in such a way that we get the unique effect of the variables, controlling for all other variables in the equation. Thus, we get a more sophisticated and nuanced look at what variables are uniquely predictive (or related to) the outcome of interest.

I have also seen aggregation used as a strategy. Instead of looking at individual characteristics and individual outcomes, researchers might aggregate to a classroom or school level. So then researchers might think they have a continuous variable (0–100% graduation rate for a school) as a function of the percent of boys or girls in a school and the average family income. In my opinion, this does tremendous disservice to the data, losing information and leading to potentially misleading results. In fact, it changes the question substantially from "what variables contribute to student completion" to "what school environment variables contribute to school completion rates." Further, the predictor variables change from, say, sex of the student to percent of students who are male or female, and from race of student to percent of students who identify as a particular race, from family socioeconomic status (SES) to average SES within the school. These are fundamentally different variables, and, thus, analyses using these strategies answer a fundamentally different question. Furthermore, in my own explorations, I have seen aggregation lead to wildly overestimated effect sizes—double that of the appropriate analysis and more. Thus, aggregation changes the nature of the question, the nature of the variables, and can lead to inappropriate overestimation of effect sizes and variance accounted for.

---

[4]Readers may be more used to reading "gender differences" rather than "sex differences"—an example of American Psychological Association style and language use betraying the meaning of words—similar to the use of "negative reinforcement" as a synonym for punishment when in fact it is not at all. I will use the term "sex" in this book to refer to physical or biological sex—maleness or femaleness. Gender, conversely, refers to masculinity or femininity of behavior or psychology. The two concepts are not synonyms, and it does harm to the concepts to conflate them (Mead, 1935; Oakley, 1972). Please write your political leaders and urge them to take action to stop this injustice!

I am sure some of you have also wondered why we cannot just compute an OLS regression equation with a binary outcome as the DV. This is a real procedure often discussed in older regression texts and is referred to as the *linear probability model,* but it is not the same as a probit model (which I will cover later). This would carry the advantages of being able to simultaneously estimate the unique effects of several independent variables (IVs) and examine relative importance in predicting the outcome, unlike the approach described above. In fact, the statistical software you use will perform this analysis if you tell it to. But there are issues with this approach. First, predicted scores (which are supposed to be predicted probabilities) can range outside the acceptable 0.00–1.00 range. Second, residuals can only be 0, −1, or 1. Thus, they are neither normally distributed nor homoscedastic. In short, and without getting into too much detail, this simply is not an appropriate analysis (Cohen, Cohen, West, & Aiken, 2002). To illustrate this issue, I used a small subset of data from the National Education Longitudinal Study of 1988 (Ingels, 1994) to predict student completion (not dropping out) from some simple variables such as race, student grade point average, and student behavior problems. We will get back to this example data set later. For now, you can see in Figure 1.1 that performing this analysis in an OLS framework produced the expected violation of assumptions. For example, the residuals[5] are not close to being normally distributed.

And thus, we come to conceptual similarities between OLS and logistic regression. Procedurally, both OLS and logistic regression are set up with a single DV and one or more IVs. Both allow us to simultaneously assess the unique effects of multiple predictor IVs (and their interactions or curvilinear components, if desired), and both allow examination of residuals for purposes of screening data for outliers, follow-up analyses, or testing of assumptions. Both can perform simultaneous entry, hierarchical or block-wise entry (groups of IVs entered at one time), and various stepwise procedures.[6] And with both, we have the ability to assess a group of IVs to

---

[5]What is a residual? A residual is many things to many people—an error of estimation, error variance, unexplained variance, the unique person effect, the distance from the regression line to the data point, $Y - \hat{Y}$ . . . All this is to say that however you interpret it, functionally it is the difference between the predicted value for an individual—their score predicted by the regression line equation—and their actual score.

[6]Many of you reading this will have been trained to have visceral negative reactions to stepwise procedures, which is ironic as just a generation earlier, they were heralded as important tools. I am of the mind that stepwise procedures have their place in the pantheon of statistical tools and that we should be knowledgeable of them and use them *when appropriate.* For most of you reading this, the answer to when these procedures are appropriate is "almost never." Indeed, a full discussion of stepwise procedures is beyond the scope of this book, but interested readers can refer to standard references for regression such as Cohen et al. (2002) and Pedhazur (1997).

Figure 1.1 Residuals From an OLS Analysis With Binary Outcome

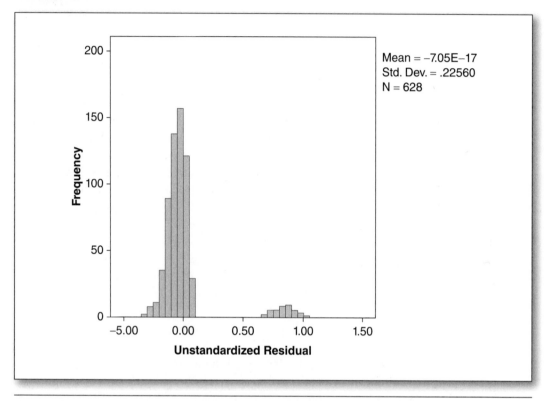

Mean = –7.05E–17
Std. Dev. = .22560
N = 628

Data Source: National Education Longitudinal Study of 1988 (NELS88), National Center for Educational Statistics (http://nces.ed.gov/surveys/nels88/).

determine which predictor is the strongest unique predictor of a particular outcome and to answer many of the types of questions that have made regression a valuable tool in quantitative methods.

OLS Regression—A Deeper Conceptual Look

Why do we call regression "ordinary least squares regression"? The ordinary least squares part refers to both the goal of the procedure and how it is calculated—the estimation method. The goal for OLS regression is to fit a straight line to the bivariate (or multivariate) scatterplot such that the line fits the data in the best way possible. Obvious, right? We would rarely want our regression line to be an inferior or misleading fit. So we have a "line of best fit" that we use as a single descriptor of the entirety of the data we are analyzing. But how does that line get placed? Well, decades ago when statisticians and mathematicians were inventing this procedure, the obvious choice to them was to place the line such that the residuals were minimized. This goal of minimizing residuals—minimizing the distance between the data and the line of best fit—is intuitive and appealing in many ways. If assumptions are met and the line is fit well, most regression analyses will produce as many negative residuals as positive residuals (because as many data points will be below the line as above the line), and they generally sum to 0.00 or some value reasonably close. To get around this issue, statisticians use the simple step of squaring each residual and then summing them to get a positive value called the "sum of squares." This removes the issue of negative and positive residuals and gets closer to the idea of raw distance, as $-2^2 = 4$ and $2^2 = 4$. Research has shown that when assumptions are met in OLS regression that (a) the estimates produced are unbiased estimates of true regression properties within the population, (b) the standard errors decrease as sample size increases, and (c) they are efficient, meaning that no other method of estimation will produce smaller standard errors (if you are interested in more on the technicalities of OLS estimation, an excellent introduction is contained in Cohen et al., 2002).

Note particularly the phrase above "when assumptions are met." Too often in research we do not know if assumptions have been met because authors do not report having tested them. In fact, I wrote an entire book on why cleaning data and testing assumptions is so important (Osborne, 2012), and regression texts such as Cohen et al. (2002) clearly make the point that when assumptions are not met (e.g., the presence of even a single extreme outlier), bad things can happen to analyses (see particularly Cohen et al., 2002, Chapter 10, or Osborne, 2012—a most excellent book, in my opinion). More on assumptions in a few paragraphs.

Maximum Likelihood Estimation—A Gentle but Deeper Look

Maximum likelihood estimation is one of those developments in statistics that has spread primarily thanks to widespread access to statistical computing. Unlike OLS estimation, which is based on set equations that researchers or software can use to arrive at a calculated solution, maximum likelihood estimation is an *iterative* procedure. In other words, the software selects starting values for coefficients, calculates a solution, and compares it with a criterion. If the solution and the criterion are farther apart than desired, new values are attempted and a new solution is found. Again, the new solution is examined and if found lacking, again is adjusted and a third solution is attempted. Hopefully, with each iteration, the solution approaches the goals of the algorithm. At some point, the last iteration will be accepted as the final estimation of effects, and that is what the researcher will see in the output. You can imagine how computationally intensive this procedure is and why it was not widely used until computing power became widely available.

Without getting into too many technical details, the goal of maximum likelihood estimation (MLE) is to find a solution that provides intercepts and slopes for predictor variables that *maximizes* the *likelihood* of individuals having scores on the dependent variable (Y) given their scores on the predictor variables (X_1, X_2, etc.). In other words, the algorithms are maximizing the likelihood that we would obtain the sample—the data, the observed scores—given the model and parameters being estimated. We have observed scores on variables for individuals within the sample that arose from some real dynamic or relationship within the population. The MLE algorithm attempts to provide a model that maximizes the likelihood of producing the results observed. In essence, both OLS and MLE are attempting to summarize the observed data. The two procedures are merely using different mathematical techniques to get to that goal.

Maximum likelihood estimation is, in my mind, similar to the somewhat counterintuitive notion of hypothesis testing and p values. The actual interpretation of a p value is the probability of obtaining the observed data if in fact the null hypothesis (H_0) is true in the population.[7] So conceptually, what MLE is trying to do is to estimate the various parameters (slopes and intercepts) that best model (or re-create) the observed data. Thus, if we have a population wherein the height of women and their shoe sizes are strongly positively related (as evidenced by the observed data), MLE will provide the coefficients and slopes that maximize the likelihood of obtaining the observed sample that contains the observed relationship between height and shoe size. MLE will repeatedly attempt estimations based on slightly different coefficients until the fit with the observed data is as good as can be—in other words, that successive iterations fail to improve the fit by an appreciable amount.

---

[7]It is not, contrary to popular belief, the probability of being wrong, the probability of getting the observed results by random chance, etc. It is also not exactly what we really want to test—which is the probability that our alternative hypothesis (H_a) is true.

◆ DIFFERENCES AND SIMILARITIES IN ASSUMPTIONS BETWEEN OLS AND LOGISTIC REGRESSION

Distributional Assumptions

Because MLE has different mathematical estimation than OLS, MLE has some different assumptions than OLS. OLS regression is a parametric technique, meaning that it requires assumptions about the distribution of the data in order to be effective (these are discussed in most regression texts, but a particularly good reference is Cohen et al., 2002; see also Osborne & Waters, 2002). Commonly used statistical tests such as ANOVA and OLS regression assume that the data come from populations that are normally distributed or that have normal distributions of residuals (errors). In contrast, because of the different estimation procedures, logistic regression is a *nonparametric* technique, meaning it does not require any particular distributional assumptions.

Linearity of the Relationship

Another assumption of OLS regression is often referred to as the "assumption of linearity." The general assumption is that the correct form of the relationship is being modeled, but in the case of OLS regression and many other analyses, the assumption is that there is a linear relationship between the DV and the IV. A similar generalization to planes and hyper-dimensional relationships is in effect for multiple regression with 2 or more IVs, but thinking too deeply about hyperdimensional generalizations of linearity gives me a bit of a headache, so I tend to stick to the 2- or 3-dimensional examples. Interestingly, I have often found relationships that are curvilinear in nature, not only in the social sciences but also in health sciences. Immediate examples that come to mind can include the relationship between arousal (i.e., stress) and performance (Loftus, Loftus, & Ketcham, 1992; Sullivan & Bhagat, 1992; Yegiyan & Lang, 2010),[8] student achievement growth curves (Francis, Schatschneider, & Carlson, 2000; Rescorla & Rosenthal, 2004), grade point average and employment in high school students (Quirk, Keith, & Quirk, 2001), dose-response relationships

---

[8]This is often attributed to Yerkes-Dodson (Yerkes & Dodson, 1908), or somewhat inaccurately referred to (sometimes by me personally) as an anxiety-performance curve. See Teigen (1994) for a historical overview of this large group of theories and studies.

(Davis & Svendsgaard, 1990), and age and life satisfaction (Mroczek & Spiro III, 2005).

For example, as Francis et al. (2000) showed, the general pattern for reaching achievement growth over time is curvilinear. In Figure 1.2, I present a growth curve modeled from their published data.

When this assumption of linearity is violated, two things happen. First, really interesting findings are overlooked, and second, OLS regression will underestimate (and mischaracterize) the true nature of the relationship. Fortunately, there are increasingly easy ways to incorporate tests for curvilinear effects as statistical software packages begin to implement curvilinear regression options.

Logistic regression is, by nature, nonlinear, as we will discuss in more detail in subsequent chapters. Specifically, the way that logistic regression converts a dichotomous or categorical variable to a dependent variable that

| **Figure 1.2** | Curvilinear Relationship Between Student Age and Reading Achievement Test Scores |

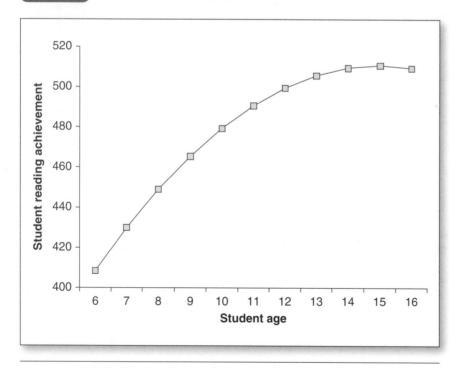

Data Source: Francis, D., Schatschneider, C., & Carlson, C. (2000). Introduction to individual growth curve analysis. In D. Drotar (Ed.), *Handbook of research in pediatric and clinical child psychology* (pp. 51–73). New York, NY: Kluwer/Plenum.

can be predicted from other binary, categorical, or continuous variables involves a nonlinear transformation. For now, envision a dependent variable that is an S-shaped curve representing the probability that an individual will be in one group or the other (like the one in Figure 1.3). Don't worry about the details of how the DV is created in logistic regression for now—we will have fun exploring that more thoroughly later. I find it interesting that although the basic character of logistic regression—the logit transformation—is curvilinear, there is a clear assumption of linearity as well. Specifically, there is an assumption that there is a linear relationship between IVs and the DV—that IVs are "linear on the logit."[9] Similar to when we create models in OLS regression, we can model relationships that are

Figure 1.3 Standard Logistic Sigmoid Function

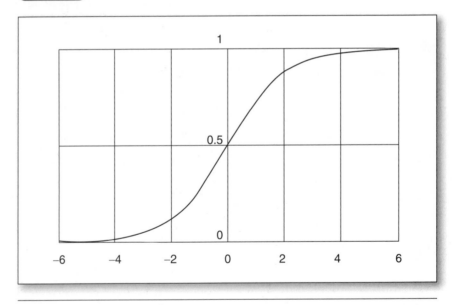

Source: Wikipedia (http://upload.wikimedia.org/wikipedia/commons/thumb/8/88/Logistic-curve.svg/320px-Logistic-curve.svg.png).

"nonlinear on the logit" easily, something we will explore in more depth in Chapter 7.

Note that "nonlinearity" includes the concept of interactions, where the effects of one variable depend on the effect of a second variable. For

[9]This is also a great phrase to drop casually into conversations. Try it and watch your social capital climb!

Figure 1.4 Relationship of School Size and Student Sex Predicting Math Achievement Test Score

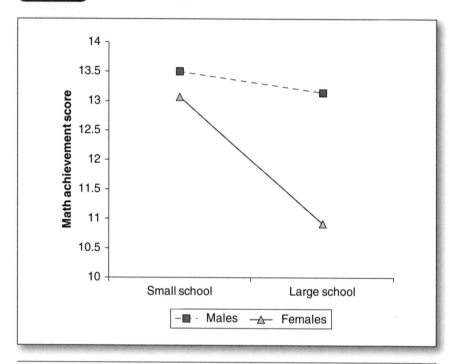

Data source: High School and Beyond data (http://nces.ed.gov/pubsearch/getpubcats.asp?sid=022).

example, there has been a lot of discussion about sex differences in math achievement test scores. This was a particular issue back in the 1980s when the National Center for Educational Statistics began their High School and Beyond study of high school students (information and data from HS&B available at http://nces.ed.gov/pubsearch/getpubcats.asp?sid=022). In the 1980s, we knew that in general, girls underperformed on mathematics achievement tests compared with boys. As Figure 1.4 shows, that general pattern, however, is not the same in all types of schools. In this example,[10] we see that there is a trend for much larger schools to have larger math achievement gaps and for smaller schools to have smaller achievement gaps.

---

[10]Note this is not a logistic regression example—we will explore interactions in logistic regression in Chapter 8. These results are from a quick hierarchical linear modeling (HLM) analysis with a continuous DV (HLM will be introduced and discussed as it relates to logistic regression in Chapter 13).

In other words, the effect of student sex differs depending on the size of the school (and probably many other variables). Again, there are many reasons for this that we will not get into, but the conclusion is interesting—that context matters. It is not simply a linear relationship, but rather a variety of relationships dependent upon the context the students find themselves in. Similarly, it is likely that when you look for them, you will find and model interaction effects when running logistic regressions. We will explore interaction effects in more detail in Chapter 8.

Perfect Measurement

It is almost a dirty little secret in statistical science that we assume perfect measurement yet rarely achieve it. In most statistical procedures, we assume we are measuring the variables of interest well, and to the extent that we are not, biases and misestimations can occur. In simple correlation and regression, the effect is usually that of underestimating the effects in question. Yet in multiple regression and more complex procedures, the effects can get unpredictable and chaotic. For example, if you are studying student achievement and attempting to control student socioeconomic status (SES), but your measure of SES is imperfect, then you are failing to fully control for the effect. This can lead other, related IVs to become overestimated if they are capturing variance that should have been removed by SES. I have dealt with this issue in more depth in other places and so will refer interested readers to those rather than recapitulating the arguments here (Nimon, Zientek, & Henson, 2012; Osborne, 2003, 2008, 2012). Logistic regression also relies upon reliable measurement of variables, and so in that respect the two are similar.

Homoscedasticity (or Constant Variance of the Residuals)

ANOVA has the assumption of equal variance across groups, and OLS regression has a similar assumption—that the variance of the residuals (or the variance of data points around the regression line) is constant across the observed range. In other words, this means that if you plot the data points around the regression line (e.g., a ZPRED vs. ZRESID plot), you should see a relatively homogenous scattering of data points around the regression line at all points.

Again, because logistic regression is not a parametric procedure, there is no assumption of homoscedasticity or equality of variance. But there are some interesting assumptions relating to sparseness that seem similar to me.

Sparseness is a concept that can be understood by imagining lots of little boxes stacked together. Each box represents a combination of the DV and IV. For example, if you are looking at blood pressure and odds of having a stroke, you have boxes for each range of blood pressure representing both people who have and who have not had strokes. In sampling from the population, you want to make sure you have your boxes filled as best you can. "Sparse" data refers to having some of these boxes unfilled or not filled enough to allow the MLE estimation to effectively form estimates. This is an interesting difference between OLS and logistic regression and we will examine assumption testing in more detail in Chapter 4.

Independence of Observations

In most analyses, we assume that observations are independent unless we are specifically modeling nested data or repeated measures. Because much of our data in the world (especially in the social sciences, but also in many other sciences, such as health sciences) comes from organisms that form hierarchies or groups, this assumption may be more or less tenable. For example, researchers sampling individuals from existing health centers or students from schools or classrooms are sampling individuals who are already more similar in many respects than individuals sampled at random from the entire population. This violates the assumption of independence of observation and may bias the results. For a brief primer on this concept, and the issues that can arise, you can refer to Osborne (2000) or refer to Chapter 13, where we discuss HLM applied to logistic regression.

SIMILARITIES BETWEEN OLS ♦ REGRESSION AND LOGISTIC REGRESSION

Summarizing the Overall Model

One of the first things many researchers look at in OLS regression is the overall model fit, usually represented with a multiple R, with associated significance test, and R^2, the overall amount of variance accounted for. This is an important statistic and represents goodness of the model. Logistic regression does not have an exact analogue to R^2. Instead we have the concept of *deviance*,[11] which represents lack of fit or deviance from

---

[11]Which is much less exciting in discussing logistic regression than in discussing social or behavioral deviance. Sorry.

the observed data. In logistic regression, we can start with deviance for the null model, or the overall amount of deviance—essentially the overall amount of deviance that can potentially exist in the dependent variable. Then we have model deviance, the deviance that remains once predictor variables have been added to the model. Deviance is reduced as significant predictors are added, and there are statistical tests for this reduction similar to that of ΔR^2, usually in the form of a χ^2 that is the difference between the null or baseline model and the final model, with degrees of freedom that represent the number of parameters estimated that changed between the two models. This test is called the *likelihood ratio test* (Hosmer & Lemeshow, 2000).

$$Deviance = -2(\ln \frac{\text{likelihood of fitted model}}{\text{likelihood of saturated model}}) \qquad \text{Eq. 1.1.}$$

So conceptually, there are ways to assess the overall model in logistic regression, but the method differs significantly in terms of what deviances are and how they are thought of. If you are familiar with other types of analyses that use maximum likelihood, you may have seen −2 log likelihood used similarly. Deviances and −2 log likelihoods are conceptually identical.

◆ WHAT IS DISCRIMINANT FUNCTION ANALYSIS AND HOW IS LOGISTIC REGRESSION SUPERIOR/DIFFERENT?

I briefly discussed the idea of performing an OLS regression analysis with the binary DV. This analysis is referred to as the linear probability model, and to recap, there are multiple issues with this approach. For example, predicted probabilities can exceed the 0.00 to 1.00 range that is conceptually valid; the residuals are highly heteroscedastic and not normally distributed. Two-group discriminant analysis was developed early in the 20th century (Fisher, 1936). In practice, this procedure was often used to classify individuals based on certain predictor variables to explore whether a researcher could account for, say, a clinician's diagnosis. In discriminant analysis, a set of predictors is used to generate a prediction equation, called the linear discriminant function, with each predictor weighted with a coefficient (just as in OLS regression), and predicted scores. While somewhat intuitive, discriminant analysis is mathematically identical to the linear probability model (Cohen et al., 2002) and thus carries the same liabilities. Thus, it is considered an anachronistic procedure and does not currently represent a best practice. Instead, researchers should use logistic regression, which is considered the successor to this procedure.

SUMMARY

Logistic regression is a relative newcomer to the statistical toolbox, particularly in the social sciences, but it is currently considered *the* best practice when dealing with outcomes that are dichotomous or categorical in nature. Through the course of this book we will explore all the various ways logistic regression is similar to, and different from, OLS regression. If you are familiar with OLS regression, you will find logistic regression a simple-to-understand cousin. The technical details "under the hood" are very different, and there are some interesting and fun nuances that an expert logistic regression user needs to master (but in fairness, there are many interesting and fun nuances that expert OLS regression users need to master as well). We will take each topic one at a time, and by the end it is my hope that you will appreciate the beauty and power of this procedure, ready to use it according to evidence-based best practices.

REFERENCES

Cohen, J., Cohen, P., West, S., & Aiken, L. S. (2002). *Applied multiple regression/ correlation analysis for the behavioral sciences.* Mahwah, NJ: Lawrence Erlbaum.

Davies, H. T. O., Crombie, I. K., & Tavakoli, M. (1998). When can odds ratios mislead? *British Medical Journal, 316,* 989–991.

Davis, J. M., & Svendsgaard, D. J. (1990). U-Shaped dose-response curves: Their occurrence and implications for risk assessment. *Journal of Toxicology and Environmental Health, Part A Current Issues, 30*(2), 71–83.

Fisher, R. (1936). The use of multiple measurements in taxonomic problems. *Annals of Eugenics, 7,* 179–188. doi: citeulike-article-id:764226

Francis, D., Schatschneider, C., & Carlson, C. (2000). Introduction to individual growth curve analysis. In D. Drotar (Ed.), *Handbook of research in pediatric and clinical child psychology* (pp. 51–73). New York, NY: Klewer/Plenum.

Holcomb, W. L., Jr., Chaiworapongsa, T., Luke, D. A., & Burgdorf, K. D. (2001). An odd measure of risk: use and misuse of the odds ratio. *Obstetrics and Gynecology, 84*(4), 685–688.

Hosmer, D. W., & Lemeshow, S. (2000). *Applied logistic regression.* Hoboken, NJ: Wiley.

Ingels, S. (1994). *National Education Longitudinal Study of 1988: Second follow-up: Student component data file user's manual.* Washington, DC: U.S. Department of Education, Office of Educational Research and Improvement, National Center for Education Statistics.

Loftus, E. F., Loftus, E., & Ketcham, K. (1992). Witness for the defense: The accused, the eyewitness, and the expert who puts memory on trial. New York, NY: St. Martin's Griffin.

Mead, M. (1935). Sex and temperament in three primitive societies. New York, NY: Morrow.

Mroczek, D. K., & Spiro III, A. (2005). Change in life satisfaction during adulthood: findings from the veterans affairs normative aging study. *Journal of Personality and Social Psychology, 88*(1), 189.

Nimon, K., Zientek, L. R., & Henson, R. K. (2012). The assumption of a reliable instrument and other pitfalls to avoid when considering the reliability of data. *Frontiers in Psychology, 3*(102).

Oakley, A. (1972). *Sex, Gender, and society.* London: Temple Smith.

Osborne, J. W. (2000). Advantages of hierarchical linear modeling. *Practical Assessment, Research & Evaluation, 7*(1).

Osborne, J. W. (2003). Effect Sizes and the disattenuation of correlation and regression coefficients: Lessons from educational psychology. *Practical Assessment, Research, and Evaluation, 8*(99).

Osborne, J. W. (2008). Is disattenuation of effects a best practice? In J. W. Osborne (Ed.), *Best practices in quantitative methods* (pp. 239–245). Thousand Oaks, CA: Sage.

Osborne, J. W. (2012). Best practices in data cleaning: A complete guide to everything you need to do before and after collecting your data. Thousand Oaks, CA: Sage.

Osborne, J. W., & Waters, E. (2002). Four assumptions of multiple regression that researchers should always test. *Practical Assessment, Research, and Evaluation, 8*(2).

Pedhazur, E. J. (1997). Multiple regression in behavioral research: Explanation and prediction. Fort Worth, TX: Harcourt Brace College.

Quirk, K. J., Keith, T. Z., & Quirk, J. T. (2001). Employment during high school and student achievement: Longitudinal analysis of national data. *The Journal of Educational Research, 95*(1), 4–10.

Rescorla, L., & Rosenthal, A. S. (2004). Growth in standardized ability and achievement test scores from 3rd to 10th grade. *Journal of Educational Psychology, 96*(1), 85.

Sullivan, S. E., & Bhagat, R. S. (1992). Organizational stress, job satisfaction and job performance: Where do we go from here? *Journal of Management, 18*(2), 353–374.

Teigen, K. H. (1994). Yerkes-Dodson: A law for all seasons. *Theory & Psychology, 4*(4), 525–547.

Yegiyan, N. S., & Lang, A. (2010). Processing central and peripheral detail: How content arousal and emotional tone influence encoding. *Media Psychology, 13*(1), 77–99.

Yerkes, R. M., & Dodson, J. D. (1908). The relation of strength of stimulus to rapidity of habit-formation. *Journal of Comparative Neurology and Psychology, 18*(5), 459–482.

2

HOW DOES LOGISTIC REGRESSION HANDLE A BINARY DEPENDENT VARIABLE?

I n what way is having an anvil dropped on your head like a logistic curve? What predicts whether students will drop out of school prior to graduating high school? Put a more positive way, what factors influence whether students are retained through high school graduation?

Imagine we had an infinite variety of anvils that we could drop on your head.[1] If we start with an infinitely tiny anvil, and gradually increase the size (and weight) of the anvils that get dropped on your head, for a long while you would not notice or care that extremely tiny things were being dropped on you. Then, suddenly, the anvils would become annoying, then painful, then pretty damaging. And just as quickly, they would become so damaging that increasing the size of the anvil really didn't matter. The result would be terminal headache beyond a certain point (unless you are Wile E. Coyote, in which case you see stars, a comically large lump grows out of your head, and then you come back for another adventure) (see Figure 2.1).

From reading the first chapter, you know that both ordinary least squares (OLS) regression and logistic regression share some important

---

[1]Something that seems to happen frequently to Wile E. Coyote in Looney Tunes cartoons, as well as to Larry the Cucumber in one of the Osborne family's favorite episodes of *Veggie Tales*.

Figure 2.1 Imaginary Relationship Between Anvil Size and Probability of Serious Injury

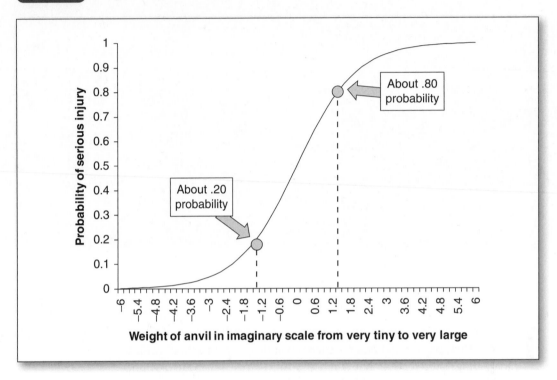

commonalities. Most relevant to this chapter, both assume a *linear* relationship between a predictor variable (or set of predictor variables) and a dependent variable. In OLS regression, it is relatively simple to imagine how that relationship is estimated. But how does a binary 0/1 or yes/no variable get handled appropriately in logistic regression? In this chapter, we will look "under the hood" so to speak, examining how counts and probabilities and odds and odds ratios and logits come to be.

The simple example we will use through this chapter is from the National Education Longitudinal Study of 1988 (NELS88) from the National Center for Educational Statistics (NCES; http://nces.ed.gov/surveys/nels88/), a survey of students in eighth grade in the United States in 1988. These students were followed for many years on thousands of variables, similar to other studies from NCES. In particular, we will predict DROP-OUT before completing 12th grade (1 = yes, 0 = no)[2] from the variable

---

[2]For those of you who are interested, I considered students who dropped out and returned as dropouts as well.

POOR (1 = the student falls below the average family income or 0 = the student falls above the average family income).[3]

PROBABILITIES, CONDITIONAL ◆ PROBABILITIES, AND ODDS

There will be a bit of hand calculation in this chapter. This is becoming rarer in statistics texts, with the modern amenities of easy access to powerful statistical computing packages. But in this case, I find it instructive and important to understanding what is happening in logistic regression. Knowing how to manipulate probabilities and odds and odds ratios and logits may help you be more successful (and accurate) when presenting your results.

Table 2.1 Cross-Tabulation of Family Income and Dropout

		Dropout		Total	Conditional probabilities	Odds	Odds ratio (change in odds)
		0 (no)	1 (yes)				
Poor	Yes (1)	7312	1244	8556	0.145	0.170	5.67
	No (0)	7821	233	8054	0.029	0.030	
Total		15133	1477	16610	0.089		

Data Source: NELS88, NCES, U.S. Department of Education (http://nces.ed.gov/surveys/nels88/).

Let's start with a simple example of student family affluence and dropout before completion of high school. Looking at Table 2.1, we can see the number of students from poor or not poor households who dropped out and who were graduated, as well as the overall numbers. It is then relatively simple to start thinking about probabilities. The probability of an event is calculated as the frequency of the event divided by the total observations (in this case, 1,477 dropouts out of 16,610 total students).

---

[3]I will remind you that I am using this public data for demonstration purposes only. I intentionally did not weight the data or do any of the methodologically important steps necessary to use these data for drawing substantive conclusions. For more on the importance of weighting complex samples such as this, I will refer you to my paper on the topic: http://pareonline.net/pdf/v16n12.pdf (Osborne, 2011).

$$\text{Probability of dropout } (P_{dropout}) = \text{number dropouts } / \text{ total students}$$

$$P_{dropout} = 1477 / 16610$$

$$P_{dropout} = 0.0889$$

When there are two categories (as with this dropout/graduated variable), the probability of a student falling into the "graduated" category is $(1 - P_{dropout}) =$

$$\text{Probability of graduated } (1 - P_{dropout}) = \text{number graduated } / \text{ total students}$$
$$or\ 1 - P_{dropout}$$

$$1 - P_{dropout} = 15133 / 16610 \ or \ 1 - 0.0889$$

$$1 - P_{dropout} = 0.9111$$

According to these data, the overall probability that any student in the eighth grade will drop out is 0.0889, and the probability that any random student will complete a high school education is 0.9111. Knowing nothing else about any student, the best we could do is guess that each student has about a 9% chance of dropping out before graduating high school and a 91% probability of staying in through completion. Of course, we know that the probabilities are not the same for all students. For example, looking at Table 2.1, it is relatively obvious that family income has an effect on the probabilities of dropping out. Thus, we can calculate *conditional probabilities,* a fancy phrase that simply means the probability of something happening within a condition. Thus, for example, we can calculate the conditional probability of dropout for students coming from "poor" households, or households with below-average income (1,244 students in this group dropped out from a total of 8,556), yielding a probability of 0.145. Likewise, we can calculate the conditional probability for those students coming from households with above-average income (233 students in this group dropped out from a total of 8,054), yielding a probability of 0.029. In other words, by knowing one piece of information about a student's background, we know a lot more about the probability of dropout. Students coming from below-average income households are much more likely to drop out than students coming from above-average income households.

In fact, those of you with a background in OLS regression might find it interesting to note that when you have dichotomous variables in OLS regression, with both variables coded 0 and 1, the conditional probabilities of dropout is the predicted variable. Putting the exact same data into an OLS regression analysis produces the following results:

| Table 2.2 | OLS Regression Results of the Family Income and Dropout Data |

	Unstandardized Coefficients		Standardized Coefficients	t	Sig.
	B	Std. Error	Beta		
(Constant)	.029	.003		9.318	.000
poor	.116	.004	.204	26.923	.000

Data Source: NELS88, NCES, U.S. Department of Education (http://nces.ed.gov/surveys/nels88/).

And it allows the following prediction equation:

Conditional probability of dropout = 0.029 + 0.116 (Poor)

As you can see from Table 2.1, when the independent variable (IV) is 0 (not poor), the conditional probability is 0.029, which matches our calculated conditional probability in Table 2.2. Likewise, when POOR = 1, the predicted probability is 0.029 + 0.116, or 0.145, the predicted probability of the other group.

As we mentioned in the previous chapter, OLS regression has been used for this type of analysis for many years, although the assumptions are difficult to meet, and the predicted probabilities can become impossible when the IV is continuous (i.e., below 0 or above 1.0). To demonstrate this, I substitute the continuous variable (family socioeconomic status [SES], which is z-scored) into the OLS regression equation, which gives us the following regression equation:

Conditional probability = 0.089—0.075(SES)

Note that because SES is z-scored, the average family income is 0.00, which gives us the conditional probability for a student dropping out when family income is average—exactly the 0.089 we calculated for the overall probability of dropout for the entire sample.

So we can calculate the conditional probability of dropout for a student who is one standard deviation below the mean by substituting −1 into the equation (above) for SES. This yields a conditional probability of 0.164, meaning that the probability of dropout for students who are coming from very poor families is much higher than average, and likewise, substituting 1 into the equation yields a conditional probability of 0.014. So far, so good. As expected from our cross-tabulation, poor students have higher probabilities of dropout than more affluent students. The problems come as we begin predicting more extreme cases. The conditional probability for a student 2 *SD* below the mean is 0.239, but for 2 *SD* above the mean is −0.061 (an impossible probability—0.00 is the lowest possible probability). The issues get more extreme as we move toward the extremes of the distribution—the conditional probability for a student coming from a very wealthy family 3 *SD* above the mean is −0.136. Functionally, this means that the probabilities are *really small,* which matches our real-world data and intuition. But the predicted probabilities still violate mathematical rules and assumptions of OLS regression.

A Brief Thought Experiment on the Logistic Curve

From these OLS regression data and common sense, we can see something that is usually presented in discussions of logistic regression but not delved into deeply: the logistic curve. Imagine a theoretical world where poverty was very strongly related to the probability that a student would drop out. As you move from average income to higher and higher poverty, the probabilities move toward 1.0, but at some point, increased poverty doesn't substantially increase the probability of dropout. There may be a threshold after which it really doesn't matter much. Conversely, as you move downward from average toward extremely low poverty, you will quickly asymptote toward 0, and after a certain level of affluence (or lack of poverty), moving toward lower levels of poverty doesn't substantially decrease the probability of dropout. This theoretical relationship is presented below in Figure 2.2. As you can see, there is a relatively narrow window of poverty where changing makes a large difference, and outside that window, the probabilities don't change a great deal. In this fictitious example, when poverty (on whatever scale we are using) reaches 1.40, the probability of a student dropping out is about .80. conversely, at −1.40, the probability is about .20. Beyond these points, the slopes flatten out, giving less change in probability despite rather large changes in *X*.

Think about this relationship in another way. Let's imagine that we were looking at the dosage of a hypothetical drug and the probability

Figure 2.2 The Logistic Curve

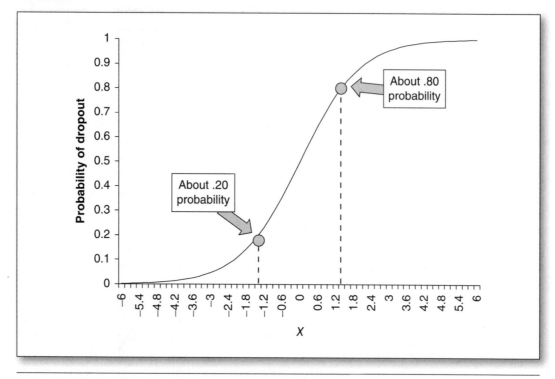

Data Source: NELS88, NCES, U.S. Department of Education (http://nces.ed.gov/surveys/nels88/).

that we could cure a disease. The drug is very effective and has no known side effects. If X is dosage and Y is the probability of cure, you might well get a similar curve. At very low doses, there are very small probabilities of cure, but as the doctors increase the dosage, there will come a point where it begins becoming effective, and as dosage increases (to a point), probability of cure will also increase. Then at some point, the benefit of increasing the dosage will level off, for any number of hypothetical reasons.

This curve, called a logistic curve (among other names), represents the conceptual underpinning of logistic regression—that the probability that something will happen can be predicted from other variables, that these relationships are usually curvilinear, and often asymptotic. There are also often ranges in the observed predictors where much of the "effect" occurs and beyond which increasingly less change is noted.

The Benefits of Odds Over Simple OLS Regression for Binary Outcomes

Returning to our issue of using OLS regression to predict binary outcomes, we can get around the issue of impossible values in OLS regression if we look at odds rather than probabilities. There are drawbacks to odds—such as being difficult for average people to interpret—but they are not constrained by the 0–1 range as probabilities are. Theoretically, odds can range from 0.00 to infinity. Odds are similar to probabilities with an important distinction: the odds of something happening (e.g., dropout) is the probability of that event divided by the probability of the event not happening:

$Odds_{(dropout)}$ = probability of dropout/probability of not dropping out.

$Odds_{(dropout)} = \pi / (1 - \pi)$

The odds of a student from a nonpoor family dropping out are about 0.03, and the odds of a student from a poor family dropping out are 0.17. Odds tend to magnify effects (some argue overestimate them), particularly as things get extreme. Although they are mathematically derived from the same data, they can give the uninformed reader the impression of larger effect sizes than is warranted because most readers interpret them as probabilities rather than odds.

The one drawback of OLS regression with this type of data remains once converted to odds—the predicted conditional odds below 0.00 can still be possible. So we have eliminated one issue—predicted odds over 1.0 are legitimate, but the problem of negative odds still remains. So the solution mathematicians and statisticians have come to is to take the natural logarithm of the odds, which has the benefit of having no restriction on minimum or maximum values. Before we talk about *logits,* the natural logarithm of the odds, let's pause and talk about one of the most commonly reported statistics from logistic regression, the odds ratio.

The Odds Ratio

I have heretofore been talking about conditional odds, and now I am going to introduce the term "odds ratio"—which is one of the standard metrics researchers use in logistic regression to understand effects.[4] Conditional

---

[4]Although I will encourage you to not use it as much as relative risk or predicted probabilities.

odds are the odds that an outcome (i.e., dropping out) will happen given a particular value of another variable (i.e., being below or above average in family income). As you can see in Table 2.1, those are interesting, but without something to compare it to, interpretation is difficult. So the odds ratio has become a standard metric reported in logistic regression. In practice, the odds ratio is the odds of the outcome at one level of X (e.g., 1) relative to the odds of the outcome at another level of X (e.g., 0). In our example in Table 2.1, we only have two levels of X: poor or not poor (1 or 0). If we calculate the ratio of those two odds, we get an odds ratio of 5.67 (0.17/0.03). The interpretation is straightforward (although we will see in the next chapter there are many ways to misinterpret odds ratios, so we will talk that over in detail). In this example, the odds of students from "poor" households dropping out are 5.67 that of students from "not poor" households. This is not a surprising statistic, given what we know of the importance of poverty in predicting educational outcomes, but it is valuable.

In general, odds ratios are calculated as the change in odds for every 1.0 increase in the IV. In the case of binary IVs, it is the comparison of those in the "1" group to those in the "0" group, as you just saw in our example in the previous paragraph. In the case of a continuous IV, the odds ratio would be the change in odds for each increase of 1.0 in the variable of interest. We will talk more about interpretation in coming chapters, but for now let's think of odds ratios as a slope—the change in the conditional odds as the IV increases one unit. It is analogous then to slope, or regression coefficient, in OLS regression. The change in one variable as another variable changes 1.0 in whatever metric the variable is measured. I think of the odds ratio as an analogue to the standardized regression coefficient (beta), as it is metric free, and generally comparable across analyses as an effect size as long as the variables are on a standard metric.

The Logit

The natural logarithm of the odds is called the *logit*, a term that might remind you of the topic of our book—*logistic* regression. And that is no coincidence. We are almost done with our exploration of some of the basics underlying logistic regression, and in this section we come to the crux of the issue—what is the thing that logistic regression is really predicting?

For those of you who are more than a few years removed from high school mathematics, let's do a brief review of a logarithm before continuing. A logarithm is actually a class of mathematical operations where numbers we are used to (which are commonly represented in something called

Table 2.3 Examples of Logarithms

Base:	1,000,000	10,000	100	1	0.01	0.0001	0.000001
2	19.93	13.28	6.64	0	−6.64	−13.28	−19.93
e (natural log)	**13.81**	**9.21**	**4.60**	**0**	**−4.60**	**−9.21**	**−13.81**
3	12.58	8.38	4.19	0	−4.19	−8.38	−12.58
4	9.97	6.64	3.32	0	−3.32	−6.64	−9.97
5	8.58	5.72	2.86	0	−2.86	−5.72	−8.58
10	6.00	4.00	1.00	0	−1.00	−4.00	−6.00

"base 10") can be represented by other bases. In brief, a logarithm is the power (exponent) a base number must be raised to in order to get the original number. Any given number can be expressed as Y to the X power in an infinite number of ways. For example, if we were talking about base 10, 1 is 10^0, 100 is 10^2, 16 is $10^{1.2}$, and so on. Thus, $\log_{10}(100) = 2$ ($100 = 10^2$) and $\log_{10}(16) = 1.2$ ($16 = 10^{1.2}$). However, base 10 is not the only option for logarithms—you can literally use any number, although base 10 is one of the more common. Another common option is the natural logarithm, where the constant e (2.7182818 . . .) is the base.[5] In this case, the natural log of 100 is 4.605 ($100 = e^{4.605}$).

As you can see in Table 2.3, the same number can be represented in a variety of ways across a variety of bases. Perhaps more germane to this discussion is the natural logarithm, of base e. If you notice, the natural logarithm of numbers above 1.0 grows from 0 toward infinity as the numbers being log transformed get larger. Interestingly, as numbers go from 1 toward 0, the log of those numbers moves toward infinity in the negative direction.

You may also notice an interesting pattern in these numbers—the log of 100 and the log of 0.01 are identical except for the sign, as are the logs of 10,000 and .0001, and 1,000,000 and 0.000001. This is because in

---

[5]Sometimes referred to as Euler's number, but usually credited to Bernoulli, who attempted to solve the following formula that was applied to calculations of compound interest: $\lim_{n\to\infty} \left(1+\dfrac{1}{n}\right)^n$, e has applications in many fields beyond economics and statistics, including being particularly useful in calculus and probability theory, physical sciences, and beyond. It has been calculated to a trillion digits thus far, and like pi, is an enigmatic and interesting number.

exponents, raising something to a negative power (X^{-1}) merely means to calculate $1/X$. Thus, the interesting property of logs is that they "pivot" at 1.0, are essentially symmetrical around 1.0, and the log of 100 and 1/100 being identical except for the sign. This is an important revelation that will help with interpreting logistic regression output as you move forward. Trust me on this, and hold on while we march forward!

SUMMARIZING SO FAR ♦

We started off with a hand calculation of simple probabilities and simple odds, and moved into the shortcomings of OLS regression in predicting dichotomous variables—aside from violations of all sorts of assumptions (usually), you can get predicted conditional probabilities (outside the 0 to 1 acceptable range) and conditional odds that are impossible (below 0.00). To handle these shortcomings, the natural logarithm of the odds can conceivably range from $-\infty$ to ∞. Thus, if we use the logit (natural logarithm of the odds) as our dependent variable, we no longer face the issues that probabilities or odds have given us. The dependent variable then becomes logit($\hat{Y}$), and we say that the regression uses a logit link function:

$$\text{Logit} = natural\,log\left(\frac{\pi}{1-\pi}\right)$$

Thus, the regression equation we calculate is:

$$\text{Logit}(\hat{Y}) = b_0 + b_1 X_1 \ldots b_k X_k$$

Where b_0 is the intercept, and b_1 is the slope, or the effect of X_1. The equation should look familiar to you if you have ever explored OLS regression—a variable is predicted from a slope and intercept (estimate of Y when $X = 0$). The only difference between this equation and the simple OLS regression equation is the *logit link*. You can think of the concept of a link in regression as a translator of sorts. In the family of regression models, the right-hand side remains relatively similar and what changes is the *link* between the dependent variable and that linear equation. In the case of logistic regression, we use the *logit link* between the dependent variable and the linear regression equation. In other words, we are converting or translating the dependent variable from its natural form, Y, to something that works more effectively, the logit(Y). There are, theoretically, an infinite number of links in regression but only a few are commonly used in the fields I am familiar with—the linear link or identity link in OLS regression (which essentially means nothing is done to the dependent variable), the logit link (where the dependent variable is converted to logits), and the probit link (which I will discuss in Chapter 9).

So this *logit link* takes care of the conceptual issues of predicting impossible values, but it does not take care of the issue that these types of analyses routinely violate assumptions of OLS regression (or the fact that the logistic curve is nonlinear, meaning that there is no ordinary least squares estimation that will fit data curvilinearly). Thus, logistic regression uses a maximum likelihood estimation (which was discussed briefly in the preceding chapter), which does not rely upon assumptions that are going to be routinely violated when performing this sort of analysis.

It is important to note, however, that when these assumptions of OLS regression are met, OLS regression and logistic regression using maximum likelihood estimation will produce virtually identical coefficients. Yet when these assumptions are not met (specifically, the binary dependent variable violates the assumption of interval or ratio measurement, there is usually heteroscedasticity of residuals, and the assumption of a linear relationship is questionable), which is usually the case with a binary dependent variable, OLS regression will produce inappropriate and/or misestimated results. All this is to say that there is a good reason to use logistic regression when you have a binary outcome—that you will get optimal results for those types of data.

◆ STILL MORE FUN WITH LOGITS, ODDS, AND PROBABILITIES

So this thing that we are going to see in logistic regression is the natural logarithm of the odds of something happening (whatever is 1 when the dependent variable is coded 0 and 1). As you can see from the table above, the log of a thing is difficult for most people who are not professional mathematicians to comprehend in a deep way (or in an accurate way). So in logistic regression, you are going to get the intercept and coefficients in a logit metric (because we are using a logic link function). But most statistical packages also give you "odds ratios" (sometimes abbreviated "OR," or in SPSS, labeled "Exp(B)" because the odds ratio is the exponentiated logit) to make interpretation a bit more straightforward. In the first part of this chapter, we worked our way conceptually and mathematically from numbers to probabilities to odds to logits. It is important to recognize that these are all essentially the same bit of information, presented in slightly different form. If you have followed to this point, you can see each is a simple mathematical transformation of the other. Because of this, it is also relatively simple to reverse the process. We can start with logits (again, the natural log of the odds of an outcome) and work our way back to conditional probabilities, which are generally easier for people to understand. This is particularly true for those of you who will be communicating to nontechnical audiences (practitioners, policymakers, or the public) and is even useful when talking to other researchers who may not be as well-versed in logistic regression as you are (or will be!).

The Logit Revisited

Most statistical programs will convert your logits to odds ratios for you, but it is valuable to understand the magic that is happening in the software. Below is a sample of the output from SPSS for this same data.

From your knowledge of probability, odds, odds ratios, and logits (natural logarithm of the odds of dropout), much of this might at this point make sense. Let's start with the constant (intercept) first. Remember I have already mentioned that SPSS calls the odds ratio "Exp(B)." In a moment it should become clear why the odds ratio is sometimes called this. For now, know it is the odds ratio. The constant is the predicted logit when $X = 0$ (when students are *not* coming from poor households). Does the 0.03 in the odds ratio (Exp[B] column) look familiar? It should. In Table 2.1, we calculated the odds of dropping out for students from non-poor households (when POOR = 0) to be 0.03. This is the same number from the same data. Recalling that logistic regression doesn't analyze odds or odds ratios, but rather logits, let's look at the left-hand column labeled "B" (regression coefficients)—the constant or intercept is −3.51. That

Table 2.4	SPSS Logistic Regression Output for POOR and DROPOUT Analysis

		B	SE	Wald	df	Sig.	Exp(B)
Step 1	poor	1.742	.073	566.339	1	.000	5.711
	Constant	−3.514	.066	2793.147	1	.000	.030

Data Source: NELS88, NCES, U.S. Department of Education (http://nces.ed.gov/surveys/nels88/).

won't look familiar yet, but it will in a moment. Recall that we moved from odds to logits by taking the natural log of the odds. In this case, you can calculate the natural log of 0.03, which turns out to be −3.51, which is what we see in this column. In other words, this is the natural log of the odds of dropping out if you are in the "0" category on the independent variable.

Now let's look at the variable of interest, POOR. The odds ratio is 5.71—which is within rounding error of what we calculated by hand, and represents the *change in odds* from POOR = 0 to POOR = 1 (the slope, expressed as an odds ratio). So far so good. And converting to logits, the natural log of 5.71 is 1.742, which is what we see under the regression coefficient column. The rest of the columns involve the tests of significance (whether the odds ratio is significantly different from 1.00, or the logit is significantly different from 0). For example, the Wald statistic is simply the square of the regression coefficient divided by the standard error of the regression coefficient:

$$\text{Wald} = \left(\frac{b}{SE_b} \right)^2 \qquad \text{Eq. 2.1.}$$

I assume you are familiar with significance testing. (You're also probably familiar with the controversy over whether it is even a useful process—I will leave that for others to discuss as we have important substantive issues to confront. We will take null hypothesis statistical testing as the standard practice of the discipline even if it has flaws, and keep moving forward.) If you have a calculator that can handle natural logs, exponents, and such (or access to Excel or similar spreadsheet programs), I encourage you to play with the output from your statistical software like this to help cement your understanding of the relationships between the numbers you are seeing on your output.

◆ WHERE IS THE LOGIT OF THE OTHER GROUP?

So to quickly review: The logit of the intercept is the natural log of 0.03, which equals −3.514. The mathematics of this are relatively straightforward. And the logit of the odds ratio (5.71) is 1.74. To get the natural log of a number, we raise e to a particular power.

$$\text{Natural log of } 5.71 = e^{1.74} \qquad \text{Eq. 2.2.}$$

And thus we say the natural log of 5.711 is 1.74. To reverse this, moving from logit to odds, we *exponentiate* the logit—in other words to convert from logit to odds, we raise *e* to the logit power: [6]

$$e^{1.74} = 5.71$$

So the logit of the Poor = 0 group is −3.514, and the exponentiation of that is 0.03. But if you look at Table 2.1 and try to find the logit for the other group (POOR = 1), it is not there, although there is an effect of poor. This is actually a little confusing (at least it was for me when I first tried to figure this all out . . .) until you think carefully about what those numbers are for POOR—they are the effect of a 1.0 increment in POOR—the slope, not the value for that group. The odds ratio is the ratio of two odds (the odds of dropping out if POOR = 1 divided by the odds of dropping out if POOR = 0), as I have already mentioned, the slope or change in odds as you move an increment of 1.0 on the independent variable from POOR = 0 to POOR = 1. This is the same concept we can find in any regression analysis, the common definition of slope. Likewise, the logit of this odds ratio is 1.742. This is the slope, or change in logits between POOR = 0 and POOR = 1. The logit and conditional odds can be found by using the regression equation to predict a logit for that group, and then converting it to odds (or probability):

$$\text{Logit } (\hat{Y}) = -3.514 + 1.742(\text{POOR})$$

Using this regression equation we can confirm that the predicted logit for POOR = 0 is −3.514, and the predicted logit for POOR = 1 is

$$\text{Logit }_{(\text{POOR} = 1)} = -3.514 + 1.742(1) \text{ or } -1.772$$

CONVERTING FROM LOGITS DIRECTLY ♦ BACK TO CONDITIONAL PROBABILITIES

I will spare you the recapitulation of the mathematics that brought us to this point and merely present the formulae for converting directly from logit (predicted logit, usually) to predicted conditional probability.

$$\text{Conditional probability} = \left(\frac{e^{logit(y)}}{1 + e^{logit(y)}} \right)$$

---

[6]Note that there is minute rounding error in all these calculations. If you are using a scientific calculator, Excel, or some similar process, you use the EXP(*X*) command, where *X* is the logit you want to convert back to an odds ratio.

which is the same as the more spreadsheet-friendly

$$\text{Conditional probability} = \left(\frac{\exp(\text{logit}(y))}{1 + \exp(\text{logit}(y))} \right)$$

So we just calculated the logit of POOR = 1 to be −1.772. Using the formula above, that converts directly to 0.145, which is the same conditional probability we calculated by hand at the beginning of this chapter.

Some Benefits of Conditional Probabilities

So why go through all these mathematical machinations? We already have what we want to know when we perform a logistic regression—what variables are significant predictors of the outcome and the magnitude of the relationship (as well as direction), right? One problem we will explore in the next chapter is the fact that odds ratios are problematic in that researchers, practitioners, and the lay public often don't intuitively understand odds—although they often think they do (Davies, Crombie, & Tavakoli, 1998; Holcomb Jr, Chaiworapongsa, Luke, & Burgdorf, 2001), and ratios of things that people don't understand are necessarily even more fraught with difficulty. Odds are not intuitive like probabilities are, and the language needed to technically describe an odds ratio is (as you can see) a bit convoluted.

The situation is not helped by authors' tendency to whitewash this important distinction and use probabilistic language when discussing odds ratios. Even sophisticated researchers will summarize odds ratios using language similar to: "boys are 4.91 times more likely to be recommended to remedial reading than girls" or "boys are 4.91 times as likely to be recommended . . ." when technically the odds ratio should be summarized as "the odds of boys being recommended are 4.91 times the odds of girls being recommended," which does not address exactly what it means for odds to be greater in one group than another. Pedhazur (1997, pp. 760–761) takes great pains to highlight this common error, as do other authors (e.g., Cohen, 2000; Davies, et al., 1998; Holcomb Jr. et al., 2001). Holcomb et al. (2001) report that 26% of authors in top-tier medical journals explicitly misinterpreted odds ratios as relative risk ratios, which are ratios of probabilities rather than odds.

In addition, odds ratios tend to exaggerate effects, as Davies et al. (1998) demonstrate. This effect is particularly egregious when the outcome being examined is not rare (e.g., occurs in more than 5% of the population) and becomes magnified as the relative risk moves away from 1.0—commonly exceeding 80%–90% inflation in my own simulations.

For this reason, some argue that reporting relative risk (conditional probability of dropout for students from poor households divided by the conditional probability of dropout for students from nonpoor households rather than the conditional odds of one group divided by the conditional odds of another group) is a better practice and is less likely to have biased estimation of effects. As an example, the relative risk in our example is:

$$Relative\ risk = 0.145/0.03 = 4.833$$

Comparing our odds ratio to relative risk, we see about a 17.2% inflation with the odds ratio, and as we see in the next chapter, this inflation gets stronger the farther from 1.00 the odds ratio gets. The other advantage is that with relative risk we can use the words "probability" and "likelihood"—words that many of us want to use to describe probabilistic relationships but really should not when discussing odds. The important point is that it is much easier to calculate relative risk and report it when you have all your statistical output in front of you than attempting to piece it together from someone's article, hoping there is enough information.

It is probably more effective to calculate relative risk directly, or, if that is not possible, calculate it from the following formula (Zhang & Yu, 1998):

$$RR = OR\ /\ [(1 - P_0) + (P_0 - OR)] \qquad \text{Eq. 2.3.}$$

where RR = relative risk, OR = calculated odds ratio, and P_0 = the proportion of nonexposed individuals (e.g., those lacking the independent variable or the reference group) that experience the outcome in question. This formula is valuable (I have actually used it in some of my publications!), but now that we are logistic regression ninja warriors, slicing and dicing probabilities, odds, odds ratios, and logits, we do not need those sorts of formulae. If you have standard logistic regression output presented in any journal article (an intercept and a slope), you should be able to directly calculate conditional probabilities for each group and relative risks. For example, knowing nothing except the regression equation for this analysis ($logit_{(y)} = -3.514 + 1.742(POOR)$), we could calculate the predicted probability for POOR = 0 (0.03) and POOR = 1 (0.145) and their ratio (4.833; note that this ratio is a probability ratio, not an odds ratio, which is larger as odds tend to inflate effect sizes).

Table 2.5 Cross-Tabulation of Family Income and Dropout in a More Expanded Form

		dropout		Total	Conditional probabilities	Odds	Predicted logit[1]	Odds ratio	Slope[2]
		.00	1.00						
poor	Yes (1)	7312	1244	8556	0.145	0.170	−1.774	5.67	1.74
	No (0)	7821	233	8054	0.029	0.030	−3.511		
Total		15133	1477	16610					

1. Natural log (probability$_{(group)}$ /1−probability$_{(group)}$)

2. Change in predicted logit as X moves from 0 to 1 or logit(group 1)—logit(group 0)

Data Source: NELS88, NCES, U.S. Department of Education (http://nces.ed.gov/surveys/nels88/).

Table 2.6 SPSS Logistic Regression Output for POOR and DROPOUT Analysis

		B	SE	Wald	df	Sig.	Exp(B)	95% CI for Exp(B)	
								Lower	Upper
Step 1	poor	1.742	.073	566.339	1	.000	5.711	4.947	6.592
	Constant	−3.514	.066	2793.147	1	.000	.030		

Data Source: NELS88, NCES, U.S. Department of Education (http://nces.ed.gov/surveys/nels88/).

Table 2.7 SAS Logistic Regression Output for POOR and DROPOUT Analysis

Analysis of Maximum Likelihood Estimates					
Parameter	df	Estimate	SE	Wald Chi-Square	Pr > ChiSq
Intercept	1	−3.5135	0.0665	2793.1509	<.0001
poor	1	1.7423	0.0732	566.3385	<.0001

Odds Ratio Estimates		
Effect	Point Estimate	95% Wald Confidence Limits
poor	5.711	4.947	6.592

Data Source: NELS88, NCES, U.S. Department of Education (http://nces.ed.gov/surveys/nels88/).

CONFIDENCE INTERVALS FOR LOGITS, ODDS ♦ RATIOS, AND PREDICTED PROBABILITIES

Confidence intervals for point estimates (means, correlations, regression coefficients, intercepts, logits, odds ratios, and probabilities, among others) are desirable because we rarely know for sure the exact population parameter (and because more journals and reviewers want to see them). In the case of simple means, we can estimate the population average from our sample, but our sample is rarely a perfect predictor of the population average. Thus we often calculate 95% confidence intervals from the mean and the standard error, which tells us the range that we are 95 confident the true population mean falls into. Similarly, with regression we can estimate intercepts and slopes, but again we need to calculate confidence intervals to honestly communicate the range the true population parameter might fall into. Most statistical programs will provide these for you, but they are not difficult to calculate:

$$\text{Confidence interval} = \text{statistic} \pm 1.96(SE_{\text{statistic}})$$

Thus, taking the logistic regression from our example in this chapter, SPSS tells us that the odds ratio is 5.711, with a 95%CI of 4.95, 6.59. This means that we are 95% confident that the real population odds ratio falls between 4.95 and 6.59. That is a relatively large range. Similarly, we could calculate the 95%CI for the logit of POOR as

$$95\%\text{CI (POOR)} = 1.742 \pm 1.96(0.073)$$

This turns out to be 1.599, 1.885. Knowing what we know about converting between logits and odds ratios, we can easily exponentiate these two numbers to check that we get the same odds ratios that SPSS served up for us. In fact, when we do this, we get 4.95 and 6.59, as expected. Perhaps more interestingly, we can also compute 95%CIs for predicted probabilities. Recall that we converted these two logits for POOR = 0 and 1 (−3.514 for POOR = 0 and −1.774 for POOR = 1) to conditional probabilities of 0.03 and 0.145. But those are only point estimates, and we might need to fit confidence intervals around them. We can produce confidence intervals around those predicted probabilities after calculating the standard error of the predicted probability:

$$SE \; \hat{\pi} = \hat{\pi} \, (1 - \hat{\pi}) * SE_{logit}$$

$$SE \; \hat{\pi} = 0.145(1-0.145) * 0.073 = 0.00905$$

And then using the standard formula for 95% confidence intervals for POOR = 1:

$$\text{Upper } 95\%CI = 0.145 + 1.96*0.00905 = 0.163$$

$$\text{Lower } 95\%CI = 0.145 - 1.96*0.00905 = 0.127$$

We can also calculate these confidence intervals for predicted probability directly from statistical output if you have the 95%CIs for predicted logit or predicted odds ratio. As mentioned earlier, it is simple to calculate a 95%CI for the logit of this group:

$$= (-1.772) \pm 1.96*SE_{logit}$$

which also ends up being −1.629 and −1.915. Converting these logits to probabilities, we get a 95%CI in probabilities of 0.128 and 0.164, both of which are reasonably close to the 0.127 and 0.163 we calculated from the predicted probability and the $SE \; \hat{\pi}$, above.

You might find all this converting and cross-converting a bit boring or bothersome or redundant. What I find comforting and interesting about it is that it reinforces confidence that you know how these numbers work and what they mean. And by successfully manipulating them, getting to the identical conclusions via multiple paths, we are confident that the math is right. This leaves you in a powerful position to communicate the results of logistic regression to your audience in the best, clearest manner possible.

ONE CONCRETE REASON WHY YOU SHOULD CARE ♦ ABOUT THIS STUFF—CLARITY OF COMMUNICATION

One of the reasons I started investigating all this "under the hood" stuff—what are we really calculating when we do logistic regression and what all those numbers mean—is because of my desire to be able to clearly communicate my findings to technical and nontechnical audiences. It is all well and good to report odds ratios (or relative risk) and their confidence intervals for simple effects like we have in these examples. It is relatively easy for people to understand that the odds of students in poor households dropping out of high school are 5.71 that of students not living in poor households. But what if you are not reporting a simple effect, but rather a curvilinear effect, or an interaction? I always try to graph those out, and when I present them in publications or at conferences, people seem a bit perplexed at what is being graphed. Concretely, if you graph out a logistic regression analysis, you are graphing in units of logits. But even those of us who use logistic regression routinely have trouble conceptualizing logits. Most researchers and consumers of research would be more comfortable talking about odds or probabilities. And now that you know how simple it is to convert from logits or odds ratios to predicted probabilities, there is no reason not to make your graphs and tables as easily comprehensible for the reader as possible.

Later in the book we will get into graphing curvilinear effects and interactions (which I think are almost always more interesting than simple effects). By understanding everything in this chapter, you will be well prepared to accurately and appropriately communicate more complex results. I will show you how to graph out curvilinear effects and interactions, and I will also show you that graphing in logits is not only confusing to readers, but also can be very misleading. So we will practice graphing the results of logistic regressions in conditional probabilities

ENRICHMENT

1. Calculate the following:

   a. Convert the following odds ratios to logits:

      i. 1.00
      ii. 3.00
      iii. 0.333333

iv. 1.50

v. 0.50

vi. Note that the natural logs of 3.00 and 0.33333 are "symmetrical," or the same number just with a negative sign (within rounding). Why are the logits for 1.50 and 0.50 not symmetrical as 3.00 and 0.33333 is?

b. Convert the following logits to conditional probabilities:

i. 0.00

ii. 0.50

iii. 1.00

iv. 2.00

v. −0.50

vi. −1.00

vii. −2.00

2. On my website for this book, under Chapter 2, there is a sample of 3328 students from the 2002 Education Longitudinal Study (ELS2002; http://nces.ed.gov/surveys/els2002/) from NCES. With help from one of my wonderful students (LaShauna Dean-Nganga), we compiled this small data set so that you can explore the same sort of calculations that I went through in this chapter. In this new example for you to work through, we are looking at student postsecondary plans (0 = not planning on attending a 4-year postsecondary institution following graduation from high school, 1 = planning on attending a 4-year postsecondary institution following high school) and a variable I am calling RICH (0 = student family income < $35,000.00 per year in 2002, 1 = student family income above $35,000.00 per year in 2002).[7]

a. Download the data file from the book website.

b. Produce a cross-tabulation of BACHPLAN versus RICH as I did in Table 2.1 (a template is provided below for your convenience to guide your calculations).

c. Compute conditional probabilities for RICH and not RICH students.

d. Compute conditional odds for RICH and not RICH students. You should see that those coming from more affluent homes are more

---

[7]Obviously I call the variable "RICH" not to indicate that a family income in the United States of $35,000.00 a year indicates wealth, but rather for a convenient label. Don't send me e-hate-mail over the label!

likely to plan on attaining their 4-year degree (and you should not be surprised by this!).

e. Compute the odds ratio.

f. In SPSS, SAS, R, or a statistical computing package of your choosing, perform the same analysis. Verify you receive the same (or similar to rounding error) odds ratio.

g. Compute the natural logarithm of the odds ratio. Verify it is the same as the B (or logistic regression coefficient for RICH) produced by your software.

h. Examine the odds ratio for the constant (intercept where $X = 0$). Verify it is identical to the conditional odds of RICH = 0 (within rounding error).

i. Reverse engineer the process. Exponentiate the logit for RICH and verify that you get the odds ratio (in Excel, e.g., the function for exponentiation is = EXP(X), where X is the odds ratio). Using the formula, convert from EXP(b) to probability.

Enrichment Table 2.1 Worksheet

		BACHPLAN		Total	Conditional probabilities	Conditional Odds	Logit	Odds ratio	Slope
		0	1						
RICH	Yes (1)								
	No (0)								
Total									

ANSWER KEY

1. a. i.   0.000
      ii.   1.099
      iii. −1.099

iv.   0.405

v.   −0.693

vi.   Because 1.50 is only 50% bigger than 1.0, whereas 0.50 is one half the size. 2.0 would be "symmetrical" with 0.50 because they represent a doubling or halving (dividing by 2 or multiplying by 2, just as 3.00 and 0.3333 are a multiplying or dividing by 3). This is a source of common errors and misinterpretations in logistic regression.

b.   i. 0.50

ii.   0.622

iii.   0.731

iv.   0.881

v.   0.378

vi.   0.269

vii.   0.119

Enrichment Table 2.2   Cross-Tabulation of RICH and BACHPLAN

		BACHPLAN		Total	Conditional probabilities	Conditional Odds	Logit	Odds ratio	Slope
		0	1						
RICH	Yes (1)	257	1563	1820	.859	6.08	1.805	1.575	0.454
	No (0)	310	1198	1508	.794	3.86	1.351		
Total		567	2761	3328					

Some notes:

The logits are the natural logarithms of the conditional odds. Interestingly, as we will see next chapter, you will not see these two logits in SPSS or SAS output. Rather, you will see the log of the odds for the intercept, and the log of the odds ratio for the slope (b) of the IV. This makes sense, as the b is the slope or effect of the IV, not the log of the odds of the other group. Once we realize that an odds ratio is a slope (the change in odds as you increase 1.0 in the IV) and that the regression coefficient is the natural log of the odds ratio or the change in logits from 0 to 1 (again, the slope), this might make things a bit clearer.

SPSS Logistic Regression Output

Enrichment Table 2.3   Variables in the Equation

		B	SE	Wald	df	Sig.	Exp(B)	95% CI for Exp(B)	
								Lower	Upper
Step 1[a]	RICH	.453	.093	23.933	1	.000	1.574	1.312	1.887
	Constant	1.352	.064	450.055	1	.000	3.865		

a. Variable(s) entered on step 1: RICH.

Alternative Statistical Computing Package Output: SAS

Enrichment Table 2.4

Analysis of Maximum Likelihood Estimates					
Parameter	df	Estimate	Standard Error	Wald Chi-Square	Pr > ChiSq
Intercept	1	1.3517	0.0637	450.0176	<.0001
RICH	1	0.4535	0.0927	23.9346	<.0001

Enrichment Table 2.5

Odds Ratio Estimates			
Effect	Point Estimate	95% Wald Confidence Limits	
RICH	1.574	1.312	1.887

SYNTAX EXAMPLES

Syntax for Performing Analysis in SPSS

```
LOGISTIC REGRESSION VARIABLES RICH
/METHOD = ENTER BACHPLAN
/SAVE = ZRESID
/PRINT = CI(95)
/CRITERIA = PIN(0.05) POUT(0.10) ITERATE(20) CUT(0.5).
```

Syntax for Performing Analysis in SAS

```
PROC LOGISTIC DATA = book.CH2_ex descending;
MODEL bachplan = rich;
output out = results p = predict;
run;
```

REFERENCES

Cohen, M. P. (2000). Note on the odds ratio and the probability ratio. *Journal of Educational and Behavioral Statistics, 25*(2), 249–252.

Davies, H. T. O., Crombie, I. K., & Tavakoli, M. (1998). When can odds ratios mislead? *British Medical Journal, 316,* 989–991.

Holcomb Jr, W. L., Chaiworapongsa, T., Luke, D. A., & Burgdorf, K. D. (2001). An odd measure of risk: use and misuse of the odds ratio. *Obstetrics & Gynecology, 98*(4), 685.

Osborne, J. W. (2011). Best practices in using large, complex samples: The importance of using appropriate weights and design effect compensation. *Practical Assessment Research & Evaluation, 16*(12), 1–7.

Pedhazur, E. J. (1997). *Multiple Regression in behavioral research: Explanation and prediction.* Fort Worth, TX: Harcourt Brace College Publishers.

Zhang, J., & Yu, K. (1998). What's the relative risk? A method of correcting the odds ratio in cohort studies of common outcomes. *Journal of the American Medical Association, 280,* 1690–1691.

3

PERFORMING SIMPLE LOGISTIC REGRESSION

SIMPLE BINARY LOGISTIC REGRESSION ♦ WITH ONE INDEPENDENT VARIABLE

In this chapter, we will use two examples—one from the medical research literature and one from the social sciences—to illustrate our first examples of a complete logistic regression analysis. I tend to use SPSS as it is more prevalent in many areas of the social sciences (and the software I have used most for the past 20 years) although SAS, STATA, R, and most other commonly used statistical computing packages will produce similar output. Throughout the rest of the book, I will alternate examples between SAS and SPSS and will provide example syntax (where necessary) for both.

The first example will look at one binary outcome (whether a patient has been diagnosed with diabetes) as a function of whether the person is considered OBESE or not (body mass index [BMI] over 30 or not). The data are taken from the National Health Interview Survey of 2010 (NHIS2010; http://www.cdc.gov/nchs/nhis.htm), which is administered by the Centers for Disease Control and Prevention. In this particular example, we will focus on 26,779 individuals who had complete data on two variables: whether the individual had ever been told he had diabetes (DIABETES, recoded to 0 = no, 1 = yes) and BMI (which ranged from 12 to 79) recoded into OBESE (0 = BMI < 30,

1 = BMI ≥ 30).[1] Later in the chapter, we will look at the same example with the independent variable (BMI) measured continuously.

The second example is carried forward from the same data as Chapter 2 wherein we examined the effect of family socioeconomic status (coded whether the family was considered POOR or not) on student dropout from school prior to completing 12th grade (DROPOUT). These data are from the National Education Longitudinal Study of 1988 (NELS88) from the National Center for Educational Statistics (http://nces.ed.gov/surveys/nels88/), a survey of students in eighth grade in the United States in 1988. Participants in this study were followed for many years on thousands of variables, similar to other studies from NCES. In particular, we will predict DROPOUT before completing 12th grade (1 = yes, 0 = no)[2] from a variable I calculated called POOR (1 = the student falls below the average family income, or 0 = the student falls above the average family income). As with the other example, later in the chapter we will consider the same analysis using family income as a continuous variable. Both example data sets will be available on the book's website (http://jwosborne.com) so that you can replicate these analyses if desired.

Example 1: The Relationship Between Obesity and Diagnosis of Diabetes

In the NHIS2010 data set, 27.92% of the sample were recorded as having a BMI of 30.0 or greater, and thus were labeled "obese" according to traditional guidelines.[3] In addition, 9.7% of respondents indicated they had ever

---

[1]A brief note on interpretation: I am using these public data sets for demonstration purposes only. I intentionally did not weight the data or do any of the methodologically important steps necessary to appropriately use data from this type of complex multistage sample for drawing substantive conclusions. Therefore, you should not draw any substantive conclusions based on these or any other analyses throughout the book. They are for illustrative purposes only. For more on the importance of weighting complex samples such as this, I will refer you to my paper on the topic: http://pareonline.net/pdf/v16n12.pdf (Osborne, 2011). The user manuals for every public data set such as the ones used in this chapter also have detailed information on the sampling frame and whether weighting is necessary.

[2]For those of you who are interested, I considered students who dropped out and returned as dropouts as well.

[3]Again, understand that this is just an example. There are now more subtle measures of obesity and differential guidelines for males and females. Those of you interested in these topics will have to indulge me in simplifying what is a fascinating and complex field for the sake of pedagogical expediency.

been diagnosed with diabetes by a physician. The simple cross-tabulation of these two variables is presented in Table 3.1.

Table 3.1 Cross-Tabulation of DIABETES With OBESE

			Diabetes		Total
			.00	1.00	
OBESE	.00	Count	18041	1256	19297
		% within OBESE	93.5%	6.5%	100.0%
	1.00	Count	6140	1342	7482
		% within OBESE	82.1%	17.9%	100.0%
Total		Count	24181	2598	26779
		% within OBESE	90.3%	9.7%	100.0%

Data Source: NHIS2010, Centers for Disease Control and Prevention.

As you can see from this table, about 9.7% of the overall sample reports having been told that they have diabetes. As with the example from the last chapter, in this simple cross-tabulation you can see that the probability of reporting this diagnosis is not the same for all individuals. Those labeled OBESE are substantially more likely to have been told that they have diabetes by a physician compared with those not labeled OBESE. A simple cross-tabulation is fine as an initial descriptive exploration of the data, but now we move into logistic regression. The first thing we want to look at in almost any inferential model is the overall model fit.

Indicators of overall model fit

As with ordinary least squares (OLS) regression, overall model fit is an important first step in assessing your model. In OLS regression, we have measures of overall model fit such as R, R^2, and significance tests for them in the form of an F test. In logistic regression there is no simple, substantively interpretable measure of overall model fit, but there is a statistic that yields a significance test for the overall model.

Table 3.2 Omnibus Tests of Model Coefficients

		Chi-square	df	Sig.
Step 1	Step	726.285	1	.000
	Block	726.285	1	.000
	Model	726.285	1	.000

Data Source: NHIS2010, Centers for Disease Control and Prevention.

In general, overall model fit looks at several pieces of information, such as omnibus chi-square test, classification tables, and pseudo-R^2 indices. None of these are important and sufficient on their own, but in aggregate they can begin the initial exploration into whether a logistic regression model is useful.

As you can see in Table 3.2, we get an overall chi-square test for the model (and for the current step and block, all of which are identical in the case of one independent variable [IV]) testing the null hypothesis that there is no association between the IVs and dependent variables (DVs; i.e., that the probabilities of experiencing the outcome is the same regardless of status on the independent variable). In this case, a $\chi^2_{(1)} = 726.29$ is significant at $p < .0001$. We thus reject the null hypothesis that there is no difference in probability of the outcome variable as a function of the independent variable, which allows us to conclude there *is* a difference in the probability of experiencing the outcome depending on where you score on the independent variable.[4]

Keep in mind that this example has a very large sample. Significance values related to chi-squared statistics (and all inferential statistics) are strongly influenced by sample size, making it possible to have very small p values even when there is a negligible effect size.

What is a −2 log likelihood? This statistic (which can also be abbreviated as "−2LL") is generally a measure of *lack of fit* (or *error variation),* conceptually the opposite of R^2 in multiple regression, which is an index of variance accounted for. Thus, the smaller the −2LL gets compared with the baseline (empty or null model), the better the model fits. −2LL is not

---

[4]Some fun, nerdly trivia on interpretation of p values: in this case, a $p < .0001$ indicates that the probability of seeing the observed results if in fact the null hypothesis was true in the population is about 1 in 10,000.

appropriate for comparing non-nested models (models that are not based on the same data set, same DV, and subsets of IVs). It is not meaningful in its absolute value, but rather is used for comparison only.

The −2 log likelihood is the product of −2 and the log likelihoods of a particular model—in practical situations, we generally care about the comparison between the initial (null) model with only the intercept in the model and the final model with all predictors in the model.

Most of us don't care about exactly how this is calculated, but it might be instructive to some of you who are particularly obsessive.[5] Conceptually, it is −2 times the natural log of the conditional probability of each group multiplied by the number of individuals in each group:

$$-2LL = -2 \ \{n_{y=1} \ {}^*\ln[(p_{(y=1)})] + n_{y=0} \ ^* \ \ln[(p_{(y=0)})]\} \qquad \text{Eq. 3.1.}$$

Thus, −2LL is affected by two different things: conditional probabilities for each group and the number of individuals in each group. This is why very large samples tend to have very large −2LLs (particularly when the larger group is in the higher-probability cell) and small samples tend to have small −2LLs.

The likelihood of the model is used to test whether all predictors' regression coefficients in the model are simultaneously zero. The larger the initial −2 log likelihood, the less tenable that hypothesis is, meaning that the more likely it is that your model is explaining some of the DV. This −2 log likelihood is also used in tests of nested models. This statistic can be compared across nested models, directly subtracted one from another, and evaluated as a chi-square statistic, with degrees of freedom equal to the difference in the number of parameters estimated. In this way, we can test whether models are significant improvements or not over previous models.

In our example, which is summarized further in Table 3.3, we can see that the −2 log likelihood is 16330.72. If I were to add a second IV to the model presented earlier, I could compare this −2 log likelihood to the new model to see if that model is significantly different (better). We will discuss this further when we get to logistic regression with multiple IVs in Chapter 8. In this case, the omnibus test of the model coefficients ($\chi^2_{(1)}$ = 726.29) is the difference between the −2 log likelihood for the empty (unrestricted/null) model (the model with no predictors) that SPSS and many statistical software packages produce (in this case, the initial −2 log likelihood is 17057.005) and the final model with the independent variable in the equation (in this case, the final −2 log likelihood is 16330.72 and the difference

---

[5]Like your author . . .

between the −2 log likelihoods is the statistic reported, 726.285, rounded). Thus, the omnibus chi-square statistic is itself a function of initial and final −2 log likelihood statistics.

The −2 log likelihood is not generally interpreted in any conceptual or practical sense and is highly influenced by sample size in addition to the goodness of the model fit, unlike R and R^2 that are standardized, substantively interpretable metrics.

Table 3.3 Model Summary

Step	−2 Log Likelihood	Cox & Snell R Square	Nagelkerke R Square
1	16330.720[a]	.027	.057

a. Estimation terminated at iteration number 5 because parameter estimates changed by less than .001.

Data Source: NHIS2010, Centers for Disease Control and Prevention.

SAS produces similar results. As you can see in the model fit results, the −2 log likelihood is 17057.005 for the baseline model (intercept only), and with the intercept and predictors (labeled covariates here in Table 3.4), the −2 log likelihood is 16330.72, an improvement in model lack of fit of 726.285. This is exactly the same number reported in the test of the global null hypothesis below, which is significant at $p < .0001$. As in the identical SPSS example above, this indicates that the IV (in this case, our obesity variable) accounts for significant variance, or improves model fit significantly.

Table 3.4 SAS Output of Same Example Predicting Diabetes From Obesity

Model Fit Statistics		
Criterion	Intercept Only	Intercept and Covariates
AIC	17059.005	16334.720
SC	17067.200	16351.111
−2 Log L	17057.005	16330.720

Testing Global Null Hypothesis: BETA = 0			
Test	Chi-Square	df	Pr > Chi-Sq
Likelihood Ratio	726.2847	1	<.0001
Score	803.7080	1	<.0001
Wald	743.9313	1	<.0001

Data Source: NHIS2010, Centers for Disease Control and Prevention.

Other statistics produced in the general model evaluation include AIC (Akaike Information Criterion). It is calculated as AIC = −2 Log Likelihood + $2((k − 1) + s)$, where k is the number of levels of the dependent variable and s is the number of predictors in the model. AIC is used for the comparison of non-nested models on the same sample. Ultimately, the model with the smallest AIC is considered the best, although the AIC value itself is not meaningful. Most researchers reporting logistic regression analyses do not report AIC routinely.

The SC refers to the Schwartz Criterion, which is a modified AIC that penalizes a model for the number of predictors (encouraging parsimony in modeling). It is used and interpreted similarly to AIC for non-nested models from the same data set and is not interpreted substantively.

The pseudo-R^2

Various scholars have attempted to introduce statistics similar to our overall model summary statistic from OLS regression: R^2 (as you see in Table 3.3, SPSS routinely reports Cox & Snell and Nagelkerke pseudo-R^2 statistics), but there remain significant challenges to this, as maximum likelihood estimation does not easily lend itself to this sort of statistic. Neither estimate of the overall effect size of this particular analysis is terribly impressive, and I tend not to report pseudo-R^2 estimates as they seem to be quite volatile. The literature on which of the many variants and options for a pseudo-R^2 statistic is inconclusive at this time, according to my reading, and thus I do not recommend any.

The classification table

Another simple way to assess the goodness of your logistic regression model is to examine the classification table. In a robust, strong model, one

Table 3.5 Classification Table[a]

	Observed		Predicted		
			Diabetes		Percentage Correct
			.00	1.00	
Step 1	Diabetes	.00	24181	0	100.0
		1.00	2598	0	.0
	Overall Percentage				90.3

a. The cut value is .500.

Data Source: NHIS2010, Centers for Disease Control and Prevention.

would want to see most of the cases on the diagonal indicating concordance between predicted and observed classification of cases. In other words, those who are observed to be 0s should be predicted to be 0s, and those observed to be 1s should be predicted to be 1s. This model pictured in Table 3.5 is not a strong model in this respect, as none of those with diabetes are classified as having diabetes from the prediction equation. While more than 90% of participants were correctly classified, this is due to the fact that every case was classified into the NON-DIABETES group, and it merely happened to be the case that 90% of the cases were observed to be in that group. What we would hope for is to have predictors that would improve the classification accuracy of our subjects. However, this does not mean that the analysis was useless. In order to be classified in the DIABETES group, the predicted probability that a case was diabetic would have to be 0.50 or higher. So the fact that no case was classified as diabetic merely means that no case had a predicted probability of .50 or higher. It does not mean that there was no variance in predicted probabilities, and it does not mean that we are not able to understand some things about the dependent variable.

In this analysis, predicted probabilities were 0.06 and 0.18 (there are only two levels of the IV, and thus only two possible predicted probabilities), so there are some individuals with much higher predicted probabilities than others. Note also that .50 is an arbitrary default that can be altered when performing this analysis. If you have a rationale for doing so, you can lower it or raise it to suit the question and context of the analysis.

How do we know if a logistic regression model is important?

As with OLS regression, everything must be taken into context. Small effects can be very important. For example, if a particular action increases the probability of cancer survival by 5%, might that be worthwhile? Or if taking a particular action improves the probability of an outcome by 1% each time it occurs, might that be important? I would argue potentially yes. Thus, it is important to report overall model fit information. The overall model statistics are primarily useful, in my mind, for two things:

a. Deciding whether it is useful to examine the individual variable statistics, and

b. Comparing nested models.

In the social sciences, it might be that the ability to correctly predict category membership is important (obviously, in some fields being able to correctly diagnose sick individuals and not diagnose healthy ones is important, and there are analogues in the social sciences), and in that case, the overall model statistics and classification tables become more important substantively than is often the case. Our first example does not provide strong classification—thus allowing us to conclude that the dichotomous BMI measure I created is not a good screening indicator for existence of diabetes. But screening is not the only reason to use logistic regression, and it does not mean that our results are uninformative or unimportant. In fact, as you will see, I think the results—faulty though they are because I did not follow appropriate procedures to model the sampling frame—might be very enlightening for understanding diabetes, if not for screening.

I also give this same advice when discussing OLS regression. If you are not explaining 33% of the variance in an outcome, does that mean that your model is weak or unimportant? I am not sure without the context.

Examining the effects of individual variables

We explored a good deal of this information in the last chapter. Therefore, we will not delve deeply into where the odds ratio and regression coefficients come from. We have a significant overall model (despite an uninspiring classification table) and as such it is appropriate to examine the individual effects. As you can see from Table 3.6, OBESE is a significant predictor ($p < .0001$, identical to the overall model fit, which is to be expected when there is only one variable in the model), with a regression

Table 3.6 Variables in the Equation

		B	SE	Wald	df	Sig.	Exp(B)	95% CI for Exp(B)	
								Lower	Upper
Step 1[a]	OBESE	1.144	.042	743.823	1	.000	3.139	2.892	3.408
	Constant	−2.665	.029	8338.001	1	.000	.070		

a. Variable(s) entered on step 1: OBESE.

Data Source: NHIS2010, Centers for Disease Control and Prevention.

coefficient (*b*) of 1.144 and an odds ratio of 3.139. This means that the odds of an obese person (an individual with a BMI ≥ 30) being diagnosed with diabetes are 3.139 that of a nonobese person. Note also that the 95% confidence interval for the odds ratio is 2.89 to 3.41,[6] meaning that we can be 95% confident that the population odds ratio is somewhere between those two values. Confidence intervals are valuable particularly in smaller samples as they demonstrate the level of confidence you can have in your point estimate (the odds ratio). This is a very large sample and thus gives us a rather narrow 95%CI. Smaller samples can yield much wider 95%CIs. We will explore volatility and replicability of logistic regression analyses in Chapter 10.

The standard error of the estimate (what SAS labels the regression coefficient) can also be instructive, as it is an indicator of the precision of the estimate of *b*. Higher standard errors indicate less precision. Another interesting bit of trivia is that the Wald statistic (which is interpreted as a chi-square) is calculated as

$$\text{Wald} = (\frac{b}{SE})^2$$

$$= (1.144051/0.041948)^2 = 743.821$$

This calculated Wald is within rounding error of the reported Wald of 743.823. You may also notice that this Wald statistic is very close to the

---

[6]95% confidence intervals are constructed as $b \pm 1.96*SE_b$. Thus, in this example, the CI in logits is 1.144 ± 1.96*.042. If you do the math, the 95%CI for logits is 1.062, 1.226. If you exponentiate both of those, you get the 95%CI in odds ratios, or 2.89, 3.41, which is within rounding error of the reported 95%CIs for the OR.

Table 3.7 SAS Output for Same Example

Analysis of Maximum Likelihood Estimates					
Parameter	df	Estimate	Standard Error	Wald Chi-Square	Pr > ChiSq
Intercept	1	−2.6647	0.0292	8338.0028	<.0001
OBESE	1	1.1441	0.0419	743.9313	<.0001

Odds Ratio Estimates			
Effect	Point Estimate	95% Wald Confidence Limits	
OBESE	3.140	2.892	3.409

Data Source: NHIS2010, Centers for Disease Control and Prevention.

overall model chi-square (743.82, compared with the model fit chi-square of 726.29). If you pay attention to simple OLS regression model fit and variable statistics, you will see parallel similarities. And rightly so. In OLS regression with only one variable, the overall model fit and the statistics for the individual IV are very similar or identical, as it is with logistic regression. However, this model fit information becomes more important as we move toward multiple independent variables. All statistical software will give an overall model fit, as well as statistics for block and/or step, as you can enter independent variables in groups and assess their overall contribution to the model. For now, with one IV, these will all be identical.

Is the constant worth paying attention to?

I find many scholars tend to ignore the constant, but this information can be useful as well. As we have explored in the previous chapter, this represents the conditional odds (and the logit) of those in the "0" or nonobese category being diagnosed with diabetes. It is a useful base rate to think about, and, in our example, it is also significantly different from 0. As we mentioned in the last chapter, you can also construct 95% CIs for this category, as well as predicting for the other category using this information.

An Example Summary of These Results

One of the most common requests from my students involves examples of reporting results in American Psychological Association or other common formats that they can use to model their own results summaries. Accordingly, I am including example summaries throughout the book as I would for a journal article or a conference presentation. In this case, I would report the following (including the summary of effects table similar to either Table 3.6 or 3.7):

Obesity was a significant predictor of Diabetes status. Entry of obesity into the model significantly improved model fit (null −2LL = 17057.01, final −2LL = 16330.72, $\chi^2_{(1)}$ = 726.29, $p < .0001$). As you can see in Table X, those who are obese are more likely to also report having been told they had diabetes (OR = 3.14, 95%CI = 2.89, 3.40). When converted to conditional probabilities, we find that those in the nonobese category have approximately a 6.51% chance of being diagnosed with diabetes while those in the obese category have approximately a 17.94% chance, representing a relative risk of 2.76.

◆ LOGISTIC REGRESSION WITH A CONTINUOUS INDEPENDENT VARIABLE

Continuous independent variables are easily incorporated into logistic regression now that we have computers to do the heavy lifting for the mathematics. And as I will point out in more detail in later chapters, converting your continuous variables to categorical is generally a bad idea and is unnecessary. I encourage you to use continuous variables in logistic regression, so let us explore how logistic regression works with continuous variables using the same example—DIABETES and BMI (the continuous variable OBESE was based upon; a histogram of BMI is presented in Figure 3.1). In this case, we will NOT convert BMI to the dichotomous OBESE variable, rather seeking to capture the added information of leaving the variable in its original metric.

Understanding the concept of the logit with a continuous variable

Our example includes odds ratios and logits that reflect the change in probability (or odds, or logits) that a change of 1.0 in the independent

Figure 3.1   Distribution of BMI

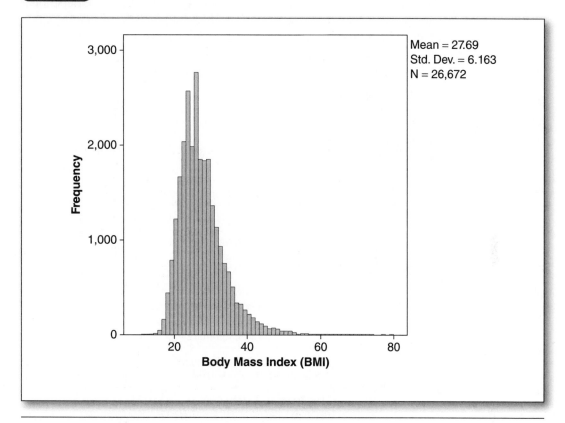

Data Source: NHIS2010, Centers for Disease Control and Prevention.

variable makes. Thus, in our first analysis, BMI was recoded into OBESE, with a 0 meaning not obese and 1 meaning obese. Thus, the change from 0 (not obese) to 1 (obese) was a large step and a dramatic comparison.[7] So we saw that the odds of being diagnosed with diabetes in the "obese" group are about 3.14 that of being diagnosed with diabetes for those in the "not obese" group. Using a continuous variable is a simple extension of this

---

[7]And also a dramatic disservice to the data. By doing this, we combine all individuals with BMI under 30, essentially saying that a person with BMI = 18 is identical to BMI = 29.95, which is not likely, and further, that individuals with BMIs of 30 and 60 are the same. Finally, we claim by doing this that individuals with BMI = 29.95 and 30.05 are very different, when in a practical sense they are probably not. I'll go into greater explanation in later chapters regarding why you should never dichotomize continuous variables.

special case. When a variable with more than two values is in the equation, the statistics reported are still related to a change of 1.0 in the independent variable. The only difference is that in this case, there are more than one of these increments present in the independent variable. And thus, the effect will take into account how many increments there are. In our example data, BMI ranges from 12 to 79, leaving us many, many increments of 1.0 in the independent variable.

Table 3.8 SPSS Model Summary Predicting DIABETES From BMI

Omnibus Tests of Model Coefficients				
		Chi-square	df	Sig.
Step 1	Step	986.981	1	.000
	Block	986.981	1	.000
	Model	986.981	1	.000

Model Summary			
Step	−2 Log likelihood	Cox & Snell R Square	Nagelkerke R Square
1	16070.024[a]	.036	.077

Data Source: NHIS2010, Centers for Disease Control and Prevention.

Table 3.9 SAS Model Summary Predicting DIABETES From BMI

Model Fit Statistics		
Criterion	Intercept Only	Intercept and Covariates
AIC	17059.005	16074.024
SC	17067.200	16090.415
−2 Log L	17057.005	16070.024

Testing Global Null Hypothesis: BETA = 0			
Test	Chi-Square	df	Pr > ChiSq
Likelihood Ratio	986.9807	1	<.0001
Score	1178.5820	1	<.0001
Wald	1013.6774	1	<.0001

Data Source: NHIS2010, Centers for Disease Control and Prevention.

As you can see in Tables 3.8 and 3.9, our omnibus test of the model shows that we can reject the null hypothesis and conclude that the independent variable is significantly related to the probability of being diagnosed with diabetes (in other words, the model with all coefficients set to 0 is a worse fit than when the coefficient is nonzero). And as before, the pseudo-R^2 estimates are relatively low, indicating that we are not accounting for all of the diabetes diagnoses in our sample. As one might expect if you read my subscripted rant on dichotomizing continuous variables earlier, by using a continuous variable (BMI) rather than categorical variable (OBESE), we are getting stronger model statistics because we are getting the full benefit of the data. Our classification table (Table 3.10) still shows poor classification performance of this one variable, however.

Table 3.10 SPSS Classification Table[a]

			Predicted		
	Observed		diabetes		Percentage Correct
			.00	1.00	
Step 1	diabetes	.00	24121	60	99.8
		1.00	2575	23	.9
	Overall Percentage				90.2

a. The cut value is .500.

Data Source: NHIS2010, Centers for Disease Control and Prevention.

Hosmer and Lemeshow test

Once we use a variable with more than two values, we can look at the Hosmer and Lemeshow test, which looks at lack of fit in the same way that the Pearson chi-square test does, except this test looks at deciles rather than all individual cells in an attempt to more accurately model lack of fit where continuous variables are concerned. The Hosmer–Lemeshow goodness-of-fit statistic is more robust than the traditional goodness-of-fit statistic used in logistic regression, particularly for models with continuous variables and studies with small sample sizes. It is based on grouping cases into deciles of risk and comparing the observed probability with the expected probability within each decile. Significant results mean that the predicted probability is significantly different from the observed probability. As you can see in Tables 3.11 and 3.12, the model actually does a relatively decent job of tracking the general pattern of where cells should be small and where they

Table 3.11 SPSS Output of the Hosmer and Lemeshow Test of Goodness of Fit

Hosmer and Lemeshow Test			
Step	Chi-square	df	Sig.
1	77.090	8	.000

Contingency Table for Hosmer and Lemeshow Test						
		Diabetes = .00		Diabetes = 1.00		Total
		Observed	Expected	Observed	Expected	
Step 1	1	2596	2560.196	79	114.804	2675
	2	2627	2574.547	91	143.453	2718
	3	2493	2487.242	153	158.758	2646
	4	2520	2487.960	146	178.040	2666
	5	2468	2456.499	186	197.501	2654
	6	2427	2469.414	266	223.586	2693
	7	2416	2423.505	259	251.495	2675
	8	2338	2373.711	328	292.289	2666
	9	2216	2299.574	449	365.426	2665
	10	2080	2048.351	641	672.649	2721

Data Source: NHIS2010, Centers for Disease Control and Prevention.

should be large. The overall significant effect from Hosmer and Lemeshow indicates that there are significant discrepancies between observed and expected groups (and hence, probabilities) across the 10 deciles of BMI, but the conditional probabilities match what we would expect: higher BMI produces higher probabilities of being diagnosed with diabetes. The reason we have a significant Hosmer and Lemeshow statistic is that we have a good deal of power to detect differences, and our model is not strong, particularly in the DIABETES = 1 group. This could be expected considering how poorly our dichotomous variable did at classifying individuals, particularly diabetic individuals.

Note that SPSS and SAS divide up the groups slightly differently (the numbers are slightly different due to the nature of the way the software groups individuals), but the results are remarkably similar. Both results indicate that the model is not a perfect fit to the data.

Table 3.12   SAS Output

| | | Partition for the Hosmer and Lemeshow Test | | | |
| | | Diabetes = 1.00 | | Diabetes = 0.00 | |
Group	Total	Observed	Expected	Observed	Expected
1	2675	79	114.81	2596	2560.19
2	2718	91	143.46	2627	2574.54
3	2646	153	158.77	2493	2487.23
4	2666	146	178.05	2520	2487.95
5	2654	186	197.51	2468	2456.49
6	2693	266	223.60	2427	2469.40
7	2675	259	251.51	2416	2423.49
8	2666	328	292.30	2338	2373.70
9	2665	449	365.44	2216	2299.56
10	2721	641	672.68	2080	2048.32

Hosmer and Lemeshow Goodness-of-Fit Test		
Chi-Square	*df*	Pr > ChiSq
77.0846	8	<.0001

Data Source: NHIS2010, Centers for Disease Control and Prevention.

The individual variable statistics

As before, we have a significant omnibus chi-square test, indicating that the variables account for some significant variation in the dependent variable, and thus that it is legitimate to examine the univariate results.

Table 3.13 SPSS Output Summarizing Variables in the Equation

		B	SE	Wald	df	Sig.	Exp(B)	95% CI for Exp(B) Lower	95% CI for Exp(B) Upper
Step 1[a]	BMI	.092	.003	1013.633	1	.000	1.096	1.090	1.102
	Constant	-4.901	.090	2939.412	1	.000	.007		

a. Variable(s) entered on step 1: BMI.

Data Source: NHIS2010, Centers for Disease Control and Prevention.

Table 3.14 SAS Output

Analysis of Maximum Likelihood Estimates					
Parameter	df	Estimate	Standard Error	Wald Chi-Square	Pr > ChiSq
Intercept	1	−4.9009	0.0904	2939.4627	<.0001
BMI	1	0.0915	0.00287	1013.6774	<.0001

Odds Ratio Estimates		
Effect	Point Estimate	95% Wald Confidence Limits
BMI	1.096	1.090 1.102

Data Source: NELS10, National Center for Educational Statistics, U.S. Department of Education (http://nces.ed.gov/surveys/nels88/).

The BMI variable statistics in Tables 3.13 and 3.14 are startlingly different from the previous analysis with the dichotomous OBESE variable. The odds ratio is now 1.096, whereas before it was 3.176. And now the *B* is 0.092, whereas before it was 1.156. Does this mean our logistic regression analysis with a continuous measure of BMI is a substantially worse model than the model with the binary OBESE variable? No. This is the most important point about interpreting results from logistic regression analyses: these statistics can only be interpreted if you know how the variables are coded.

Let's examine the Wald statistic. In the last analysis, it was 726.29 and was significant at $p < .0001$. The Wald in this analysis is larger by a good amount—1013.63. So what is going on? Remember that the effect is now spread across dozens of increments of 1.0, rather than one. So for every increment of 1.0 in BMI, the odds of being diagnosed with diabetes increase. Every increase in BMI of 1.0 results in odds of being diagnosed that are 1.097 that of those with a BMI 1.0 lower—at any point in the scale, at least according to this simple linear analysis where we assume that the effect is linear on the logit. In future chapters, we will explore nonlinear effects where increments may not be equal across the entire range of a variable or may be radically different depending on the status of a third variable. As we will see later, to the extent that this assumption of linearity is incorrect, I am potentially misestimating these statistics.

The complexity of using a continuous variable is not great, but it does take a little thought and some careful narrative so that readers not used to seeing continuous variables in logistic regression interpret the results appropriately. We now know that increasing BMI is associated with increasing odds of diabetes—but an increase in odds of .097 is not impressive to the casual reader, even a reader who understands that increase is for each increase of 1.0 in BMI. So let's compare the probability or odds of being diagnosed with diabetes at two arbitrarily chosen points: the 25th percentile and 75th percentile of BMI (about 23 and 31).[8]

By inserting these numbers into the regression equation:

$$\text{Logit}(\hat{Y}) = -4.90 + 0.092(\text{BMI})$$

we get predicted logits of −2.784 (BMI = 23) and −2.048 (BMI = 31). By converting these to predicted probabilities, we observe conditional probabilities of 0.058 and 0.114, respectively. In other words, we can say that the probability of being diagnosed with diabetes of individuals at the 75th percentile of BMI is about 2 times that of individuals at the 25th percentile. Of course, this is an arbitrary comparison as I am not a researcher

---

[8]Of course, if this was your research, you might choose two points that are less arbitrary and more meaningful.

with expertise in this area. I could just as easily compare those at the 10th and 90th percentiles (about BMI of 21 and 36), which yields predicted probabilities of 0.049 and 0.170, and the conclusion that those with BMI of 36 are 3.47 times more likely to be diagnosed with diabetes than those at BMI = 21.

Example Summary of This Analysis

Body mass index (BMI) was a significant predictor of Diabetes status. Entry of obesity into the model significantly improved model fit (null −2LL = 17057.01, final −2LL = 16070.02, $\chi^2_{(1)}$ = 986.98, $p < .0001$). As you can see in Table X, increased BMI is associated with increased probabilities of being diagnosed with diabetes ($b = 0.092$, $SE_b = 0.003$, $p < .0001$). When converted to conditional probabilities we find that those in the 25th percentile for BMI (BMI = 23) have a predicted logit of −2.784, which corresponds to a conditional probability of 0.058, and those in the 75th percentile (BMI = 31) have a predicted logit of −2.048, which corresponds to a conditional probability of 0.11. The relative risk of being diagnosed with diabetes for those in the 75th percentile is therefore 1.90 compared to those in the 25th percentile.

Example 2: The Relationship Between Family Poverty and Dropping Out of School Prior to Graduation

You have already seen some of these data relating to family poverty and dropout from high school, so I will briefly review the full logistic regression analysis, and then replicate the analysis with the continuous family socioeconomic status variable (SES), as I did in the first example. As you recall, these data are from the National Education Longitudinal Study of 1988 (NELS88; http://nces.ed.gov/surveys/nels88/). Since we have seen that both SAS and SPSS produce nearly identical results I will not replicate each analysis in both software package, but from this point on I will alternate between the two packages so that both are represented.

In this analysis (summarized in Table 3.15), we have an initial −2 log likelihood for the empty model of 9967.242 and 9205.454 once POOR is entered into the model. This gives us an omnibus test of the model of $\chi^2_{(1)}$ = 761.788, $p < .0001$. Why does the chi-square difference have one degree of freedom? As mentioned briefly earlier, when comparing nested models such as this, the difference in −2 log likelihood from the null and final models can be interpreted as a chi-square with degrees of freedom equal to the number of variables that entered the model (more technically, the difference in parameters estimated, which is the same thing in this sort of analysis). In this case, we only entered one variable into the model, so the *df* = 1. If we had simultaneously entered several, the degrees of freedom for the chi-square test would be equal to that number.

Table 3.15   Summary of Analysis of NELS88 Dropout and Poverty Data

Omnibus Tests of Model Coefficients				
		Chi-square	*df*	Sig.
	Step	761.788	1	.000
Step 1	Block	761.788	1	.000
	Model	761.788	1	.000

Model Summary			
Step	−2 Log likelihood	Cox & Snell R Square	Nagelkerke *R* Square
1	9205.454[a]	.045	.099

Data Source: NELS88, National Center for Educational Statistics, U.S. Department of Education (http://nces.ed.gov/surveys/nels88/).

Table 3.16   Classification Table[a]

			Predicted		
	Observed		dropout		Percentage Correct
			.00	1.00	
	dropout	.00	15133	0	100.0
Step 1		1.00	1477	0	.0
	Overall Percentage				91.1

a. The cut value is .500.

Data Source: NELS88, National Center for Educational Statistics, U.S. Department of Education (http://nces.ed.gov/surveys/nels88/).

Similar to the diabetes analyses earlier in the chapter, the overall classification table in Table 3.16 yielded 91.1% of cases classified correctly, but this is only because 91.1% of the cases were nondropouts. The predicted probabilities were not high enough to classify any student as a likely dropout based on these analyses. In the next example, we will explore a logistic regression analysis where there is a more interesting classification table.

Importantly, the overall model is significant, meaning that probabilities of dropout are influenced by family poverty. Thus, we can examine the variable statistics, presented in Table 3.17.

Table 3.17 Variables in the Equation

| | | B | SE | Wald | df | Sig. | Exp(B) | 95% CI for Exp(B) | |
								Lower	Upper
Step 1[a]	poor	1.742	.073	566.339	1	.000	5.711	4.947	6.592
	Constant	−3.514	.066	2793.147	1	.000	.030		

a. Variable(s) entered on step 1: poor.

Data Source: NELS88, National Center for Educational Statistics, U.S. Department of Education (http://nces.ed.gov/surveys/nels88/).

As we have seen in Chapter 2, those from households classified as POOR are more likely to drop out prior to completing high school. Specifically, the odds of dropout for students from poor households are 5.71 that of students from non-poor households. In this case, as before, we also requested 95% confidence intervals, which range from 4.947 to 6.592, and are interpreted the same as in the previous chapter: we are 95% sure the odds ratio in the population is between these two numbers.

Example Summary of This Analysis

Poverty was a significant predictor of dropout status. Entry of POOR into the model significantly improved model fit (null −2LL = 9967.242, final −2LL = 9205.454, $\chi^2_{(1)}$ = 761.79, $p < .0001$). As you can see in Table X, those who are from high poverty families are more likely to drop out of high school (OR = 5.71, 95%CI = 4.95, 6.59). When converted to conditional probabilities, we find that those in the nonpoor homes have approximately a 0.029% chance of withdrawing from high school prior to graduation while those in the high-poverty category have approximately a 14.54% chance, representing a relative risk of 5.01.

PREDICTING DROPOUT FROM ♦ A CONTINUOUS FAMILY SES VARIABLE

Let's see what happens when we use family SES as a continuous variable rather than split into a somewhat arbitrary binary variable. As before, the −2 log likelihood for the empty model is 9967.242—something that should not change as it reflects the lack of fit in the model before ANY independent variables are entered. Once SES is entered into the equation, the −2 log likelihood for the overall model is 8739.91, markedly lower than the binary POOR variable (meaning there was a better improvement in fit with the continuous variable than the binary variable; change in −2LL was 1227.33 for the continuous variable vs. 761.788 for the binary POOR variable).

Table 3.18 SAS Output Summary Predicting DROPOUT From Family SES

Model Fit Statistics		
Criterion	Intercept Only	Intercept and Covariates
AIC	9969.242	8743.911
SC	9976.960	8759.346
−2 Log L	9967.242	8739.911

Testing Global Null Hypothesis: BETA = 0			
Test	Chi-Square	df	Pr > ChiSq
Likelihood Ratio	1227.3312	1	<.0001
Score	1167.5133	1	<.0001
Wald	1018.3531	1	<.0001

Data Source: NELS88, National Center for Educational Statistics, U.S. Department of Education (http://nces.ed.gov/surveys/nels88/).

As you can see in Table 3.18, we have a significant improvement in the model once family SES is entered into the equation. We can thus examine the variable statistics. Remembering that SES is now a continuous variable, we again are going to have to adjust how we interpret the results. Recall that in the last example, BMI ranged from 12 to 79, giving us many increments of 1.0. In these data, SES is continuous, but it is created and scaled to match the standard normal distribution (z scores with a mean of 0.00 and a SD of 1.0). Thus, instead of dozens of increments of 1.0, we will have only a handful, as each increment now represents 1 standard deviation rather than 1 on a scale with a broad range. Again, it is important to understand the nature of your variables in interpreting the results of a logistic regression.

What is nice about using z-scored continuous variables is that the 1.0 increment is consistent across all variables—and the interpretation is simple, as each increment of 1.0 means an increase of 1.0 standard deviations

Figure 3.2 Distribution of Family SES

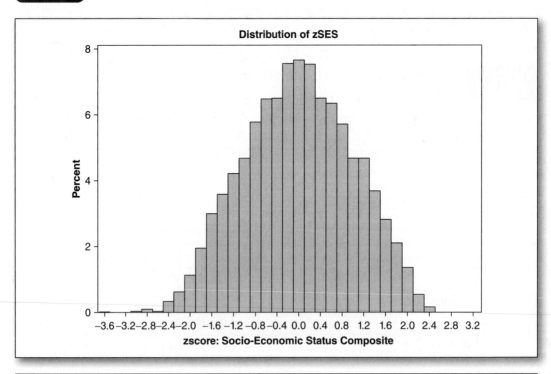

Data Source: NELS88, National Center for Educational Statistics, U.S. Department of Education (http://nces.ed.gov/surveys/nels88/).

in the independent variable. This is directly analogous to the standardized regression coefficient in OLS regression, where each variable is converted to the standard normal distribution and therefore the betas are directly comparable. Another nice aspect of using standard normal distributions is that the intercept (0.00) is set to the mean of the distribution, rather than a number that may not be useful or even possible (i.e., BMI = 0.00 is not possible). *Thus this will be considered a best practice moving forward—all continuous variables should be standardized through being converted to the standard normal distribution.*[9]

As with the first example in this chapter, the odds ratios and regression coefficients need to be interpreted carefully. But first, let's keep in mind that POOR and SES are coded in different directions. In POOR, the higher number reflected poverty in the household. In the variable SES, higher numbers reflect less poverty, so the coefficients will be in the opposite direction of POOR—higher numbers should relate to lower odds of dropout.

Let's start with interpreting the odds ratio for these results: for each 1 *SD* increase in family SES, the odds of dropout are 0.353 that of students with family SES 1 *SD* lower. In other words, compared with students with a score of 0 (median SES), the odds of dropout for students coming from

| **Table 3.19** | SAS output Summarizing Variable Statistics Predicting DROPOUT From Family SES |

Analysis of Maximum Likelihood Estimates					
Parameter	df	Estimate	Standard Error	Wald Chi-Square	Pr > ChiSq
Intercept	1	−2.7395	0.0372	5409.5698	<.0001
zSES	1	−1.0408	0.0326	1018.3531	<.0001

Odds Ratio Estimates			
Effect	Point Estimate	95% Wald Confidence Limits	
zSES	0.353	0.331	0.376

Data Source: NELS88, National Center for Educational Statistics, U.S. Department of Education (http://nces.ed.gov/surveys/nels88/).

---

[9]Indeed, DeMaris (1993) advocated this 20 years ago.

a family with SES of 1.0 standard deviations higher are 0.353 (about one third as large). But let's examine the full range of SES: what are the odds of dropout for a student with a family SES of −2.0 (two standard deviations below average) compared with 2.0 (two standard deviations above average)? Using the prediction equation:

$$\text{Logit}(Y) = -2.740 - 1.041(\text{SES})$$

We can calculate predicted logits of −0.658 and −4.822, which translates to predicted probabilities of 0.34 and 0.008—a very dramatic difference.[10] If you do the math, the probability of dropout for those coming from very poor households (SES = −2) is *42.72 times that of students from very affluent families* (SES = 2).

Let's practice good statistical habits right from this chapter and calculate 95% CIs for our predicted probabilities. Recall that 95% CIs can be calculated by using the equation we covered previously:

$$95\%\text{CI} = \text{predicted logit} \pm 1.96(SE_{\text{logit}})$$

For students from low SES families, we get a 95% CI in logits of (−0.72, −0.59), which translates to predicted probabilities of (0.327, 0.356). For students from high-SES families, we get a 95% CI in logits of (−4.89, −4.76), which translates to predicted probabilities of (0.0075, 0.0085). Thus, because we have very small standard errors, our confidence intervals are relatively close to our point estimates. Remember, I suggest always reporting 95% confidence intervals to give your reader as much information as possible!

Aside from this rather dramatic comparison, we can again see the value of using continuous variables, as we did in the first example. In these analyses, the Wald statistic was 566.34 when using the variable POOR, a binary version of the continuous SES variable. When using the original continuous variable, we have a Wald that is almost double—1018.35.

Example Summary of This Analysis

Family socioeconomic status (SES) was a significant predictor of dropout status. Entry of SES into the model significantly improved model fit (null

---

[10]See? All that math we did in the previous chapter is already paying off!

$-2LL = 9967.24$, final $-2LL = 8739.91$, $\chi^2_{(1)} = 1227.33$, $p < .0001$). As you can see in Table X, increased family SES is associated with a substantial decrease in dropout ($b = -1.04$, $SE_b = 0.033$, $p < .0001$). When converted to conditional probabilities we find that students from families two standard deviations below the mean have a predicted logit of -0.66, which corresponds to a conditional probability of 0.34 (95%CI $= 0.33, 0.36$), and those from families two standard deviations above the mean had a predicted logit of -4.82, which corresponds to a conditional probability of 0.008 (95%CI $= 0.0057, 0.0085$). The relative risk of dropping out for students at 2 SD below the mean compared with those 2 *SD* above the mean is 42.72.

ARE CLASSIFICATION TABLES EVER USEFUL? ♦

In these two examples, the effects have been strong in most ways of looking at a logistic regression analysis with the exception of the classification tables. In many areas of research, these are not going to be critical. But in cases where it is important to posit that your model is correctly classifying individuals into the observed groups, there are a couple issues that we want to explore. First is the cutoff score.

Logistic regression, as all regression models, produces predicted values for each individual. In this case, we are looking at predicted conditional probabilities, which are then used to classify individuals. Thus, we have two factors influencing the goodness of classification tables: the strength and accuracy of the model, and the cutoff scores. By default, most programs use a predicted probability of 0.50 as the cutoff for placing cases in one group or the other for comparison to the observed groupings. It may be the case that .50 is not an appropriate cutoff score for placing individuals into groups. For example, in the second example where we are predicting dropout from POOR, the predicted probabilities are 0.029 and 0.145. No cases are going to be placed into the "dropout" group with a threshold of .50. When using the continuous SES variable, predicted probabilities ranged from 0.002 to 0.744. As you can see in the histogram in Figure 3.3, few cases surpass the .50 probability threshold, and thus only a handful of cases were classified as dropout.

But what if .50 was not a reasonable cutoff score? Let us set the cutoff score at 0.25. At this, the classification table looks like Table 3.20.

Figure 3.3 Distribution of Predicted Probabilities

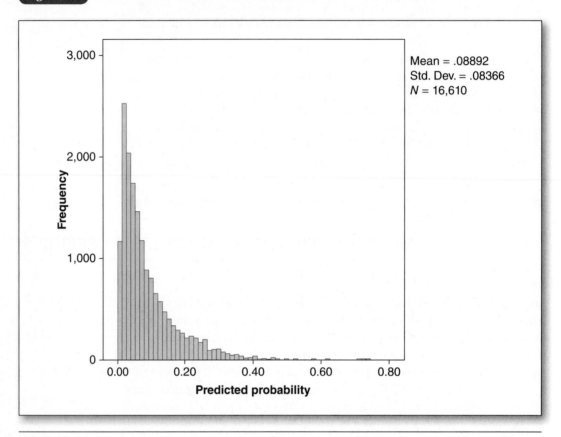

Data Source: NELS88, National Center for Educational Statistics, U.S. Department of Education (http://nces.ed.gov/surveys/nels88/).

Table 3.20 Classification Table[a]

	Observed		Predicted		
			dropout		Percentage Correct
			.00	1.00	
Step 1	dropout	.00	14436	697	95.4
		1.00	1176	301	20.4
	Overall Percentage				88.7

a. The cut value is .250.

Data Source: NELS88, National Center for Educational Statistics, U.S. Department of Education (http://nces.ed.gov/surveys/nels88/).

Table 3.21 Classification Table[a]

	Observed		Predicted		
			diabetes		Percentage Correct
			.00	1.00	
Step 1	diabetes	.00	294	806	26.7
		1.00	183	2413	93.0
	Overall Percentage				73.2

a. The cut value is .500.

Data Source: NHIS2010, Centers for Disease Control and Prevention.

You may note that more students are being classified as predicted dropouts—and in fact with this guideline about 20% of dropouts are now correctly classified as dropouts. Unfortunately, 4.6% of nondropouts are now misclassified as dropouts, dropping the overall accuracy from 91.1% to 88.7%. But it might be the case that in your research it is critically important to get the classification of one group as good as possible and that it is more permissible to have misclassifications in the other group.

This is probably not the best path to improving your classification table, but I did want to point out that it might not be reasonable to have .50 as a cutoff score for classification (note that fiddling with this parameter does not change any other aspect of the analysis). A more desirable path would be to find variables that are more strongly related to the outcome. In later chapters we will explore multiple independent variables, which can help improve the power of your model.

For example, when I go back to the diabetes data from the first example, and imagine my goal is to be the most accurate in predicting which patients have diabetes, not which are diabetes-free, I can add insulin use to the equation (along with age, smoking status, race, and BMI) and achieve the classification table in Table 3.21.

In this example, I am 93% accurate in identifying individuals with diabetes but only 26.7% accurate in nondiabetic patients.[11] This table may or may not be of particular interest to your research, and depending on your focus, it may be critical for you to identify one group with greater accuracy or to be as accurate overall as possible.

---

[11]You may note that the sample size dropped dramatically—that is because only a small percentage of patients had data on insulin usage. We'll talk more about missing data later in the book!

In SAS, the default classification table gives a bit more information, which relates to the above discussion. You have the option, as you do in SPSS, to specify a specific cut score for assignment to predicted category. With the default SAS output, you also get the classification tables for a variety of cut scores, along with sensitivity, specificity, and false positive/negative rates.

Table 3.22 Classification Table

Prob Level	Correct		Incorrect		Percentages				
	Event	Non-Event	Event	Non-Event	Correct	Sensitivity	Specificity	False POS	False NEG
0.000	1477	0	15133	0	8.9	100.0	0.0	91.1	.
0.020	1455	2526	12607	22	24.0	98.5	16.7	89.7	0.9
0.040	1364	5622	9511	113	42.1	92.3	37.2	87.5	2.0
0.060	1230	7993	7140	247	55.5	83.3	52.8	85.3	3.0
0.080	1108	9739	5394	369	65.3	75.0	64.4	83.0	3.7
0.100	981	10949	4184	496	71.8	66.4	72.4	81.0	4.3
0.120	864	11836	3297	613	76.5	58.5	78.2	79.2	4.9
0.140	744	12544	2589	733	80.0	50.4	82.9	77.7	5.5
0.160	654	13078	2055	823	82.7	44.3	86.4	75.9	5.9
0.180	582	13495	1638	895	84.8	39.4	89.2	73.8	6.2
0.200	490	13816	1317	987	86.1	33.2	91.3	72.9	6.7
0.220	423	14094	1039	1054	87.4	28.6	93.1	71.1	7.0
0.240	334	14331	802	1143	88.3	22.6	94.7	70.6	7.4
0.260	262	14548	585	1215	89.2	17.7	96.1	69.1	7.7
0.280	203	14667	466	1274	89.5	13.7	96.9	69.7	8.0
0.300	157	14788	345	1320	90.0	10.6	97.7	68.7	8.2
0.320	116	14876	257	1361	90.3	7.9	98.3	68.9	8.4
0.340	92	14940	193	1385	90.5	6.2	98.7	67.7	8.5
0.360	67	14988	145	1410	90.6	4.5	99.0	68.4	8.6
0.380	46	15022	111	1431	90.7	3.1	99.3	70.7	8.7
0.400	37	15040	93	1440	90.8	2.5	99.4	71.5	8.7
0.420	25	15067	66	1452	90.9	1.7	99.6	72.5	8.8
0.440	22	15083	50	1455	90.9	1.5	99.7	69.4	8.8
0.460	21	15092	41	1456	91.0	1.4	99.7	66.1	8.8
0.480	12	15112	21	1465	91.1	0.8	99.9	63.6	8.8
0.500	12	15114	19	1465	91.1	0.8	99.9	61.3	8.8

Prob Level	Correct		Incorrect		Percentages				
	Event	Non-Event	Event	Non-Event	Correct	Sensitivity	Specificity	False POS	False NEG
0.520	11	15114	19	1466	91.1	0.7	99.9	63.3	8.8
0.540	6	15127	6	1471	91.1	0.4	100.0	50.0	8.9
0.560	5	15127	6	1472	91.1	0.3	100.0	54.5	8.9
0.580	5	15127	6	1472	91.1	0.3	100.0	54.5	8.9
0.600	3	15130	3	1474	91.1	0.2	100.0	50.0	8.9
0.620	2	15130	3	1475	91.1	0.1	100.0	60.0	8.9
0.640	2	15130	3	1475	91.1	0.1	100.0	60.0	8.9
0.660	2	15130	3	1475	91.1	0.1	100.0	60.0	8.9
0.680	2	15130	3	1475	91.1	0.1	100.0	60.0	8.9
0.700	2	15130	3	1475	91.1	0.1	100.0	60.0	8.9
0.720	1	15130	3	1476	91.1	0.1	100.0	75.0	8.9
0.740	1	15132	1	1476	91.1	0.1	100.0	50.0	8.9
0.760	0	15133	0	1477	91.1	0.0	100.0	.	8.9

Data Source: NHIS2010, Centers for Disease Control and Prevention.

HOW SHOULD WE INTERPRET ♦ ODDS RATIOS THAT ARE LESS THAN 1.0?

One significant problem with odds ratios is that they are asymmetrical. They can theoretically range from 0.00 to ∞, but a value of 1.0 means there is no difference in risk or odds (i.e., there is no effect of the independent variable). Thus, the entire infinity of decreasing (inverse) relationships must fit between 0.000001 and 0.99999, while that same infinity of positive relationships fits in a much larger space between 1.00001 and ∞. As you saw in the DROPOUT and POOR example, that relationship was positive—odds of dropout increase as you move from nonpoor to poor households, and the odds ratio was impressive: 5.711. What if we had reversed the variable so that we were studying *affluence* (0 = poor households and 1 = affluent households)? The odds ratio would have been 0.175. Reversing the coding of a variable (swapping 0 and 1) merely inverts the odds ratio (thus, 0.175 = 1/5.711). An odds ratio of 20.00 is therefore equivalent to an odds ratio of 0.05 in magnitude. But from a psychological and interpretation point of view, odds ratios below 1.0 tend to seem less impressive and (in my experience) are more likely to be misinterpreted.

Two issues arise here. First, use of directional language such as "individuals in group 1 are X times *more likely* to experience a specific outcome than in group 2" or "individuals in group 2 are X times *less likely*. . . ." Leaving for a moment the difficulty with cogently describing an odds ratio, the difficulty here comes in the common mistake people make in describing decreasing ratios. If you have an odds ratio of 5.71, as we did, it is straightforward to say something like "students from poor households are 5.71 times more likely to withdraw from school than students." But if we had coded the variables differently, as suggested earlier, we would have gotten an odds ratio of 0.175. This means the exact same thing—that students from affluent households are much less likely to drop out.

Yet these odds ratios less than 1.0 can be treacherous to interpret. Authors often want to say things like "students from affluent households are 0.175 times *less likely to drop out* than students from high-poverty households," but in fact that is not the case. 0.175 times less likely implies 0.815 times *as likely*—a much smaller effect than is actually the case. Psychologically, people do not generally view 0.175 and 5.71 as being equal in magnitude, just as people often do not view 0.01 and 100 as the same magnitude, although they are in terms of odds ratios.

So what to do about this? First, we need to be careful how we talk about odds ratios. My advice has always been to use "as likely" rather than less or more likely. Another way of staying clear of trouble is to use language like "the odds of GROUP X having an outcome is <odds ratio> that of GROUP Y." So using our previous example, saying "the odds that students from affluent households will drop out of school are 0.175 that of students from poor households" is preferable to using terminology like "less likely." But it is not solving the problem of people perceiving that as a less impressive effect than 5.71. This dilemma brings us to the second issue: the psychological impact of ratios and accurately conveying effect sizes when the effect sizes themselves vary depending on whether they are increasing or decreasing odds.

Taking a more extreme example, imagine a drug that made the risk of experiencing a cancer relapse OR = 0.001 compared with people who do not take the drug. Mathematically, that is identical to saying that taking the drug makes you 1,000 times less likely to experience relapse or that not taking the drug makes you 1,000 times more likely to have a relapse. But are they perceptually identical? No. Further elaborating, let us say you have two drugs. One produces an OR = 0.001 and one an OR = 0.01. Even the most technically proficient of us will view these as pretty close (i.e., really small). However if the direction of the independent variable were arbitrarily reversed, the ORs would be 1,000 and 100, respectively, and most people

Figure 3.4 The Nonlinear Relationship Between Odds Ratios Above 1.0 and Below 1.0

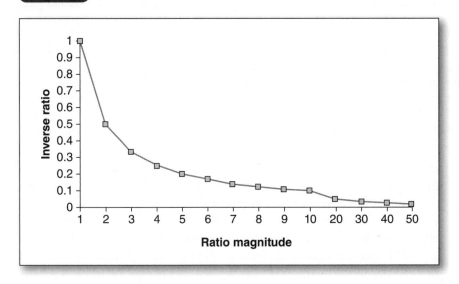

would interpret those as "pretty large," but in the latter case, it is much more apparent that the magnitude of the effect is a magnitude different.

Thus another practical recommendation is to refrain from reporting ORs less than 1.0. It would make sense to standardize the reporting of this effect size so that all ratios be reported as >1.0. Analyses that result in ratios less than 1.0 would take the inverse of the OR, and reverse the categories or the description of the results to keep the conclusion consistent.[1]

Another, perhaps preferable method of dealing with this issue is to convert odds or logits to predicted probabilities for each group, as we did in the last chapter (and as we will do with more urgency in later chapters when looking at interactions and curvilinear effects). This has the laudable effect of reducing the exaggeration of effect size that odds ratios can have under certain circumstances and helping avoid issues like interpreting an odds ratio of 0.175 as being "0.175 times *less likely*" for something to happen. So

---

[1]Pedhazur (1997) suggests an alternative solution to this issue—taking the natural log (ln) of all ORs. This has the effect of moving the "null effect" point from 1.0 to 0.0 and removing the lower bound so that effect size distribution is symmetrical. The drawback to this elegant solution is that it changes the effect from substantively interpretable (relative risk or odds ratio) to something much more complex to interpret—the natural log of a relative risk or an odds ratio. Thus I would not recommend this solution.

Table 3.23 Variables in the Equation

		B	SE	Wald	df	Sig.	Exp(B)
Step 1[a]	RICH	−1.742	.073	566.339	1	.000	.175
	Constant	−1.771	.031	3335.136	1	.000	.170

a. Variable(s) entered on step 1: RICH.

Data Source: NELS88, National Center for Educational Statistics, U.S. Department of Education (http://nces.ed.gov/surveys/nels88/).

taking the same data as presented in example 2, but recoding POOR to RICH (0 = not affluent, 1 = affluent), you can see we get the expected odds ratio of 0.175. But instead of using the standard interpretation as discussed earlier, we can create predicted probabilities for both groups, illustrating the effect more directly. In this case, the predicted logits for nonaffluent students is −1.774 and for affluent students is −3.513. These convert to predicted probabilities of 0.029 and 0.145 (as we saw in Chapter 2), and it is readily apparent that there is a large discrepancy between the two groups and is thus less easy to misinterpret regardless of the direction of the effect.

SUMMARY

In this chapter, we covered a lot of ground—from assessing the overall goodness of a model to some of the benefits of using continuous variables (where your data has continuous variables) rather than engaging in the common practice of dichotomizing. Along the way, I argued that any continuous variable should be converted to the standard normal distribution before using it in logistic regression so as to standardize interpretation of those variables. Furthermore, I suggested that variables should be coded in such a way that odds ratios end up above 1.0 for ease of interpretation.

We will explore other good reasons for these recommendations in coming chapters.

ENRICHMENT

In addition to the data sets, which are housed on the website for the book (so that you can reproduce the analyses presented in this chapter if you like; www.sagepub.com/osbornebplr), we can explore the NELS88 data set (http://nces.ed.gov/surveys/nels88/) that you can use to test whether you have mastered the content of this chapter. Both data sets are subsamples of the much larger original data, and neither is weighted appropriately. Thus, you should not use these data for any purpose other than exploring the ideas presented in this chapter.

If you want to reproduce the analyses from this chapter, download the data from the book website.

1. What predicts whether students will report using marijuana?

In some of the NCES surveys, they asked students interesting questions such as whether they used alcohol, smoked, used drugs, or had sex. Although these are self-report data, they are interesting to play with, as getting data on these illicit activities from minors is often difficult (at least in the United States).

Download the data set from the book website. The dependent variable (EVERMJ) is coded 0 = never tried marijuana, 1 = tried marijuana at least once.

a. Does SEX (1 = male, 2 = female) predict reported marijuana use? If so, are males or females more likely to report having tried it?

b. Does student race (RACEBW; 0 = Caucasian/White, 1 = Black/ African American) predict reported marijuana use? If so, are White (Caucasian) or Black/African American students more likely to report having tried it?

c. A long time ago, I calculated a variable I called "BADCNT," which counted the number of bad things a student reported having happened in school that year. These included things like being assaulted, having things stolen, being offered drugs, and other stressful events. This variable ranges from 0 to 6, with most students having experienced none of these or one of these types of events. According to common theories of marijuana (and other drug use), stressful events might make students more likely to try marijuana. Your final challenge in this chapter is to see whether this "continuous" variable predicts reported marijuana use. Contrary to my recommendation above, we will NOT convert this variable to the standard normal distribution as it is already in a substantively interpretable metric: number of events experienced.

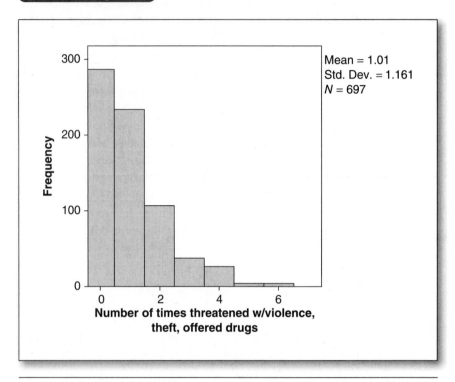

Enrichment Figure 3.1 Distribution of BADCNT Variable

Data Source: NELS88, National Center for Educational Statistics, U.S. Department of Education (http://nces.ed.gov/surveys/nels88/).

If there is a significant effect, describe the nature of the effect, keeping in mind that this is a continuous variable.

d. Calculate a predicted logit for BADCNT = 0 and for BADCNT = 4. Convert the predicted logits back to conditional probabilities for BADCNT = 0 vs. 4.

ANSWER KEY

Mastery example: What predicts whether students will report using marijuana?

a. When SEX is entered into the prediction equation for EVERMJ, there is a tendency for females to be less likely to report having tried it (OR = 0.733) but that trend is not significant (95%CI = 0.496, 1.08,

$p < .118$). Thus, we cannot conclude that sex is a significant predictor of whether a student reports trying marijuana.

b. When RACEBW is entered into a prediction equation for EVERMJ, Black/African American students are substantially less likely to report having tried marijuana (OR = 0.394, 95%CI = 0.174, 0.890). Because the 95% confidence interval does not contain 1.00 (and because $p < .025$), we can reject the null hypothesis and assert that race is significantly related to reported marijuana use. Specifically, the odds that Black students report trying marijuana are about .40 that of White students. Put another way (by calculating the inverse of this OR), the odds that White students will are report using marijuana are about 2.5 times that of Black/African American students.

c. There is a significant relationship between stressful events experienced by students and reported marijuana use. Specifically, the odds ratio is 1.426 (95%CI 1.212, 1.677). Because the confidence interval does not contain 1.00, and $p < .0001$,[2] we can reject the null hypothesis and assert that stressful events do relate to reported marijuana use. Specifically, for each new event (as BADCNT increases by 1.0), the odds that a student will report trying marijuana are 1.426 that of students with one less stressful event.

Enrichment Table 3.1 Variables in the Equation

		B	SE	Wald	df	Sig.	Exp(B)
Step 1[a]	BADCNT	.355	.083	18.375	1	.000	1.426
	Constant	−1.564	.141	122.869	1	.000	.209

a. Variable(s) entered on step 1: BADCNT.

1. Using the regression line equation: logit(y) = −1.564 + 0.355(BADCNT)

2. BADCNT = 0: predicted logit = −1.564, predicted conditional probability = 0.17

[2]In SPSS, p values are usually truncated to 3 decimal places. So in my output, I see .000 for the p. We cannot report a probability less than 0.000, and so I usually advise my students to add a 1 to the end of that number just to make sure you do not violate fundamental laws of mathematics. Alternatively, you can adjust your output to get more specific details on p values.

3. BADCNT = 1: predicted logit = −1.209, predicted conditional probability = 0.23

4. BADCNT = 2: predicted logit = −0.854, predicted conditional probability = 0.30

5. BADCNT = 3: predicted logit = −0.499, predicted conditional probability = 0.38

6. BADCNT = 4: predicted logit = −0.144, predicted conditional probability = 0.46

7. People with BADCNT = 4 are 2.68 times more likely to report having tried marijuana compared to those with BADCNT = 0.

SYNTAX EXAMPLES

SPSS syntax for producing Hosmer and Lemeshow analyses with continuous variables:

```
LOGISTIC REGRESSION VARIABLES dropout
/METHOD = ENTER Zbyses
/PRINT = GOODFIT CI(95)
/CRITERIA = PIN(0.05) POUT(0.10) ITERATE(20) CUT(0.5).
```

In this case, the /PRINT = GOODFIT command produces that particular output.

SAS syntax for producing logistic regression analyses with Hosmer and Lemeshow analyses:

```
PROC LOGISTIC DATA = book.Ch03_NELS descending;
MODEL dropout = zbyses
/lackfit ctable;
output out = results p = predict ;
run;
```

In this case, the LACKFIT command produces these results (CTABLE produces the classification table). You can customize how many categories are produced, but this produces the default ~10 categories.

SAS command for producing the histogram:

```
proc univariate data = BOOK.Ch03_NELS;
var zbyses;
histogram;
run;
```

REFERENCES

DeMaris, A. (1993). Odds versus probabilities in logit equations: A reply to Roncek. *Social Forces, 71*(4), 1057–1065. doi: 10.2307/2580130

Osborne, J. W. (2011). Best practices in using large, complex samples: The importance of using appropriate weights and design effect compensation. *Practical Assessment Research & Evaluation, 16*(12), 1–7.

Pedhazur, E. (1997). *Multiple regression in behavioral research.* New York, NY: Harcourt Brace.

4

A PRACTICAL GUIDE TO TESTING ASSUMPTIONS AND CLEANING DATA FOR LOGISTIC REGRESSION

L ogistic regression is a nonparametric technique. Does that mean that data cleaning is less important (or not important at all)?

There is good news and bad news. The good news is that parametric assumptions like normality and homoscedasticity are not relevant in logistic regression. The bad news is that basics like data cleaning (e.g., outliers), missing data, linearity, independence of observations, perfect measurement, and sparseness of data still matter. In the course of this chapter, we will cover how these basic data cleaning chores can be accomplished and how your analyses can benefit if you do so.

You have now learned that logistic regression contains some conceptual and procedural similarities to ordinary least squares (OLS) regression. In Chapter 1, we discussed one of the primary differences: that the nature of the dependent variable must be discrete—generally dichotomous (but not necessarily!). We briefly covered the notion that logistic regression uses maximum likelihood estimation rather than OLS estimation, which you may be more familiar with.

The result of this is that there are different assumptions that we must check and attend to when performing logistic regression than OLS/multiple regression. We briefly reviewed some of these assumptions in Chapter 1 and will now explore them in more depth in this chapter.

As with all inferential statistics, failure to meet the assumptions of the test you are performing can lead to significantly biased parameter estimates and errors of inference. In this chapter, we will cover the basic assumptions and how to test them:

- Independence of observations
- No inappropriately high collinearity between predictors
- Fully represented (no sparse) data matrix
- Perfect measurement
- Accurate model specification, which includes
  o linearity link function, and
  o additivity of the terms
- Data free from inappropriately influential cases

Note that the last one is not technically specified in most analyses as an explicit assumption, but it should be the unstated yet tested assumption for all analyses. We will spend substantial time in this chapter on how to explore your data for inappropriately influential data points (such as outliers).

♦ INDEPENDENCE OF OBSERVATIONS

People (and most creatures, for that matter) tend to exist within organizational structures, such as families, schools, business organizations, churches, towns, states, and countries. In education, students exist within a hierarchical social structure that can include family, peer group, classroom, grade level, school, school district, state, and country. Workers exist within production or skill units, businesses, and sectors of the economy, as well as geographic regions. Health care workers and patients exist within households and families, medical practices and facilities (e.g., a doctor's practice, or hospital), counties, states, and countries. Many other communities exhibit hierarchical data structures as well. Any sample can include nested data explicitly or accidentally.

Nested data present several problems for analysis. First, people or creatures that exist within hierarchies tend to be more similar to each other than people randomly sampled from the entire population. For example, students in a particular third-grade classroom are more similar to each other than to students randomly sampled from the school district as a whole or from the national population of third graders. This is because students are not randomly assigned to classrooms from the population, but rather are assigned to schools based on geographic factors. Thus, students within a particular classroom tend to come from a community or community segment that is more homogeneous in terms of morals and values, family background, socioeconomic status, race or ethnicity, religion, and even educational preparation than the population as a whole. Further, students within a particular classroom share the experience of being in the same environment—the same teacher, physical environment, and similar experiences, which may lead to increased homogeneity over time.

This discussion could be applied to any level of nesting, such as the family, the school district, county, state, or even country. Based on this discussion, we can assert that individuals who are drawn from an institution, such as a classroom, school, business, or health care unit, will be more homogeneous than if individuals were randomly sampled from a larger population. Herein lies the first issue for analysis of this sort of data. Because these individuals tend to share certain characteristics (environmental, background, experiential, demographic, or otherwise), observations based on these individuals are not fully independent. However, most analytic techniques require independence of observations as a primary assumption for the analysis. Because this assumption is violated in the presence of hierarchical data, statistical procedures that do not explicitly model nested data (e.g., hierarchical linear modeling, which we will explore in later chapters) produce standard errors that are too small (unless these so-called design effects are incorporated into the analysis). In turn, this leads to an inappropriately increased probability of rejection of a null hypothesis than if (a) an appropriate statistical analysis were performed or (b) the data included truly independent observations.

In logistic regression this is referred to as overdispersion or underdispersion (depending on whether the data are unexpectedly clustered or unexpectedly diverse).

COLLINEARITY OF INDEPENDENT VARIABLES ◆

In almost any analysis, but particularly in regression type analyses, having variables that are highly collinear can cause serious problems for your analysis, including extremely large standard errors. There are several ways this can happen: (a) variables that are perfectly (or almost perfectly) correlated with each other, such as accidentally entering a variable and its z-scored analogue, or a variable and a log transform of that variable; or (b) entering variables that are linear combinations of each other (e.g., entering subscale scores and a total score, or entering all possible dummy variables representing a categorical variable). These are generally easily dealt with. Other examples of collinearity issues are slightly more complex, such as when variables are highly correlated (e.g., $r \geq .80$) but are conceptually distinct variables. In cases such as these, it might be desirable to remove one or the other from the analysis, or to combine the variables in some way. Another option might be to model the variables in latent variable modeling software (e.g., AMOS, EQS, Lisrel) where highly correlated observed variables can be modeled as representatives of latent constructs.

♦ FULLY REPRESENTED DATA MATRIX

A related issue specific to logistic regression is that of *sparse data,* where one cell in a data array is empty. For example, when I was looking at the probability of a student dropping out of high school prior to completion of 12th grade, I was looking at family socioeconomic status (SES) and student achievement test scores but encountered a problem that might be predictable in hindsight—students in the highest achieving category were not represented in the lowest family SES ranges, leading to potentially sparse data if these had been categorical rather than continuous variables.

When sparse data occurs in categorical variables—when there are cells that have zero cases in them—odds can go toward infinity (either infinitely small or large), and the logit can go toward infinity as well.[1]

So what do you do when you have sparse data? You can recode the variable to collapse cells if it makes sense to do so. A more desirable option is to ensure your sample has full representation in all possible combinations of groups while planning your sampling framework.

Another related situation is *complete (or quasi-complete) separation,* where there is perfect (or near-perfect) separation of groups. In other words, when group membership is perfectly, or almost perfectly predicted, the logistic regression analysis has trouble computing estimates. More importantly, complete separation almost never occurs, especially in social sciences research, and thus should be viewed with suspicion. It is likely that there is something wrong with the analysis, which could include a variable that is perfectly correlated with the dependent variable.

---

[1]Thus, another advantage of using continuous variables or ordinal variables is that when sparseness occurs we can use predictions from adjacent values to "fill in" the information. When using categorical variables, we cannot assume anything about the relationship between two adjacent cells.

Figure 4.1 Example of Sparse Data

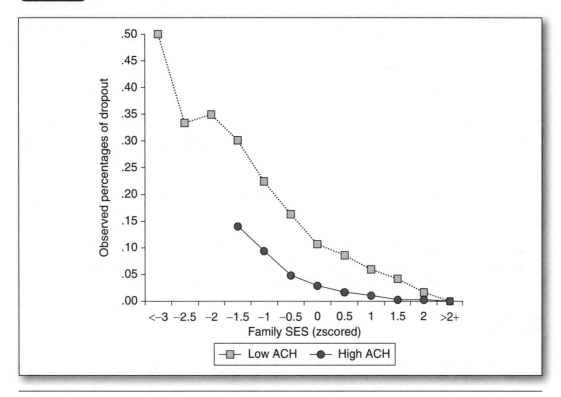

Data Source: National Education Longitudinal Study of 1988 (NELS88), National Center for Educational Statistics, U.S. Department of Education (http://nces.ed.gov/surveys/nels88/).

PERFECT MEASUREMENT ◆

Although not often discussed, in most statistical analyses we assume the variables are measured without error. Authors usually focus on the independent variable, but if cases are miscategorized in the dependent variable, then that also is a source of error in the model. The independent variables are also assumed to be measured without error, although this is almost always an assumption that is violated. I explore issues of measurement error in my 2012 book (Osborne, 2012). In the context of common parametric statistics, I was able to show that even levels of reliability that are generally considered "good" measurement produce underestimation of effect sizes.

Unreliable measurement has other deleterious effects when more than one predictor is in the equation. Imagine an equation where we are predicting whether a student drops out of high school prior to graduation from student achievement and family SES. Achievement and SES tend to be moderately correlated, so when both are in the equation, their unique effects are diminished when well measured. However, if one is poorly measured, the shared variance will not be properly accounted for, and the effect of the other variable could be inflated over where it should be.

To provide an example of the effect of poor measurement on simple logistic regression, we return to the example of DROPOUT (recoded into GRADUATED to keep the logit positive and the odds ratio over 1.0) and family SES (measured as a continuous variable) from Chapter 2. Recall that using the original data, students from families with SES of 1.0 higher have odds of graduating that are 2.83 that of students 1.0 SD lower.

We will assume SES and graduation are both perfectly measured and that this represents the gold standard against which we will compare the effects of poorer measurement. To simulate poorer measurement, I randomly selected 25%, 50%, or 75% of the cases to have SES replaced with a random number generated from a standard normal distribution with a mean of 0 and SD of 1.0.[2] As confirmation, after these scores were randomly

Table 4.1 Family SES and Odds of Graduating High School

% replaced by random numbers		B	SE	Wald	df	Sig.	Exp(B)
Original	zSES	1.041	.033	1018.355	1	.000	2.831
	Constant	2.740	.037	5409.564	1	.000	15.480
25%	SES_25	.748	.030	624.180	1	.000	2.112
	Constant	2.544	.033	6115.089	1	.000	12.737
50%	SES_50	.491	.029	296.872	1	.000	1.634
	Constant	2.423	.030	6688.529	1	.000	11.282
75%	SES_75	.235	.028	73.123	1	.000	1.265
	Constant	2.348	.028	7138.306	1	.000	10.463

Data Source: NELS88, National Center for Educational Statistics. U.S. Department of Education (http://nces.ed.gov/surveys/nels88/).

[2]The correlation between the original SES variable and the randomly generated variable was $r = .015$.

replaced by random numbers, the correlation between the original SES variable and the new "less reliably measured" SES variable was $r = .75, .52,$ and .27 for the 25%, 50%, and 75% replacement conditions, respectively.

As you can see in Table 4.1, when 25% of SES values are replaced by random numbers (simulating poorer reliability), the odds ratio decreases from 2.83 to 2.11, and the logit decreases from 1.04 to 0.75. Similarly, less reliable measurement (50% or 75% of values substituted with random values) results in more attenuation. Thus, it is clear that poor reliability in logistic regression has the same deleterious effect on accuracy of the estimates that is does in other common analyses.

MODEL IS CORRECTLY SPECIFIED—NO ◆ IMPORTANT VARIABLES OMITTED, NO EXTRANEOUS VARIABLES INCLUDED

This may sound like esoteric statistical blathering,[3] but in point of fact, these assumptions address the essence of what most of us are doing—trying to figure out what variables predict what outcomes. In order to do this, we assume that (a) the link function we are using—the logistic transformation of the original conditional probabilities—is the appropriate transform, (b) the linear link function is appropriate, (c) the terms are additive, (d) all important variables are in the equation, and (e) no irrelevant variables are in the equation.

The Logit Link Function Is Appropriate

Regarding the first point, when we are performing logistic regression, we are using the logit link function—transforming the data via the natural log of the odds. There are other possible transforms for dichotomous outcomes, including the probit transform, which is reviewed in Chapter 9 in this book. The choice to use probit versus logistic transforms of conditional probabilities seems largely to be dependent upon traditions within a particular discipline. Regardless of which you choose (and both tend to reveal similar results, as you will see in Chapter 9), the point is that by doing logistic regression, you are assuming that the essential transform at the heart of the link function—the log of the odds—is appropriate. If you perform probit, you assume that link function is appropriate.

---

[3]"Esoteric blathering" is a nicer phrase than many use regarding things I talk about.

The Relationships Are "Linear on the Logit"

In Chapter 1, I introduced the fun phrase "linear on the logit," which I have unabashedly adopted from other authors such as Menard (2010). The essence of this assumption is that after we use the logit link function with our data, the relationship between the independent variables and the logit of the dependent variable is linear. Similarly, when one uses probit regression, one assumes the relationship will be linear following that transform. In comparison, in OLS regression, we merely assume that the variables will be linearly related without any particular transformation (although I often find fun curvilinear relationships all types of regression and devote a chapter to this sort of thing later in the book!). Technically, the link function used in OLS regression is a 1 (the mathematical identity).

$$\text{Logit}(\hat{Y}) = a + b_1 X_1 + b_2 X_2 + \ldots + b_k X_k \qquad \text{Eq. 4.1.}$$

Equation 4.1 specifically posits that the logit of the conditional probabilities of the dependent variable is equal to a linear weighted combination of the predictors.[4]

One example of violating this assumption is that some variables in most areas of science are not *linearly* related to each other. Gravitational attraction, for example, between two objects is inversely proportional to the square of the distance, which is a curvilinear relationship. The effect of age on the probability of certain disease states is curvilinear as well—in some cases, staying flat for many decades of life and then accelerating rapidly at a certain point (e.g., the probability of being diagnosed with Alzheimer's disease). It is also the case that social constructs such as wealth and socioeconomic status are not linearly related to outcomes such as academic success across the entire range of the variable. For example, it is possible that the change in predicted achievement comparing students from families making $25,000 a year versus $50,000 a year is probably much more dramatic than comparing students from families making $1,925,000 versus $1,950,000. And finally, acquisition of reading and language skills is not linear—as Figure 4.2 shows.

All this is to say that just like in OLS regression, while it might be reasonable to assume your variables are linear to the logit, it is also smart to test for curvilinear relationships.

---

[4]Again let's review the fact that it is not the actual values of the dependent variable that matter, but the probability of being in one group versus the other. Thus, although we sometimes talk about the logit transform of the dependent variable, we are really talking about the probability of membership.

| Figure 4.2 | Curvilinear Relationship Between Student Age and Reading Achievement Test Scores |

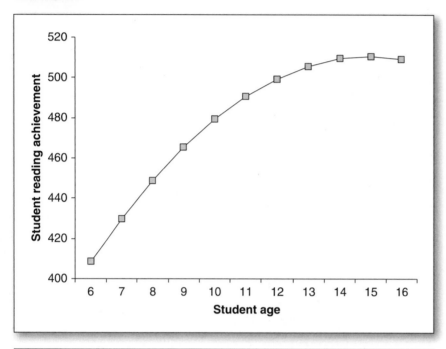

Data Source: NELS88, National Center for Educational Statistics, U.S. Department of Education (http://nces.ed.gov/surveys/nels88/).

It is also possible that poor coding of variables can artificially lead to curvilinearity. For example, in some U.S. government data, family income is coded unevenly (such as the example in Table 4.2 from the Early Childhood Longitudinal Study [ECLS], from the National Center for Educational Statistics [NCES])[5].

You can see that in this case a continuous variable—family income in dollars—has been broken into uneven categories. At the lower end, income is classified into blocks of $5,000 each,[6] while at the top end, the blocks are $25,000, $100,000, each, or more. This can serve to convert a linear relationship to curvilinear, or could also be used to convert a curvilinear to

---

[5]http://nces.ed.gov/pubs2002/2002135_2.pdf

[6]In other studies I have seen more egregious examples of this same thing, where at the lower end income was broken into $1,000 or $2,500 increments, with $100,000 increments at the top end of the scale.

Figure 4.3 Curvilinear Relationship Between Infant Age in Months and Number of Words in Vocabulary

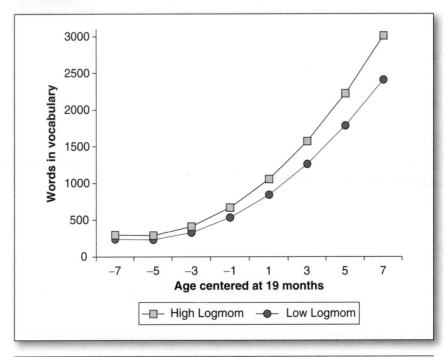

Data Source: Huttenlocher, Haight, Bryk, Seltzer, and Lyons (1991) as featured in Raudenbush and Bryk (2002, p. 171) but reanalyzed by Osborne.

Table 4.2 Total Household Income as Categorized in the ECLS-K Data Set From NCES

1 $5,000 or less	8 $35,001 to $40,000
2 $5,001 to $10,000	9 $40,001 to $50,000
3 $10,001 to $15,000	10 $50,001 to $75,000
4 $15,001 to $20,000	11 $75,001 to $100,000
5 $20,001 to $25,000	12 $100,000 to $200,000
6 $25,001 to $30,000	13 $200,001 or more
7 $30,001 to $35,000	

Data Source: ECLS, National Center for Educational Statistics, U.S. Department of Education (http://nces.ed.gov/pubs2002/2002135_2.pdf).

linear relationship. To be sure, it seems to violate some of our basic assumptions about measurement—converting what was a nice example of ratio measurement to a variable that does not even meet the criteria for interval level data. One must be careful converting continuous variables to categorical, as I explore further in Chapter 5.

Effects of Independent Variables Are Additive in Nature

The assumption implicit here (represented by our regression line equation in Equation 4.1) is that the independent variables are additive in nature—that they are (a) able to be added, and (b) not multiplicative, exponential, or related in other nonlinear (nonadditive) ways. This assumption may be violated when there are interactions present but not modeled. Again, this is something we will delve into in later chapters, but in brief, when an interaction between two variables occurs, it is an example of a multiplicative relationship, not an additive relationship, and failure to appropriately model it results in model misspecification (and loss of potentially important information). A classic pharmaceutical example of an interaction is that taking a sedative usually has a particular effect and ingesting alcohol usually has a particular effect, and doing both at the same time has a multiplicative, not additive, effect. In other words, the two effects do not simply add up; they often create dramatically stronger effects.

Another example of this multiplicative type of relationship is that in the health sciences, age and smoking status may interact to predict whether someone is diagnosed with Alzheimer's, and perhaps coffee drinking interacts in a different way. In the social sciences, family SES and school climate can interact. As I showed in one of my papers on hierarchical linear modeling (Osborne, 2000), poverty prevalent in a school has an independent, interactive effect with family poverty in predicting achievement test scores of individual students—in other words, the environment matters! As you can see below in Figure 4.4, family SES matters, generally allowing students coming from higher SES families to outscore students from lower SES families—but this effect depends upon the environment of the school. Students in low-poverty schools tend to outscore students in high-poverty schools. And the interaction of these two variables means that the effect of school poverty influences the effect of family SES. Family SES makes a larger difference in low poverty schools and less of a difference in high poverty schools. Of course, this is an example from OLS regression as there is a continuous variable, but when we get to

Figure 4.4 Interaction of Family SES and School Poverty Rate

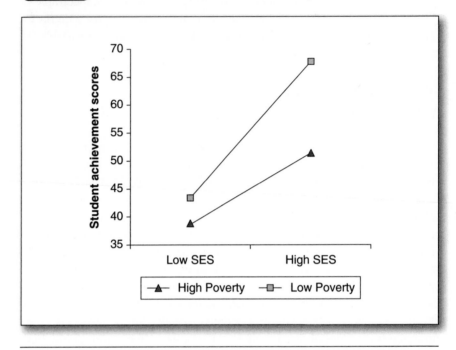

Data Source: NELS88, NCES, U.S. Department of Education (http://nces.ed.gov/surveys/nels88/).

exploring interactions in logistic regression, we will see multiplicative effects like this.

All Important Variables Are Included in the Analysis

There is more to specification of the model than making sure that the logit link function is appropriate and that you have correctly modeled the nature of the relationship (i.e., curvilinear or interactive relationships). We also must assume that you have included all relevant and important variables in the model. In many sciences, it is a challenging task to measure, gather, and include all the myriad possible important variables related to an outcome. However, it is possible that omission of important variables can lead to misestimation of the model. Thus researchers must carefully consider what variables *need* to be included in the analysis and include them as possible.

No Extraneous Variables Are Included in the Analysis

Extraneous variables are variables that are not relevant to the current analysis—variables that are not related to the dependent variable. This is not to say that every variable that ends up not significant should be considered extraneous! There is a difference between variables that are not significant predictors of the dependent variable and those that do not account for significant variance once other variables are controlled for. Let us define extraneous variables as any variable that has *no significant zero-order (simple) relationship to the dependent variable.*[7]

How do extraneous variables get into regression equations? The obvious answer is that you, the person performing the analysis, put them there. It is possible that theory led you to conclude this extraneous variable should be in there, or prior research, or a hunch. It is possible that you are using stepwise entry, where the software is choosing variables to enter based on statistical criteria (although most stepwise procedures either add or eliminate variables based on their relationship to the dependent variable so that this should be a relatively rare occurrence using stepwise entry).[8]

Why are extraneous variables problematic? You might think it is better to have them in the equation confirming that they are not significant rather than risk leaving a significant variable out. In many cases they are innocuous, despite consuming degrees of freedom (you will see in Chapter 10 that small samples do not fare well in logistic regression, so I always recommend large samples for these sorts of analyses). Perhaps more importantly, however, extraneous variables can lead to *suppressor effects.* Suppressor effects are errors of inference—the conclusion that a variable is significant when in fact it should not be. Specifically, extraneous variables (variables with no simple/zero-order relationship to the dependent variable) can create suppressor effects when they are related to other IVs in the equation. In essence, they can create a situation where certain variables are only

---

[7]A zero-order relationship is the relationship between that variable and the dependent variable when no other variables are covaried or are in the analysis.

[8]Stepwise procedures need to be used cautiously, as they can lead you to unreproducable conclusions based on quirks in your particular data set. Stepwise entry is usually considered an exploratory technique, requiring replication on an independent sample. In many areas of the social sciences, stepwise entry of any kind is (perhaps wrongly) demonized and considered unacceptable. Another fault of stepwise procedures, in my mind, is the fact that stepwise procedures will never find curvilinear or interaction effects, which I as I have mentioned before, are often the most interesting results.

significant when the extraneous variables are in the equation. This of course creates a misleading outcome. To prevent this, no variable without a significant zero-order relationship to the dependent variable should be included in the equation—unless they are needed to build interaction or curvilinear effects. It is possible, for example, that a particular variable is not significant by itself, but it is part of a significant interaction. In that case, this variable is not significant by itself but does not meet the definition of extraneous as it has an important role in defining the interaction.

Detection of violations of this assumption

There are five aspects to this assumption. We cannot test whether the logit link function is appropriate, you have to assert it. Likewise, there is no way to test whether an unmeasured variable that might be important is omitted.[9] There are ways to examine whether variables might be extraneous—principally, if they have no zero-order relationship to the dependent variable, and are not part of an interaction or higher-order term.

As I have mentioned several times, we will get into modeling curvilinear effects in a separate chapter. However, at this point it is worthwhile to point out a few methods of exploring whether there is curvilinearity present in your data. First and foremost, theory and common sense is always a good guide. I tend to believe that many things in social science (and health sciences as well) are curvilinear in nature, and so I routinely check for these effects. They are easily tested by entering the independent variable (IV), IV^2, and IV^3 terms into an equation. In my experience, adding squared and cubed terms tends to capture a good amount of any present curvilinearity. Those preferring a more strategic approach to this issue may enjoy exploring Box-Tidwell transformations (Box & Tidwell, 1962). Some prominent regression authors and texts (i.e., Cohen, Cohen, West, & Aiken, 2002, pp. 239–240) suggest Box-Tidwell as a method of easily exploring whether any variables have nonlinear effects.

The essential process for Box-Tidwell is to (a) perform an initial analysis with the independent variables of interest in the regression equation, (b) transform all independent variables of interest via Box-Tidwell, below, (c) enter them into the regression equation simultaneously along with the original untransformed variables, and (d) see which of the transformed variables (if any) are significant. The Box-Tidwell transformation is:

$$V_i = X_i(\ln X_i). \qquad \text{Eq. 4.2.}$$

---

[9]There are ways to analyze residuals with other variables that are measured but not included in an analysis to see if they are candidates for entry, but that is a topic for another day.

If the variable V is a significant predictor when X is in the equation, there is probably a significant curvilinear component to that variable.

$$\text{Logit}(\hat{Y}) = b_0 + b_1 X_1 + b_2 V_1 \qquad \text{Eq. 4.3.}$$

Note that your variable must not have any values that are undefined when taken as a natural log, and thus it is my recommendation in other papers as here to anchor the variable at 1.0 (add or subtract a constant to all cases so that the minimum value for the variable is 1.0).

One nice thing about this process is that you then get a good estimate of the nature of the curvilinear effect,

$$\hat{\lambda} = \frac{B_2}{B_1} + 1, \qquad \text{Eq. 4.4.}$$

where b_2 is taken from the second analysis and b_1 is taken from the initial analysis without the V_i in the equation. You can do successive iterations of this process as well, entering $X^{\text{lambda-hat}}$ in place of the original X_i in both the original steps and the calculation of V_i, but in my opinion that tends to overfit the model unnecessarily. Our data in the social sciences are not the same character and nature as in the physical sciences and manufacturing, for example.

The final step in this process is to substitute $X^{\text{lamda hat}}$ where X_i had been in the final analysis. I will also suggest that anytime you incorporate curvilinearity or interactions, you should graph the results for the reader. We will explore this more fully in Chapters 7 and 8.

Detecting the presence of nonadditive (i.e., interaction) effects is similarly guided by theory or exploration. Interaction effects can be of many different varieties, and I am not aware of any simple way to test for them other than merely to test for them. For continuous predictors, the procedure is to center the variables (per best practices in using continuous variables) and create a new interaction term by multiplying the two variables together. Thus, if you have two independent variables X_1 and X_2, you can multiply them together and add them (along with the original variables) into the regression equation to test whether the interaction term is significant. We will of course discuss this in greater detail later in the book.

$$\text{Logit}(\hat{Y}) = b_0 + b_1 X_1 + b_2 X_2 + b_3 X_1 X_2 \qquad \text{Eq 4.5.}$$

In summary, model specification is an assumption that: (a) the relevant important variables are in the equation, (b) irrelevant variables are not in the equation, (c) the logit link function (transform) is the appropriate way to model the data, (d) the variables are linear on the logit (or that nonlinearity is appropriately modeled), and (e) the variables are additive in nature (or that interactions are modeled appropriately).

◆ NORMALITY OF ERRORS, DISTRIBUTIONAL ASSUMPTIONS

There are no distributional assumptions regarding logistic regression, and as such, it is not necessary to worry about non-normally distributed residuals. However, it is sometimes the case that highly non-normal independent variables can distort parameter estimates (sometimes because they contain highly influential outliers, rather than the non-normality itself).

To provide an example of how logistic regression might be influenced by non-normality in the independent variables, we return to the example of DROPOUT (recoded into GRADUATED to keep the logit positive and the odds ratio over 1.0) and family SES (measured as a continuous variable) from Chapter 2. Recall that using the original data, students from families with SES of 1.0 higher have odds of graduating that are 2.83 that of students 1.0 *SD* lower.

SES as it is originally constituted has a skew of −0.04 and kurtosis of −0.53, which is well within the bounds of what is reasonable for social science data (Figure 4.5). When we transform this normal variable to be decidedly non-normal by applying a $\log_{10}$ transform (and then converting to z-scores to maintain a constant metric with a different distribution), we end up with the same variable but non-normal (skew = −0.85, kurtosis = 1.78) (Figure 4.6). You can see in Table 4.3 that highly non-normal variables can have some effect on the odds ratio and logit, *slightly* attenuating them.

Table 4.3 Family SES and Odds of Graduating High School

Non-normality and logistic regression

		B	SE	Wald	df	Sig.	Exp(B)
Original	zSES	1.041	.033	1018.355	1	.000	2.831
	Constant	2.740	.037	5409.564	1	.000	15.480
Step 1	zlogSES	.860	.027	1026.500	1	.000	2.364
	Constant	2.633	.034	6051.755	1	.000	13.913

Data Source: NELS88, NCES, U.S. Department of Education (http://nces.ed.gov/surveys/nels88/).

Figure 4.5 Distribution of Family SES

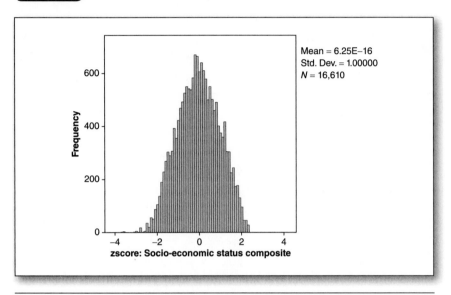

Data Source: NELS88, NCES, U.S. Department of Education (http://nces.ed.gov/surveys/nels88/).

This leads to unstandardized residuals that look like this:

Figure 4.6 Family SES Skewed by Applying a Log Transform

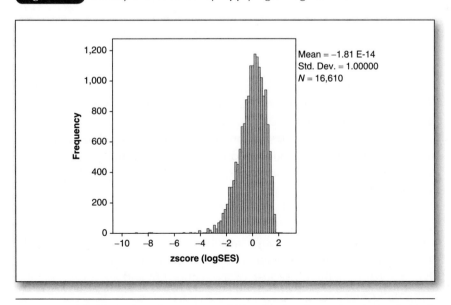

Data Source: NELS88, NCES, U.S. Department of Education (http://nces.ed.gov/surveys/nels88/).

And it leads to standardized residuals that look like this:

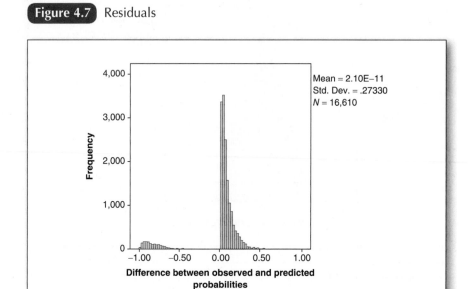

Figure 4.7 Residuals

Data Source: NELS88, NCES, U.S. Department of Education (http://nces.ed.gov/surveys/nels88/).

Thus, it is evident that normal distribution of residuals even for a very normally distributed variable is not a tenable expectation.

As you can see in this last graph, the non-normality led to some residuals that were far off—standardized residuals ranged from −7.38 to 12.16. −2 log likelihood for this analysis was 8842.75, while for the original analysis it was 8739.91—not a huge increase in lack of fit but a notable (and significant) one. What is more striking is that the parameter estimates (logit, odds ratio) are attenuated. This may be due to the increased error variance that the extreme non-normality would produce. In other words, it is possible I created substantial outliers when creating the non-normal variable, which is the root cause of the reduced fit and attenuated parameter point estimates.

Figure 4.8 Standardized Residuals

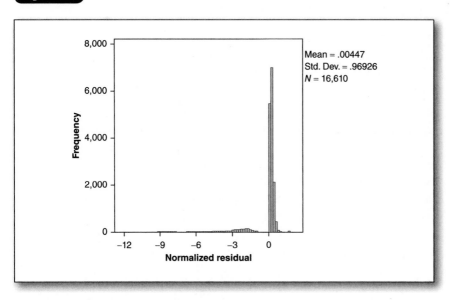

Data Source: NELS88, NCES, U.S. Department of Education (http://nces.ed.gov/surveys/nels88/).

Figure 4.9 Example With Some Extreme Standardized Residuals

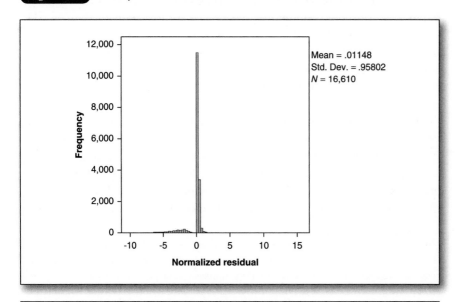

Data Source: NELS88, NCES, U.S. Department of Education (http://nces.ed.gov/surveys/nels88/).

♦ EXPLORING DATA FOR INAPPROPRIATELY INFLUENTIAL CASES

Give me a lever long enough and a fulcrum on which to place it, and I shall move the world.

—Attributed to Archimedes

It is the goal of this part of the chapter to help you explore whether there are individual cases that are inappropriately influencing your analysis. Let us start with the assumption that each case should contribute relatively equally to overall model fit/lack of fit and that each case should contribute relatively equally to estimation of parameter estimates (e.g., intercept, slopes). If a particular case is disproportionately influential, then I argue it might be grounds for removing it from the analysis.

Examining Residuals

Of course one traditional way of identifying cases that are potentially inappropriately influential is to look at standardized (or studentized)[10] residuals. In OLS regression the residual is conceptualized by the distance of a data point from the regression line, and operationalized by subtracting the predicted score from the actual score ($Y - \hat{Y}$). In logistic regression the residual is the difference between the predicted probability of the individual and the observed conditional probability for that individual.

In OLS regression, residuals are independent of $\hat{Y}$, and when homoscedasticity assumption is met, residuals can be directly compared. In my book on outliers I generally recommend looking at cases that have standardized residuals of ± 3.00 (which equates to a 0.13% chance of being a legitimate member of the population of interest) for illegitimate influence.

However, in logistic regression, residuals (both size and variance) are dependent on the predicted probability $\hat{Y}$, and as such use of these residuals is more challenging.

Studentized residuals in logistic regression are an index of how much each case contributes to the overall deviance statistic (an index of lack of fit, conceptually similar to error variance in my mind). Thus, higher

---

[10]Standardized residuals are residuals divided by the standard deviation of the residuals). Studentized residuals in OLS regression are often very similar to standardized residuals except in the presence of very unusual data points. They are computed by dividing each residual by the standard deviation of the residuals without that particular case in the SD statistic. This can be important in that cases with very high residuals can inflate the standard deviation of the residuals and thus make extreme cases look less extreme.

deviance residuals would be candidates for examination. Deviance statistics are often more normally distributed than standardized residuals and less unstable as predicted probabilities approach 0.00 or 1.00 (as mentioned above concerning leverage statistics). To make things confusing, SPSS calls deviance residuals (the change in model deviance if a case was excluded) studentized residuals, whereas in OLS regression studentized residuals are $(Y - \hat{Y})/SD_{res}$, where the SD_{res} is the SD of the residuals without that case in the analysis. SAS calls deviance residuals "deviance residuals." To further complicate things, SPSS also has "deviance residuals," which are residuals based on the model deviance.

In this section, we will explore whether standardized residuals are useful in improving model specification. We will explore the concept of how much each case contributes to the overall model lack of fit (e.g., standardized residuals and DfBetas in SPSS, DIFCHISQ in SAS) next.

Taking the example at hand, the standardized residuals range from −10.87 to 1.70, as the graph in Figure 4.10 shows.

The problem with many aspects of data cleaning in logistic regression is that influential cases are not always distributed evenly across groups. For example, graphing the residuals separately by group reveals that the nongraduated group (dropouts) had the extreme residuals (see Figure 4.11, page 106).

In other words, as family SES increased, the odds of dropping out should have dropped dramatically, but these individuals dropped out, producing

Figure 4.10 Normalized Residuals

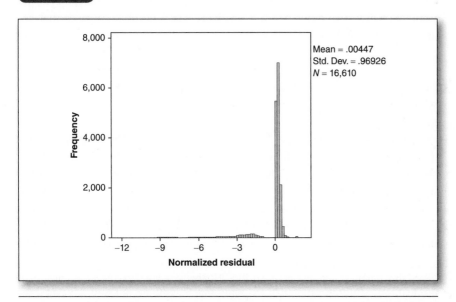

Mean = .00447
Std. Dev. = .96926
N = 16,610

Data Source: NELS88, NCES, U.S. Department of Education (http://nces.ed.gov/surveys/nels88/).

Figure 4.11 Normalized Residuals Separated by Group

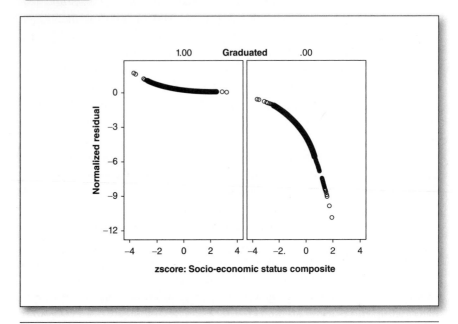

Data Source: NELS88, NCES, U.S. Department of Education (http://nces.ed.gov/surveys/nels88/).

relatively extreme standardized residuals. One must be thoughtful in analyses such as these as we want to maintain a sample that is generalizable to the population. On the other hand, a relatively small number of cases that are aberrant can mask an effect or cause it to be misestimated. To be overly conservative, I removed all cases with residuals below −4. Removal of these 240 cases a stronger effect of SES (Wald = 1264.35 compared with 1018.36 prior to removal of these outliers). In addition, the effect size increased somewhat dramatically (logit increasing from 1.04 to 1.45, OR increasing from 2.83 to 4.25).

DIFCHISQ is a metric available in SAS that specifies the change in overall chi-square goodness of fit attributable to deleting a particular case. This is similar in concept to other indices of individual leverage or effect—in particular, SPSS's implementation of *studentized residuals,* which in logistic regression is defined as the change in the model deviance if a case is excluded.[11]

Looking at the same analysis in SAS, you can see that some individual cases, if deleted, would improve model fit disproportionately (and

---

[11]SAS also includes an option called RESCHI that specifies the Pearson chi-square residual for each observation that indicates which cases are not well accounted for by the present model.

Table 4.4 Effects of Various Data Cleaning Strategies

		B	SE	Wald	df	Sig.	Exp(B)	95% CI for Exp(B)	
								Lower	Upper
Original analysis	zbyses	1.041	.033	1018.355	1	.000	2.831	2.656	3.018
	Constant	2.740	.037	5409.564	1	.000	15.480		
Standardized residuals > −4	zbyses	1.448	.041	1264.353	1	.000	4.253	3.927	4.606
	Constant	3.297	.050	4273.465	1	.000	27.040		
DIFCHISQ < 10	zbyses	3.8487	.0658	3425.8904	1	.000	5.859	5.317	6.457
	Constant	1.7681	.0496	1272.8977	1	.000	46.931		
Leverage < 0.00054	zbyses	1.105	.037	894.636	1	.000	3.018	2.808	3.245
	Constant	2.759	.038	5207.367	1	.000	15.790		
Cook's < 0.0016	zbyses	1.341	.038	1230.734	1	.000	3.821	3.545	4.118
	Constant	3.118	.046	4583.401	1	.000	22.612		
DfBetas > −0.001 and < 0.00079	zbyses	1.148	.039	862.190	1	.000	3.151	2.919	3.402
	Constant	3.049	.044	4829.914	1	.000	21.101		

Note: DIFCHISQ results produced via SAS; all others produced via SPSS.

Data Source: NELS88, NCES, U.S. Department of Education (http://nces.ed.gov/surveys/nels88/).

significantly as chi-square of ≈ 4 is statistically significant with one degree of freedom).[12] In particular, most of the cases with very high deletion differences seem to be coming from the nongraduated, or dropout, group. In this analysis, the DIFCHIs ranged from a low of 0.002 to over 118, and that the dropout group again contained the cases that seemed to be contributing to the model misfit. The 95th percentile was about 5.16, and to be conservative we can delete all cases over 20 (the 99th percentile was around 19.14) to start. This removed 152 cases from the analysis.

---

[12]This is similar to looking at modification indices in structural equation modeling.

Figure 4.12 DIFCHISQ Plotted by Group

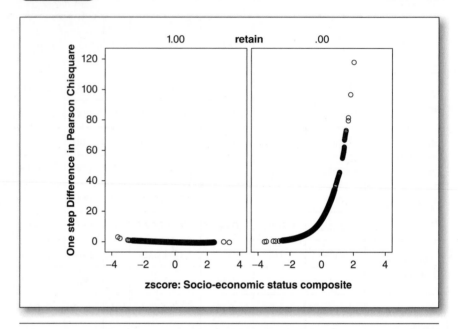

Data Source: NELS88, NCES, U.S. Department of Education (http://nces.ed.gov/surveys/nels88/).

Table 4.5 SAS Output Without Data Cleaning

Analysis of Maximum Likelihood Estimates					
Parameter	*df*	Estimate	Standard Error	Wald Chi-Square	Pr > ChiSq
Intercept	1	2.7395	0.0372	5409.5698	<.0001
zbyses	1	1.0408	0.0326	1018.3531	<.0001

Odds Ratio Estimates		
Effect	Point Estimate	95% Wald Confidence Limits
zbyses	2.831	2.656	3.018

Data Source: NELS88, NCES, U.S. Department of Education (http://nces.ed.gov/surveys/nels88/).

Table 4.6 SAS Output With Some Data Cleaning

Analysis of Maximum Likelihood Estimates					
Parameter	*df*	Estimate	Standard Error	Wald Chi-Square	Pr > ChiSq
Intercept	1	3.0877	0.0452	4659.9160	<.0001
zbyses	1	1.3105	0.0376	1216.0141	<.0001

Odds Ratio Estimates			
Effect	Point Estimate	95% Wald Confidence Limits	
zbyses	3.708	3.445	3.991

Data Source: NELS88, NCES, U.S. Department of Education (http://nces.ed.gov/surveys/nels88/).

As you can see from the tables above, showing the original analysis and then the analysis with the removal of a small percentage of the cases, the effect (Wald) is stronger, as are the point estimates. Lowering the cutoff to DIFCHI = 10, we remove 289 cases, and the results are even more dramatic:

Table 4.7 SAS Output With Less Conservative Data Cleaning

Analysis of Maximum Likelihood Estimates					
Parameter	*df*	Estimate	Standard Error	Wald Chi-Square	Pr > ChiSq
Intercept	1	3.8487	0.0658	3425.8904	<.0001
zbyses	1	1.7681	0.0496	1272.8977	<.0001

Odds Ratio Estimates			
Effect	Point Estimate	95% Wald Confidence Limits	
zbyses	5.859	5.317	6.457

Data Source: NELS88, NCES, U.S. Department of Education (http://nces.ed.gov/surveys/nels88/).

There is a clear art to examining these types of diagnostics, not a specific formula. Different types of diagnostics give you different information, and you as a thoughtful researcher must examine potential data points to see if they are appropriate to keep in the data set or inappropriate and candidates for separate analysis or removal.

◆ LEVERAGE AND INFLUENCE IN LOGISTIC REGRESSION

The concept of leverage is the concept that no single data point should wield disproportionate influence over the outcome of the analysis. As you know, a data point substantially outside the distribution of other data points can have disproportionate influence on many statistics, such as the mean, the standard deviation, error variance, correlation, and so forth. In a data set with 100 cases, each case should ideally have 1/100th influence on the outcome. In reality that is, of course, not the case, and analysis of leverage can give a researcher a way to examine just how great the disparity is across data points.

Indicators of leverage in OLS regression generally follow a simple, predictable pattern: the farther a point from the centroid of a distribution, the more leverage over the results that data point is likely to have. However, leverage in logistic regression is not so clear cut and depends somewhat on the predicted probability of the case as Hosmer and Lemeshow (2000) showed. Specifically, it appears that leverage of points is dependent upon the predicted probability of a point. Leverage is a concern primarily for data points with predicted probabilities between 0.10 and 0.90. Any data point with a predicted probability of between 0.00 and 0.09 or between 0.91 and 0.99 probably does not have reliable indicators of leverage in logistic regression.

In logistic regression, indicators of leverage range from 0.00 (has no influence on the logistic regression parameters) to 1.00 (completely determinant of the parameters or complete influence). Of course, raw values for leverage tend to get smaller as sample size gets larger, so absolute cutoff values are impractical. Rather, one can look at the distribution of leverage values for relatively extreme scores and consider examining them for undue influence. Some guidance proposed by Agresti and Finlay (1997) regarding OLS regression that I think is probably reasonable to apply to logistic regression is to use $3K/N$ (where K is the number of independent variables in the equation and N is the sample size) as a guide for deciding where individual data points begin to have excessive or inappropriate leverage. Again, as this is merely a guide, researchers must examine suspect cases thoughtfully prior to eliminating them. Another method of examining leverage values might be to convert them to z-scores and look for z-score values.

Predicted probabilities ranged from 0.256 to 0.998, with a large majority of cases above 0.90, as the histogram (see Figure 4.13) shows. Removing all cases with predicted probabilities of less than 0.10 or greater than 0.90 left us with only 5,165 cases (out of 16,610) for which we could examine leverage. Of these cases, leverage ranged from 0.00008 to 0.00189. Expected cutoff values for leverage should be $3K/N$, in this case 3/16610 or 0.00018. Examining only those cases within the 0.10–0.90 predicted probability range, you can see that both groups are relatively congruent in that cases with relatively low SES tended to have higher leverage. Let us remove cases that are within the appropriate predicted probability range and exceeds 0.00054, which is three times the calculated expected leverage and corresponds to approximately the 95th percentile in leverage scores. To do this, I kept all cases with predicted probabilities of less than 0.10 or greater than 0.90 and all those in between those two numbers with leverage values less than 0.00054. This filtering removed 312 cases from the analysis. As you can

Figure 4.13 Predicted Probability Distribution

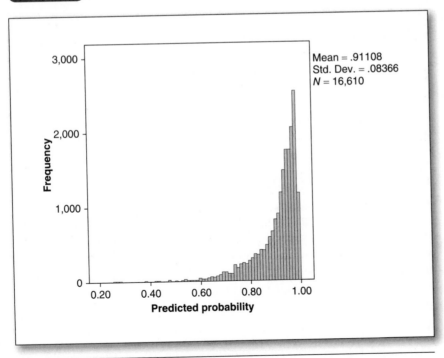

Mean = .91108
Std. Dev. = .08366
N = 16,610

Data Source: NELS88, NCES, U.S. Department of Education (http://nces.ed.gov/surveys/nels88/).

Figure 4.14 Leverage Plotted by Group

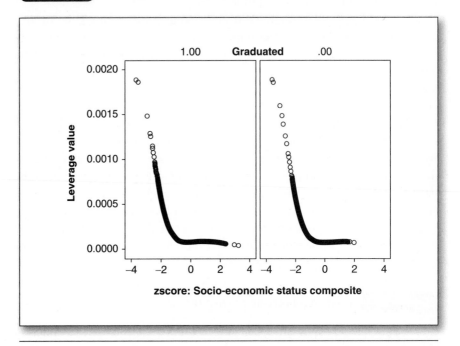

Data Source: NELS88, NCES, U.S. Department of Education (http://nces.ed.gov/surveys/nels88/).

see in Table 4.4 this improved the model slightly over the original baseline but not nearly as much as filtering based on standardized residuals or DIF-CHISQ, probably partly due to the inability to trust the reliability of leverage values in a large portion of the sample.[13]

Cook's Distance (Influence)

In SPSS, for example, Cook's Distance/influence for logistic regression is operationalized as a measure of how much the residuals of all cases would change if a case were removed from the analysis. In our SES and retention example, the Cook's Distance (influence) analogue ranged from 0.0000001 to 0.00835, with the 95th percentile at 0.00082 and the 99th percentile at 0.0016.

---

[13]As an aside, I also performed the analysis including all cases, filtering on the same leverage value, which produced virtually identical results for this analysis.

Figure 4.15 Distribution of Cook's Distance Analogue

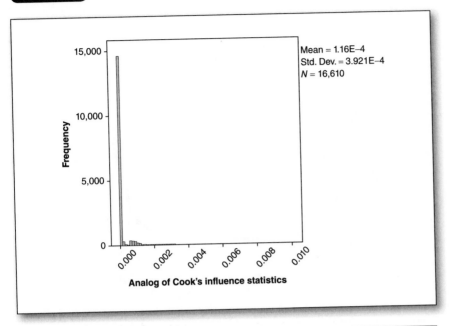

Data Source: NELS88, NCES, U.S. Department of Education (http://nces.ed.gov/surveys/nels88/).

This statistic also has a different pattern depending on which group the student is in, which makes sense. Those who graduated and are from unexpectedly low SES families are relatively more unusual and thus have more influence on the parameter estimates. Likewise, in the not graduated group, those coming from high SES families have more influence.

Reinforcing the fact that leverage and Cook's Distance represent different pieces of information, only 6 cases out of 16,610 met both criteria for having unreasonable leverage and being in the top 1% of Cook's influence. Similar to removing those with undesirably high leverage, removing the 167 cases representing the top 1% of distance resulted in a larger effect size than the baseline, but not as impressive an effect as other methods.[14]

---

[14]As an example of "more is not always better," removing cases with Cook's distance scores at the 95th percentile rather than the 99th percentile did not improve the model. In fact, the model was weaker when more cases were removed.

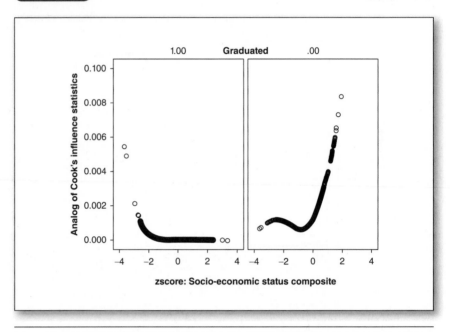

Figure 4.16 Cook's Distance Plotted by Group

Data Source: NELS88, NCES, U.S. Department of Education (http://nces.ed.gov/surveys/nels88/).

♦ DFBETAS

Examining how the regression coefficients change (change in logit) divided by the standard error of the regression coefficient (DfBeta, in many software packages) will also provide insight into this issue. One challenge with DfBeta is that you get a DfBeta for each parameter (intercept, each regression coefficient) in the model, and the parameters can move negatively and positively, so you must examine extremes of movement in both directions or take the absolute value of the DfBeta. For the purpose of this chapter, I examined DfBetas for the slope (SES), but it would be appropriate for you to examine both slope(s) and intercept.

DfBetas for slope ranged from −0.00283 to 0.0010. Because these can be extreme in both directions, we will pay attention to both the 1st percentile (−0.0010) and the 99th percentile (0.00079). Removing the 350 cases that exceed those thresholds produced modest beneficial effects.

You can also note different patterns for each group: For the graduated students, there are only extreme DfBetas at the very low end of SES, whereas there appear to be extreme DfBetas at both ends in the dropout group.

Figure 4.17   Distribution of DfBeta for Family SES

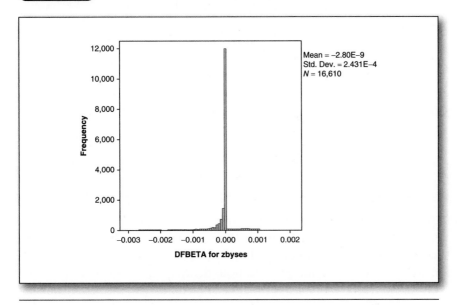

Data Source: NELS88, NCES, U.S. Department of Education (http://nces.ed.gov/surveys/nels88/).

Figure 4.18   DfBetas Plotted by Group

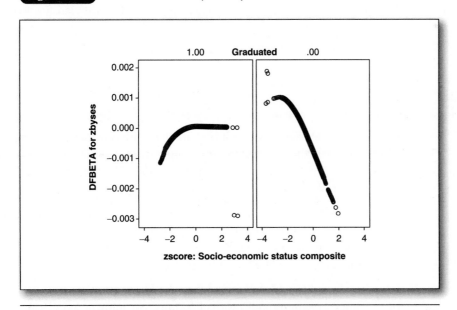

Data Source: NELS88, NCES, U.S. Department of Education (http://nces.ed.gov/surveys/nels88/).

The Relationship Between DfBetas and Other Measures of Influence/Leverage

Of note, only 19 cases had DfBetas in excess of this cutoff and leverage exceeding the $3K/N$ cutoff. In contrast, there was substantial overlap between Cook's distance and DfBeta. This is not surprising as both indices look at how individual cases influence parameter estimates. Thus, it might be beneficial to consult multiple indicators of influence/leverage in order to improve your analyses.

SUMMARY

Thanks to maximum likelihood estimation, logistic regression is robust to some violation assumptions that OLS regression can be highly influenced by, like assumptions of normal distribution of residuals and homoscedasticity. However, it is important to note that in some cases non-normality of independent variables can adversely influence the estimation of parameters.

Regression diagnostics are not assumptions per se, such as diagnostics that look at influence and leverage, but are nonetheless important to examine to get good (generalizable) estimation of population parameters. As the examples above show, judicious use of leverage and influence statistics to eliminate the most inappropriately influential cases can improve parameter estimates, sometimes dramatically.

ENRICHMENT

1. Using the NELS data set described in this and previous chapters (predicting whether a student graduated [GRADUATE] in school from family SES [zBYSES]), reproduce the data cleaning examples presented in the chapter.

   a. If you test this analysis for linearity, be sure to add a constant to the SES (or zSES) variable to make sure there are no values in the variable that are 0 or negative—a good practice is to anchor the variable at 1.0 to eliminate these issues).

2. Using the Diabetes and body mass index (BMI) example from previous chapters, examine indicators of leverage or influence (DfBetas,

leverage, Cook's distance, standardized residuals) to see if you believe any cases are unreasonably influential.

a. If so, compare results of the logistic regression analysis with them in and removed from the data set.

b. Download from www.sagepub.com/osbornebplr.

c. Test whether it is reasonable to assume BMI is "linear on the logit" with diabetes via Box-Tidwell as discussed in this chapter. Be sure to add a constant to the variable if using zBMI as negative or zero values are undefined when taking a natural log.

3. Using the marijuana data set described in Chapter 3, check whether assumptions were met when predicting EVERMJ from BADCNT.

a. Download from www.sagepub.com/osbornebplr.

b. If there are any inappropriately influential cases, compare the results of the logistic regression analysis with them in and with them removed from the data set.

c. Test whether it is reasonable to assume BADCNT is "linear on the logit" with EVER_MJ via Box-Tidwell.

ANSWER KEY

2. BMI and Diabetes
Analysis of Influence and Leverage

Some examples of the types of analyses described in the chapters follow. They are not comprehensive, nor are they entirely objective—there are few hard and fast rules in data cleaning, so your conclusions may differ from mine. In this data set, with almost 27,000 data points, data cleaning may be challenging for two reasons: first, because there are so many data points you might think any individual data point might make little difference. And in fact, this might be true. It is also true that if 1% of the data points are aberrant, the analysis could be seriously misspecified.

As a reminder, the overall logistic regression analysis produces the following results with all cases in the analyses (this will serve as our baseline for comparison):

Enrichment Table 4.1   Initial Results of Relationship Between BMI and Diabetes

Omnibus Tests of Model Coefficients				
		Chi-square	df	Sig.
	Step	986.981	1	.000
Step 1	Block	986.981	1	.000
	Model	986.981	1	.000

Model Summary			
Step	−2 Log likelihood	Cox & Snell R Square	Nagelkerke R Square
1	16070.024[a]	.036	.077

a. Estimation terminated at iteration number 5 because parameter estimates changed by less than .001.

Hosmer and Lemeshow Test			
Step	Chi-square	df	Sig.
1	77.090	8	.000

Contingency Table for Hosmer and Lemeshow Test						
		diabetes = .00		diabetes = 1.00		Total
		Observed	Expected	Observed	Expected	
	1	2596	2560.196	79	114.804	2675
	2	2627	2574.547	91	143.453	2718
	3	2493	2487.242	153	158.758	2646
	4	2520	2487.960	146	178.040	2666
Step 1	5	2468	2456.499	186	197.501	2654
	6	2427	2469.414	266	223.586	2693
	7	2416	2423.505	259	251.495	2675
	8	2338	2373.711	328	292.289	2666
	9	2216	2299.574	449	365.426	2665
	10	2080	2048.351	641	672.649	2721

Variables in the Equation								
		B	*SE*	Wald	*df*	Sig.	Exp(B)	95% CI for Exp(B)	
								Lower	Upper
Step 1ᵃ	BMI	.092	.003	1013.633	1	.000	1.096	1.090	1.102
	Constant	−4.901	.090	2939.412	1	.000	.007		

a. Variable(s) entered on step 1: BMI.

Data Source: NHIS2010, Centers for Disease Control and Prevention.

Standardized Residuals

Standardized residuals from this analysis ranged from −2.98 to 5.92, as the plot below shows:

Enrichment Figure 4.1 Standardized Residuals by Group

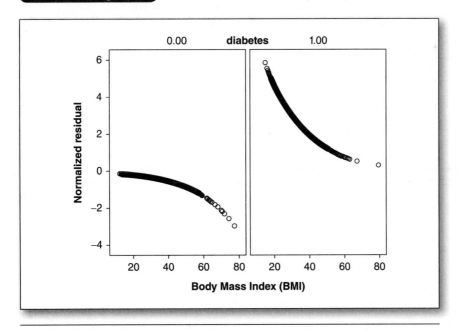

Data Source: NHIS2010, Centers for Disease Control and Prevention.

Not surprisingly, the largest standardized residuals occur for those with very low BMI and who are diagnosed with diabetes. They also tend toward extremes for those with very high BMI who are claiming not to be diagnosed with diabetes, although they do not exceed −3.00. As I used |4| in my chapter as a guideline for starting to clean standardized residuals, we get a modest improvement in the analysis from removing less than 100 individuals:

Enrichment Table 4.2 Variables in the Equation

| | | B | SE | Wald | df | Sig. | Exp(B) | 95% CI for Exp(B) | |
								Lower	Upper
Step 1[a]	BMI	.108	.003	1303.501	1	.000	1.115	1.108	1.121
	Constant	−5.519	.096	3290.266	1	.000	.004		

a. Variable(s) entered on step 1: BMI.

Data Source: NHIS2010, Centers for Disease Control and Prevention.

Using zRE =3.50 as a cutoff, we remove about 500 cases and end up with a marginally improved analysis, although at a cost:

Enrichment Table 4.3 Variables in the Equation

| | | B | SE | Wald | df | Sig. | Exp(B) | 95% CI for Exp(B) | |
								Lower	Upper
Step 1[a]	BMI	.132	.003	1637.750	1	.000	1.141	1.134	1.149
	Constant	−6.461	.108	3597.956	1	.000	.002		

a. Variable(s) entered on step 1: BMI.

Data Source: NHIS2010, Centers for Disease Control and Prevention.

Cook's Influence Statistics

Cook's statistics range from 0.00001 to 0.015.

As you can see by the more nuanced analysis above (produced by paneling scatterplots of zBMI by Cook's influence statistics as a function of

Enrichment Figure 4.2

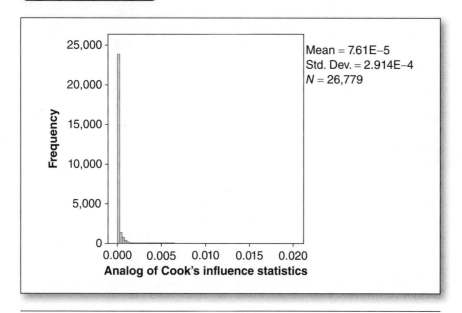

Data Source: NHIS2010, Centers for Disease Control and Prevention.

Enrichment Figure 4.3   Cook's Influence by Group

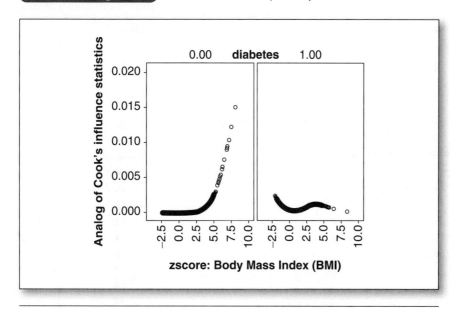

Data Source: NHIS2010, Centers for Disease Control and Prevention.

diabetes status), most of the influential data points (according to this metric) fall in the nondiabetes category—specifically, those with very high BMI but who claim not to have diabetes. If we remove any cases beyond the 99th percentile for this statistic (in this case, retaining all cases with <0.001), overall model fit (−2LL) is now 15,023, more than 1,000 lower than with those ~270 cases in the analysis. The Hosmer and Lemeshow test, however, increased from about 77 to more than 195, which is not desirable. Finally, the model statistics are interesting:

Enrichment Table 4.4 Variables in the Equation

		B	SE	Wald	df	Sig.	Exp(B)	95% CI for Exp(B)	
								Lower	Upper
Step 1[a]	BMI	.099	.003	891.717	1	.000	1.104	1.097	1.111
	Constant	−5.182	.103	2548.097	1	.000	.006		

a. Variable(s) entered on step 1: BMI.

Data Source: NHIS2010, Centers for Disease Control and Prevention.

The Wald statistics for BMI decreased slightly (from more than 1,000 in the original model), but the B and odds ratio increased slightly

Leverage

Recall from above that only cases with predicted probabilities between 0.10 and 0.90 have reliable indicators of leverage. This makes this analysis less useful as only 8,098 of the almost 27,000 cases had predicted probabilities in this range. However, when examined the leverage values for this subgroup ranged from 0.00004 to 0.002, and the expected reasonable leverage value would be 0.000112 using the $3K/N$ formula discussed above. Thus, even in this subgroup there might be cases with inappropriate leverage. However, we would probably have to include all cases with predicted probabilities above 0.90 or below 0.10 regardless of leverage value, and then remove cases between these two values with leverage substantially above. For example, among these cases, the 95th percentile is 0.0005, which would be a reasonable cut score. Removing these cases (about 390) results in a −2LL of 15447.80, again reduced from the noncleaned analysis, and perhaps more promisingly, a Hosmer and Lemeshow statistic of 42.66, lower than the original.

Enrichment Figure 4.4

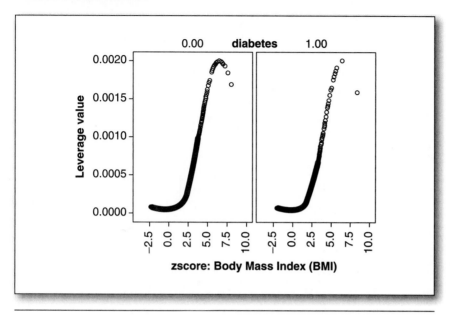

Data Source: NHIS2010, Centers for Disease Control and Prevention.

Enrichment Table 4.5   Variables in the Equation

		B	SE	Wald	df	Sig.	Exp(B)	95% CI for Exp(B)	
								Lower	Upper
Step 1ª	BMI	.108	.004	907.011	1	.000	1.114	1.107	1.122
	Constant	−5.378	.110	2389.546	1	.000	.005		

a. Variable(s) entered on step 1: BMI.

Data Source: NHIS2010, Centers for Disease Control and Prevention.

Finally, the statistics above seem a bit improved, along the lines of what one might expect if data cleaning were having a laudable effect.

DfBetas

There are DfBetas estimated for each parameter in an equation—the intercept and each independent variable effect. You have to decide which

Enrichment Figure 4.5 DfBetas for BMI Effect by Diabetes Group

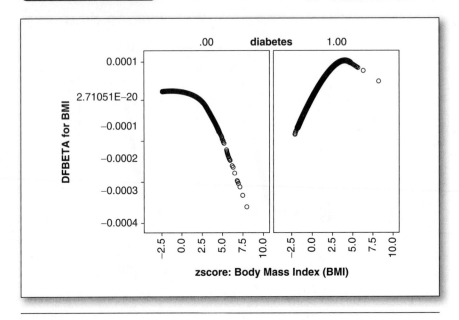

Data Source: NHIS2010, Centers for Disease Control and Prevention.

(or both) of the parameters are more important to data clean. In this case, let's explore the DfBetas for the independent variable, which range from −0.00035 to 0.00010.

As you can see, the DfBetas in each group trend in the opposite direction—negative for the non-diabetic group and positive for the diabetic group. The lowest DfBetas are over 19 *SD* below the average, and the highest ones are over 5 *SD* above the average. Thus, I elected to remove those that were extreme (below the 5th percentile from the nondiabetic group and above the 95th percentile from the diabetic group) as:

```
temp.
select if ( (diabetes=0 and DFB1_1 > -0.0000126) or
(diabetes=1 and dfb1_1 < .0000843)).
LOGISTIC REGRESSION VARIABLES diabetes
/METHOD=ENTER BMI
/SAVE=PRED COOK LEVER DFBETA ZRESID DEV
```

```
/PRINT=GOODFIT ITER(1) CI(95)
/CRITERIA=PIN(0.05) POUT(0.10) ITERATE(20) CUT(0.5).
```

This produced a desirable improvement to the model: with 25452 cases in the analysis, the −2LL was 14622.99, with a Hosmer and Lemeshow chi-square of 34.35. Furthermore, the classification table showed an unexpected movement toward accurately classifying almost 5% of the diabetic cases, which was not the case before. Finally, the regression equation showed stronger effects than other models, with an enhanced Wald statistic.

Enrichment Table 4.6

Classification Table[a]				
		Predicted		
Observed		diabetes		Percentage Correct
		.00	1.00	
Step 1	diabetes .00	22983	0	100.0
	1.00	2347	122	4.9
	Overall Percentage			90.8

a. The cut value is .500.

Data Source: NHIS2010, Centers for Disease Control and Prevention.

Variables in the Equation									
		B	SE	Wald	df	Sig.	Exp(B)	95% CI for Exp(B)	
								Lower	Upper
Step 1[a]	BMI	.168	.004	1462.260	1	.000	1.183	1.173	1.194
	Constant	−7.019	.133	2767.818	1	.000	.001		

a. Variable(s) entered on step 1: BMI.

Data Source: NHIS2010, Centers for Disease Control and Prevention.

Using Pearson Chi-Square Deletion Difference in SAS

Using the syntax as follows:

PROC LOGISTIC DATA=book.Ch03 descending
plots(MAXPOINTS=NONE)=(ROC dfbetas(unpack) influence(unpack) leverage(unpack));
   MODEL diabetes = BMI
   /lackfit ctable ;
   output out=book.results p=predict CBAR=cbar DIFchisq=DIFCHI
RESCHI=reschi dfbetas=_ALL_ H=leverage ;
   run;

we can examine the individual impact on overall model fit for each case, as discussed earlier. In this analysis we receive the following graph, showing some cases with disproportionate effects on overall lack of model fit.

Most of the extreme scores are coming from the diabetic group, and the mean of the entire group is 0.97, but ranges from 0.023 to 35.01. Ninety-five percent of the cases are below 8.12, which is very close to the 10.00 cutoff I

Enrichment Figure 4.6 Range of Chi-Square Deletion Difference Values

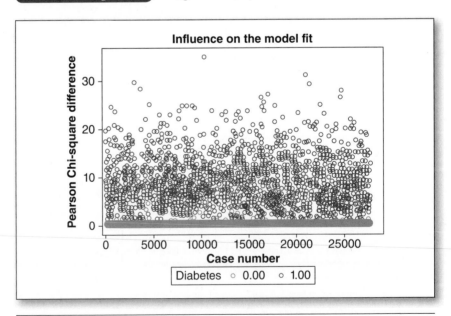

Data Source: NHIS2010, Centers for Disease Control and Prevention.

often use when examining modification indices for structural equation modeling. Thus, removing cases with DIFCHI (the name I gave this variable in the SAS analysis) greater than 10.00, −2LL drops from the original 16070.024 to 9897.69. Interestingly, while that overall model fit index dropped, the Hosmer and Lemeshow goodness-of-fit test increased from the original 77.08 to 792.94. To complicate matters, the Wald for BMI was 1852.20, a marked improvement over previous examples. In addition, the parameter estimates indicate stronger effects. Thus, this deletion of approximately 1,000 cases (out of 26,779) has seemed to improve the model rather dramatically.

2c. Testing nonlinearity of BMI and diabetes

In order to test for nonlinearity using Box-Tidwell we transform BMI as follows (I used the original data not the cleaned data for this analysis—if you remove outliers, your results may differ!):

$$BT\_BMI = BMI*ln(BMI)$$

And enter BT_BMI into the logistic regression equation after entering BMI. Recall that if BT_BMI has a significant effect after BMI is in the equation that is an indication of curvilinearity.

My results indicate there is a significant curvilinear component. When BMI is in the equation and BT_BMI is added, the −2LL decreases ($\chi^2 = 115$,

Enrichment Table 4.7

Analysis of Maximum Likelihood Estimates					
Parameter	df	Estimate	Standard Error	Wald Chi-Square	Pr > ChiSq
Intercept	1	−7.5614	0.1251	3651.5852	<.0001
BMI	1	0.1575	0.00366	1852.2022	<.0001

Odds Ratio Estimates			
Effect	Point Estimate	95% Wald Confidence Limits	
BMI	1.171	1.162	1.179

Data Source: NHIS2010, Centers for Disease Control and Prevention.

$p < .0001$), the Hosmer and Lemeshow chi-squared test drops from 77.09 to 17.50, and most importantly, the BT_BMI variable is significant.

Enrichment Table 4.8 Variables in the Equation

		B	SE	Wald	df	Sig.	Exp(B)	95% CI for Exp(B)	
								Lower	Upper
Step 1[a]	BMI	.950	.084	128.169	1	.000	2.585	2.193	3.046
	BT_BMI	−.190	.019	104.847	1	.000	.827	.798	.858
	Constant	−11.167	.621	322.967	1	.000	.000		

a. Variable(s) entered on step 1: BT_BMI.

Data Source: NHIS2010, Centers for Disease Control and Prevention.

Thus, we will return to this example in the future to examine the curvilinear nature of the relationship between BMI and diabetes!

SYNTAX EXAMPLES

Example SPSS SYNTAX for Requesting Standardized Residuals, Cook's Distance, Leverage Statistics, Etc.

```
LOGISTIC REGRESSION VARIABLES diabetes
/METHOD=ENTER BMI
/SAVE=PRED COOK LEVER DFBETA ZRESID DEV
/PRINT=GOODFIT ITER(1) CI(95)
/CRITERIA=PIN(0.05) POUT(0.10) ITERATE(20) CUT(0.5).
```

Example SPSS Syntax for Selecting or Filtering Cases

```
temp.
select if (zre_1 gt -4).
LOGISTIC REGRESSION VARIABLES Graduate
/METHOD=ENTER Zbyses
```

```
/SAVE=PRED COOK LEVER DFBETA SRESID ZRESID DEV
/PRINT=GOODFIT CI(95)
/CRITERIA=PIN(0.05) POUT(0.10) ITERATE(20) CUT(0.5).
```

This is the "classic" way of temporarily selecting certain cases for analysis—without the TEMP command, select removes cases permanently from the data set. With the TEMP command, it only removes it for the first analysis. The more recent method is FILTER:

```
USE ALL.
COMPUTE filter_$=(ZBMI < 3 and ZBMI > -3).
FILTER BY filter_$.
EXECUTE.
```

The FILTER command keeps the cases in the data set but removes them from any analyses until the USE ALL command returns them to analyses. It is a nice, safe compromise to select, but you have to remember to return cases to the data if you want to analyze the entire sample again.

Example SAS Syntax for Requesting Extensive Plots and Leverage/Influence Statistics

```
PROC LOGISTIC DATA=book.Ch03 descending
plots(MAXPOINTS=NONE)=(ROC dfbetas(unpack)
influence(unpack) leverage(unpack) );
   MODEL diabetes = BMI
   /lackfit ctable ;
   output out=book.results p=predict CBAR=cbar
DIFchisq=DIFCHI RESCHI=reschi dfbetas=_ALL_ H=leverage ;
   run;
```

Example SAS Syntax for Deleting Particular Cases and Saving in a New Data File Called "Remove"

```
data remove;
set BOOK.results;
if DIFCHI > 10 then delete;
;
run;
```

Example SAS Syntax for Examining Univariate Distributions of Variables, Such as DIFCHI.

```
proc univariate data=remove;
var DIFCHI;
histogram;
run;
```

REFERENCES

Agresti, A., & Finlay, B. (1997). *Statistical methods for the social sciences*. New York, NY: Pearson.

Box, G. E. P., & Tidwell, P. W. (1962). Transformation of the independent variables. *Technometrics, 531–550*.

Cohen, J., Cohen, P., West, S., & Aiken, L. S. (2002). *Applied multiple regression/correlation analysis for the behavioral sciences*. Mahwah, NJ: Lawrence Erlbaum.

Hosmer, D. W., & Lemeshow, S. (2000). *Applied logistic regression*. New York, NY: Wiley.

Huttenlocher, J., Haight, W., Bryk, A., Seltzer, M., & Lyons, T. (1991). Early vocabulary growth: Relation to language input and gender. *Developmental Psychology, 27*(2), 236.

Menard, S. W. (2010). Logistic regression: From introductory concepts to advanced concepts and applications. Thousand Oaks, CA: Sage.

Osborne, J. W. (2000). Advantages of hierarchical linear modeling. *Practical Assessment, Research & Evaluation, 7*(1).

Osborne, J. W. (2012). Best practices in data cleaning: A complete guide to everything you need to do before and after collecting your data. Thousand Oaks, CA: Sage.

Raudenbush, S. W., & Bryk, A. S. (2002). *Hierarchical linear models: Applications and data analysis methods* (Vol. 1). Thousand Oaks, CA: Sage.

5

CONTINUOUS PREDICTORS

Why Splitting Continuous Variables
Into Categories Is Undesirable

When I was in graduate school my advisor and I were exploring self-esteem effects in college undergraduate samples. In one project, my advisor directed me to split students at the median into "high self-esteem" and "low self-esteem" groups and do 2 × 2 analysis of variance (ANOVA) analyses (self-esteem by experimental condition).

Unfortunately for researchers in this area, individuals with truly low self-esteem are scarce—most individuals rate their global self-esteem relatively high. This is probably a good thing. We generally want people to feel good about themselves, but when you have a variable (like global self-esteem) that theoretically ranges from 1 to 4 with a median of 3.14, one must wonder what it means to split a variable like that into "low" and "high" groups. We did this as a median split but could also have used the mean, or an objective criterion such as 2.50 (but that would have left us with almost nobody in the "low" group!).

So the question is, were we really capturing "low self-esteem" and "high self-esteem"? Or were we studying "very high self-esteem" as compared with "moderately high self-esteem"? And ultimately, would we have been better off leaving the variable continuous?

There is a long tradition of splitting people into easily analyzed groups in various sciences. Health sciences researchers split people into "sick" and "healthy" or "obese" and "normal weight," despite the fact that people vary on a continuum from very healthy to very ill or from very underweight to very overweight. In the social sciences, we categorize people as "low income" or not, "successful" or not, old and young, depressed or not, into different racial and ethnic groups, and so on, again despite most variables being continuous in nature. In fact we can even argue about whether states such as dropping out of school, being a tobacco user, being male or female, or even "being dead" are categorical or continuous.

The traditional position of many researchers has been that it is easier for readers to understand analyses that compare one group versus another rather than relationships between variables. Yet I suspect that it is the case that it is merely easier for those researchers to conceptualize their results that way because of tradition, training, or mindset. People of all walks of life are used to considering relationships. People without high school diplomas know that the more they push on the accelerator in the automobile, the faster they tend to go, the more alcohol they drink the more inebriated they get, the lower the thermometer drops the more layers of different types of clothing they need to wear to be comfortable, and so forth. In fact, I might argue that it is artificial and unfamiliar for nontechnical audiences to think in dichotomous terms. Even death, the ultimate binary outcome, in some cultures is thought of as more of a continuous, evolving developmental process.

When I studied epidemiology, I disliked the tendency of those epidemiologists I worked with to want to group cases into two categories. For example, we were taught to group people into "high blood pressure" or "normal blood pressure" groups and analyze their risk of heart attack. It was certainly interesting to see that individuals above a certain threshold had increased odds of experiencing a heart attack relative to individuals below that threshold, but I never felt comfortable splitting a continuous variable such as blood pressure into two categories. My tendency was to want to study the relationship with blood pressure as a continuous variable.

◆ WHAT IS CATEGORIZATION AND WHY DOES IT EXIST?

Let's start with a definition. Categorization is the practice of splitting individuals measured on a continuous (ratio, interval, or at least ordinal) scale into two or more groups.[1] The most common type of categorization is dichotomization, often through a "median split" or use of another cutoff

---

[1]You may have noticed that in this and previous chapters I use the term "continuous" rather liberally—such as with the variable BADCNT, which as a count variable was not technically continuous. I am using the term to refer to variables that are not binary or categorical. Thank you for your patience with this liberty.

point such as the mean or a conceptually important cut score.[2] A median split is a common methodological procedure (MacCallum, Zhang, Preacher, & Rucker, 2002) that groups objects or individuals by whether they fall above or below the median. Dichotomization can use other cutoff points (Cohen, 1983), but the median is often preferred as it technically represents the exact middle of a distribution (i.e., 50% of the scores will fall above and 50% will fall below regardless of the shape of the distribution) and is a superior measure of the center of a distribution even when there is substantial non-normality present. Other indicators of centrality (e.g., mean) are more strongly influenced by non-normality and outliers, which could result in relatively uneven groups if used to split a sample.

Dichotomization and median splits are a special case of *k-group* splits where researchers convert a continuously measured variable into a variable represented by *k* number of groups. For example, some researchers (and governmental agencies) tend to use tertiles (grouping into three groups based on where the 33.33rd and the 66.67th percentiles fall, such as low-, medium-, and high-income groups), quartiles (grouping into four groups, usually at the 25th, 50th, and 75th percentiles), deciles (grouping into 10 groups of relatively equal size or span), and so forth. In all types of *k-group* splits, the researcher is converting a continuous variable into a categorical variable, which can cause significant loss of information and increase error variance (Knüppel & Hermsen, 2010). I'll demonstrate that point a little later. Obviously, as *k* gets larger, the damage done to the original continuous variable diminishes—for example, a $k = 1,000$ would be much better than $k = 10$, which in turn is better than $k = 2$. And $k = N$ (i.e., the number of groups equals the number of data points in a distribution) is equivalent to the original continuous variable.

The origins of this practice are difficult to trace. Relatively few articles have been written about the procedure itself compared with the hundreds of thousands of times it has been utilized in peer-reviewed journal articles. My assumption is that the technique is probably rooted in the late 19th century and early 20th century, when scholars were constructing inferential statistical tests such as Student's *t* test and the Pearson product-moment correlation (Pearson, 1901; Student, 1908), or was borrowed from early epidemiology and health sciences, where groups were often split into two (as discussed earlier) for easier manual computation of odds ratios and relative risk. Prior to the wide availability of statistical computing software, some of these calculations, particularly for procedures with continuous variables, were onerous and difficult (Cohen, 1983). Furthermore, in many branches of science, there were traditions of using analyses requiring categorical

---

[2]Such as a cutoff for diagnosis of an exceptionality.

independent variables (e.g., ANOVA or odds ratios [ORs]). Therefore, a tradition of simplifying computations through dichotomization developed (e.g., refer to Blomqvist, 1951). Early statisticians seemed to be well aware that they were compromising quality and power for convenience, but their choices were limited to what was possible with hand calculations. For example, Peters and Van Voorhis (1940, p. 398) explicitly pointed out that computing correlations using dichotomous variables sacrifices large portions of the true population effect size (particularly if the groups are unequal, as highlighted in Cohen, 1983).

This important point seems to have been lost over the years as the acceptance of this methodology continued. Subsequent generations of scholars were trained in the tradition of quantitative analysis, perhaps without questioning whether there are better ways to conduct analyses. By the early 1970s, as researchers had access to statistical computing, scholars began calling for the end to this practice, reminding scientists of the forgotten costs of this procedure: substantial underestimation of effects. Researchers began calling for the widespread use of regression techniques as an alternative to this practice many decades ago (Humphreys & Fleishman, 1974).

Traditions and mythologies in statistics seem to be tenacious once established. The advisor I refer to at the beginning of this chapter, although an extremely smart woman, had difficulty getting beyond her own training and tradition to see the potential downsides of such practices. Likewise, the professors teaching the epidemiology courses I took thought it a silly idea to use continuous variables in their analyses. They do not appear to be alone (Fitzsimons, 2008), although I hope readers of this book will be among the growing number of researchers to eschew this anachronistic practice.

◆ HOW WIDESPREAD IS THIS PRACTICE?

While writing my last book on data cleaning, I surveyed the broad scientific literature and found that dichotomization in the particular form of median split methodology can be found referenced in more than 340,000 articles catalogued by Google Scholar, spanning such important topics as the following[3]:

- Alzheimer's disease
- HIV interventions

---

[3]This is, sadly, only a brief summary of the 340,000 articles I found using median split methodology. This does not include other dichotomization techniques that may not involve median splitting, or other techniques for converting continuous variables to categorical.

- Diabetes
- Personality and mortality due to cardiovascular disease
- Androgyny
- Problem solving
- Facial recognition
- Acculturation to new situations
- Spatial learning in female meadow voles
- Therapy for bipolar disorder
- Leadership
- Gene expression and cancer treatment
- Empathy
- Humor and coping with stress
- Environmental knowledge
- Meal variety and caloric intake
- Aggressive behavior
- Acculturation to Latino culture and cancer risk
- Memory and gene expression
- Maternal anxiety and fetal outcomes
- Postmenopausal estradiol treatment and intellectual functioning
- Social support and coping with pain
- Internet purchasing behavior
- False memories
- Depression in asylum seekers
- Entrepreneurial behavior
- Burnout
- Unconscious decision making
- Goal orientation and motivational beliefs
- Condom usage in adolescent populations
- Maternal responsiveness and infant attachment
- Body image
- Brain growth in children with autism
- Disability due to pain
- Attitudes toward female business executives
- Service quality expectations
- Glaucoma
- Effectiveness of physical therapy on osteoarthritis of the knee
- Loneliness and herpes latency
- The subjective effects of alcohol consumption
- Creativity
- Impulsive buying behavior

As I mentioned earlier, scholars have been vocal about the deleterious effects of dichotomization and similar techniques for many decades (e.g., Cohen, 1983; Peters & Van Voorhis, 1940) in fields such as psychology/social science (MacCallum et al., 2002), medical research (Royston, Altman, & Sauerbrei, 2006), pharmaceutical research (Fedorov, Mannino, & Zhang, 2009), stock market forecasting (Lien & Balakrishnan, 2005), and consumer research (Fitzsimons, 2008). Despite these recent efforts, the practice persists to this day as a common occurrence (e.g., DeCoster, Iselin, & Gallucci, 2009). For example, McCallum et al. (2002) found that 11.5% of articles in two highly respected psychology journals contained analyses that had at least one continuous variable converted to a dichotomous variable. There is no way to estimate how much damage this practice is doing to the fields in which they occur.

◆ WHY DO RESEARCHERS USE DICHOTOMIZATION AND SIMILAR TECHNIQUES?

Attempting to understand why smart, sophisticated researchers publishing in good journals continue to use this practice (and perhaps why reviewers and editors continue to allow it), DeCoster and colleagues (2009) surveyed more than a hundred authors of recent articles in respected journals who used this practice to attempt to understand the reasoning behind these dichotomization decisions. Some of the myths surrounding the continued use of dichotomization seem to include three general categories of proposed benefits (see also Fitzsimons, 2008):

- Ease of analysis/interpretation
- Distributions of the continuous variables/improved measurement
  - o Analyses are easier to compute
  - o Variables are more reliable when dichotomized
  - o Dichotomization helps deal with outliers and non-normality of continuous variables
- Prior precedent within the field

I hope that by the end of this chapter you are convinced that none of these arguments are compelling enough to embrace the disadvantages of this procedure. I will address the last rationale first. Prior precedent and tradition is important, but no field advances by blindly clinging to outdated practice. So let's continue evolving and improving by looking for best practices.

Not only are scientists still using the procedure, researchers are still arguing that these types of conversions have a legitimate and useful place in quantitative methodology. For example, Westfall (2011) argued that in certain applications, dichotomization can improve power in biopharmaceutical research (e.g., gene expression analysis, multiple endpoints for clinical trials),[3] and others argue it can enhance ease of interpretation for readers in criminology and psychiatric research (Farrington & Loeber, 2000).[4] Although there may be particular situations in particular fields where this is not a terrible practice, I suspect that it is difficult to show it is *preferable* to maintaining a continuous variable in its original form. In other words, I cannot imagine a situation where it can convincingly be demonstrated to be a best practice. Thus, I think evidence is on the side of letting dichotomization slip into the history books as an anachronistic practice, due to all the drawbacks of this practice that this chapter will demonstrate.

The Evils of Cutoff Scores

OK, "evil" may be too strong a word, but one of the major practical, conceptual, and statistical issues with converting a continuous variable to a categorical variable is the cutoff score—the point at which you decide an individual is in one group or another.

From a practical point of view, we do this all the time. As teachers, we decide when a product or performance is "good enough" or an A, A–, or B+. As parents we are constantly making judgments about whether something is "healthy" or not for our children,[5] and as researchers, it often helps

---

[3]I am not sure dichotomization can *legitimately* improve power in any line of research, given the inflation of error variance. But later in this chapter I show how *inappropriate* applications of this methodology (such as extreme groups analysis) can *illegitimately* inflate effect sizes and power.

[4]It may not surprise you to learn that I disagree with this point. Farrington makes the point that in logistic regression dichotomous variables are more interpretable. I hope that by the end of this chapter you will be fully persuaded that this is complete baloney. Furthermore, when dichotomization of control variables occurs, biased effects in any analysis can result (Chen, Cohen, & Chen, 2007) as the effects of these covariates are not completely removed from the analysis due to dichotomization. All in all, this is a very weak argument, in my opinion, that promotes the use of a very poor practice.

[5]But most teachers and parents I know are sophisticated enough to know that cutoff scores are not absolute. Most teachers will tell you they dislike having to make summary categorical judgments about students, and most parents know a little of an "unhealthy" treat is fine—everything in moderation.

to group things together to impose some sort of simplistic order. In order to make these categorical decisions, we need something against which we compare the performance or qualities of the thing we are judging. This is a cut score, and the issue is not limited to logistic regression but is found everywhere from driver's license exams and professional licensure to clinical diagnoses for mental or physical illnesses.

From a conceptual point of view, however, the mere act of creating a cutoff score is difficult to justify. Continuing with the blood pressure example, let's define anyone with a diastolic blood pressure (DBP; that's the second number in the traditional 120/75 type of blood pressure measurement) over 80 as having "high blood pressure" and anyone under 80 as "normal blood pressure." We're essentially saying that someone with a DBP of 81 is in a completely different category than someone with a DBP of 79, despite the fact that in reality those are probably not *meaningfully* different (particularly given the difficulties of measuring things like blood pressure precisely), and the risks of adverse outcomes for these two individuals are probably not materially different. Further, we are saying that someone with a BDP of 81 is the same as someone with a DBP of 120, or that someone with a DBP of 79 is the same as someone with DBP of 50. I doubt many doctors or epidemiologists would agree with either of those assertions, however.

In reality, when doing this sort of cut-score conversion from a continuous to categorical variable, a researcher is creating groups with a tremendous amount of variance *within each group,* often more than the variance between the two groups (especially when the cut score is near the center of the distribution). Looking at Figure 5.1, you can see that when there is a continuous variable that is converted to a dichotomous variable, we end up with a lot of individuals in Group A that are, on the surface very different from each other. For example, in Group A we can have individuals who vary up to 3 or more standard deviations from each other, and the same is true for Group B. Yet the irony is that two individuals who were extremely similar—let's say individuals at −0.05 and 0.05 (who are in fact only 0.10 standard deviations from each other) are now classified into two completely different groups. This is what I mean by creating a lot of within-group variance—by which I mean error.

So why not simply do a correlation between DBP and age of heart attack or use logistic regression to predict incidence of heart attack based on DBP as a continuous variable? As you saw in previous chapters, it is not terribly difficult to incorporate continuous variables into logistic regression. Taking another example of age, it doesn't make sense to say that all people under 65 years of age are the same, and all people over 65 years old are the same, yet it is often the case in research that this is exactly what we do.

Figure 5.1 Visual Depiction of Dichotomizing a Normally Distributed Variable

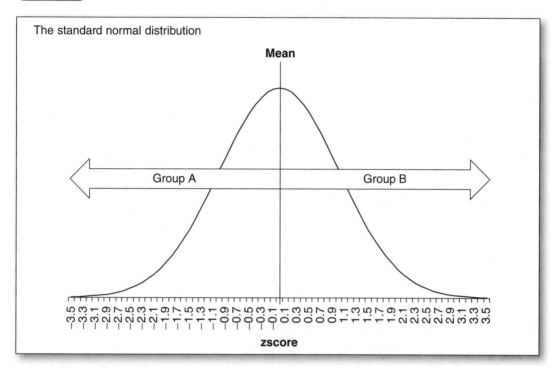

We're potentially giving away a lot of useful information, creating excessive within-group (error) variance, eliminating interesting effects like curvilinear effects, and perhaps creating false distinctions between individuals.

ARE ANALYSES MORE EASILY INTERPRETED ◆ WITH DICHOTOMOUS VARIABLES?

Some researchers seem to be under the impression that certain types of analyses are much more easily interpretable by nontechnical audiences if dichotomous variables are used. So, for example, this argument holds that it is more confusing for a reader to ponder a correlational relationship such as: "As socioeconomic status increases, student achievement test scores tend to increase." Instead, this argument posits that this type of finding is more easily received as "rich students score higher than poor students." Leaving aside the notion that Type II errors are more likely in the latter case (reducing rather than enhancing the clarity of the literature), most consumers of research

I have talked to[6] seem equally able to digest both types of finding if presented clearly. Some particular authors (Farrington & Loeber, 2000) seem to think that logistic regression is more easily interpretable with dichotomous predictors (but see strong dissenting opinion by Fitzsimons, 2008). This idea is again rooted in tradition and origins of the technique, where the earliest epidemiologists such as John Snow (1855) made simple hand calculations of 2 × 2 matrices (e.g., drank water from the Broad Street Pump or not; contracted cholera or not) calculating odds ratios.

To be fair, it is often a simple 2 × 2 analysis that leads to important insight and new paths to understanding phenomena. But as with other traditional analyses (such as certain types of correlations or internal consistency estimates), they are not superior to more complex analyses, merely *more easily calculated*. Thus, I argue it is as easy for a reader to read "Individuals drinking more frequently from the Broad Street pump had increased odds of contracting cholera relative to those drinking less frequently" as it is to read "The odds of contracting cholera for those having ever drank from the Broad Street well were 3.20 times that of those who had never drank from that well."

◆ ARE ANALYSES WITH DICHOTOMOUS VARIABLES EASIER TO COMPUTE?

To be sure, there are times when dichotomization creates simplicity in formulae, leaving researchers easier computations (Cohen, 1983). Yet this argument seems a bit silly in the 21st century when we have cell phones in our pockets with more power than some of the mainframe computers on which I first ran statistical analyses in graduate school. Most statistical software provides analyses for either categorical or continuous variables with the same few mouse clicks or lines of code. In my opinion, this is not a rationale for all the drawbacks that dichotomization brings.

◆ ARE DICHOTOMOUS VARIABLES MORE RELIABLE?

One of the most common reasons authors cite for performing dichotomization relates to the misperception that this can improve measurement,

---

[6]I have a long history of working with nonresearchers like teachers, policymakers, and health care professionals. They all seem to be able to digest results generated by continuous variables easily.

including refining crude/unreliable measurement, dealing with irregular or non-normal distributions, or the presence of outliers (DeCoster et al., 2009). Let's take each of these related arguments in order.

Dichotomization Improves Reliability of Measurement

The myth here is founded on the argument that measurement becomes more reliable under dichotomization because (a) all members of each group have identical scores, and (b) measurement is more replicable lumping people into two groups (i.e., it is more likely that a person in the "high depression" or "low depression" group will be in that same group at a following measurement, whereas it is unlikely that a second administration of a depression inventory would produce an identical score). This argument is misguided on several counts.

It is true that reliable measurement is important to research and that one hallmark of reliable measurement is repeatedly assigning the same score to an individual (assuming their underlying trait has not changed). However this argument assumes that being assigned to a different group (e.g., first being assigned to the "depressed" group and then to the "nondepressed group") is equivalent in importance to receiving a different score on whatever depression inventory is being used (e.g., 38 vs. 39). This is an obvious mischaracterization of the principle. In the first case, there is supposedly a meaningful difference between being assigned to one group versus the other, whereas there may not be a meaningful difference between a score of 38 and 39 on a depression inventory. Following this logic, the ultimate reliability would be achieved from putting everyone in a single group, assigning everyone the same score, repeatedly. Perfect reliability is thusly achieved, from this perspective. But clearly that is not a desirable strategy from a scientific or statistical point of view. Reliable measurement is important—*sine qua non* in research, in fact—but validity is also important. In fact, dichotomization creates neither reliable nor valid measurement.

The reason we care about reliable measurement is that more reliable measurement means that there is *less error variance* in the analysis. To the extent that measurement is unreliable, we have increased error variance, which undermines our ability to detect effects and causes underestimation of effect sizes. So let's think this process through. First, referring back to Figure 5.1, transforming a continuous variable into a categorical variable produces a tremendous amount of error variance. All the variance within each group is now error variance. If we were to calculate residuals (actual score vs. predicted or assigned score), those residuals under dichotomization would be much larger than when a variable is left in its original state—one strike against categorization producing more reliable (i.e., less error-filled) measurement.

Second, we may still have a good deal of individuals crossing boundaries into different groups *when there is little meaningful change*. If we perform a median or mean split, more of the sample lies very close to the cutoff point than far away from it. If we have less than perfect measurement (and we almost always do), it is likely that repeated measurements would lead to a good number of cases moving across the cutoff score to the other category due to minor fluctuations.[7] When a variable is kept continuous, these minor fluctuations are largely ignorable (e.g., a grade point average moving from 2.99 to 3.01 is not a big deal, but if 3.0 is the cutoff for dichotomization, that minor fluctuation has a large effect). Yet under dichotomization, differences between being in one group or the other have artificially large implications—and group membership for a large portion of the sample may be influenced by random fluctuation around the cutoff score.

Further exacerbating this problem, recall that most dichotomization procedures use the median or mean to assign individuals to groups. In other words, we are placing a cut score at the point of the distribution where the sample is densest, leaving the highest possible proportion of individuals to randomly fall on one side or other of the cut score due to random fluctuations in measurement rather than meaningful differences. All in all, categorization does not seem to be able to improve measurement reliability in any meaningful way and perhaps undermines one of the original arguments for using this procedure.

Let us also look at the issue of error variance, which is quantified by the residual, or the difference between expected (predicted) scores and actual scores. In ANOVA-type analyses, we can look at the difference between individual scores and group averages, and in regression-type analyses, we can similarly look at the difference between a predicted score and an actual score. It simply does not make sense to argue that dichotomization (i.e., assigning everyone below the median a score of "1" and everyone above the median a "2") would reduce error, as we now have vast differences between individual scores and the group mean, whereas each individual would be much closer to their predicted score in a regression equation.

---

[7]In fact, the randomness of individuals being close on one side or the other of a cut score is the basis for regression discontinuity analysis. In regression discontinuity analyses, the assertion is that individuals closely clustered around a cut score are *not meaningfully different because it is primarily random chance that determines which side of the cut score an individual falls.* This highlights the fallacy of the myth that dichotomization improves reliability of measurement.

Let me demonstrate this with a concrete example.[8] Starting with two highly correlated variables from the Education Longitudinal Study of 2002 (Ingels et al., 2004; http://nces.ed.gov/surveys/els2002/): 10th-grade math achievement test score (BYTXMIRR) and 12th-grade math achievement test score (F1TXM1IR), we can explore the effects of dichotomization on reliability. Both variables are reasonably normally distributed, as Figures 5.2 and 5.3 show (both skew close to 0.00). Furthermore, the two variables, as one might expect, are very strongly correlated ($r_{(13,394)} = .89$, $p < .0001$, with 10th-grade math scores accounting for 79.7% of the variance in 12th-grade math scores) as Figure 5.3 shows. In other words, students who score higher on 10th-grade math assessments are likely to score higher on 12th-grade math assessments.

Figure 5.2 10th-Grade Math Scores

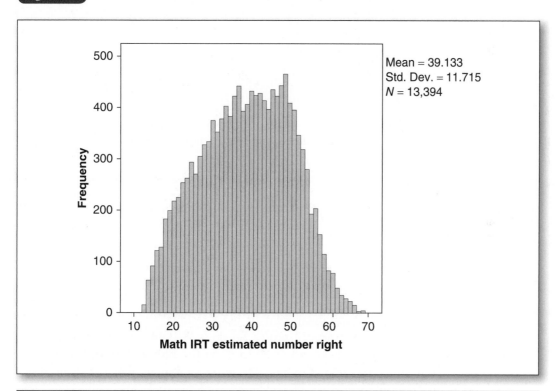

Mean = 39.133
Std. Dev. = 11.715
N = 13,394

Source: Osborne, *Best Practices in Data Cleaning*. SAGE, 2012 (Figure 11.1, p. 240). Data obtained from: Ingels et al. (2004). *Education Longitudinal Study of 2002: Base Year Data File User's Manual.*

---

[8]Just to be upfront about this example, it is borrowed directly from my last book on data cleaning (Osborne, 2012).

Figure 5.3 12th-Grade Math Scores

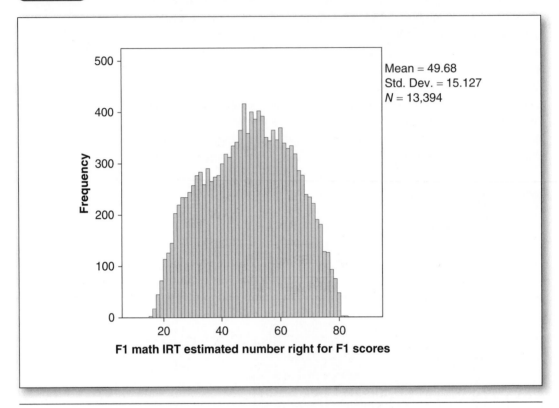

Mean = 49.68
Std. Dev. = 15.127
N = 13,394

Source: Osborne, *Best Practices in Data Cleaning*. SAGE, 2012 (Figure 11.2, p. 240). Data obtained from: Ingels et al. (2004). *Education Longitudinal Study of 2002: Base Year Data File User's Manual.*

As you can see in Figure 5.4, there is not a tremendous amount of error variance in this analysis—only 20.3% of the variance is unaccounted for, and the residuals are relatively small, as Figure 5.5 shows. The average (unstandardized or raw) residual is 4.93, with a standard deviation of 4.70 (recall scores on these variables range from 12.52 to 69.72 for 10th grade and 15.20 to 82.54 for 12th grade). If dichotomization truly does improve reliability of measurement, the size of the residuals should diminish after splitting students into "low performers" and "high performers." To test this, I performed a median split on the 10th-grade variable and performed an ANOVA with 12th-grade achievement as the dependent variable. As you can see in Figure 5.6, when 10th graders are dichotomized into "low" and "high," the dispersion of the

Figure 5.4 Correlation Between 10th- and 12th-Grade Math Scores

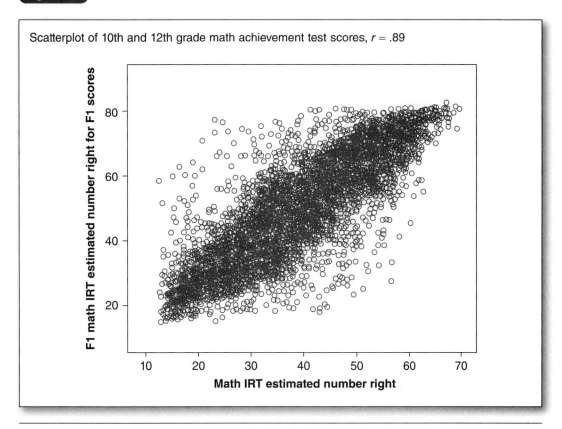

Scatterplot of 10th and 12th grade math achievement test scores, $r = .89$

Source: Osborne, *Best Practices in Data Cleaning.* SAGE, 2012 (Figure 11.3, p. 241). Data obtained from: Ingels et al. (2004). *Education Longitudinal Study of 2002: Base Year Data File User's Manual.*

12th-grade scores within each group is now much larger than the dispersion around any given point in Figure 5.4.

Once the variable is dichotomized, we come to the same conclusion: low math performers in 10th grade tend to score lower in 12th grade than high math performers (average scores = 38.45 [*SD* = 10.56] and 60.91 [*SD* = 9.69], respectively, $F_{(1,13387)} = 16433.22$, $p < .0001$, $\eta^2 = .55$). And in fact, 10th-grade math performance still has a strong effect on 12th-grade math performance, with the dichotomous 10th-grade math performance variable accounting for 55% of the variance in 12th-grade math performance. This is a 30.99% reduction in effect size, and the residuals (presented in Figure 5.7) show an equal increase. The average residual is now 8.26,

Figure 5.5 Residuals From Simple Regression Predicting 12th-Grade Math Scores From 10th-Grade Math Scores

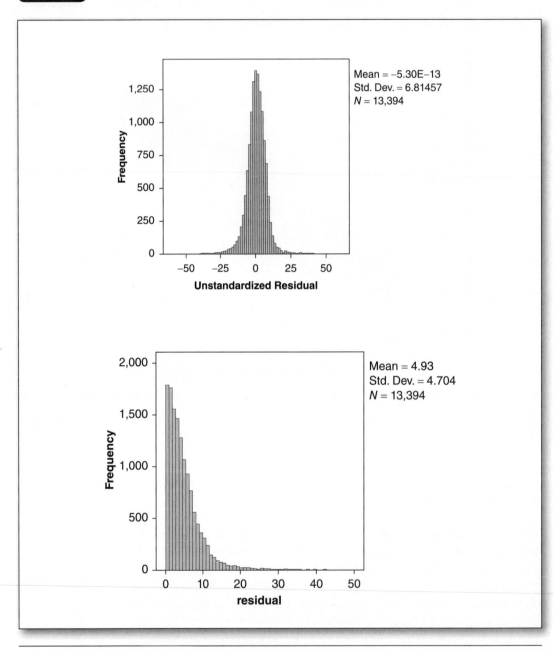

Source: Osborne, *Best Practices in Data Cleaning.* SAGE, 2012 (Figure 11.4, p. 241). Data obtained from: Ingels et al. (2004). *Education Longitudinal Study of 2002: Base Year Data File User's Manual.*

Figure 5.6 Scatterplot Following Dichotomization

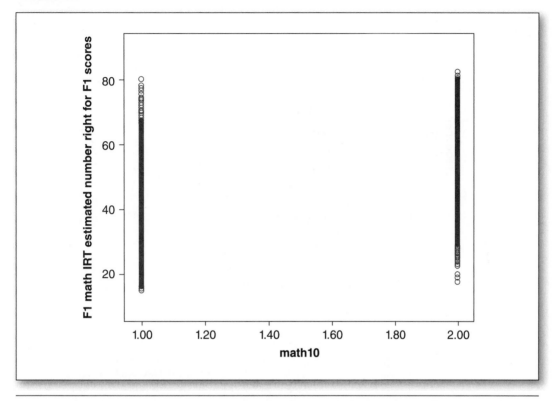

Source: Osborne, *Best Practices in Data Cleaning*. SAGE, 2012 (Figure 11.5, p. 242). Data obtained from: Ingels et al. (2004). *Education Longitudinal Study of 2002: Base Year Data File User's Manual.*

with a standard deviation of 5.87. Thus, this simple dichotomization almost doubled the average size of the residuals while simultaneously decreasing the variance explained.

Keep in mind this is an unusually strong relationship, and most researchers do not deal with effect sizes this large. Imagine how more modest effects would fare. How many researchers would experience Type II errors (failing to find a significant effect when in fact there is an effect in the population) after giving away one third of their effect sizes?

The other argument, that measurement is more reliable because of the reliability of repeated categorization, is also shown to be false in this analysis. Again, even with this tremendously strong correlation between the two administrations of the math test, 13.3% of the students change classification

Figure 5.7 Residuals Following Dichotomization

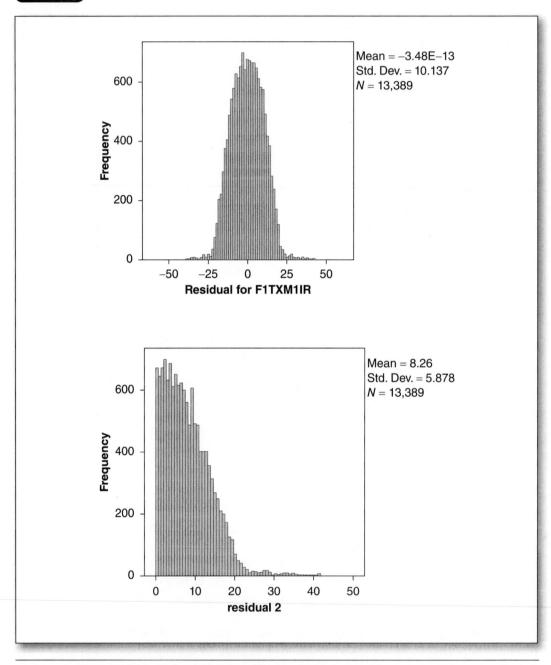

Source: Osborne, *Best Practices in Data Cleaning.* SAGE, 2012 (Figure 11.6, p. 243). Data obtained from: Ingels et al. (2004). *Education Longitudinal Study of 2002: Base Year Data File User's Manual.*

from "low" to "high" or from "high" to "low" between 10th and 12th grade.[9] Does this mean that more than 1,700 students in this sample got qualitatively more or less adept at math? Probably not. As mentioned earlier in the footnote discussing regression discontinuity analysis, this changing of categories is most often caused by minor variation in performance near the cut score (or random measurement error), where most students are, rather than by students who meaningfully change performance levels. Note also that this problem would be more pronounced as the reliability of the original variable becomes less perfect.

By taking the absolute value of the distance of each individual from the median (BYTXMIRR-39.63) and comparing distances between people who switched classification from "low" to "high" math achiever or the opposite direction, it is clear that this exactly what is happening. The average distance for people switching classification was 3.91 points ($SD = 3.57$) (mostly around the cut score), whereas for those who maintained their classification consistently the average distance was 10.72 ($SD = 6.27$; significant effect $F_{(1,13387)} = 1992.48$, $p < .0001$, $\eta^2 = .13$), indicating these individuals were much farther, on average from the cut score. This example supports some important conclusions about dichotomization.

First, even with very strong relationships between variables and excellent measurement properties, categorization reduces effect sizes dramatically—in this example, the percent variance accounted for dropped from about 79% to 55%. This is not surprising considering effect sizes are generally a ratio of variance accounted for to error (unexplained) variance, and by dichotomizing, we dramatically increased error variance. In this simple example, errors (residuals) almost doubled in size *on average*.

Second, approximately one in seven students in this sample switched classification from high to low or low to high-achievement categories between 10th and 12th grade despite the particularly good measurement and strong correlation between these variables. Finally, those who move categories are those closest to the median, therefore creating the appearance of large differences in performance when in fact these changes are due to *relatively small, perhaps inconsequential changes* consistent with random fluctuation rather than meaningful improvement or decline.

This does not support common assertions about the benefits of categorization.

---

[9]Not surprisingly, an equal number of students moved from high- to low-performing categories as moved the other way: 890 moved from the low to high group, while 886 moved the other way . This is consistent with random fluctuation around a fixed point rather than some other meaningful change in performance.

♦ DOES DICHOTOMIZATION EFFECTIVELY DEAL WITH NON-NORMALITY OR OUTLIERS?

The logic of this argument is that if you have a highly skewed distribution, splitting the participants into two groups based on the median eliminates the nasty issues that non-normal data can bring. You no longer have skew, just two groups—extreme scores, or outliers are no more. But at what cost?

I have published on transforming and normalizing data, issues that outliers bring to parametric analyses, and other issues around data cleaning (e.g., Osborne, 2010; Osborne, 2012; Osborne & Overbay, 2004). My immediate response, as outlined in these publications, is to encourage use of a data transformation to deal with variables that are not normally distributed. Further, my inclination regarding outliers is to examine the potential cause of them and fix them where appropriate. Other options, as examined in Chapter 7 of my book on data cleaning (Osborne, 2012), are probably more desirable than merely ignoring the fact and dichotomizing as outliers and extreme scores can arise from many sources. If you have non-normal data, such as outliers that are substantially outside the general distribution of a variable, you are merely *increasing the within-group variance* when dichotomizing. In other words, you are creating even more error variance by attempting to deal with extreme scores in this manner than by appropriately dealing with extreme scores or non-normal data.

Let us also keep in mind that logistic regression does not assume normal distributions of any variable, or residuals, so this is not a good rationale for dichotomizing your data.

To explore this issue, we will explore a data set on university size and average faculty salary. This particular data set, which I often use in classes and have used in previous publications, are 1,161 institutions in the United States collected on the size of the institution (number of faculty) and average faculty salary by the American Association of University Professors (available at www.sagepub.com/osbornebplr) in 2005. As Figure 5.8 shows, the variable *number of faculty* is highly skewed (NUM_TOT; skew = 2.58, kurtosis = 8.09). Faculty salary (associate professors) was more normally distributed to begin with, with a skew of 0.36 and kurtosis of 0.12. The initial correlation between the two variables of $r_{(1161)} = 0.49$, $p < .0001$ (coefficient of determination or percent variance accounted for of 24.0%) improved to $r_{(1161)} = 0.66$, $p < .0001$ (coefficient of determination or % variance accounted for of 0.44, or an 81.50% increase) after improving normality of the faculty variable by

Figure 5.8 Distribution of Faculty Size

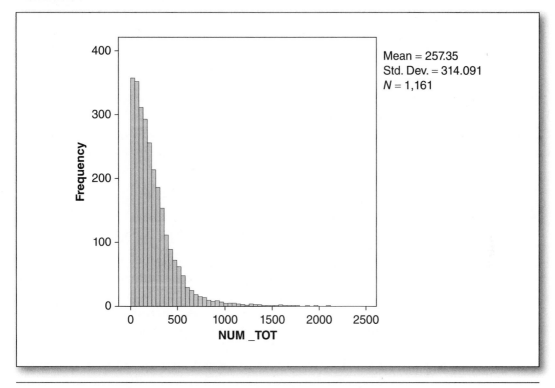

Source: Osborne, *Best Practices in Data Cleaning.* SAGE, 2012 (Figure 11.7, p. 245). Data obtained from: Ingels et al. (2004). *Education Longitudinal Study of 2002: Base Year Data File User's Manual.*

Box-Cox transformation (Osborne, 2010). Likewise, the average residual was 48.49 (*SD* = 38.92) before this transformation and 42.94 (*SD*=33.46) after.[10]

Instead of performing this data transformation, let us imagine we dichotomized the number of faculty variable through median split (this variable ranged from 7 to 2,261, with a median of 132.0). Following dichotomization, the correlation is indeed somewhat improved over the untransformed data $r_{(1161)}$ = 0.57, p < .0001 (coefficient of determination or percent variance accounted for of 33.0%). But rather than demonstrate the potential of this method, this analysis highlights the weakness. The normalized version of this continuous variable (following Box-Cox transformation) yielded an effect size one third *stronger* than dichotomization

---

[10]This analysis is discussed in greater depth in Chapter 8 of Osborne (2012) for those of you interested in the details.

(coefficient of determination = 44%). Similarly, the residuals present following dichotomization are closer in magnitude to the untransformed data than the appropriately transformed data (average residual from the dichotomized analysis was 46.88, $SD = 35.11$). Thus, I would suggest that even in the case of severe non-normality in your data such as this variable, appropriate transformation yields is still a better practice (in this case, 33.33% stronger effect size over dichotomized data). Similarly, appropriately dealing with outliers will be a more satisfactory solution than dichotomization.

There is some evidence that nonparametric analyses, such as logistic regression, also suffer reduced effect sizes from dichotomization (Farrington & Loeber, 2000), as I will demonstrate later.

♦ EXTREME GROUPS ANALYSIS: GENERALLY ILL-ADVISED AND OFTEN DISHONEST

A less common but more problematic type of dichotomization is that of extreme-groups analysis (Preacher, Rucker, MacCallum, & Nicewander, 2005), wherein researchers may choose individuals that represent extremes of a distribution. For example, we could choose people who score above or below a certain IQ cutoff (such as those below IQ = 80 and those above IQ = 120), or my advisor and I could have chosen the 25 individuals with the lowest self-esteem and the 25 individuals with the highest self-esteem for comparison or intervention. The latter approach, called *post-hoc* subgrouping, is particularly to be avoided, as I will explain later.

There are some benefits to this approach, properly applied, in terms of efficiency where resources prohibit use of large numbers of participants, and enhanced power and effect size. Many mixed-methods researchers practice purposeful sampling, wherein they seek to gather interesting individuals to understand important processes. Mixed-methods and qualitative researchers are constrained by how much effort goes into analysis of each case. This justification tends to fall flat when looking at a purely quantitative analysis, as there is little difference in performing a logistic regression analysis with 50 or 50,000 cases.

When using this approach without strong justification, it appears that a researcher is merely attempting to artificially (and unethically) inflate apparent effect sizes. I label this as unethical and dishonest as the effect size from this sort of analysis is rarely representative of the effect size in the general population, because the comparison is between two groups at different extremes of a distribution. Thus it is my assertion that extreme groups analysis is rarely defensible and should be used with great caution.

As you have probably surmised by now, it is my opinion that this is not a viable alternative to using continuous variables. While I have argued that dichotomization generally is not a good strategy, this particular version of dichotomization is not easily defensible and should be avoided.

SOME OTHER DRAWBACKS OF DICHOTOMIZATION ♦

Curvilinearity and Interactions Will Be Masked or Undetectable

There are times when variables have nonlinear relationships. As I often tell my students, interactions and nonlinear relationships are among the more interesting results we can find (as we will explore later in this book). It seems unrealistic to expect all things in nature to be linearly related. However, conversion of variables from continuous to dichotomous effectively eliminates the opportunity to look for curvilinear relationships, potentially eliminating interesting effects. It seems a shame to lose this possibility (and more accurate representation of the true nature of the effect) through artificially dichotomizing a continuous variable (Farewell, Tom, & Royston, 2004; Maxwell & Delaney, 1993).

Interactions are not necessarily destroyed by categorization, but as error variance is increased and effect sizes are decreased, interactions (already more difficult to detect than simple effects in many cases) become more likely to be overlooked merely by virtue of loss of power rather than for lack of being there (see Aiken & West, 1991 for more on testing interactions in ordinary least squares regression).

The Variable Is by Nature Categorical

To be sure, there are probably instances where individuals cluster together, creating the illusion of categorical groups (MacCallum et al., 2002). If a variable is truly categorical, why is it being measured continuously? What the researcher probably means when asserting that the variable is "by nature categorical" is that the sample is not evenly distributed across the entire range of the variable. But then, is dichotomization an appropriate response to this natural clustering? I tend not to think so, particularly when we require no assumption that variables correspond to the normal distribution. And even in the case where individuals clearly cluster into well-defined and separated groups, care must be taken to accurately categorize. This may involve more than two groups, split at points not necessarily represented by the median, and so on. If it happens that there are clear, nonoverlapping clusters of individuals, it is possible that multinomial logistic regression would be appropriate, a topic we will discuss later in the book as well. But note again, if you are taking groups of individuals—even groups that cluster together—clusters have variance, and by eliminating the continuous measurement you are likely increasing error variance and causing all sorts of unfortunate effects as we have already explored.

Spurious Statistical Significance

If you accept the argument and considerable evidence that dichotomization increases error variance, then a less reliable covariate necessarily is a less effective covariate. Type I error rates might be increased by utilizing dichotomized covariates that fail to adequately remove the effects of the variable had it been left continuous (Maxwell & Delaney, 1993). Along the same lines, prediction equations/models can be significantly biased when artificial dichotomization is used (Hin, Lau, Rogers, & Chang, 1999), as can the goodness of fit of predictive modeling (Lien & Balakrishnan, 2005).

◆ DICHOTOMIZATION OF VARIABLES AND LOGISTIC REGRESSION

Of course, this is a book devoted to all the fun and excitement you can have with logistic regression, so we have to come back to how this issue specifically influences a logistic regression analysis. It might be no surprise at this point that my position on this point is that if you have continuous measurement, you should keep your variable continuous. So let's talk about some of the ways that this issue relates specifically to logistic regression.

First, some authors have argued that dichotomization can increase apparent effect sizes in logistic regression (I will refrain from citing the offenders). It definitely is true that dichotomization can *inappropriately* misrepresent a variable's effect size by altering the nature of an increment of 1.0, which is the basis of the odds ratio and logit slope. Logistic regression calculates effects as the change in the probabilities and odds, and so on, in the dependent variable as a function of a change of 1.0 in the independent variable. When a variable is dichotomous, you have only one increment.

When a variable is continuous, you can have dozens, hundreds, or thousands of increments of 1.0. Thus, if you have a variable such as percentage correct on a test as an independent variable, with perhaps 50 increments of 1.0, you can get highly significant effects that look very small (odds ratio of, say 1.05). Changing this variable to z-scores changes the interpretation from an increment of 1.0 percentage points to 1.0 standard deviations and changes the odds ratio, not because the actual effect changes, but merely because we are changing how many increments of 1.0 there are in the variable (perhaps 6 rather than 50, in this hypothetical example). Similarly, dichotomizing changes the interpretation yet again. Where there were potentially 50, or 6 increments accounting for the effect, now there is only 1: above the cut point versus below the cut point. At this point, the odds ratio may be substantially larger, inappropriately so only because of the dichotomization, making this variable look substantially more important than when it was continuous or z-scored. But this is an illusion and a purposeful misrepresentation of the nature of the effect. No true scientist or scholar should ever accept that as a reason to make a particular decision!

So we have three possibilities in the previous paragraph of how to deal with a continuous variable: leaving it as measured, converting to the standard normal distribution (z-scores), and converting to a dichotomous variable. If my lengthy arguments from earlier in the chapter hold, dichotomizing continuous variables in logistic regression should simultaneously decrease effect sizes (increased error variance) while inappropriately increasing the appearance of the effect size. The other option, converting to z-scores, not only preserves the effect size and error variance, but makes your continuous variable more easily interpretable. Thus, the latter option is the best practice, as I will show.

In Table 5.1, I present some simple examples from the Education Longitudinal Study of 2002[11] wherein I use logistic regression to predict whether a student graduated from high school or dropped out prior to completion of 12th grade as a function of 10th-grade math achievement test score. Reading achievement ranges from 12.52 to 69.72, with a standard deviation of 11.88. Thus, left as is, the original variable has about 50 increments of 1.0 to account for the effect of graduating. As Table 5.1 shows, math is a significant predictor of graduation/dropout. For every increase of 1.0 in math, the odds of graduating are 1.07 that of those who scored one point lower (which obviously seems like a small effect size to individuals who do not understand the nuances of continuous variables in logistic regression). As expected, converting math scores to z-scores has no effect on the analysis model statistics, which are identical. However, because we have redefined

---

[11]http://nces.ed.gov/surveys/els2002/

how many increments of 1.0 there are (in this case, about 4 in the observed range), each increment of one standard deviation leads to an increase in the odds of graduating of 2.19. Note that this seems to be an inflation of effect size but is defensible as it keeps the original variable intact, accounts for the same amount of variance, and when performed on ALL continuous variables, allows for direct comparisons of odds ratios across predictors.

The third line in the table shows how dichotomization (mean split) can inappropriately inflate the apparent effect size. In this case, the odds ratio inflates to 4.16; however, the Wald and model chi-square dropped dramatically. This represents an *inappropriate* inflation of apparent effect size.

Extreme groups analysis can inappropriately increase apparent effect size through eliminating individuals in the center of the distribution. In this case, choosing students more than one standard deviations from the mean not only eliminates a majority of the sample but inappropriately inflates both variance accounted for and apparent odds ratio. This comparison eliminates the majority of the sample, making it nonrepresentative and changes the definition of the comparison from the original (1 point or one standard deviation increase) to represent a comparison between those substantially below the mean only to those substantially above the mean.

Inhibiting Accurate Meta-Analysis of Results

Widespread dichotomization has implications for researchers as the methodology of meta-analysis becomes more widely used. As Hunter and

Table 5.1 Illusory Effects of Dichotomization on Logistic Regression

Model	Wald for Math	Model Chi-Square	Odds Ratio	95% CI Odds Ratio
Math continuous	516.96	585.44	1.068***	1.062, 1.074
Math z-scored	516.96	585.44	2.187***	2.044, 2.339
Math median split	371.49	453.22	4.161***	3.599, 4.810
Math Extreme groups (± 1 SD)	239.65	393.77	10.002***	7.473, 13.388

Note: *** $p < .0001$. N = 15,892, N = 5,953 for extreme groups analysis; because of decreased N in extreme groups analysis model chi-square comparison is not valid.

Data Source: National Education Longitudinal Study of 2002 (ELS2002), National Center for Educational Statistics, U.S. Department of Education (http://nces.ed.gov/surveys/els2002/).

Schmidt (1990) point out, dichotomization has the potential to significantly bias the results of the analysis (compared with what analyses with the original data would have shown).

WHAT ABOUT OTHER K-GROUPS ♦ CATEGORIZATION SCHEMES?

As mentioned briefly earlier, dichotomization is currently unfortunately common. However, it is not the only method of converting continuous type variables to categorical type variables. Also mentioned in the literature are variations containing 3, 4, 5, or 10 groups. And there are probably other variations. So the natural question becomes whether it is better to use three or four groups rather than two. In theory, as you move from two groups toward more groups, the damage that categorization causes is reduced. So deciles are better than dichotomies. Yet unless there is a very good rationale, it seems to me like a lot of work for no demonstrable benefit and high risk for loss of precision and power. Practically, as we take categorization to extremes, we approach the results we would have obtained from the original continuous variable. It just seems to me like a solution in search of a problem and not worth the time and effort.

SO WHAT ARE BEST PRACTICES FOR LOGISTIC ♦ REGRESSION WITH CONTINUOUS VARIABLES?

There seem to be two challenges with using continuous variables in a logistic regression framework: interpreting the individual variable results and comparing results across variables in an attempt to determine which variables are the strongest (or most important) predictors of an outcome. For example, I could have in the same analysis grade point average (GPA; which usually varies from 0.00 to 4.00, giving us four theoretical increments of 1.0) and SAT score (which can traditionally range from 200 to 800 on a given scale, giving us hundreds of theoretical increments). If both variables were left in their original state, and if they had identical effects, the difference in number of increments would make GPA look like a much stronger predictor of the outcome than SAT score. Further, even if SAT has a very strong effect, the odds ratio and logit will appear very small because that strong effect is being sliced up into many more increments.

I believe the answer to both issues is to standardize all continuous variables through conversion to the standard normal distribution. To highlight

the benefits of this approach, I will again use ELS2002 data and two continuous variables with different ranges. We will predict retention in high school
(opposite coding of dropout to keep odds ratios over 1.00) from family
socioeconomic status (SES; which ranges from −2.11 to 1.98 with a mean of
0.04 and *SD* of 0.75[12]) and from 10th-grade standardized math test performance (which ranges from 12.52 to 69.72, with a mean of 38.06 and a *SD*
of 11.88). The results of the initial analysis are presented in Table 5.2.

Table 5.2 Predicting Student Retention From Family SES and Standardized Test Scores

		B	*SE*	Wald	*df*	Sig.	Exp(B)	95% CI for Exp(B)	
								Lower	Upper
	BYSES	.643	.052	149.943	1	.000	1.902	1.716	2.108
Step 1[a]	BYTXMIRR	.053	.003	264.534	1	.000	1.054	1.047	1.061
	Constant	.896	.111	64.556	1	.000	2.449		

a. Variable(s) entered on step 1: BYSES2, BYTXMIRR.

Data Source: ELS2002, National Center for Educational Statistics, U.S. Department of Education (http://nces.ed.gov/surveys/els2002/).

If these results are reported without proper context, one might assume
that family SES has a much stronger effect on retention or withdrawal than
academic performance (as measured by standardized test scores). However,
SES has many times fewer increments of 1.0. If we follow my suggestion in
this analysis and convert both variables to the standard normal distribution
(I will convert SES as well because it is not exactly a standard normal distribution), then both variables are expressed on the same scale with a
similar number of increments, making them more directly comparable. This
is particularly true when the distributions of the continuous variables contain the same number of standard deviations. For example, if two variables
both conform to the standard normal distribution, then both should range
from about −3.0 to 3.0, six standard deviations. Realizing no two variables
will have exactly the same distributions, this is a good approximation of
standardization. Furthermore, and perhaps more importantly, this gives us

---

[12]This looks almost like a standard normal distribution but seems restricted to
a −2 to 2 range rather than a −3 to 3 range. I have seen this in other Institute of
Education Sciences/National Center for Education Statistics data sets as well.

a standard interpretation of the odds ratio—the change in odds for a one-standard-deviation increase in the predictor.

In Table 5.3, you can see that once both variables are put on exactly the same metric, student achievement is a stronger predictor of retention than family SES.

Table 5.3 Predicting Student Retention From Family SES and Standardized Test Scores Converted to a Standard Normal Distribution

| | | B | SE | Wald | df | Sig. | Exp(B) | 95% CI for Exp(B) | |
								Lower	Upper
Step 1[a]	zBYSES2	.482	.039	149.943	1	.000	1.620	1.499	1.750
	zBYTXMIRR	.625	.038	264.534	1	.000	1.868	1.732	2.014
	Constant	2.926	.042	4859.361	1	.000	18.656		

a. Variable(s) entered on step 1: zBYSES2, zBYTXMIRR.

Data Source: ELS2002, National Center for Educational Statistics, U.S. Department of Education (http://nces.ed.gov/surveys/els2002/).

To be clear, this procedure does change the interpretation of the results slightly. In this case, we now interpret the odds ratio and logit as the change in odds of retention for each one standard deviation increase in the predictors (controlling for other variables in the equation). Thus, we can compare the relative effects of one standard deviation increase for every continuous variable.

I suspect this also makes things easier on the reader as all analyses that use this approach can be interpreted in terms of increases of one standard deviation, rather than having to interpret variables with wildly different ranges. This approach is similar to the common approach in multiple regression of interpreting standardized regression coefficients when comparison across variables is desirable for the same reason.

There are other advantages of using variables that are converted to the standard normal distribution. For example, it is usually a best practice to center variables when exploring interaction terms (which we will get to later in the book), and so instead of manually centering each variable without standardizing the dispersion of each variable, conversion to *z*-scores accomplishes this in addition to making variable effects directly comparable.

Another benefit of this approach is that the intercept can be substantively interpretable and interesting. When the intercept is left at 0.00 it is often outside the reasonable or even theoretical range of a variable (i.e., blood pressure or SAT test score). When all variables are centered or converted to z-scores, the intercept becomes substantively meaningful—it is the average (mean) of each continuous variable, and thus instead of an intercept representing the odds of something happening for a group of people who do not exist, it represents the odds of something happening for those who are average (or coded as "0") on all variables in the equation.

♦ BEST PRACTICES IN REPORTING RESULTS FROM CONTINUOUS VARIABLES: CONDITIONAL PROBABILITIES

One of the reasons some researchers probably like dichotomized variables is that it makes for easy talking points: "the odds of group A having the outcome were <odds ratio> that of group B." There are no easy talking points with continuous variables. However, we as researchers can easily make them when reporting results. It is simple to make conceptually meaningful comparisons. For example, looking at the BMI and diabetes analyses, it would be easy to compare someone with a very healthy BMI (e.g., 20) to someone with a very unhealthy one (e.g., 40), or low BMI (e.g., 1 SD below the mean) to high BMI (1 SD above the mean). We will perform this comparison in the enrichment exercises later. Instead, let's look at math achievement and GRADUATE in the ELS2002 data we were exploring earlier. As shown in Figure 5.2, the math scores ranged from 12.52 to 69.72, with a mean of 38.06 and a SD of 11.88. With no objective or conceptual points that are obvious to compare (like BMI or GPA might have), let us just choose to compare those who score 1 SD below the mean to those who score 1 SD above the mean for purposes of communicating the results to our audience. According to these statistics, 26.18 is 1 SD below the mean, and 49.93 is 1 SD above the mean. The analysis of these data result in a regression line equation:

$$\text{Logit}(\hat{Y}) = 0.2803 + 0.0659(\text{Math})^{13}$$

Using the regression line equation and our estimates for ± 1 SD, we get predicted logits of 2.00544 and 3.57099, respectively. But our audience (and

---

[13]Once again, I am violating American Psychological Association (APA) format by including more decimals than ideal for precision of calculation.

Table 5.4 SAS Output Predicting GRADUATE From Math Achievement Test Score

Analysis of Maximum Likelihood Estimates					
Parameter	df	Estimate	Standard Error	Wald Chi-Square	Pr > ChiSq
Intercept	1	0.2803	0.0944	8.8127	0.0030
BYTXMIRR	1	0.0659	0.00290	516.9596	<.0001

Odds Ratio Estimates			
Effect	Point Estimate	95% Wald Confidence Limits	
BYTXMIRR	1.068	1.062	1.074

Data Source: ELS2002, National Center for Educational Statistics, U.S. Department of Education (http://nces.ed.gov/surveys/els2002/).

most of us, indeed!) might have difficulty conceptualizing what a predicted logit is. Converting these to predicted probabilities, we can then say that the probability of graduating is 0.8814 for those 1 *SD* below the mean and 0.9726 for those 1 *SD* above the mean in 10th-grade math scores. In other words, students who are 1 *SD* above average in math in 10th grade are 11% more likely to stay in school through graduation than those 1 *SD* below average. These are numbers that average readers (and researchers) can understand.

But best practices include using z-scored predictors where possible! Let's do the same analysis with math converted to *z*-scores, as authors have advocated for decades (DeMaris, 1993). Let me foreshadow the conclusion of this section by telling you that the results should be identical regardless—for most things. As you remember from earlier, this analysis produces identical model fit and Wald so we will skip directly to the regression line equation and predicted conditional probabilities. The analysis gives us a regression line equation of:

$$\text{Logit}(\hat{Y}) = 2.7873 + 0.7824(z\text{Math})$$

One nice aspect of using *z*-scored variables is that we can simply use ±1 for the values we substitute into the equation, producing predicted logits of 2.0049 and 3.5697, which are very close to the predicted logits from

Table 5.5 SAS Output With Normalized Math Achievement

Analysis of Maximum Likelihood Estimates					
Parameter	df	Estimate	Standard Error	Wald Chi-Square	Pr > ChiSq
Intercept	1	2.7873	0.0376	5509.5882	<.0001
zBYTXMIRR	1	0.7824	0.0344	516.9596	<.0001

Odds Ratio Estimates			
Effect	Point Estimate	95% Wald Confidence Limits	
zBYTXMIRR	2.187	2.044	2.339

Data Source: ELS2002, National Center for Educational Statistics, U.S. Department of Education (http://nces.ed.gov/surveys/els2002/).

the previous equation, and of course, convert to very close approximations of the other predicted probabilities. So we emerge with two important conclusions. First, functionally, it does not matter whether you convert continuous variables to z-scores or not, you get identical (to several decimal places) predicted probabilities. Therefore, there is little reason *not* to use them in most cases. They improve the reader's ability to understand and interpret the results.

The second conclusion, which I alluded to when first mentioning the advantages of using z-scores, is that the intercept is now the mean rather than some potentially impossible or meaningless point. For example, in the first analysis the intercept is a math score of 0.00, but the lowest math score was over 12. Thus, it is irrelevant and meaningless as it does not fall within the observed range of scores. With an intercept of 0.28 logits, the first equation tells us that someone with a score of 0 in math has about a 0.57 probability of staying in school to graduate. Of course, it makes sense that very poorly performing students have lower expectations of graduation, but this is nonsensical as nobody scored that poorly.

On the other hand, when using the z-scored variable, we get a third data point as a free bonus—the mean, which has a logit of 2.79, with a predicted probability of about 0.94. Thus, we now know the predicted probability of someone with a score of −1 *SD* (0.88), average (0.94), and +1 *SD* (0.97).

SUMMARY

Conversion of continuous to categorical variables has a long tradition within quantitative research—primarily due to the fact that hand calculations were necessary for much of our history. This is no longer an issue with the ubiquitous access of most researchers to statistical computing software. Researchers have also claimed that dichotomization makes interpretation easier, variables more reliable, helps remedy non-normality, and can enhance effect sizes.

I strongly believe that interpretation is no easier with dichotomous variables than with appropriately handled continuous variables. I think I have argued convincingly that reliability is actually harmed in measurable and important ways when continuous variables are converted to dichotomous variables and that it does not remedy non-normality (which is unnecessary in logistic regression at any rate).

Finally, I have attempted to persuade you that increased effect sizes through dichotomization is either illusory (decreased variance accounted for while apparently increasing odds ratios, which points toward inappropriate inflation of effect sizes) or dishonest (as in the case of extreme groups analysis).

Finally, I recommended and demonstrated the simple, easy way to handle continuous variables through conversion to *z*-scores. This puts every continuous variable on the same metric and allows for direct comparison between predictors. It also leaves the researcher optimally prepared to explore interactions between predictors and to have an intercept that is substantively interpretable rather than ignorable or nonsensical.

ENRICHMENT

Download the data set from www.sagepub.com/osbornebplr. You can also download some SPSS syntax that was used to create the dichotomized and extreme groups variables from the same website.

1. Reproduce the analyses included in the chapter. Play with different extreme groups comparisons (e.g., ± 1.5 or 2 *SD*) to see how you can easily (and inappropriately) inflate the odds ratio.

2. Using the data set downloaded from #1 above, explore the results of a logistic regression predicting GRADUATE (whether a student

stayed in high school to graduate or not) from BYSES (family socio-economic status) under the following conditions:

a. Original BYSES variable

b. BYSES converted to z-scores

c. Compute predicted probabilities for individuals 1 SD above and below the mean from the analysis with the original BYSES variable (4a, above). Then do the same for BYSES converted to z-scores (4b, above). The predicted probabilities should be close. Are they?

d. BYSES median split

e. BYSES extreme groups analysis comparing students more than 1 SD from the mean (zBYSES < −1 vs. zBYSES > 1).

3. Using the DIABETES and BMI data set used in previous chapters, explore the results of a logistic regression predicting DIABETES from BMI under the following conditions:

a. Original BMI variable

b. BMI converted to z-scores

c. Compute predicted probabilities for individuals 1 SD above and below the mean from the analysis in 5a, above. Then do the same for individuals ±1 SD from the equation in analysis 5b, above. The predicted probabilities should be close. Are they?

d. BMI median split

e. BMI extreme groups analysis comparing students more than 1 SD from the mean (zBMI < −1 vs. zBMI > 1).

Answers for these analyses are presented at the end of this chapter for reference.

4. Look through the best journals in your field, and see if you can find an example of where an author dichotomized a continuous variable. How did they justify doing this? Do you agree it was a legitimate analytic strategy?

5. Using one of your own (or your advisor's) data sets, explore how dichotomization can alter/damage power and effect sizes.

ANSWER KEY

Enrichment problem #3: We know some of the results of these analyses from previous examples in previous chapters. Let's review:

3a. With an overall model chi-square of 986.98, the overall model is significant. The logit is positive, and the OR is 1.096, meaning that for every increment of 1.0 in BMI, the odds of reporting having diabetes are 1.096 that of individuals with 1.0 BMI lower.

Enrichment Table 5.1 Variables in the Equation

		B	SE	Wald	df	Sig.	Exp(B)	95% CI for Exp(B)	
								Lower	Upper
Step 1[a]	BMI	.092	.003	1013.633	1	.000	1.096	1.090	1.102
	Constant	−4.901	.090	2939.412	1	.000	.007		

a. Variable(s) entered on step 1: BMI.

Data Source: NHIS2010, Centers for Disease Control and Prevention.

3b. With an overall model chi-square of 986.98, the overall model is significant and identical to the previous model. However, we can see markedly different point estimates with the z-scored variable (despite identical Wald statistics). With a logit of 0.56 and OR of 1.76, these effects look much stronger.

Enrichment Table 5.2 Variables in the Equation

		B	SE	Wald	df	Sig.	Exp(B)	95% CI for Exp(B)	
								Lower	Upper
Step 1[a]	zBMI	.564	.018	1013.633	1	.000	1.758	1.698	1.821
	Constant	−2.366	.023	10836.597	1	.000	.094		

a. Variable(s) entered on step 1: zBMI.

Data Source: NHIS2010, Centers for Disease Control and Prevention.

3c. Calculating predicted probabilities for individuals at 1.0 and −1.0 standard deviations from the mean from the analyses in #3a we get the following:

- The mean for BMI is 27.69, with a *SD* of 6.167, yielding a BMI of 21.523 for −1 *SD* and 33.857 for +1 *SD*.
- Using the regression line equation of logit(Y) = −4.900966 + 0.091522(BMI) we calculate predicted logits of −2.9311 and −1.8023, respectively (I am purposely using more decimals than APA suggests for precision of calculation).
- Converting these to predicted probabilities, we get 0.0506 for −1 *SD* and 0.1416 for +1 *SD*.

Calculating from the equation in 3b for ±1 *SD*, we use −1 and +1 as values because the variable is already *z*-scored.

- Using the regression line equation of logit(Y)= −2.366292 + 0.564428(zBMI), we calculate predicted logits of −2.9307 and −1.8019, respectively (which are close to the previous predicted logits to rounding error).
- Converting these to predicted probabilities, we get 0.0507 and 0.1416, respectively.
- Thus we can see that both these analyses are predicting the same conditional probabilities for the same values of BMI regardless of whether the predictor variable is left in the original metric or converted to *z*-score

3d. The median for BMI is 26.62, and thus converting the continuous variable to a binary variable (0 = below median, 1 = above median) we get a model chi-square of 727.82 (substantially less than in the previous analyses) and a stronger logit and odds ratio. Compare the OR of 3.262 in this analysis to the RR of 2.79 in the previous analyses (comparing −1 *SD* to +1 *SD*). In point of fact, this analysis is in line with what an appropriate analysis such as in 3a or 3b, but with a much weaker effect due to the inflated error variance. In fact, if you calculate predicted logits for each group we get −2.954 for the "low BMI" group and −1.772 for the "high BMI" group, which correspond to predicted probabilities of 0.0495 and 0.145, which are similar to those acquired from previous two analyses. The calculated RR from these numbers is 2.93 (again, compare to 2.79 for the appropriate analysis).

Enrichment Table 5.3 Variables in the Equation

		B	SE	Wald	df	Sig.	Exp(B)	95% CI for Exp(B)	
								Lower	Upper
Step 1[a]	BMI_hilo	1.182	.047	641.970	1	.000	3.262	2.977	3.574
	Constant	−2.954	.040	5555.153	1	.000	.052		

a. Variable(s) entered on step 1: BMI_hilo.

Data Source: NHIS2010, Centers for Disease Control and Prevention.

3e. Examining an (inappropriate) extreme groups analysis (where we define "low" as those individuals below −1 *SD* from the mean and "high" as those over 1 *SD* from the mean), we see a model chi-square of 655.03, which is significant at *p* < .0001 (as all previous models have been). We also see highly magnified logit and odds ratios. It is easy to understand why—we eliminated over half the sample in the middle of the distribution, inappropriately inflating the apparent effect.

Enrichment Table 5.4 Variables in the Equation

		B	SE	Wald	df	Sig.	Exp(B)	95% CI for Exp(B)	
								Lower	Upper
Step 1[a]	BMI_ext	2.232	.109	420.020	1	.000	9.318	7.527	11.535
	Constant	−3.466	.102	1164.956	1	.000	.031		

a. Variable(s) entered on step 1: BMI_ext.

Data Source: NHIS2010, Centers for Disease Control and Prevention.

REFERENCES

Aiken, L. S., & West, S. (1991). *Multiple Regression: testing and interpreting interactions* Thousand Oaks, CA: Sage.

Blomqvist, N. (1951). Some tests based on dichotomization. *The Annals of Mathematical Statistics, 22*(3), 362–371.

Chen, H., Cohen, P., & Chen, S. (2007). Biased odds ratios from dichotomization of age. *Statistics in Medicine, 26*(18), 3487–3497.

Cohen, J. (1983). The cost of dichotomization. *Applied Psychological Measurement, 7*(3), 249–253.

DeCoster, J., Iselin, A., & Gallucci, M. (2009). A conceptual and empirical examination of justifications for dichotomization. *Psychological Methods, 14*(4), 349.

DeMaris, A. (1993). Odds versus probabilities in logit equations: A reply to Roncek. *Social Forces, 71*(4), 1057–1065. doi: 10.2307/2580130

Farewell, V., Tom, B., & Royston, P. (2004). The impact of dichotomization on the efficiency of testing for an interaction effect in exponential family models. *Journal of the American Statistical Association, 99*(467), 822–831.

Farrington, D. P., & Loeber, R. (2000). Some benefits of dichotomization in psychiatric and criminological research. *Criminal Behaviour and Mental Health, 10*(2), 100–122. doi: 10.1002/cbm.349

Fedorov, V., Mannino, F., & Zhang, R. (2009). Consequences of dichotomization. *Pharmaceutical Statistics, 8*(1), 50–61.

Fitzsimons, G. (2008). Death to dichotomizing: Editorial. *Journal of Consumer Research, 35,* 5–8.

Hin, L. Y., Lau, T. K., Rogers, M. S., & Chang, A. M. Z. (1999). Dichotomization of continuous measurements using generalized additive modelling—application in predicting intrapartum Caesarean delivery. *Statistics in Medicine, 18*(9), 1101–1110. doi: 10.1002/(sici)1097–0258(19990515)18:9<1101::aid-sim99>3.0.co;2-q

Humphreys, L., & Fleishman, A. (1974). Pseudo-orthogonal and other analysis of variance designs involving individual-differences variables. *Journal of Educational Psychology, 66*(4), 464–472.

Hunter, J., & Schmidt, F. (1990). Dichotomization of continuous variables: The implications for meta-analysis. *Journal of Applied Psychology, 75*(3), 334–349.

Ingels, S., Pratt, D., Rogers, J., Siegel, P., Stutts, E., & Owings, J. (2004). *Education Longitudinal Study of 2002: Base year data file user's manual.* Retrieved from http://nces.ed.gov/surveys/els2002/.

Knüppel, L., & Hermsen, O. (2010). Median split, k-group split, and optimality in continuous populations. *AStA Advances in Statistical Analysis, 94*(1), 53–74.

Lien, D., & Balakrishnan, N. (2005). On regression analysis with data cleaning via trimming, winsorization, and dichotomization. *Communications in Statistics—Simulation and Computation, 34*(4), 839–849.

MacCallum, R., Zhang, S., Preacher, K., & Rucker, D. (2002). On the practice of dichotomization of quantitative variables. *Psychological Methods, 7*(1), 19–40.

Maxwell, S., & Delaney, H. (1993). Bivariate median splits and spurious statistical significance. *Psychological Bulletin, 113*(1), 181–190.

Osborne, J. W. (2010). Improving your data transformations: Applying Box-Cox transformations as a best practice. *Practical Assessment Research & Evaluation, 15*(12), 1–9.

Osborne, J. W. (2012). *Best practices in data cleaning: A complete guide to everything you need to do before and after collecting your data.* Thousand Oaks, CA: Sage.

Osborne, J. W., & Overbay, A. (2004). The power of outliers (and why researchers should ALWAYS check for them). *Practical Assessment, Research, and Evaluation, 9*(6).

Pearson, K. (1901). Mathematical contribution to the theory of evolution. VII: On the correlation of characters not quantitatively measurable. *Philosophical Transactions of the Royal Society of London, A 195,* 1–47.

Peters, C., & Van Voorhis, W. (1940). *Statistical procedures and their mathematical bases*. New York, NY: McGraw-Hill.

Preacher, K., Rucker, D., MacCallum, R., & Nicewander, W. (2005). Use of the extreme groups approach: A critical reexamination and new recommendations. *Psychological Methods, 10*(2), 178.

Royston, P., Altman, D., & Sauerbrei, W. (2006). Dichotomizing continuous predictors in multiple regression: A bad idea. *Statistics in Medicine, 25*(1), 127–141.

Snow, J. (1855). *On the mode of communication of cholera*. London: John Churchill.

Student. (1908). The probable error of a mean. *biometrika, 6,* 1–25.

Westfall, P. H. (2011). Improving power by dichotomizing (even under normality). *Statistics in Biopharmaceutical Research, 3*(2), 353–362. doi:10.1198/sbr.2010.09055

6

USING UNORDERED CATEGORICAL INDEPENDENT VARIABLES IN LOGISTIC REGRESSION

We have thus far explored simple logistic regression with a single dichotomous variable and with a single continuous variable. As you are well aware, there are different types of measurement that we all learn about in our basic methodology courses (from most desirable to least): ratio, interval, ordinal, and nominal. The focus of this chapter is on the last category, nominal measurement (which I also refer to as a categorical or polytomous variable). What differentiates them, briefly, is whether they contain three different ingredients:

1. Ordinality: Higher numbers indicate more of that trait/characteristic.

2. Equal intervals: Distance between numbers is the same across the range of measurement.

3. A "true" zero point that represents the complete absence of the quality being measured.

ORDINALITY

In all measurement, we assume higher numbers relate to increasing amounts of something. In our examples thus far, for example, we have looked at increasing family socioeconomic status (SES) and how it might influence the probability that a student would drop out or graduate high school. In coding SES, we assume that higher numbers mean more SES, and lower numbers mean less. In early chapters of the book we had the variable POOR, which was coded 0 for not poor and 1 for poor—the simplest example of this assumption of measurement. In this case, the higher number indicates more POORNESS than the lower number.

◆ EQUAL INTERVALS

This might seem a silly issue—how can the difference between 4 and 5 be different than between 10 and 11? They are both a difference of 1.0, right? In many of the sciences, this is something we don't have to consider. Inches and pounds and degrees and velocity are all measured on scales that have equal intervals. One inch and one pound and one degree difference is the same regardless of where we are in the range of measurement. But what about IQ? Some authors have argued that the difference between 100 and 110 IQ is not the same as between 40 and 50—both are increments of 10, but both have profoundly different implications for the expectations and lives of those two individuals. It is questionable whether the difference between student projects that receive an F versus a D– would be the same as between A– and A. There has certainly been debate in the measurement literature about whether differences between points on Likert-type scales meet this criterion (e.g., the difference between 1 "strongly agree" and 2 "agree" is the same as between 2 "agree" and 3 "neutral"). In order to meet this condition, it must be reasonable to assert that increments are identical across the entire range of a scale.

◆ TRUE ZERO POINT

This characteristic of measurement refers to whether a scale or construct has a meaningful, legitimate 0 point that truly means the complete absence of what is being measured. In theory, weight has a meaningful 0 point—the complete absence of weight. This is of course a theoretical construct, as everything on the planet (perhaps even things that particle physicists talk about) has some weight. Distance is another example of something with a conceptually meaningful zero point. Constructs including zero in their range of possible numbers do not always meet this characteristic. For example, temperature measured on Fahrenheit and Celsius scales do NOT meet this goal. Their zero points are important, but they are not a true zero in the sense of complete absence of something. Kelvin, on the other hand, has a theoretically meaningful zero point that means the complete absence of molecular motion or where entropy reaches its minimum value. Social science constructs can meet this criterion as well. Income can be 0, meaning you can have no income. The score on a final exam can be 0, the number of days absent can be 0. However, constructs such as GRE scores, IQ, and self-esteem might not have a true zero point that is meaningful.

DIFFERENT CLASSIFICATIONS OF MEASUREMENT ♦

Ratio measurement incorporates all three of these characteristics: higher numbers indicate more of something, there are equal increments between numbers, and zero is a true absence of something, even if it is not theoretically possible to find an example of an individual with an observed 0. Weight is a good example—even zygotes have weight, but the construct of weight has a meaningful true zero. Thus, weight is ratio measurement. When a scale meets the criteria for ratio measurement, you can interpret ratios of numbers, such as the fact that 500 kg is exactly twice as heavy as 250 kg and half as heavy as 1,000 kg.[1] Because IQ does not have a true zero point, we cannot conclude that someone with an IQ of 150 is twice as smart as someone with an IQ of 75 and only half as smart as someone with an IQ of 300. Number of cigarettes smoked is ratio measurement as it has a true zero point, and so we can say that smoking two packs a day is twice as much as one pack a day.

Interval measurement incorporates ordinality and equal intervals—but not a true zero. So for example, temperature measured in Celsius is interval. One degree is one degree regardless of whether it is at −200 on the scale or +200. However, we cannot say that 100 degrees Celsius is twice as hot as 50 because zero does not indicate complete absence of temperature. In general, it is nice to have ratio measurement but most statistical techniques are perfectly fine with interval measurement.

Ordinal measurement is merely a rank ordering, containing only the characteristic that higher numbers mean more of something. So if you take the three medalists from the last Olympics in the 10,000 meter race and me, the gold medal winner could be assigned a 4 (fastest), the silver medal

---

[1]However, we should note that the perception of weight is not ratio. Dropping a 50-kg weight on your foot is not necessarily twice as painful as dropping a 25-kg weight on your foot, and not necessarily half as painful as the 100-kg weight. Don't ask me how I know this.

winner a 3 (second fastest), the bronze medalist a 2 (third fastest), and I would get a 1 (fourth fastest). However, there is no way to know how far apart each individual is. We only know their relative ranking. Odds are I am very, very far from the bronze medal winner, and those other three are relatively closely matched.

In the social sciences, we often measure things using a Likert-type scale. Using this type of scale, we can generally say that higher numbers mean more positive attitudes toward something, but we cannot say that the difference between 1 and 2 is the same as between 4 and 5, merely that 1 is lower than 2 which is lower than 3 and so on. Ranking the wealthiest people in a country (or best students in a graduating class) is interesting to some—it puts people in order from first to last. But we do not know how much distance there is between the first and second person, or between the 99th and 100th person. It might be that the wealthiest person has $100 billion and the second has "only" $50 billion, and it may be that the third wealthiest person has $49.9 billion. Rank connotes only order, not relative distance. Many statistical techniques are robust enough to deal effectively with this level of measurement, but it is not ideal.

In *nominal measurement,* numbers are assigned to groups in an ad hoc fashion to represent groups. It is merely a label. In this way, I might assign racial categories in my data numeric codes:[2] 1 for Black/African American, 2 for White/Caucasian, 3 for Asian/Pacific Islander, 4 for Hispanic/Latino individuals, and so forth. Individuals assigned a 2 do not have more "race" than those assigned a 1, and those assigned a 3 do not have more than those assigned a 1 or 2. It is merely a label, a placeholder. Thus, one cannot simply place variables with this sort of measurement in a regression equation and expect sensible results, as it violates the expectations of measurement and contains none of the characteristics mentioned earlier.

So what is one to do with a nominal (polytomous, categorical) variable? The traditional method of dealing with this sort of issue has been to create dummy, effects, or contrast coded variables that represent the variable. For example, let's imagine the race variable, mentioned earlier, has four categories. We can represent that nominal variable through three binary variables (variables like this can be represented by k-1 variables, where k represents the number of groups) that then allow us to assess certain comparisons and capture the overall effect of the variable of interest.

---

[2] I am aware that in many disciplines there is great controversy over the validity of the concept of racial groupings. I share this concern and am merely using this as a convenient (and common) example, whether you agree or disagree with the process or details of grouping individuals into race-based groups.

DUMMY CODING ♦

"Dummy" variables are binary 0–1 variables that computer programmers have used for decades to represent the presence or absence of a state or condition. We in statistics have adopted the language and technique to code a set of "dummy" variables that represent the variable of interest. When using this sort of coding, there are several steps if one is doing this manually. Cohen, Cohen, West, and Aiken (2002, Chapter 8) provide excellent technical guidance in this area, and as such this will be but a brief overview of the issues.

Define the Reference Group

The first step when you have multiple groups like our race variable is to decide what group is the reference group—the group others will be compared with. This is essentially a planned comparison (like you would do in analysis of variance [ANOVA]), meaning there are k-1 degrees of freedom for comparisons. In our case, with four groups we have three possible independent comparisons we can make. So what makes the most sense? That depends on your research question. If Caucasian individuals are in the majority and are the group that it makes sense to compare the other groups with, make them the comparison group. If our research was concerning how Asian American individuals compare with other groups, we would make them the reference group. Hardy (1993) suggested that the reference group should:

a. make sense, being a control group, for example, or a group that represents some sort of standard reference, routine, or dominant group;

b. be coherent and well defined, not an "other group" or heterogeneous catch-all group such as "multiracial" or "other race" might be in this case; and

c. not have a small sample size compared with the other groups.

Set Up the Dummy Coded Variables

Knowing we have k-1 possible comparisons, represented by k-1 dummy variables, we need to create them and set them up appropriately.

I often encourage students learning this technique to use a table as shown in Table 6.1:

Table 6.1 Setting Up Dummy Coded Variables

Race category:	DUM1	DUM2	DUM3
Caucasian	0	0	0
Black/African American	1	0	0
Asian	0	1	0
Hispanic/Latino	0	0	1

Let's imagine that it makes sense for Caucasian individuals to be the reference group. They get assigned a 0 on all three dummy variables. Black/African American individuals get assigned a 1 on the first dummy coded variables, and 0 on all other. Asian individuals are assigned a 1 on the second dummy coded variable and 0 on all others, and Hispanic or Latino individuals are assigned a 1 on the third dummy variable and 0 on all others. When all three variables are entered into the regression equation at the same time, they completely capture the race variable and also allow for simple contrasts. Because of how the dummy variables were set up, when all variables are in the equation, DUM1 is the effect comparing Caucasian individuals to Black/African American individuals, DUM2 is the comparison between Caucasian and Asian individuals, and so on. In fact, in ordinary least squares (OLS) regression, the unstandardized regression coefficient represents the actual mean difference between the two group means as you would see in ANOVA-type analyses. A significant effect for any of the three dummy variables indicates a significant mean difference between the reference group and the group that is assigned a 1 on that variable.

In logistic regression, the unstandardized regression coefficient for each dummy variable will represent the logit difference between the reference group (which is the constant) and the group who has a "1" on that dummy variable. Using the regression equation, it is then simple to compute predicted logits and convert to predicted probabilities as we have done in previous chapters.

Let's look at a specific example from our Diabetes data set from the National Health Interview Survey (NHIS) data set we have introduced in previous chapters. In these data, we have only the first three racial categories: Caucasian, African American, and Asian, which we will set up as two

Table 6.2 Example of Dummy Coded Logistic Regression

		B	SE	Wald	df	Sig.	Exp(B)	95% CI for Exp(B)	
								Lower	Upper
	DUM1	.457	.049	85.504	1	.000	1.579	1.433	1.740
Step 1[a]	DUM2	−.277	.099	7.811	1	.005	.758	.624	.920
	Constant	−2.303	.024	9105.996	1	.000	.100		

a. Variable(s) entered on step 1: DUM1, DUM2.

Data Source: National Health Interview Survey of 2010 (NHIS2010), Centers for Disease Control and Prevention.

dummy variables with Caucasian as the reference group as they are the largest group. As a point of reference, 9.1% of Caucasian, 13.6% African American, and 7.0% of Asian individuals reported being diagnosed with diabetes, representing our observed conditional probabilities.

As you can see in Table 6.2, the logistic regression with dummy variables mirrors what we would expect from knowing the conditional probabilities. DUM1 is significant, with a logit of 0.46 and an odds ratio of 1.58. As mentioned earlier, we would interpret this as indicating that the group represented by DUM1 (African American individuals) has odds of being diagnosed with diabetes that are 1.57 that of the reference group (Caucasians). Further, DUM2 is significant, with a logit of −0.28 and an odds ratio of 0.75, indicating that Asian individuals have lower conditional probabilities of being diagnosed with diabetes.

With a regression equation of:

$$\text{Logit } (\hat{Y}) = -2.303 + 0.457(\text{DUM1}) - 0.277(\text{DUM2})$$

we can create predicted logits for each group. By using our formula for converting from predicted logits to predicted conditional probabilities, we see that this analysis reproduces the observed probabilities well.

You might be wondering what would happen if we constituted the dummy variables differently—for example, representing African American individuals as the reference group, as they tend to have higher rates of diabetes. In Table 6.4, I created DUM3 and DUM4 variables to test this using the same data, making African American individuals the reference group, DUM3 representing Caucasian individuals, and DUM4 representing Asian individuals.

Table 6.3 Creating Predicted Conditional Probabilities for Each Group From the Logistic Regression Equation

Race category:	DUM1	DUM2	Predicted logit	Predicted probability
Caucasian	0	0	−2.303	.0909
Black/African American	1	0	−1.846	.1363
Asian	0	1	−2.580	.0704

Data Source: NHIS2010, Centers for Disease Control and Prevention.

Table 6.4 Diabetes Analyses With African Americans as Reference Group

		B	SE	Wald	df	Sig.	Exp(B)	95% CI for Exp(B)	
								Lower	Upper
Step 1[a]	DUM3	−.457	.049	85.504	1	.000	.633	.575	.698
	DUM4	−.734	.106	48.440	1	.000	.480	.390	.590
	Constant	−1.846	.043	1834.484	1	.000	.158		

a. Variable(s) entered on step 1: DUM3, DUM4.

Data Source: NHIS2010, Centers for Disease Control and Prevention.

Recalling that both Caucasian and Asian individuals should have lower odds of being diagnosed with diabetes according to the observed probabilities, we see this reflected in the results of this new analysis. Both Caucasian (DUM3) and Asian (DUM4) variables have negative logits and odds ratios significantly ($p < .001$) below 1.0. In this case, the regression equation is:

$$\text{Logit } (\hat{Y}) = -1.846 - 0.457(\text{DUM3}) - 0.734(\text{DUM4})$$

We can similarly use this regression equation and the way the two variables were coded to produce predicted logits and probabilities that should lead back to the same predicted conditional probabilities based on group membership despite the alternative coding. As you can see, the predicted probabilities are similar, and both are close estimates of the observed probabilities. Thus, it does not matter, particularly, how you constitute the dummy variables—in all cases you will should able to reproduce the original observed probabilities. What does make a difference in how you code the dummy variables is what you can say about the data. In this case, we can say both Caucasian and Asian individuals have significantly lower odds of being diagnosed with diabetes, but we cannot say whether Caucasian and Asian individuals were significantly different from each other.

| Table 6.5 | Creating Predicted Conditional Probabilities for Each Group From the Logistic Regression Equation |

Race category:	DUM3	DUM4	Predicted logit	Predicted probability
Caucasian	1	0	−2.303	.0909
Black/African American	0	0	−1.846	.1363
Asian	0	1	−2.580	.0704

Data Source: NHIS2010, Centers for Disease Control and Prevention.

ALTERNATIVES TO DUMMY CODING ♦

It is perfectly fine to create dummy coded variables and enter them into the logistic regression equation as I did in the example above. The nice aspect of this is that through taking control of the situation you know exactly what the comparisons are. However, statistical software packages have some features in logistic regression routines that attempt to make these sorts of coding efforts easier.[3] For example, SPSS has

---

[3] I find it ironic that there is such inconsistency across routines within the same package. For example, in SPSS logistic regression, it is a simple point and click procedure to specify categorical variables and the way to contrast the groups. It is also a simple click to enter interaction (multiplicative) terms into the analysis. However, in OLS regression, these options are not evident as of this writing. Categorical variables must be converted manually as described earlier, and interaction terms similarly must be created manually. If any of you reading this has any influence within the statistical computing software community, please beg them for modernization and homogenization of experience!

the following contrast options: indicator, simple, difference, Helmert, repeated, polynomial, and deviation.

Indicator contrasts simply indicate the presence or absence of category membership, with the reference group represented as a row of 0s. This sounds like dummy coding as described earlier, and indeed when the reference group is set to "first"—which is the Caucasian group, the results are identical to the dummy coded analysis described earlier, as you can see in Table 6.6.

The only difference between the two analyses is that there is a row for RACE and the two rows below that represent the chosen two contrasts. One issue with using predesigned contrasts is that given the race variable as I coded it (1 = Caucasian, 2 = Black/African American, 3 = Asian), the only choices for reference group are first and last, meaning I cannot replicate the other analysis with Black/African American as the reference group without recoding race. If I do that, recoding Black/African American to be first or last, and then set that group to be reference, it replicates the other analysis.

Simple contrast is described in the SPSS documentation as comparing each category of the predictor variable with the reference category (usually the last category). Again, this sounds similar to dummy coding or indicator contrasts. However, simple contrasts produce slightly different results because the intercept is an unweighted average of all levels rather than the value for the reference group. In other words, this contrast is answering a slightly different question than indicator contrasts (dummy coding). What this does is compare each group (except the reference group) with the average of the entire sample rather than simply the reference group. In this example, this result is not substantially different from the dummy coded example with Caucasian as the reference group because 77% of the sample is Caucasian, and the other two groups have averages above and below the Caucasian group. In other words, the overall sample is similar to the average of the Caucasian group by happenstance only. Using this contrast coding scheme can answer important questions but can also produce very different results from dummy coding if the reference group and the overall sample have very different means. For example, when Asian is set as the reference group, the results look very different. In theory you should be able to use this output to reproduce the same predicted probabilities as with dummy codes, but to do that you must know the respective weights that the software is using, which is not always easy. If you use syntax you can ask for all output, which will provide you with the categorical variable codings. In the case of the simple contrast with Caucasian as the reference group, SPSS assigned the codes in Table 6.7,

Table 6.6 Using Different Contrasts in SPSS Logistic Regression

		B	SE	Wald	df	Sig.	Exp(B)	95% CI for Exp(B)	
								Lower	Upper
Indicator-Caucasian ref	Race			100.877	2	.000			
	Race (1)	.457	.049	85.504	1	.000	1.579	1.433	1.740
	Race (2)	−.277	.099	7.811	1	.005	.758	.624	.920
	Constant	−2.303	.024	9105.996	1	.000	.100		
Simple-Caucasian ref	Race			100.877	2	.000			
	Race (1)	.457	.049	85.504	1	.000	1.579	1.433	1.740
	Race (2)	−.277	.099	7.811	1	.005	.758	.624	.920
	Constant	−2.243	.036	3866.907	1	.000	.106		
Simple-Asian ref	Race			100.877	2	.000			
	Race(1)	.277	.099	7.811	1	.005	1.320	1.086	1.603
	Race(2)	.734	.106	48.440	1	.000	2.084	1.695	2.563
	Constant	−2.243	.036	3866.907	1	.000	.106		
Difference-Caucasian ref	Race			100.877	2	.000			
	Race(1)	.457	.049	85.504	1	.000	1.579	1.433	1.740
	Race(2)	−.506	.099	25.894	1	.000	.603	.496	.733
	Constant	−2.243	.036	3866.907	1	.000	.106		
Helmert	Race			100.877	2	.000			
	Race(1)	−.090	.058	2.390	1	.122	.914	.816	1.024
	Race(2)	.734	.106	48.440	1	.000	2.084	1.695	2.563
	Constant	−2.243	.036	3866.907	1	.000	.106		
Polynomial	Race			100.877	2	.000			
	Race(1)	−.196	.070	7.811	1	.005	.822	.716	.943
	Race(2)	−.486	.054	82.066	1	.000	.615	.553	.683
	Constant	−2.243	.036	3866.907	1	.000	.106		
Repeated	Race			100.877	2	.000			
	Race(1)	−.457	.049	85.504	1	.000	.633	.575	.698
	Race(2)	.734	.106	48.440	1	.000	2.084	1.695	2.563
	Constant	−2.243	.036	3866.907	1	.000	.106		
Deviation	Race			100.877	2	.000			
	Race(1)	.397	.044	82.066	1	.000	1.487	1.365	1.621
	Race(2)	−.337	.066	25.894	1	.000	.714	.627	.813
	Constant	−2.243	.036	3866.907	1	.000	.106		

Data Source: NHIS2010, Centers for Disease Control and Prevention.

Table 6.7 Categorical Variables Codings

		Frequency	Parameter coding		Predicted logit	Predicted probability
			(1)	(2)		
Race	1.00	20781	−.333	−.333	−2.304	.0908
	2.00	4571	.667	−.333	−1.847	.1363
	3.00	1648	−.333	.667	−2.580	.0704

Data Source: NHIS2010, Centers for Disease Control and Prevention.

and using the regression equation that corresponds with this analysis we can again recapture the conditional probabilities.

Thus, it is the case that most contrasts, if done correctly, should produce the correct predicted probabilities. The issue in choosing contrasts is whether it answers the correct question.

Difference (Reverse Helmert) Contrasts

In this contrast, the effects of each category are compared with the average of all the previous categories (with the exception, of course, of the first group, which is the reference group in this scheme). Thus, in our example, Caucasian individuals (which are coded as 1) are necessarily the reference group. Black/African American individuals (coded 2) are compared with Caucasian, and then Asian individuals (coded 3) are compared with *the average of the Caucasian and Black/African American individuals*. I honestly do not see the value of this particular type of contrast, but I am sure it was invented to solve a particular problem. The issue, as I see it, is that of making sure the contrasts again make sense. Why would it make sense to compare Asian individuals to all others? And if we had coded the variable as follows: 1 = Asian, 2 = Black/African American, and 3 = Caucasian, then the first contrast would be Asian versus Black/African American, and the second would be the average of those two categories versus Caucasian. Because Asian and Black/African American individuals averaged together come to roughly the same average as Caucasian, that contrast might be nonsignificant, and we might falsely conclude that Caucasian individuals are not significantly different from other racial groups when in fact they are, just not when averaged. You will see this is in fact the case when we use Helmert contrasts, below.

Table 6.8   Coding of Difference Contrast

		Frequency	Parameter coding	
			(1)	(2)
Race	1.00	20781	−.500	−.333
	2.00	4571	.500	−.333
	3.00	1648	.000	.667

Data Source: NHIS2010, Centers for Disease Control and Prevention.

I would recommend using this contrast only with great caution and only when it truly does make sense to compare groups with the average of previous groups.

Helmert contrasts are contrasts where the effects of each category are compared with the mean of subsequent categories—in other words, it is the opposite of the previous (Difference or reverse Helmert) contrasts. As you can see in Table 6.9, this contrast is the opposite of the previous contrast, which is why they are often called Helmert and reverse Helmert contrasts. In this case, the first group is compared with the average of all other groups, the second is compared with the average of following groups, and so forth. The last group is by default the reference, leaving us with a nonsignificant contrast between Caucasian and other groups, which creates a misperception that there are no significant differences between these groups when in fact there are.

Polynomial contrasts are contrasts that test whether there is a linear, quadratic, cubic, etc. effect across the groups. Of course in our case, as there are only three groups, there are only two possible effects: linear and

Table 6.9   Helmert Codings

		Frequency	Parameter coding	
			(1)	(2)
Race	1.00	20781	.667	.000
	2.00	4571	−.333	.500
	3.00	1648	−.333	−.500

Data Source: NHIS2010, Centers for Disease Control and Prevention.

quadratic. As you can see in Table 6.10, these are indeed significant although I am not sure what to make of linear and quadratic effects when thinking of race as a variable.

Repeated contrasts look at adjacent categories, comparing group 1 versus 2, group 2 versus 3, group 3 versus 4, and so forth. As you can see in Table 6.11, this produces the expected significant contrasts between the three groups, with a particularly large contrast between Black/African American and Asian, which is again not surprising as that comparison is between the two most different groups. In some cases, this might be a sensible contrast if the categories were ordered in some way. In unordered groupings, it is not necessarily the case that adjacent groups are the contrast that makes sense. Again, you the researcher must be thoughtful about choice of contrast.

Deviation Contrasts

Typically referred to as effects coding, in this coding scheme the comparison group is assigned a −1 rather than all 0s, which leads to the comparison

Table 6.10 Polynomial Codings

		Frequency	Parameter coding	
			(1)	(2)
Race	1.00	20781	−.707	.408
	2.00	4571	.000	−.816
	3.00	1648	.707	.408

Data Source: NHIS2010, Centers for Disease Control and Prevention.

Table 6.11 Repeated Contrast Codings

		Frequency	Parameter coding	
			(1)	(2)
Race	1.00	20781	.667	.333
	2.00	4571	−.333	.333
	3.00	1648	−.333	−.667

Data Source: NHIS2010, Centers for Disease Control and Prevention.

being between each group assigned a 1 and the overall grand mean. As you can see in Table 6.12, both of these contrasts are significant, largely because the overall grand mean (population probability, the intercept) is largely composed (about 77%) of Caucasian individuals. Thus, the contrasts are mostly (in this case) contrasts with Caucasian groups. As this is the default analysis in SAS, I will explore this more in detail below.

Table 6.12   Deviation Contrast (Effects) Codings

		Frequency	Parameter coding	
			(1)	(2)
race_new	1.00	20781	−1.000	−1.000
	2.00	4571	1.000	.000
	3.00	1648	.000	1.000

Data Source: NHIS2010, Centers for Disease Control and Prevention.

SAS CONTRASTS ♦

By default, SAS uses effects coding (Deviation contrasts in SPSS), where the reference category is assigned a −1 and the other categories are then compared to this category with 0 and 1. Thus, as you can see in Table 6.13, using this scheme we constitute the analysis, but the difference is that using this coding scheme each of the two groups (Black/African American and Asian) are compared with the grand mean (overall effect in the population, or the intercept) rather than from the reference group. Thus, we are asking a slightly different question of the data than simple dummy coding.

Note that the exponentiated logit of the intercept (0.106) when converted to probability is equal to 0.0958, which is a close approximation of the overall probability of being diagnosed in the population. This is what each group is being compared with for significant effect. Exponentiated odds ratios and significance tests for the two contrasts test whether members of those groups are significantly different from the population estimate (the intercept), not Caucasians. To get those estimates, we can examine the second table, which asks slightly different questions.

To explore what this is, exactly, we can examine the predicted logits, exponentiated logits (odds) for each group, and then create our own custom odds ratios (and conditional probabilities).

Table 6.13 SAS Example Using Effects Coded Variables

Analysis of Maximum Likelihood Estimates							
Parameter		df	Estimate	Standard Error	Wald Chi-Square	Pr > ChiSq	Exp(Est)
Intercept		1	−2.2435	0.0361	3866.9071	<.0001	0.106
race_new	2.00	1	0.3971	0.0438	82.0663	<.0001	1.487
race_new	3.00	1	−0.3373	0.0663	25.8940	<.0001	0.714

	Odds Ratio Estimates		
Effect	Point Estimate	95% Wald Confidence Limits	
race_new 2.00 vs. 1.00	1.579	1.433	1.740
race_new 3.00 vs. 1.00	0.758	0.624	0.920

Data Source: NHIS2010, Centers for Disease Control and Prevention.

Using the regression equation:

$$\text{Logit } (\hat{Y}) = -2.2435 + 0.3971(\text{EFF1}) - 0.3373(\text{EFF2})$$

and using the codings presented in Table 6.12 for each group (remember, the reference group of Caucasian has −1 values, not 0), we can create predicted logits:

Table 6.14 Effects Coding for Race Variable

Class-Level Information			
Class	Value	Design Variables	
	1.00	−1	−1
race_new	2.00	1	0
	3.00	0	1

Data Source: NHIS2010, Centers for Disease Control and Prevention.

| Table 6.15 | Predicted Logits, Odds, and Conditional Probabilities for Each Group | | | | |

	EFF1	EFF2	Logit	Odds	Probability
Caucasian	−1	−1	−2.3033	0.099929	0.09085
African American	1	0	−1.8464	0.157804	0.136296
Asian	0	1	−2.5808	0.075713	0.070384

Data Source: NHIS2010, Centers for Disease Control and Prevention.

Using the conditional odds in Table 6.15, we can see where SAS is getting the odds ratios for the various comparisons. For the first (Caucasian vs. Black/African American), we can divide the odds for the two groups and come up with 1.579, the ratio of the odds of having diabetes for the two groups. Likewise, the ratio of Asian to Caucasian yields 0.758. Note that we can easily produce these custom odds ratios from SPSS output as well. We can also produce relative risk estimates of 1.50 and 0.77 for African American and Asian groups. What these mean is that Black/African American individuals are 1.50 times as likely to get diabetes as Caucasian individuals, and Asian individuals are only 0.77 times as likely.

The reason why these are different than the exponentiated logits is that those logits are comparing the group in question with the grand mean (population probability or intercept) rather than the other group, which is often *not the question we want to answer.* Indeed, we do not have significance tests in this example for the questions we actually want to answer! More often, we want to know how one group differs from another. By taking a few moments to produce this table, we can then answer the appropriate question, and make the answer clearer to the reader.

DUMMY CODING IN SAS ◆

Predictably, you can use my preferred mode of coding, dummy coding, with either SPSS or SAS or the program of your choice and get the same result. Invoking the correct commands (outlined in the Syntax Examples section), you get the following dummy coding, which is identical to the dummy codes we initially used with SPSS:

Table 6.16 SAS Dummy Codings of Race Variable

Class-Level Information			
Class	Value	Design Variables	
race_new	1.00	0	0
	2.00	1	0
	3.00	0	1

Data Source: NHIS2010, Centers for Disease Control and Prevention.

And equally predictably, we get identical results, with the odds ratios (exponentiated predicted logits) reflecting the same predictions above. What is notable is that in this analysis, the exponentiated logits are identical to the odds ratios for the contrasts between the groups because the reference group is Caucasian, not the intercept (as it is with effects coding), making interpretation of dummy coded analyses more direct and

Table 6.17 Results of SAS Dummy Coded Example

Analysis of Maximum Likelihood Estimates							
Parameter		df	Estimate	Standard Error	Wald Chi-Square	Pr > ChiSq	Exp(Est)
Intercept		1	−2.3033	0.0241	9105.9961	<.0001	0.100
race_new	2.00	1	0.4569	0.0494	85.5043	<.0001	1.579
race_new	3.00	1	−0.2775	0.0993	7.8112	0.0052	0.758

	Odds Ratio Estimates		
Effect	Point Estimate	95% Wald Confidence Limits	
race_new 2.00 vs. 1.00	1.579	1.433	1.740
race_new 3.00 vs. 1.00	0.758	0.624	0.920

Data Source: NHIS2010, Centers for Disease Control and Prevention.

straightforward (in my opinion). Note also that both analyses (effects and dummy coding) ended in the same place, with identical odds ratios and predicted probabilities when identical comparison groups were used and appropriate calculations were performed.

There are other methods of contrasts in SAS, including specifying custom contrasts, but this example and the examples coming before lead to an important point—in many cases, the different coding schemes lead us to this sort of table, which allows us to create and present odds ratios and relative risk in ways that make sense to all readers. I have never needed anything other than well-planned dummy or effects coded variables and expect most readers will likewise be suitably served with these options, particularly if you then construct appropriate odds ratios and relative risk estimates between groups.

SUMMARY

Unordered categorical independent variables are not difficult to incorporate into logistic regression analyses as long as you are thoughtful about your goal for that variable. You must determine what sorts of comparisons between which groups makes the most sense and work with the software of your choice to produce the contrasts that best approximate sensible questions of interest.

Note that one issue I do not address in this chapter is that of the number of contrasts appropriate. It is routine for the number of contrasts to be limited to one fewer than the number of categories. Thus, if we have three groups, only two orthogonal contrasts are possible as there are only two degrees of freedom. Performing more than that increases the odds of Type I error and should be avoided unless you control for Type I error rates in some way.

ENRICHMENT

1. Download the NHIS data set containing RACE and DIABETES from the book website (www.sagepub.com/osbornebplr) and reproduce the contrasts reported earlier. After producing an analysis, produce predicted probabilities for each group and compare with observed probabilities. Are your analyses accurately reflecting the observed

probabilities? Produce the type of relative risk/odds ratio estimates produced in the final table.

2. Download the NHIS data set referenced in question 1. Perform similar analyses using SMOKE_CAT (Smoking status: 0 = nonsmoker, 1 = former smoker, 2 = occasional current smoker, 3 = everyday smoker) to predict DIABETES. Using an appropriate coding scheme, answer the following questions:

   a. Does smoking status have any overall impact on whether individuals report being diagnosed with diabetes?

   b. Do nonsmokers have significantly different diabetes risk than former, occasional, or daily smokers?

   c. Can you tell if former smokers have significantly different diabetes risk than either occasional or daily smokers using the same coding scheme from 2b? If not, what type of coding scheme would you have to use? Perform this analysis comparing model and variable statistics.

   d. Can you tell if occasional smokers have different diabetes risk than daily smokers using the same coding scheme as 2b? If not, what type of coding scheme would you have to use? Perform this analysis comparing model and variable statistics.

   e. Report odds ratios and relative risk ratios for all the questions above if significant.

3. If I have a variable that is categorical and binary (like SEX), does it matter whether I use dummy, effects, Helmert, reverse Helmert, simple, or any other coding scheme? Why or why not?

ANSWER KEY

2. An initial exploration of the data via crosstabs reveals an interesting effect:

It appears that nonsmokers, occasional smokers, and daily smokers are at lower risk for diabetes than former smokers. Let us see if the appropriate analyses reinforce these observations.

Enrichment Table 6.1   smoke_cat * Diabetes Cross-Tabulation

			diabetes		Total
			.00	1.00	
smoke_cat	.00	Count	14618	1338	15956
		% within smoke_cat	91.6%	8.4%	100.0%
	1.00	Count	5190	879	6069
		% within smoke_cat	85.5%	14.5%	100.0%
	2.00	Count	1205	100	1305
		% within smoke_cat	92.3%	7.7%	100.0%
	3.00	Count	3902	371	4273
		% within smoke_cat	91.3%	8.7%	100.0%
Total		Count	24915	2688	27603
		% within smoke_cat	90.3%	9.7%	100.0%

Data Source: NHIS2010, Centers for Disease Control and Prevention.

Effects Coded Analyses

Performing the appropriate analyses using effects coding: the effects coding in Enrichment Table 6.2, we see the overall model is significant (indicating that smoking has some effect on diabetes overall):

Enrichment Table 6.2   Class-Level Information

Class	Value	Design Variables		
smoke_cat	0.00	−1	−1	−1
	1.00	1	0	0
	2.00	0	1	0
	3.00	0	0	1

Data Source: NHIS2010, Centers for Disease Control and Prevention.

Enrichment Table 6.3 Testing Global Null Hypothesis: BETA = 0

Test	Chi-Square	df	Pr > ChiSq
Likelihood Ratio	184.4167	3	<.0001
Score	200.5000	3	<.0001
Wald	195.7161	3	<.0001

Data Source: NHIS2010, Centers for Disease Control and Prevention.

All three effects coded contrasts are significant at $p < .05$, but the last one is just barely so, which raises suspicion in such a large sample that this

Enrichment Table 6.4 SAS Output

Analysis of Maximum Likelihood Estimates							
Parameter		df	Estimate	Standard Error	Wald Chi-Square	Pr > ChiSq	Exp(Est)
Intercept		1	−2.2522	0.0316	5095.5284	<.0001	0.105
smoke_cat	1.00	1	0.4765	0.0408	136.7367	<.0001	1.610
smoke_cat	2.00	1	−0.2368	0.0801	8.7505	0.0031	0.789
smoke_cat	3.00	1	−0.1008	0.0497	4.1131	0.0426	0.904

	Odds Ratio Estimates		
Effect	Point Estimate	95% Wald Confidence Limits	
smoke_cat 1.00 vs. 0.00	1.850	1.690	2.026
smoke_cat 2.00 vs. 0.00	0.907	0.734	1.120
smoke_cat 3.00 vs. 0.00	1.039	0.921	1.172

Data Source: NHIS2010, Centers for Disease Control and Prevention.

is likely a very small effect. Indeed, we can see in the odds ratio estimates that former smokers are at much higher risk for diabetes than nonsmokers. Occasional smokers seem to have slightly lower odds, and daily smokers seem to have *slightly* inflated odds.

In order to fully explore the results, let us produce a table similar to Table 6.13 in the chapter. Using the regression line equation from the analysis above:

$$\text{Logit}(\hat{Y}) = -2.2522 + 0.4765(\text{EFF1}) - 0.2368(\text{EFF2}) - 0.1008(\text{EFF3})$$

we can produce the following table:

Enrichment Table 6.5

	EFF1	EFF2	EFF3	Logit	Odds	Probability
Nonsmoker	−1	−1	−1	−2.3911	0.091529	0.083854
Former smoker	1	0	0	−1.7757	0.169365	0.144835
Occasional smoker	0	1	0	−2.489	0.082993	0.076633
Daily smoker	0	0	1	−2.353	0.095083	0.086828

Data Source: NHIS2010, Centers for Disease Control and Prevention.

From the table, we can estimate risk ratios for nonsmokers versus former smokers (former smokers have RR = 1.73), occasional smokers (occasional smokers have RR = 0.91), and daily smokers (daily smokers have RR = 1.04). While significant, the last two group comparisons are modest in effect, while the first comparison is notable.

The problem with this analysis is that, while we can accurately calculate the probabilities and relative risks, and so on, for each group, the significance tests for effects coded analyses are testing whether any group is significantly different than the intercept or the probability for the overall group/population. Thus, each contrast is being compared with the overall probability of 9.7%. This is not the question originally posed. In order to test this question, we really need dummy coding, which compares each group with the reference group, not the intercept.

Dummy Coded Analyses

Performing the analysis with dummy coding produces the following contrasts:

Enrichment Table 6.6 Class-Level Information

Class	Value	Design Variables		
smoke_cat	0	0	0	0
	1	1	0	0
	2	0	1	0
	3	0	0	1

Data Source: NHIS2010, Centers for Disease Control and Prevention.

and identical model fit statistics (e.g., chi-square of 184.42, $p < .0001$):

Enrichment Table 6.7 Testing Global Null Hypothesis: BETA = 0

Test	Chi-Square	df	Pr > ChiSq
Likelihood ratio	184.4167	3	<.0001
Score	200.5000	3	<.0001
Wald	195.7161	3	<.0001

Data Source: NHIS2010, Centers for Disease Control and Prevention.

Further, these analyses produce identical odds ratio estimates for contrasts of each group with group "0"—the nonsmokers as the analysis before, but now the statistical tests are answering the correct question. In point of fact, neither occasional or daily smokers have significantly different probabilities of diabetes than nonsmokers, as you can see in the significance tests below, although former smokers are at significantly higher risk.

Enrichment Table 6.8 SAS Output With Reference Category "0"

Analysis of Maximum Likelihood Estimates							
Parameter		df	Estimate	Standard Error	Wald Chi-Square	Pr > ChiSq	Exp(Est)
Intercept		1	−2.3911	0.0286	7008.2150	<.0001	0.092
smoke_cat	1	1	0.6154	0.0463	176.4519	<.0001	1.850
smoke_cat	2	1	−0.0980	0.1079	0.8245	0.3639	0.907
smoke_cat	3	1	0.0380	0.0614	0.3840	0.5355	1.039

	Odds Ratio Estimates		
Effect	Point Estimate	95% Wald Confidence Limits	
smoke_cat 1 vs. 0	1.850	1.690	2.026
smoke_cat 2 vs. 0	0.907	0.734	1.120
smoke_cat 3 vs. 0	1.039	0.921	1.172

Data Source: NHIS2010, Centers for Disease Control and Prevention.

Replicate the predicted probabilities above using the new coding scheme and logistic regression equation:

Enrichment Table 6.9

	Dum1	Dum2	Dum3	Logit	Odds	Probability
Nonsmoker	0	0	0	−2.3911	0.091528947	0.083853889
Former smoker	1	0	0	−1.7757	0.169364853	0.144834909
Occasional smoker	0	1	0	−2.4891	0.082984619	0.076625852
Daily smoker	0	0	1	−2.3531	0.095073976	0.086819683

Data Source: NHIS2010, Centers for Disease Control and Prevention.

From this, we can again calculate that former smokers are 1.72 times[4] as likely to get diabetes as nonsmokers, which is statistically significant, that occasional smokers are about 0.91 times as likely to get diabetes, and that daily smokers are about 1.04 times as likely to get diabetes compared with nonsmokers. Neither of these last two estimates are significant, as mentioned earlier, meaning that only former smokers have significantly different probabilities than nonsmokers.

Do former smokers have different risk of diabetes than occasional or daily smokers? In order to answer the next question, whether former smokers have different diabetes risk than current (occasional or daily) smokers, we can see from the above analyses that the relative risks for these comparisons are 0.53 and 0.60 for occasional and daily smokers compared with former smokers (respectively). However, the current coding scheme would not allow for significance tests of these questions. Because there are only three possible contrasts available when there are four groups, it is not really legitimate to re-run the analysis with a different coding scheme as we have already used the three contrasts available. So note that it is not generally appropriate to do the next analysis if you have done the former.

To answer these questions (rather than the former questions) and see whether these are significant, we can re-run the analyses with "1" as the reference group, as in Enrichment Table 6.10.

Note that through all these analyses, the same model fit statistics have been observed no matter the contrasts (chi-square of 184.42). This is an important epiphany that there is only so much variance the variable as a whole will account for, regardless of coding.

Enrichment Table 6.10 SAS Output With Reference Group "1"

Parameter		df	Estimate	Standard Error	Wald Chi-Square	Pr > ChiSq	Exp(Est)
					Analysis of Maximum Likelihood Estimates		
Intercept		1	−1.7757	0.0365	2370.1717	<.0001	0.169
smoke_cat	0	1	−0.6154	0.0463	176.4519	<.0001	0.540
smoke_cat	2	1	−0.7134	0.1103	41.8485	<.0001	0.490
smoke_cat	3	1	−0.5773	0.0654	77.8422	<.0001	0.561

Data Source: NHIS2010, Centers for Disease Control and Prevention.

---

[4]Note probabilistic language indicates I am reporting relative risk.

Back to the question at hand, you can see that all three groups (non-smoker, occasional, and daily smokers) are significantly different than former smokers, thus indicating that those relative risk ratios are significantly different than 1.0.

Do occasional and daily smokers have different relative risks for diabetes? Finally, the relative risk for daily versus occasional smokers is 1.13 (OR = 1.46), which is not significant at $p < .05$. Thus we cannot conclude that occasional and daily smokers have different probabilities for diabetes.

Enrichment Table 6.11 SAS Output With Reference Group "2"

Testing Global Null Hypothesis: BETA = 0			
Test	Chi-Square	df	Pr > ChiSq
Likelihood Ratio	184.4167	3	<.0001
Score	200.5000	3	<.0001
Wald	195.7161	3	<.0001

			Analysis of Maximum Likelihood Estimates				
Parameter		df	Estimate	Standard Error	Wald Chi-Square	Pr > ChiSq	Exp(Est)
Intercept		1	−2.4891	0.1041	572.0696	<.0001	0.083
smoke_cat	0	1	0.0980	0.1079	0.8245	0.3639	1.103
smoke_cat	1	1	0.7134	0.1103	41.8485	<.0001	2.041
smoke_cat	3	1	0.1360	0.1174	1.3425	0.2466	1.146

	Odds Ratio Estimates		
Effect	Point Estimate	95% Wald Confidence Limits	
smoke_cat 0 vs. 2	1.103	0.893	1.363
smoke_cat 1 vs. 2	2.041	1.644	2.533
smoke_cat 3 vs. 2	1.146	0.910	1.442

SYNTAX EXAMPLES

SPSS syntax for recoding the original race variable in the NHIS data set and for receiving contrasts in output (in this example it is asking for REPEATED contrasts):

```
recode RACERPI2 (1=1) (2=2) (4=3) into race_new.
** race recode: 1= white, 2=black, 3=asian.

LOGISTIC REGRESSION VARIABLES diabetes
/METHOD=ENTER race_new
/CONTRAST (race_new)=Repeated
/print=all
/CRITERIA=PIN(.05) POUT(.10) ITERATE(20) CUT(.5).
```

Another example gives us DEVIATION coding with Caucasian (1) as the reference group:

```
LOGISTIC REGRESSION VARIABLES diabetes
/METHOD=ENTER race_new
/CONTRAST (race_new)=Deviation(1)
/CRITERIA=PIN(.05) POUT(.10) ITERATE(20) CUT(.5).
```

In this syntax below, we recode Smoking into a more manageable categorical variable, and then into dummy coded variables. Note the use of the DO IF loop—only do this for individuals with a valid (nonmissing) smoking status. We do not want to include them in the dummy coded variables:

```
recode smkstat2 (4=0) (3=1) (2=2) (1=3) into smoke_cat.
*** smoking recode 0= nonsmoker 1=former, 2=occasional,
3=every day.
execute.
do if (smoke_cat ge 0).
compute dum1=0.
compute dum2=0.
compute dum3=0.
if (smoke_cat=1) dum1=1.
if (smoke_cat=2) dum2=1.
if (smoke_cat=3) dum3=1.
end if.
execute.
```

SAS syntax for effects coding

```
proc logistic data=Book.Ch06 descending;
class race_new (ref=first);
model diabetes=race_new /expb;
run;
proc logistic data=Book.Ch06 descending;
class smoke_cat (ref=first);
model diabetes=smoke_cat /expb;
run;
```

To get dummy coding in SAS use the "/param=ref" statement:

```
proc logistic data=Book.Ch06 descending;
class smoke_cat (ref=first) /param=ref;
model diabetes=smoke_cat /expb;
run;
```

To get dummy coding in SAS that uses a different reference group, make sure your categorical variable is a STRING variable, and then simply specify the value. For example, Former smoker is "1" in our data:

```
proc logistic data=Book.Ch06 descending;
class smoke_cat (ref='1') /param=ref;
model diabetes=smoke_cat /expb;
run;
```

REFERENCES

Cohen, J., Cohen, P., West, S., & Aiken, L. S. (2002). *Applied multiple regression/ correlation analysis for the behavioral sciences*. Mahwah, NJ: Lawrence Erlbaum.

Hardy, M. A. (1993). *Regression with dummy variables* (Vol. 93). Thousand Oaks, CA: Sage.

7

CURVILINEAR EFFECTS IN LOGISTIC REGRESSION

My high school science teacher, Larry Josbeno, was not only a brilliant teacher, but he also was fond of lousy physics jokes. One of his favorites related to Zeno's paradoxes and was a variant of what is apparently a classic mathematical joke[1]:

A group of boys are lined up on one wall of a dance hall, and an equal number of girls are lined up on the opposite wall 10 meters apart. Both groups are then instructed to advance toward each other by one half the distance separating them every 10 seconds (i.e., if they are distance d apart at time 0, they are $d/2$ at time = 10, $d/4$ at time = 20, $d/8$ at time = 30, and so forth). A mathematician, a physicist, and an engineer are asked when they would meet at the center of the dance hall. The mathematician said they would never actually meet because the series is infinite. The physicist said they would meet when time equals infinity. The engineer said that within 1 minute they would be close enough for all "practical" purposes.

Enthusiastic adolescent laughter ensued, predictably. Thank you, Mr. Josbeno! But what does this have to do with curvilinear independent variables? Like many things in life, if we were to explore the relationship between time and distance between our girls and boys, the relationship is not linear, as Figure 7.1 shows. And curvilinearity is the topic of this chapter!

In previous chapters, we talked about the assumption that logistic regression is "linear on the logit," meaning that the logits and independent variables are linearly related. I have also asserted that in many areas of science, this assumption may not be tenable. I believe that if we routinely

---

[1]See Paul Field and Eric W. Weisstein, "Zeno's Paradoxes," from MathWorld—A Wolfram Web Resource (http://mathworld.wolfram.com/ZenosParadoxes.html).

Figure 7.1 Zeno's Paradox in the High School Dance

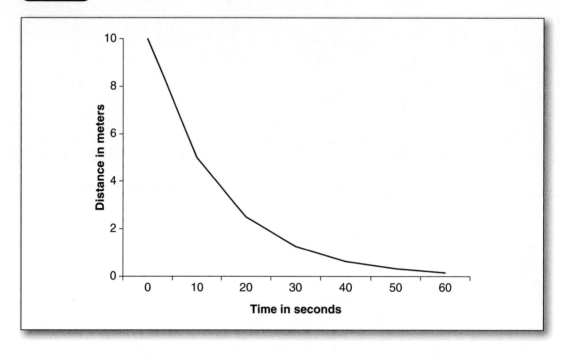

looked for curvilinear relationships, we would find many. In fact, while writing this chapter, I had to explore surprisingly few examples to produce the curvilinear results shown below.

In this chapter, we will briefly review the concept of curvilinearity, how to test for curvilinearity more formally, how to account for curvilinearity in your logistic regression analyses, and how to graph curvilinear effects.[2]

◆ A BRIEF REVIEW OF THE ASSUMPTION OF LINEARITY

Recall from previous chapters that we assume that the logistic transformation on our binary/categorical dependent variable produces a linear relationship between independent variable(s) and the logit of the dependent variable. If one were to use probit regression (or any other link function

---

[2]I believe graphical representations of complex findings like curvilinear effects and interaction effects (where found) are critical to effectively communicating the results of research to the audience of interest.

[note we cover probit regression in Chapter 9]), one assumes the relationship will be linear following that transform.

One example in this chapter will be the effect of age on the probability of certain disease states. We will begin by returning to our National Health Interview Survey (NHIS) 2010 (http://www.cdc.gov/nchs/nhis/nhis_2010_data_release.htm) data on diabetes and look at the relationship between age of the patient and the probability of diagnosis with diabetes.

ILLEGITIMATE CAUSES OF CURVILINEARITY ◆

In this chapter, I am most concerned with modeling legitimately curvilinear relationships. As I briefly mentioned in Chapter 4 on assumptions, there are several potential sources of curvilinearity that are not, in my mind, legitimate: model misspecification (omission of important variables), converting interval or ratio variables to ordinal variables with unequal intervals, and uncleaned data (i.e., containing influential data points).

Model Misspecification: Omission of Important Variables

When discussing the assumption that we have correctly specified the model, we introduced the assumption that we have included all relevant and important variables in the model and have not included extraneous variables. It is possible that omission of important variables can lead to either of these situations. Thus, theory and prior research should help guide you in designing research that accounts for important variables (i.e., prior academic experiences in studying education, prior health events in studying current health status).

Violating Equal Intervals in Coding Continuous Variables

It is also possible that poor coding of variables can artificially lead to curvilinearity. Specifically, when researchers take what are conceptually continuous variables (i.e., income, age, or achievement) and create categories for convenience, they might convert ratio or interval measurement to ordinal measurement with unequal categories. I previously introduced the fact that in some government databases, family income is coded unevenly (such as this example from the Early Childhood Longitudinal Study [ECLS] from the National Center for Educational Statistics [NCES])[3]:

| Table 7.1 | Total Household Income as Categorized in the ECLS-K Data Set From NCES |

1 $5,000 or less	8 $35,001 to $40,000
2 $5,001 to $10,000	9 $40,001 to $50,000
3 $10,001 to $15,000	10 $50,001 to $75,000
4 $15,001 to $20,000	11 $75,001 to $100,000
5 $20,001 to $25,000	12 $100,000 to $200,000
6 $25,001 to $30,000	13 $200,001 or more
7 $30,001 to $35,000	

Data Source: *User's Manual for the ECLS-K First-Grade Public-Use Data Files and Electronic Code Book* (NCES 2002–135), National Center for Educational Statistics, U.S. Department of Education.

You can see that a continuous variable that could conceptually be ratio measurement (with a true zero point and equal intervals)—family income in dollars—is in this case broken into uneven categories. At the lower end, income is classified into blocks of $5,000 each,[4] while at the top end, the blocks are $25,000, $100,000 each or more. This process can serve to collapse sparse categories or groups into larger groups, convert a linear relationship to curvilinear, or could also be used to convert a curvilinear to linear relationship.[5] To be sure, it seems to violate some of our basic assumptions about measurement and is thus undesirable. One must be careful converting continuous variables to categorical, as we discovered in Chapter 5.

In the case of our first example, age and diabetes, we have a continuous variable (age) that has an interesting curvilinear relationship to the probability of being diagnosed with diabetes, as you can see in Figure 7.2.

---

[3]http://nces.ed.gov/pubs2002/2002135_2.pdf

[4]In other studies, I have seem more egregious examples of this same thing, where at the lower end income was broken into $1,000 or $2,500 increments, with $100,000 increments at the top end of the scale.

[5]However, as we explored in previous chapters, it is usually better to leave a continuous variable as a continuous variable, transforming if necessary.

Figure 7.2   Age and Probability of Diabetes Diagnosis

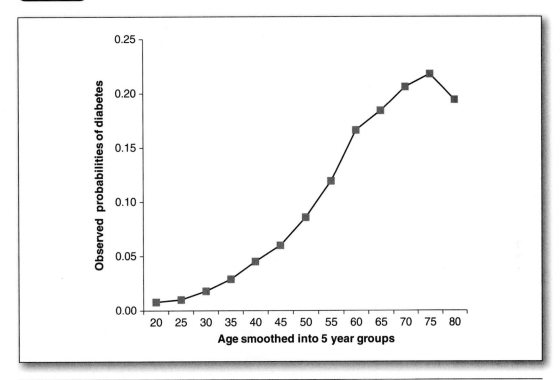

Data Source: National Health Interview Survey of 2010 (NHIS2010), Centers for Disease Control and Prevention.

To follow the previous point, if I group individuals into decades, the curve does change somewhat, although it retains much of general nature, as Figure 7.3 shows. In Figure 7.4, I moved all under 65 into one category and had much smaller age categories above 65. You can see that again changes the nature of the curve.

Poor Data Cleaning

As also mentioned previously, I have occasionally seen curvilinear effects arise (or masked) merely because of poor data cleaning—a prominent outlier in one range of the data where there are few other cases can pull the regression line in that area out of linearity, leading to the appearance of a curvilinear effect when in fact it is merely poor data cleaning.

Figure 7.3 Diabetes and Age Grouped Into Decades

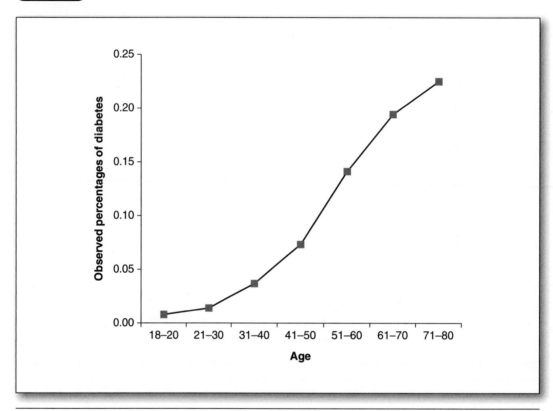

Data Source: NHIS2010, Centers for Disease Control and Prevention.

I suppose it is also possible for highly non-normal data to have the appearance of curvilinearity when in fact it is just another example of poor data cleaning.

Thus, I would argue that prior to examining data for curvilinear effects, one should be sure that the measurement of the variable is defensible (i.e., that you are not creating or masking curvilinearity), that appropriate variables are modeled in the equation, and that you have done due diligence in data cleaning. Once you have satisfied those basic steps (which should probably be part of any analysis regardless of whether curvilinearity is suspected), it is time to explore whether curvilinear effects exist in the data. There are examples of how data cleaning can reveal an existing curvilinear effect at the end of the chapter.

Figure 7.4 Age and Diabetes in Uneven Categories

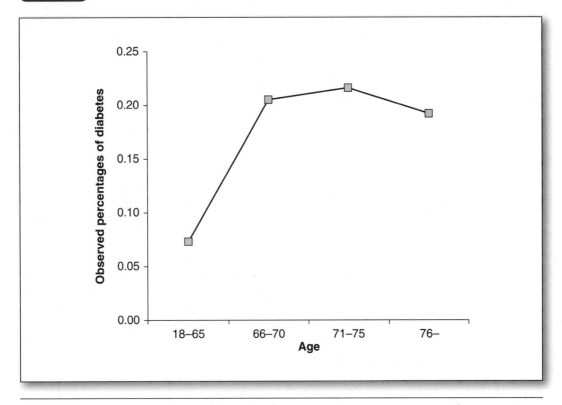

Data Source: NHIS2010, Centers for Disease Control and Prevention.

DETECTION OF NONLINEAR EFFECTS ♦

Theory

First and foremost, theory and common sense are always good guides. I tend to believe that many things in social science (and health sciences as well) are curvilinear in nature, and so I routinely check for these effects. If prior research has indicated curvilinear effects or if there is good cause to suspect that the effect might not be uniform across the entire range of a variable, it is probably worth taking a few minutes to test.

Ad Hoc Testing

They are easily tested by entering X, X^2, and X^3 terms into an equation. In my experience, if there is curvilinearity, adding squared and cubed terms tends to capture much of the curvilinearity if there is any.

Box-Tidwell Transformations

Those preferring a more strategic approach to this issue may enjoy exploring Box-Tidwell transformations (Box & Tidwell, 1962), introduced in Chapter 4 as a more methodical approach to testing and specifying curvilinear effects (and more importantly, linearizing relationships). Many prominent regression authors and texts (i.e., Cohen, Cohen, West, & Aiken, 2002, pp. 239–240) suggest Box-Tidwell as a method of easily exploring whether any variables have nonlinear effects.

The essential process for Box-Tidwell, already described in Chapter 4, is to (a) perform an initial analysis with the independent variables of interest in the regression equation, (b) transform all independent variables of interest via Box-Tidwell, below, (c) enter them into the regression equation simultaneously along with the original untransformed variables, and (d) see which of the transformed variables (if any) are significant. The Box-Tidwell transformation is:

$$V_i = X_i(\ln X_i). \qquad \text{Eq. 7.1.}$$

If the variable V is a significant predictor when X is in the equation, there is a significant curvilinear component to that variable.

$$\text{logit}(\hat{Y}) = b_0 + b_1 X_1 + b_2 V_1 \qquad \text{Eq. 7.2.}$$

One nice thing about this process is that you then get a good estimate of the nature of the curvilinear effect:

$$\hat{\lambda} = \frac{b_2}{b_1} + 1 \qquad \text{Eq. 7.3.}$$

where b_2 is taken from the second analysis and b_1 is taken from the initial analysis without the V_i in the equation. You can do successive iterations of this process as well, entering $X^{\text{lambda-hat}}$ in place of the original X_i in both the original steps and the calculation of V_i, but in my opinion, that tends to overfit the model unnecessarily. Our data in the social sciences are not the same character and nature as in the physical sciences and manufacturing, for example.

The final step in this process is to substitute $X^{\text{lamda-hat}}$, where X_i had been in the final analysis. I will also suggest that anytime you incorporate curvilinearity or interactions, you should graph the results for the reader.

CURVILINEAR LOGISTIC REGRESSION ◆
EXAMPLE: DIABETES AND AGE

As a baseline, the unaltered age variable from Figure 7.1 was entered into the logistic regression equation, meaning that the logit and odds ratio reflect increments of 1.0 years, not 1.0 standard deviations as was previously suggested because age in years is a meaningful metric. This model had a −2 log likelihood of 16196.924, which was significant at $\chi^2_{(1)} = 1527.24$, $p < .0001$.

Adding Quadratic and Cubic
Terms to the Logistic Regression Analysis

To demonstrate the ad hoc method of exploring curvilinearity, I often add the squared (X^2) and cubed (X^3) terms to the regression equation. With X in the equation, if X^2 is significant that indicates that there is a quadratic (one-bend) curve present in the relationship. With both X and X^2 in the equation, if X^3 is significant, then the curve is cubic (two bends). This procedure, in my experience, captures a reasonable approximation of many curvilinear relationships. Given the generally imprecise nature of

Table 7.2 Relationship of Age and Diabetes—Linear Model Only

		B	SE	Wald	df	Sig.	Exp(B)	95% CI for Exp(B)	
								Lower	Upper
Step 1[a]	AGE	.045	.001	1381.895	1	.000	1.046	1.044	1.048
	Constant	− 4.631	.074	3890.651	1	.000	.010		

a. Variable(s) entered on step 1: AGE_P.

Data Source: NHIS2010, Centers for Disease Control and Prevention.

measurement in the social sciences (compared with physical or biomedical sciences, or manufacturing, for example), it is important to honor the quality of the data and be careful not to overfit the data beyond what could be expected to generalize.

In this example, both the squared and cubed terms were significant when entered into the equation, but when the cubic term was entered into the equation, it represented a very small ($X^2 = 14.14$, $p < .0001$) increment and so was not included in this example for simplicity. The first step was identical to what is reported above. When Age^2 was entered into the equation, the −2 log likelihood was reduced by 298.45 to 15898.47, which was significant at $X^2_{(1)} = 298.45$, $p < .0001$.[6]

To graph this equation, you would create the logistic regression equation from Table 7.3:

Table 7.3 Predicting Diabetes From Age and Age^2

		B	SE	Wald	df	Sig.	Exp(B)	95% CI for Exp(B)	
								Lower	Upper
Step 1[a]	AGE	.19402	.010	405.285	1	.000	1.214	1.191	1.237
	AGE²	−.001301	.000	253.400	1	.000	.999	.999	.999
	Constant	− 8.56625	.275	971.730	1	.000	.000		

Data Source: NHIS2010, Centers for Disease Control and Prevention.

$$\text{Logit}(\hat{Y}) = -8.56625 + .19402(\text{Age}) - .001301(\text{Age}^2) \qquad \text{Eq. } 7.4[7].$$

Procedurally, creating predicted logits and conditional probabilities when looking at curvilinear effects is no different than any simple algebra

---

[6]Recall that when examining nested models such as this, the difference in the −2 log likelihood is evaluated as a chi-squared statistic with degrees of freedom equal to the number of variables entered on that step. In this case, only one variable was entered, so the chi-squared has one degree of freedom. Most statistical software packages will perform this test for you if you enter the terms on successive steps.

[7]Note that by default SPSS gives only a certain number of decimals—SAS tends to give more. For precision in this sort of application, I like to examine four or five decimals (because we are using logits, in which decimals make a difference!). Double-clicking on the table in the output will allow you to adjust the precision of the output.

example where you must substitute a value (or several values) of X and compute a predicted Y. In this case, we can substitute in a range of numbers from 20 to 80, getting predicted logits that can then be converted to predicted probabilities.

As you can see from Figure 7.5, the quadratic line (long dashes with triangles) is a better fit to the actual data (squares with dotted line), although not perfect.

As you can also see from Figure 7.5, graphing the logit (log of the odds of having diabetes in any five-year group) and the predicted logit from the linear and quadratic equations produce similar results in that the curvilinear analysis is much closer to the actual smoothed data than the linear analysis.

One reason why I like to graph predicted probabilities (as I have advocated for several times in the book already) is that the logit graphs often misrepresent the actual nature of the curve. For example, looking

Figure 7.5 Observed Log Odds of Diabetes, Predicted Logit, and Logit From Quadratic Analysis

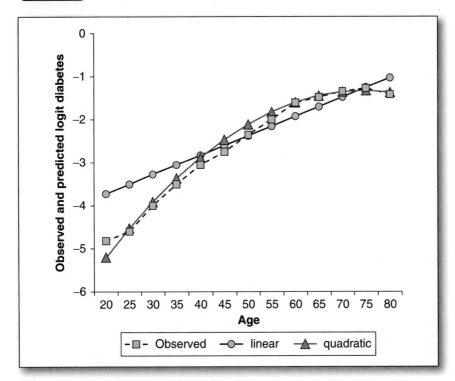

Data Source: NHIS2010, Centers for Disease Control and Prevention.

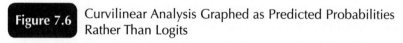

Figure 7.6 Curvilinear Analysis Graphed as Predicted Probabilities Rather Than Logits

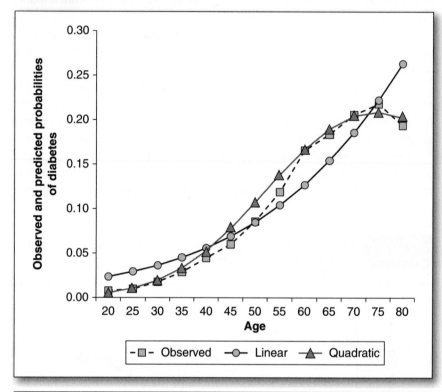

Data Source: NHIS2010, Centers for Disease Control and Prevention.

at Figure 7.6, you can see that the observed probability of being diagnosed with diabetes is relatively flat, and then accelerates later in life. Graphing the logit, however, leads to the impression that diabetes rates accelerate early in life and then level out later in life—the opposite of the observed trend.

You can also observe one other interesting thing—remember that logistic regression is "linear on the logit"—meaning that there is assumed to be a linear relationship between the log of the odds of being diagnosed with diabetes and the independent variable (age). In Figure 7.4, when the logit is being graphed, that linear relationship is evident. However, when logits are converted to probabilities, the "linear" relationship is slightly curvilinear. A logarithmic transformation is a nonlinear transform—in this case, taking a nonlinear relationship and making it linear. This highlights the important reminder that we do *not* assume the relationship is linear between the conditional probabilities of being diagnosed and the independent variable. Only the logit is assumed to be linearly related.

AN EXAMPLE SUMMARY OF THIS ANALYSIS ♦

In order to explore the curvilinear relationship between diabetes and age, squared and cubed versions of the age variable were created and entered sequentially (on individual steps) into the analysis. The linear version of age accounted for significant improvement in the model ($-2LL = 16196.92$, $\chi^2_{(1)} = 1527.24$, $p < .0001$). As expected, with only this variable in the analysis, increasing age is associated with increased probability of diabetes ($b = 0.045$, $SE_b = 0.001$, $p < .0001$). When Age^2 was entered into the equation, the -2 log likelihood was reduced by 298.45 to 15898.47, which was significant at $\chi^2_{(1)} = 298.45$, $p < .0001$. (I would summarize both analyses in a single table that combined Tables 7.2 and 7.3 for the convenience of the reader. I would also include a graph similar to Figure 7.6 that simply graphed the curvilinear effect rather than all three lines, which I have mostly included for pedagogical reasons.) As you can see in Figure 7.6, the probability of being diagnosed with diabetes is relatively low and slow to accelerate in relatively young adults, but it begins to rise more rapidly from ages 40–75, at which point it seems to asymptote and then decline slightly.

ESTIMATING CURVILINEAR RELATIONSHIPS ♦ USING BOX-TIDWELL TRANSFORMATIONS

Imagining we were to go about curve estimation more methodically, we could have performed Box-Tidwell initially rather than my old-fashioned ad hoc (and very trustworthy) method. The first step is to estimate the logistic regression equation with the variable of interest in it, as we did earlier. The next step is to create a new version of the variable V that represents $X\ln(X)$ and add it to the equation containing X. The results of this new analysis are interestingly similar to that of the ad hoc analysis earlier when the squared term was entered into the equation as Figure 7.7 illustrates. After entering V, we get a -2 log likelihood of 15914.87, representing an improvement in model fit of $\chi^2_{(1)} = 282.05$, $p < .0001$. According to the

Figure 7.7 Box-Tidwell Transformation of Age

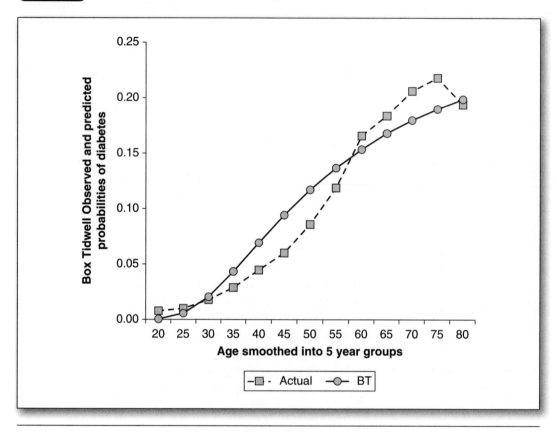

Data Source: NHIS2010, Centers for Disease Control and Prevention.

procedure outlined earlier in the chapter, this significant increment indicates a curvilinear effect, which is not surprising given what we already know of this relationship. We then estimate λ as the ratio of the original regression weight for age divided by the coefficient for V plus 1 or:

$$\hat{\lambda} = \frac{b_2}{b_1} + 1$$ Eq. 7.5.

I estimate $\hat{\lambda} = (-0.135/.045) + 1 = -2$. When age is transformed in this way and entered into the regression equation, we get −2 log likelihood of 16041.62 (better than the simple linear model but slightly worse than the ad hoc quadratic model above), with a Wald of 819.99, which is slightly better than the combined Wald statistics of the previous analysis.

Table 7.4 Variables in the Equation

		B	SE	Wald	df	Sig.	Exp(B)	95% CI for Exp(B)	
								Lower	Upper
Step 1[a]	age_ BTtransform	−2569.175	89.720	819.991	1	.000	.000	.000	.000
	Constant	−.995	.038	674.019	1	.000	.370		

a. Variable(s) entered on step 1: age_BTtransform.

Data Source: NHIS2010, Centers for Disease Control and Prevention.

Box and Tidwell (and other authors) suggest an iterative approach wherein you substitute the newly transformed variable throughout and perform the regression equation again to see if there is any tweaking that is needed to the lambda. In this case, V and $V \ln V$ were so highly collinear (correlation exceeding 0.99) that it was not possible to perform another iteration.

DATA CLEANING AND CURVILINEAR EFFECTS ♦

Curvilinearity can be caused by unreasonably influential scores, or it can easily be masked by them. Thus, it is important to establish whether a curvilinear effect is being caused by, or masked by, these data quality issues. Turning to our data on marijuana use, we will see an example of how removing 20 out of 540 cases can reveal a curvilinear relationship between marijuana use and student achievement test scores. In this data set (National Education Longitudinal Study of 1988 [NELS88]), all students completed achievement tests, which were combined into single composites at 8th, 10th, and 12th grade. We are using the example of the 8th-grade achievement test score, which has been converted to z-scores.

Let us start off with the fact that there is no significant relationship between student achievement test scores at 8th grade and whether the student admitted to using marijuana, as you see in the abbreviated tables (Table 7.5).

| Table 7.5 | Logistic Regression Equation as Linear, Squared, and Cubic Terms Are Entered Into the Equation |

		B	SE	Wald	df	Sig.	Exp(B)	95% CI for Exp(B)	
								Lower	Upper
Step 1	zBYACH	−.197	.107	3.351	1	.067	.821	.665	1.014
	Constant	− 1.164	.103	126.848	1	.000	.312		
Step 2	zBYACH	−.177	.120	2.167	1	.141	.838	.662	1.060
	zBYACH2	−.039	.102	.149	1	.699	.961	.787	1.174
	Constant	− 1.131	.134	71.266	1	.000	.323		
Step 3	zBYACH	.055	.212	.067	1	.795	1.057	.697	1.602
	zBYACH2	.078	.134	.340	1	.560	1.081	.831	1.407
	zBYACH3	−.132	.101	1.723	1	.189	.876	.719	1.067
	Constant	−1.199	.145	68.669	1	.000	.302		

Data Source: NELS88, National Center for Educational Statistics. U.S. Department of Education.

As you can see in Table 7.5, the 95% CIs include 1.0. Although the effect is in the expected direction (students with increasingly high achievement are less likely to admit using marijuana than those with lower achievement test scores), the significance test and CIs do not allow us to conclude there is a significant relationship. Furthermore, adding the squared term for achievement does not improve the situation. In this analysis, neither the linear nor quadratic terms are significant at $p < .05$. Finally, when the cubed term enters the equation, we are left with non-significant results.

After examining some of the typical diagnostic tools available in SPSS (e.g., standardized residuals and DfBetas), the standardized residuals are all within a reasonable range as you can see in Figure 7.8.

However, the DfBetas (shown in Figure 7.9) do seem to have some relatively large values, and so I selected cases with DfBetas for the intercept that were greater than the 1st percentile and less than the 99th percentile. This eliminated 20 of 540 cases, as mentioned earlier but led to a different result. As you can see in Table 7.6, the linear effect is still non-significant (perhaps more so than before).

Figure 7.8　Standardized Residuals From Marijuana and Achievement Analysis

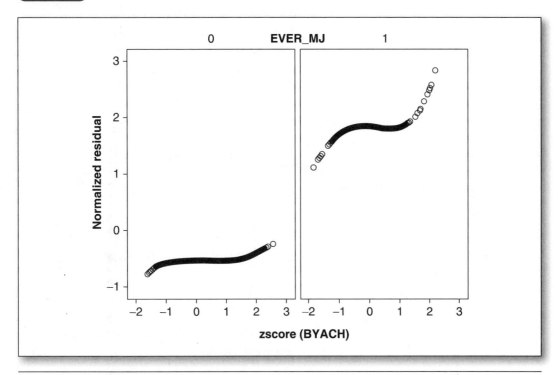

Data Source: NELS88, National Center for Educational Statistics. U.S. Department of Education.

Table 7.6　Variables in the Equation

		B	SE	Wald	df	Sig.	Exp(B)	95% CI for Exp(B)	
								Lower	Upper
Step 1	zBYACH	−.112	.113	.995	1	.318	.894	.717	1.115
	Constant	−1.350	.111	146.777	1	.000	.259		
Step 2	zBYACH	−.135	.127	1.137	1	.286	.874	.682	1.120
	zBYACH2	.039	.105	.142	1	.706	1.040	.847	1.277
	Constant	−1.384	.146	90.512	1	.000	.250		
Step 3	zBYACH	.296	.227	1.695	1	.193	1.344	.861	2.097
	zBYACH2	.285	.148	3.682	1	.055	1.329	.994	1.778
	zBYACH3	−.247	.110	5.075	1	.024	.781	.630	.968
	Constant	−1.546	.166	87.138	1	.000	.213		

Data Source: NELS88, National Center for Educational Statistics. U.S. Department of Education.

Figure 7.9 DfBetas Graphed by Group

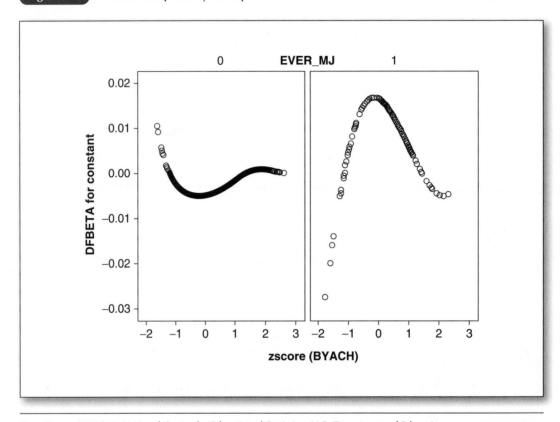

Data Source: NELS88, National Center for Educational Statistics. U.S. Department of Education.

And likewise the quadratic effect is also nonsignificant, but the cubic effect is significant, leaving us with a regression line equation of:

$$\text{Logit}(\hat{Y}) = -1.546 + 0.296(\text{zBYACH}) + 0.285(\text{zBYACH}^2) - 0.247(\text{zBYACH}^3)$$

As you can see in Figures 7.10 and 7.11, the curvilinear nature of this relationship is both interesting and somewhat intuitive—and the curve is similar regardless of whether it is expressed in logits or probabilities. In this example, data cleaning revealed an intuitive and interesting curvilinear relationship that was masked by a relatively small number of influential individuals.

Figure 7.10 Curvilinear Relationship Between Marijuana Use and Achievement in Logits

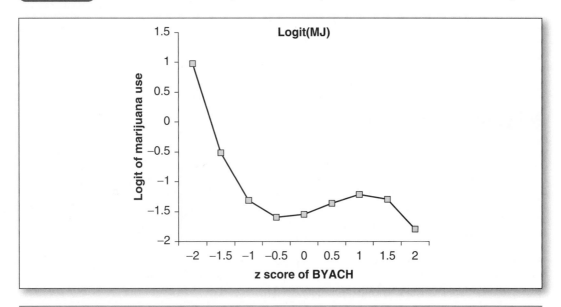

Data Source: NELS88, National Center for Educational Statistics. U.S. Department of Education.

Figure 7.11 Curvilinear Relationship Between Marijuana Use and Achievement in Conditional Probabilities

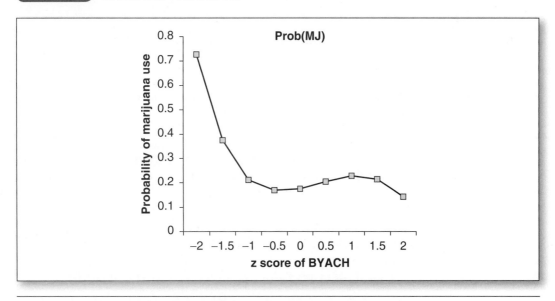

Data Source: NELS88, National Center for Educational Statistics. U.S. Department of Education.

◆ SAS ANALYSES USING DIFCHISQ

Using the same example and data, we can see that using DIFCHISQ can be equally powerful. Performing the same analysis in SAS, we achieve the same results with noncleaned data:

Table 7.7 SAS Results Prior to Cleaning the Data

Analysis of Maximum Likelihood Estimates					
Parameter	df	Estimate	Standard Error	Wald Chi-Square	Pr > ChiSq
Intercept	1	−1.1986	0.1446	68.6692	<.0001
zBYACH	1	0.0551	0.2122	0.0673	0.7953
zBYACH2	1	0.0783	0.1343	0.3399	0.5599
zBYACH3	1	−0.1321	0.1007	1.7229	0.1893

Odds Ratio Estimates		
Effect	Point Estimate	95% Wald Confidence Limits
zBYACH	1.057	0.697	1.602
zBYACH2	1.081	0.831	1.407
zBYACH3	0.876	0.719	1.067

Data Source: NELS88, National Center for Educational Statistics. U.S. Department of Education.

However, looking at the DIFCHISQ results presented in Figure 7.12, we can see that there are a very few cases that seem to have a relatively large influence on the lack of fit for the model.

Removing six cases where DIFCHISQ was greater than 5.0 (remember that about 4 is significant for an χ^2 with one degree of freedom) produced a significant model presented in Table 7.8.

$$\text{Logit}(\hat{Y}) = -1.1514 + 0.2683(\text{zBYACH}) - 0.0214(\text{zBYACH}^2) - 0.3168(\text{zBYACH}^3)$$

Figure 7.12 DIFCHISQ Results From EVER_MJ and zBYACH

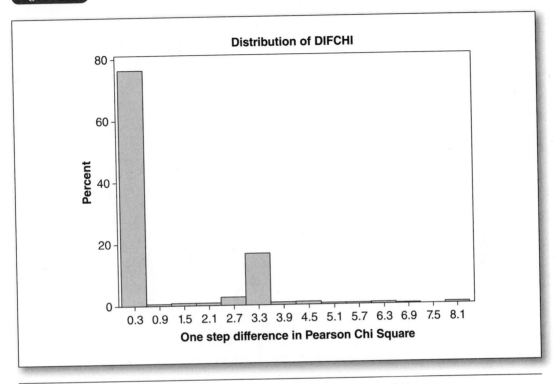

Data Source: NELS88, National Center for Educational Statistics. U.S. Department of Education.

Table 7.8 SAS Results Using DIFCHISQ < 5 to Clean Data

Analysis of Maximum Likelihood Estimates					
Parameter	df	Estimate	Standard Error	Wald Chi-Square	Pr > ChiSq
Intercept	1	−1.1514	0.1449	63.1217	< .0001
zBYACH	1	0.2683	0.2421	1.2283	0.2677
zBYACH2	1	−0.0214	0.1401	0.0234	0.8784
zBYACH3	1	−0.3168	0.1314	5.8118	0.0159

Data Source: NELS88, National Center for Educational Statistics. U.S. Department of Education.

Figure 7.13 Curvilinear Relationship Between Student Achievement and Marijuana Use After SAS Cleaning With DIFCHISQ < 5 and < 4

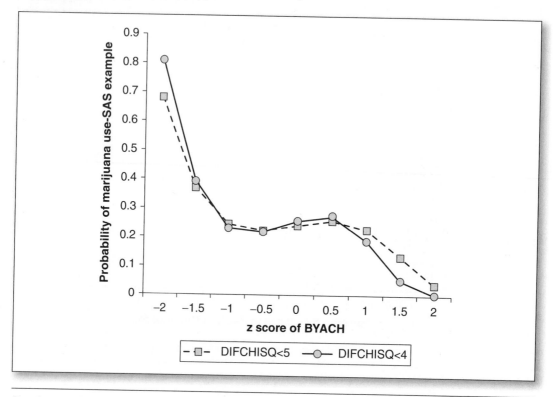

Data Source: NELS88, National Center for Educational Statistics. U.S. Department of Education.

The dashed line in Figure 7.13 represents the effect when the data are cleaned by keeping all cases with DIFCHISQ < 5, and the solid line represents a more aggressive cleaning keeping only cases with DIFCHISQ < 4 (removing 6 cases vs. 12 cases out of 540, respectively).

◆ ADVANCED TOPICS IN CURVILINEAR REGRESSION: ESTIMATING MINIMA AND MAXIMA AS WELL AS SLOPE AT ANY POINT ON THE CURVE

Although we will explicitly discuss logistic regression in this section because that is the focus of this book, these principles should work with any type of regression. In fact, Aiken and West (1991, see pp. 72–76) explicitly discuss this issue in their excellent treatise on interactions in OLS regression.

Any regression line equation can be manipulated with calculus according to simple rules to allow post-hoc probing. In complex curvilinear equations this can be particularly fun, as you can estimate where the curve reaches a minimum or maximum, or you can estimate the slope at any particular point on the curve to estimate how fast the probabilities are changing.[8]

Those of you who have taken (and remember) basic calculus[9] will remember that taking the first derivative of any equation allows you to estimate slope. So, for example, taking a simple linear equation from our AGE and DIABETES equation, discussed earlier, our original equation was:

$$\text{Logit}(\hat{Y}) = -4.631 + 0.45X \qquad \text{Eq. 7.6.}$$

or expressed more fully:

$$\text{Logit}(\hat{Y}) = -4.631X^0 + 0.45X^1 \qquad \text{Eq. 7.7.}$$

Being more specific, the intercept has an X raised to the 0 power, which is 1 (anything raised to the 0 power is 1), and thus it is often eliminated from the regression equation by convention. Further, the X is raised to the first power, and anything raised to the first power is itself. This might seem like more detail than is needed, but once we start adding quadratic and cubic terms, or taking derivatives, this starts to make some sense. For example, the quadratic equation for AGE and DIABETES is

$$\text{Logit}(\hat{Y}) = -8.56625X^0 + 0.19402X^1 - 0.001301X^2 \qquad \text{Eq. 7.8.}$$

The simple rules for taking a derivative are that you multiply each term by the exponent of the X, then reduce that exponent by 1. The first term will drop out, as anything multiplied by 0 is 0. Thus, taking the derivative of the first equation, we get:

$$\frac{d(\text{logit}(\hat{Y}))}{dx} = (1)0.45X^0$$

---

[8] As many authors have pointed out (Aiken & West, 1991 pp. 73–75; DeMaris, 1993), technically what you are estimating is the slope of a line *tangent to* the point where we are estimating the value for the first derivative. For our purposes these concepts are identical.

[9] Unfortunately, we cannot include an entire course in calculus here. Please refer to good calculus references if you are not familiar with this concept.

which simplifies to:

$$\frac{d(\text{logit}(\hat{Y}))}{dx} = 0.45$$

In other words, because this is a *linear* equation, not a curvilinear equation, the slope is constant across the entire regression: 0.45. Perhaps it's not the most surprising or illuminating outcome, but it is a simple example of a derivative. Let's move to the curvilinear example. The derivative for the quadratic formula is (dropping the constant and simplifying):

$$\frac{d(\text{logit}(\hat{Y}))}{dx} = 0.19402 - 2(0.001301X) \text{ or}$$

$$\frac{d(\text{logit}(\hat{Y}))}{dx} = 0.19402 - 0.002602X$$

Once we have this first derivative, we can look for the point where the slope is 0 (the minimum or maximum) by setting $\frac{d(\text{logit}(\hat{Y}))}{dx}$ equal to 0 and solving for X. We get:

$0 = 0.19402 - 0.002602X$; by adding $0.002602X$ to both sides we get:

$0.002602X = 0.19402$; solving for X we get:

$X = 74.57$ years

Looking at the curve from earlier in the chapter (Figure 7.14) this makes sense, as visually we can see that the curve levels off around that point and then curves downward.

Note that we are predicting the change in the logit($\hat{Y}$). When the logit = 0, that is where the probabilities are 50%, or the odds are 1.0: in other words, there is no difference between the groups, and the slope is 0.

We can also estimate slopes of the tangent lines (in logits) at particular values of X. For example, let us look again at the first derivative of the quadratic equation, and estimate the slope at two other time points (we already know the slope around Age = 75): Age = 25 and Age = 50. By substituting these into the equation, we get slopes of 0.12897 for Age = 25 and 0.06392 for Age = 50. This suggests that the odds of having diabetes are increasing faster at age 25 than 50. Looking at the graph of logits, that

Figure 7.14 Calculating the Inflection Point of a Curve

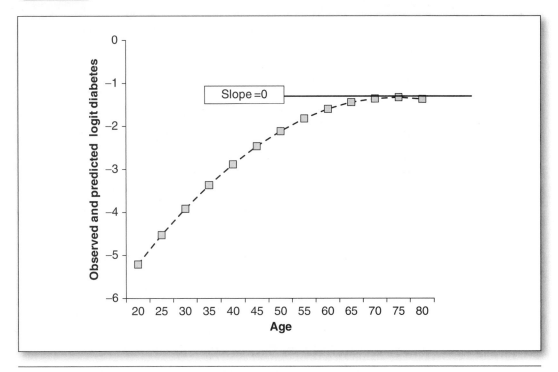

Data Source: NELS88, National Center for Educational Statistics. U.S. Department of Education.

seems to hold. However, looking at the graph of the predicted conditional probabilities (Figure 7.15), it does not. The change in probabilities seems to be much slower at age 25 than age 50. Thus we must be careful to be clear when reporting post hoc probes of these types of analyses, but they can be useful at times.

In the other example, predicting marijuana use from student achievement, the logit and probability curves are similar. This is also a cubic curve, meaning it has two points where the slope is equal to 0. The original equation (after DIFCHISQ = 5 cleaning) was:

$$\text{Logit}(\hat{Y}) = -1.1514 + 0.2683(\text{zBYACH}) - 0.0214(\text{zBYACH}^2) - 0.3168(\text{zBYACH}^3)$$

$$\frac{d(\text{logit}(\hat{Y}))}{dx} = 0.2683 - 0.0428(\text{zBYACH}) - 0.9504(\text{zBYACH}^2)$$

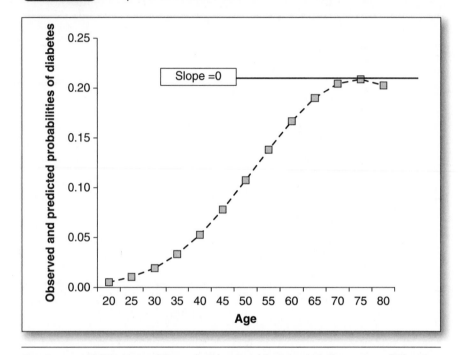

Figure 7.15 The Same Inflection Point Is Apparent When Results Are Graphed as Probabilities

Data Source: NELS88, National Center for Educational Statistics. U.S. Department of Education.

This produces two *extrema:* at −0.55 and at 0.51, both of which seem reasonable given the graph in Figure 7.16 (graphed in logits rather than predicted probabilities).

We could again predict slopes at particular points using the first derivative. With this example, let us examine the following three points: −1.75, 0, and 1.75. Substituting into the equation, we get slopes of: −2.57, 0.27, and −2.72, respectively. This tells us that the logits are decreasing relatively steeply in the extremes of the distribution and are relatively flat in the center of the distribution of achievement scores.[10]

---

[10]There are interesting examples of application of this technique throughout various literatures in science. For example, Boyce and Perrins (1987) used this type of technique of locating extrema to understand and estimate the optimal clutch size for Great Tits (*parus major,* the bird, although I could see how this particular phrasing could lead to confusion) in varying environmental conditions. Apparently there is a curvilinear relationship between clutch size (number of eggs laid) and number of chicks that survive to breed as adults, and this curve is also influenced by whether the year was "bad" or "good" for the birds.

Figure 7.16 Calculating Inflection Points in a Cubic Curve

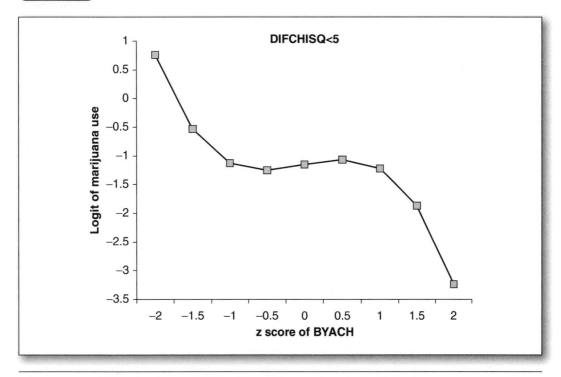

Data Source: NELS88, National Center for Educational Statistics. U.S. Department of Education.

In general this procedure should allow reasonable estimation of extrema (minima and maxima) for curves expressed either as logit or probability. Note that while these calculations give us very exact estimates (our diabetes equation has an inflection point at AGE = 74.75 years), the precision of estimates through this method is only as good as the data. This is a warning all statisticians using regression or linear modeling need to keep in mind! One can model complex, beautiful curves with poor-quality, biased, or error-filled data and the results are only as good as the ingredients.

The question of expressing slopes in terms of probabilities and more advanced statistical and calculus prospects are beyond the scope of this chapter.

Further, there have been discussions of how to test whether individual point estimates for slope are significantly different from 0. For example, Aiken and West (1991, pp. 77–78) discuss this in regards to OLS regression. I have some reservations about probing the data too much, as that (a) increases the risk of overinterpreting the data, unless it is a very large and representative sample, and (b) this too is beyond the scope of this chapter. Perhaps if you encourage all your colleagues and friends to buy the book I will add more of these advanced topics in a second edition!

SUMMARY

This chapter explored how to model curvilinear effects in logistic regression. As I have shown, it is relatively simple to find curvilinear effects. There are several more examples in the Enrichment section. This chapter became more focused on data cleaning than I had originally planned due to the number of examples I came across that highlighted the efficacy of simple, very conservative data cleaning in revealing or strengthening curvilinear effects. In fact, I had intended to include an example of a curvilinear effect that was due to extreme scores (certainly a possibility!) but was unable to find one in the data sets I was working with. One of the reasons there are so many examples at the end of the chapter relative to other chapters is that as I kept searching for a counter example (removing inappropriately influential scores removed a curvilinear effect), I repeatedly came across relatively powerful and interesting examples of how data cleaning enhanced curvilinear effects. After trying many different modes of data cleaning (standardized residuals, different DfBetas, DIFCHISQ, etc.), I failed to find a reasonable example that used appropriate data cleaning to remove a curvilinear effect. Of course I could manufacture an artificial example, and perhaps I will in the future. At this point, there are two main messages from this chapter.

First, checking analyses for curvilinear effects is not terribly difficult nor is it particularly time-consuming. In a few minutes you can create quadratic and cubic terms for important variables, and in a few seconds an analysis can demonstrate whether there might be a nonlinear effect. Some few minutes more spent data cleaning may amplify or attenuate the effect, and you may end up with a very interesting result.

Second, the unintentional message of this chapter reinforces the message from Chapter 4—that cleaning your data in very simple, conservative ways can lead to surprising and unexpected results. I encourage you to explore the data you have, particularly if you have not looked for curvilinear effects before.

If you are familiar with simple calculus concepts, you can glean interesting details from well-modeled curvilinear equations (such as where the curve flattens out and turns the opposite direction). If you enjoyed this

chapter, you will enjoy the next chapter, where we get into multiple predictors, interactions, and even curvilinear interactions![11]

ENRICHMENT

1. Download the data and reproduce the age and diabetes analyses in
   the chapter. Perform routine data cleaning and compare your results
   following data cleaning with those reported in the chapter.

2. Using the same diabetes data as above, perform a curvilinear analysis on body mass index (BMI). After performing this analysis, clean
   the data and perform the analysis on the cleaned data.

3. Using the ELS2002 data predicting dropout/retention from 10th-
   grade math achievement test scores, perform an analysis examining
   any curvilinear effects of math achievement on retention. Clean the
   data, and perform the analysis on cleaned data. Does the result hold?

4. Using the ELS2002 data, perform a curvilinear logistic regression
   analysis of dropout/retention from family socioeconomic status
   (zBYSES). Does the curvilinear effect hold after data cleaning?

5. The NELS88 data regarding marijuana use and achievement scores
   are on the web site for the book.

ANSWER KEY

1. Results of Age and Diabetes Analyses Following Routine Data Cleaning

As with the next example (BMI and DIABETES), the model becomes
stronger with a bit of data cleaning. For example, examining the standardized residuals from this analysis, we see standardized residuals up to 11.

Eliminating 178 cases with standardized residuals over 5 (to be very
conservative) produces improved model fit. As you can see in the abbreviated results, below, the −2LL is reduced 1839.84 with the uncleaned data

---

[11]You may think we were performing analyses that included multiple predictors in
this chapter—and in a sense we did, as there were multiple terms being entered as
predictors. However, technically, BMI, BMI^2, and BMI^3 are all different aspects of the
same variable. So in my mind we were still performing univariate analyses.

Enrichment Figure 7.1 Standardized Residuals From AGE and DIABETES Analysis

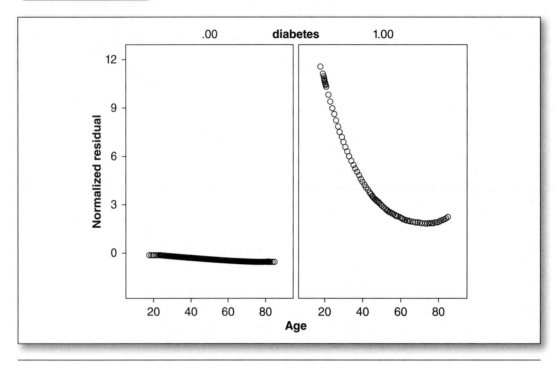

Data Source: NHIS2010, Centers for Disease Control and Prevention.

and 2581.065 once a small fraction of the cases with extreme residuals are removed. While these numbers are not from nested models and thus not directly comparable, they are instructive.

Enrichment Table 7.1 Original Model Without Data Cleaning

Omnibus Tests of Model Coefficients		Chi-square	df	Sig.
Step 1	Step	14.140	1	.000
	Block	14.140	1	.000
	Model	1839.838	3	.000

Data Source: NHIS2010, Centers for Disease Control and Prevention.

		B	SE	Wald	df	Sig.	Exp(B)	95% CI for Exp(B)	
								Lower	Upper
Step 1[a]	age	.041	.040	1.040	1	.308	1.042	.963	1.128
	age2	.002	.001	4.405	1	.036	1.002	1.000	1.003
	age3	.000	.000	14.577	1	.000	1.000	1.000	1.000
	Constant	−6.063	.689	77.384	1	.000	.002		

Variables in the Equation

a. Variable(s) entered on step 1: age3

Data Source: NHIS2010, Centers for Disease Control and Prevention.

Enrichment Table 7.2   Cleaned Data

Omnibus Tests of Model Coefficients

		Chi-square	df	Sig.
Step 1	Step	27.416	1	.000
	Block	27.416	1	.000
	Model	2581.065	3	.000

Data Source: NHIS2010, Centers for Disease Control and Prevention.

Variables in the Equation

		B	SE	Wald	df	Sig.	Exp(B)	95% CI for Exp(B)	
								Lower	Upper
Step 1[a]	age	.740	.085	76.432	1	.000	2.096	1.776	2.475
	age2	−.009	.001	43.089	1	.000	.991	.988	.993
	age3	.000	.000	24.682	1	.000	1.000	1.000	1.000
	Constant	−20.590	1.634	158.700	1	.000	.000		

a. Variable(s) entered on step 1: age3.

Data Source: NHIS2010, Centers for Disease Control and Prevention.

Enrichment Figure 7.2 Comparison of AGE and DIABETES Before and After Data Cleaning

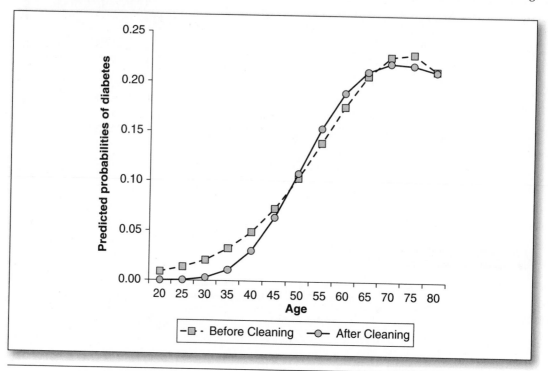

Data Source: NHIS2010, Centers for Disease Control and Prevention.

As you can see in Enrichment Figure 7.2, I modeled the cubic terms for the original data despite it being a very small effect to maintain parallel analyses. This figure also highlights that a bit of data cleaning in these data produces a more pronounced effect of age—which matches what the model statistics indicate.

Despite the fact that I focused on standardized residuals of a certain extreme magnitude, other indicators (DfBetas, DIFCHISQ) should produce similar results.

2. Results for BMI and DIABETES

The original analyses with all cases is promising: there is a significant overall effect, a significant linear effect, and a significant quadratic (but not cubic effect).

Recall the simple linear analysis for these two variables, shown in Enrichment Table 7.3.

Enrichment Table 7.3 Initial Results for BMI and Diabetes

Omnibus Tests of Model Coefficients				
		Chi-square	df	Sig.
	Step	986.981	1	.000
Step 1	Block	986.981	1	.000
	Model	986.981	1	.000

Data Source: NHIS2010, Centers for Disease Control and Prevention.

Variables in the Equation									
		B	SE	Wald	df	Sig.	Exp(B)	95% CI for Exp(B)	
								Lower	Upper
Step 1[a]	BMI	.092	.003	1013.633	1	.000	1.096	1.090	1.102
	Constant	−4.901	.090	2939.412	1	.000	.007		

a. Variable(s) entered on step 1: BMI.

Data Source: NHIS2010, Centers for Disease Control and Prevention.

This indicates that there is a strong linear effect. However, if we suspect that there is a curvilinear effect, we can enter the squared a cubed terms to explore whether that is tenable. Without cleaning the data, the results are interesting—entering the squared term results in a significant improvement in model fit over simply the linear analysis:

Enrichment Table 7.4 BMI and Diabetes Curvilinear Effect

Omnibus Tests of Model Coefficients				
		Chi-square	df	Sig.
	Step	114.907	1	.000
Step 1	Block	114.907	1	.000
	Model	1101.888	2	.000

Data Source: NHIS2010, Centers for Disease Control and Prevention.

(Continued)

Enrichment Table 7.4 (Continued)

		B	SE	Wald	df	Sig.	Exp(B)	95% CI for Exp(B)	
								Lower	Upper
	BMI	.273947	.019	218.858	1	.000	1.315	1.268	1.364
Step 1[a]	BMI2	−0.002613	.000	98.678	1	.000	.997	.997	.998
	Constant	−7.904	.316	627.524	1	.000	.000		

Variables in the Equation

a. Variable(s) entered on step 1: BMI2. Note that I have asked SPSS to provide more decimals than routine to get better precision. You can double-click on the output and get the same precision of results, which is important when graphing these types of outcomes.

Data Source: NHIS2010, Centers for Disease Control and Prevention.

In this analysis, the cubic term does not significantly improve the model ($X^2 = 1.197, p < .27$).

Examining standardized residuals from this analysis revealed some cases with standardized residuals over 9.0, clearly extreme scores, as Enrichment Figure 7.3 shows:

Enrichment Figure 7.3

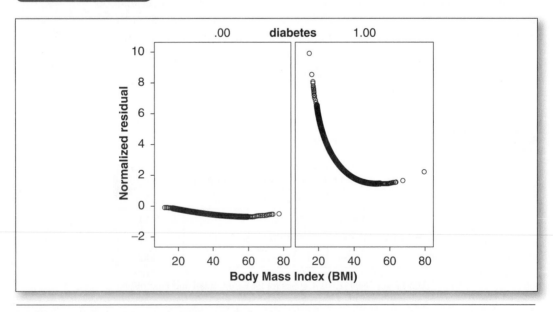

Data Source: NHIS2010, Centers for Disease Control and Prevention.

Removing cases with standardized residuals over 4.0 takes our sample from 26,779 to 26,407, removing 372 cases, just over 1%. However, the results are striking:

Enrichment Table 7.5 Curvilinear Effects of BMI on Diabetes Following Data Cleaning

		Chi-square	df	Sig.
Model 1	Step	1499.272	1	.000
	Block	1499.272	1	.000
	Model	1499.272	1	.000
Model 2	Step	415.846	1	.000
	Block	415.846	1	.000
	Model	1915.118	2	.000
Model 3	Step	108.072	1	.000
	Block	108.072	1	.000
	Model	2023.190	3	.000

Omnibus Tests of Model Coefficients

		B	SE	Wald	df	Sig.	Exp(B)	95% CI for Exp(B) Lower	95% CI for Exp(B) Upper
Model 1	BMI	.119	.003	1462.817	1	.000	1.126	1.119	1.133
	Constant	−5.922	.101	3453.559	1	.000	.003		
Model 2	BMI	.554	.026	465.272	1	.000	1.741	1.655	1.830
	BMI2	−.006	.000	285.639	1	.000	.994	.993	.995
	Constant	−13.276	.444	893.151	1	.000	.000		
Model 3	BMI	1.4446	.097	223.232	1	.000	4.240	3.508	5.125
	BMI2	−0.0298	.002	146.228	1	.000	.971	.966	.975
	BMI3	.000202	.000	99.033	1	.000	1.000	1.000	1.000
	Constant	−23.937	1.218	385.905	1	.000	.000		

Variables in the Equation

Data Source: NHIS2010, Centers for Disease Control and Prevention.

Enrichment Figure 7.4

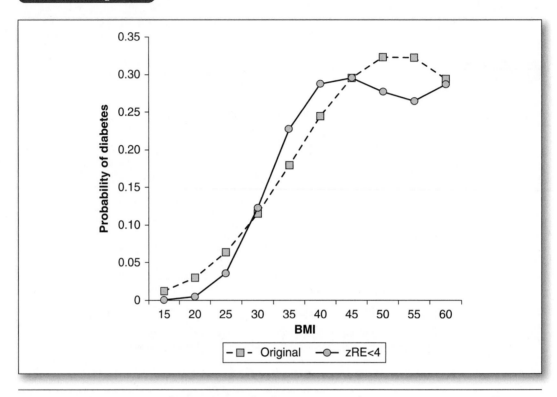

Data Source: NHIS2010, Centers for Disease Control and Prevention.

Again, the simple cleaning of data provides a clearer picture of the results.

Cleaning the Data Using DIFCHISQ

Performing the same analysis in SAS, requesting DIFCHISQ produces similar, predictable results. The DIFCHISQ results range up to over 98, which is very high for a single case. The 95th percentile is 7.01, and the 99th percentile is 17.75, so let us start with 14 as a reasonably conservative cut-off point for cleaning the data. This removed 366 cases, again a relatively small number given the overall size of the sample.

For the sake of succinctness, I entered all three terms on the same step in SAS as we knew the results would be significant for all three terms:

Enrichment Table 7.6 Same Analysis With DIFCHISQ Data Cleaning

Model Fit Statistics		
Criterion	Intercept Only	Intercept and Covariates
AIC	14803.834	12595.777
SC	14812.012	12628.488
−2 Log L	14801.834	12587.777

Data Source: NHIS2010, Centers for Disease Control and Prevention.

Testing Global Null Hypothesis: BETA=0			
Test	Chi-Square	*df*	Pr > ChiSq
Likelihood Ratio	2214.0575	3	<.0001
Score	2083.5613	3	<.0001
Wald	1410.3200	3	<.0001

Data Source: NHIS2010, Centers for Disease Control and Prevention.

Analysis of Maximum Likelihood Estimates					
Parameter	*df*	Estimate	Standard Error	Wald Chi-Square	Pr > ChiSq
Intercept	1	−27.1144	1.3341	413.0726	<.0001
BMI	1	1.6609	0.1051	249.9350	<.0001
BMI2	1	−0.0346	0.00267	168.1633	<.0001
BMI3	1	0.000235	0.000022	116.0424	<.0001

Data Source: NHIS2010, Centers for Disease Control and Prevention.

This data cleaning produces a slightly different curve from the others:

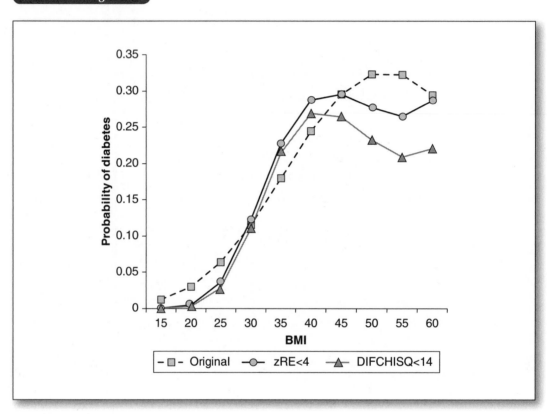

Data Source: NHIS2010, Centers for Disease Control and Prevention.

4. SES and Retention

In this example, I used two different indicators for data cleaning—standardized residuals and DIFCHISQ. Below is an example of what you might see. First, the original analysis (Enrichment Table 7.7).

Enrichment Table 7.7   SES and Retention Curvilinear Analysis Without Data Cleaning

Model 1			
Test	Chi-Square	df	Pr > ChiSq
Likelihood Ratio	441.0694	1	<.0001
Score	411.9929	1	<.0001
Wald	389.9710	1	<.0001
Model 2			
Test	Chi-Square	df	Pr > ChiSq
Likelihood Ratio	449.9023	2	<.0001
Score	433.9340	2	<.0001
Wald	353.6993	2	<.0001
Model 3			
Test	Chi-Square	df	Pr > ChiSq
Likelihood Ratio	453.2357	3	<.0001
Score	437.9948	3	<.0001
Wald	365.9897	3	<.0001

Data Source: NHIS2010, Centers for Disease Control and Prevention.

Model 1					
Parameter	df	Estimate	Standard Error	Wald Chi-Square	Pr > ChiSq
Intercept	1	2.7841	0.0378	5413.6761	<.0001
zBYSES	1	0.7217	0.0365	389.9710	<.0001
Model 2					
Intercept	1	2.7216	0.0433	3949.2397	<.0001
zBYSES	1	0.7909	0.0463	291.9829	<.0001
zBYSES2	1	0.0973	0.0338	8.2752	0.0040
Model 3					
Parameter	df	Estimate	Standard Error	Wald Chi-Square	Pr > ChiSq
Intercept	1	2.7582	0.0480	3303.3788	<.0001
zBYSES	1	0.8809	0.0677	169.4428	<.0001
zBYSES2	1	0.0615	0.0369	2.7786	0.0955
zBYSES3	1	−0.0471	0.0255	3.4259	0.0642

Data Source: NHIS2010, Centers for Disease Control and Prevention.

Following modest cleaning, eliminating DIFCHISQ > 10, we have much stronger results (Enrichment Figure 7.6).

Enrichment Table 7.8 Retention and SES Following Data Cleaning Eliminating DIFCHISQ >10

Testing Global Null Hypothesis: BETA = 0			
Test	Chi-Square	df	Pr > ChiSq
Likelihood Ratio	1346.7934	3	<.0001
Score	1120.1784	3	<.0001
Wald	218.6174	3	<.0001

Data Source: NHIS2010, Centers for Disease Control and Prevention.

Analysis of Maximum Likelihood Estimates					
Parameter	df	Estimate	Standard Error	Wald Chi-Square	Pr > ChiSq
Intercept	1	8.5346	0.5146	275.0821	<.0001
zBYSES	1	13.8257	1.2869	115.4211	<.0001
zBYSES2	1	8.8874	0.9990	79.1443	<.0001
zBYSES3	1	1.8043	0.2397	56.6467	<.0001

Data Source: NHIS2010, Centers for Disease Control and Prevention.

Thus, we begin with an effect that was only significant in a linear sense and end with some rather strong curvilinear effects by modest data cleaning.

Enrichment Figure 7.6

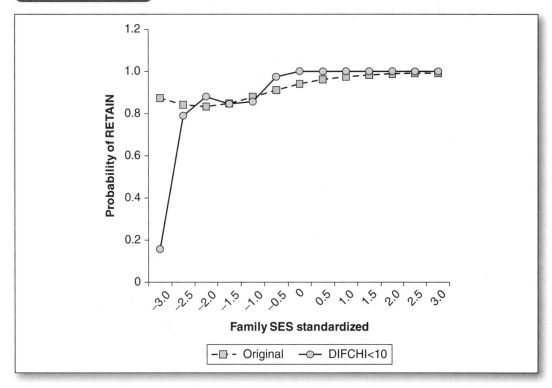

Data Source: NHIS2010, Centers for Disease Control and Prevention.

SYNTAX EXAMPLES

Example SPSS Syntax to create squared and cubed terms for exploring curvilinearity:

```
compute zBYACH2=zBYACH**2.
compute zBYACH3=zBYACH**3.
execute.
```

Example SPSS Syntax to perform logistic regression entering squared and cubed terms on separate steps:

```
LOGISTIC REGRESSION VARIABLES EVER_MJ
/METHOD=ENTER zBYACH
/METHOD=ENTER zBYACH2
/METHOD=ENTER zBYACH3
/SAVE=DFBETA ZRESID
/PRINT=CI(95)
/CRITERIA=PIN(0.05) POUT(0.10) ITERATE(20) CUT(0.5).
```

Example SAS syntax to enter variables one at a time on separate steps:

```
PROC LOGISTIC DATA=book.ELS2002 descending ;
MODEL GRADUATE = ZBYSES;
;
run;
PROC LOGISTIC DATA=book.ELS2002 descending ;
MODEL GRADUATE = ZBYSES ZBYSES2
;
run;
PROC LOGISTIC DATA=book.ELS2002 descending ;
MODEL GRADUATE = ZBYSES ZBYSES2 ZBYSES3
/selection=none sequential;
run;
```

The above syntax might not be the most elegant, but it allows for direct comparison of separate models by comparing change in −2LL and regression equation at each step. There are options if you use stepwise entry methods to accomplish this with one command (such as the "sequential" command), but stepwise entry methods have the potential to produce problematic outcomes under certain circumstances (like a regression model that includes zBYSES and zBYSES^3 but not zBYSES^2). Thus, I prefer the above method that provides absolute control to the analyst.

REFERENCES

Aiken, L. S., & West, S. (1991). *Multiple regression: Testing and interpreting interactions* Thousand Oaks, CA: Sage.

Box, G. E. P., & Tidwell, P. W. (1962). Transformation of the independent variables. *Technometrics,* 531–550.

Boyce, M. S., & Perrins, C. M. (1987). Optimizing great tit clutch size in a fluctuating environment. *Ecology, 68*(1), 142–153. doi: 10.2307/1938814

Cohen, J., Cohen, P., West, S., & Aiken, L. S. (2002). *Applied multiple regression/ correlation analysis for the behavioral sciences.* Mahwah, NJ: Lawrence Erlbaum.

DeMaris, A. (1993). Odds versus probabilities in logit equations: A reply to Roncek. *Social Forces, 71*(4), 1057–1065. doi: 10.2307/2580130

8

LOGISTIC REGRESSION WITH MULTIPLE INDEPENDENT VARIABLES

Opportunities and Pitfalls

Those individuals who visit doctors are more likely to die than those who do not—a significant and replicable correlation in the literature. Do we have an epidemic of homicidal doctors rampaging through our society? Or is it, perhaps, an artifact of another variable? Perhaps people who are more ill, and therefore more likely to die, are those most likely to visit doctors. Or perhaps there is a curvilinear effect, such that those most likely to visit doctors are either very health conscious or very ill, and the former group are much less likely to die and the latter group much more likely to die. Regardless of what is truly going on, we cannot begin to think about answering these questions with the techniques we have explored thus far. In this chapter, we will explore logistic regression with multiple independent variables and the nonlinear (interaction) effects of those multiple variables.

We have been exploring different examples from publicly available data throughout the book thus far. One example that I was excited to explore was the finding from Chapter 6 that former smokers had higher probability of being diagnosed with diabetes than nonsmokers or current smokers. On the surface, this seems a bit nonsensical—why would smoking status and diabetes be linked, and why would only former smokers be at higher risk for diabetes? My naïve theory (remember, I am a psychologist, not an epidemiologist or medical doctor) was that those who quit smoking were more likely to gain weight, which is a primary predictor of diabetes (as we saw in previous chapters with our body mass index [BMI] analyses). Of course, we also have analyses showing that age is a predictor of diabetes. So perhaps older folks are more likely to quit smoking and are also more likely to be diagnosed with diabetes, and perhaps there is really no direct relationship between smoking cessation and diabetes; rather, perhaps it is an artifact related to age.

Our other examples, such as predictors of graduation or dropout in high school, might be equally intriguing and simultaneously unsatisfying. For example, our findings that student achievement and family socioeconomic status predict whether a student graduates high school are interesting but don't explain why. If the previous examples have felt unsatisfying, if you have found yourself saying, "Yeah, but what about . . ." every time you read an example, that is a good sign. In most sciences, outcomes we care about are determined by complex sets of factors, and our statistical models need to at least attempt to represent those complexities. In this chapter, we begin putting together models that allow us to look at multiple predictors and also interactions between predictors, which allow us to look at phenomena in more interesting ways. By the end of this chapter, you will be modeling outcomes as a function of multiple predictors, their interactions, and perhaps even curvilinear interactions!

◆ THE BASICS OF MULTIPLE PREDICTORS

In simple logistic regression[1] analyses, we have thus far modeled a single predictor as:

$$\text{Logit}(\hat{Y}) = b_0 + b_1 X_1$$

Which of course can be generalized (and was introduced in Chapter 2) to look like this:

$$\text{Logit}(\hat{Y}) = b_0 + b_1 X_1 \ldots b_k X_k$$

---

[1]Note that the same principles apply for ordinary least squares (OLS) regression, which are covered in superb fashion in many other places. I will not reproduce them here, but interested readers should refer to Aiken and West (1991); Cohen, Cohen, West, and Aiken (2002); and Pedhazur (1997).

Indeed, when we talked about dummy coding variables in Chapter 6 and curvilinear effects in Chapter 7, we already introduced the procedural aspects of adding more than one "variable" to the equation, although in those examples we were adding multiple things to an equation in order to represent different aspects of a *single variable*. In this case, let us assume that we are truly adding a second, conceptually distinct variable to the equation.

WHAT ARE THE IMPLICATIONS OF THIS ACT? ◆

When we only have one variable in a logistic regression equation, we can answer the question: "Does this variable have a significant/important relationship to the outcome?" The simple act of including two or more predictor variables in a logistic regression equation allows us to answer an important and interesting question: "What is the *most important* predictor of the outcome?"

When looking at simple (one-predictor) equations, it is difficult to assess relative importance of variables. Sure, family socioeconomic status (SES) is important to academic outcomes, but is it *more important or less important* than prior academic achievement? And perhaps even more intriguing, are SES and achievement independent predictors of SES, or do they interact in some way such that the effect of achievement is dependent upon level of SES, or vice versa?

When two or more variables are in the logistic regression equation, the effect of each variable is assessed controlling for all other variables in the equation. In other words, what we are getting is an estimate of the *unique* effect of a particular variable above and beyond the effects of all other variables in the equation, which can be very informative and useful. Let us take a concrete example predicting high school graduation we have explored from previous chapters.

When looking at family SES,[2] we see that variable accounts for a significant amount of variance in graduation. The initial $-2\log$ likelihood for the model was 9967.24, and once SES entered the equation, it was reduced to 8739.91, a reduction of 1227.33 ($\chi^2_{(1)} = 1227.33$, $p < .0001$). The variable statistics are represented in Table 8.1.

It should not be surprising that SES is a significant predictor of graduation, with an odds ratio of 2.83, and a 95% CI of 2.66–3.02. We have seen this information before in previous chapters. Similarly, we can look at

---

[2]Converted to *z*-scores.

Table 8.1 Simple Logistic Regression Equation With Only SES in the Equation

		B	SE	Wald	df	Sig.	Exp(B)	95% CI for Exp(B)	
								Lower	Upper
Step 1	zSES	1.041	.033	1018.355	1	.000	2.831	2.656	3.018
	Constant	2.740	.037	5409.564	1	.000	15.480		

Data Source: National Education Longitudinal Study of 1988 (NELS88), National Center for Educational Statistics, U.S. Department of Education.

whether eighth-grade achievement test scores[3] predicts graduation. Again, starting with a −2 log likelihood of 9967.24, once ACH is in the equation −2LL is reduced to 8475.86, a reduction of 1491.38 ($\chi^2_{(1)}$ = 1491.38, $p < .0001$). At first glance, the two models both seem strong, with ACH having a bit larger of an effect (i.e., the model misfit was improved more by adding that variable than the other variable with only the intercept in the equation). The variable statistics reflect this as well (Table 8.2).

In this case, the odds ratio is a bit higher (3.89, 95% CI of 3.58, 4.23). Of course, this tells us important information—that both variables are strongly related to graduation. But SES and achievement also tend to be strongly correlated—in this case, the simple correlation between the two variables exceeds $r = .50$, meaning there is substantial overlap in the two variables. It looks as though achievement is the more important predictor from these first simple analyses, but we can do better. We can actually evaluate the unique, independent predictive effects of these two variables.

Table 8.2 Simple Logistic Regression Equation With Only ACH in the Equation

		B	SE	Wald	df	Sig.	Exp(B)	95% CI for Exp(B)	
								Lower	Upper
Step 1	zACH	1.359	.043	1003.838	1	.000	3.891	3.577	4.232
	Constant	2.955	.045	4326.004	1	.000	19.194		

Data Source: NELS88, National Center for Educational Statistics, U.S. Department of Education.

---

[3]Also converted to z-scores.

Note also that combining multiple predictors into a single equation eliminates thorny issues such as the increased chance of Type I errors inherent
in performing several simple logistic analyses. Thus, combining variables
into a single equation has many benefits from controlling Type I error rate
to being able to ask more nuanced questions of the data.

Entering both variables in the same equation yields a significant overall
model. With the initial −2 log likelihood of 9967.24, the model summary shows
a final −2 log likelihood of 8062.99, a reduction of 1904.25 ($X^2_{(2)}$ = 1904.52,
$p < .0001$). This overall model fit improvement has two degrees of freedom
because we entered two variables. Note also that entering the two variables
does *not* produce the same change in −2 log likelihood as simply adding the
effects from the simple logistic regression analyses. The two effects mentioned
above (1491.38 and 1227.33) add to 2718.71, but the change when both are
entered simultaneously was 1904.25, a difference of 814.46. This reflects the
fact that the two predictors are correlated, and thus account for overlapping
variance. If they were perfectly orthogonal (uncorrelated) then there would be
no difference between the added effects of the separate analyses and the
model change when both are entered into the regression equation.

As you can see from Table 8.3, both variable effects are attenuated
somewhat over what they were in the simple regression analyses. The point
estimates for the odds ratios, for example, dropped about 0.8 and 0.9,
respectively.

In OLS regression, these unique effects are captured by semipartial
correlations, which are routinely less than zero-order (simple) correlations.
These are similarly partial or corrected effects—effects corrected for (or
partialing out) other variables. Thus, when student achievement is covaried,
the odds ratio for SES is 2.00, $p < .0001$. Likewise, when SES is covaried,
the odds ratio of ACH is 2.90, $p < .0001$.

Table 8.3 Logistic Regression With Both SES and ACH in the Equation

		B	SE	Wald	df	Sig.	Exp(B)	95% CI for Exp(B)	
								Lower	Upper
	zSES	.695	.036	381.240	1	.000	2.004	1.869	2.149
Step 1	zACH	1.066	.046	543.383	1	.000	2.904	2.655	3.176
	Constant	3.119	.048	4145.332	1	.000	22.613		

Data Source: NELS88, National Center for Educational Statistics, U.S. Department of Education.

Thus, we interpret all effects in the equation as unique effects of that variable controlling for all other variables in the same equation. We can perform the same analysis of residuals and other diagnostic tests we examined in Chapter 4 with multiple predictors, of course, to ensure we have the most generalizable representation of the results.

We do not have to be limited to two predictor variables. We can add student sex (coded 0 = female, 1 = male) to the equation (as shown in Table 8.4).

In this case, sex is not a significant predictor of graduation, once the other variables are in the equation.

Table 8.4 Variables in the Equation

		B	SE	Wald	df	Sig.	Exp(B)	95% CI for Exp(B)	
								Lower	Upper
Step 1	zSES	.693	.036	376.976	1	.000	1.999	1.864	2.144
	zACH	1.069	.046	542.835	1	.000	2.913	2.663	3.187
	sex	−.055	.059	.875	1	.350	.947	.844	1.062
	Constant	3.147	.057	3005.791	1	.000	23.265		

Data Source: NELS88, National Center for Educational Statistics, U.S. Department of Education.

◆ EXAMPLE SUMMARY OF PREVIOUS ANALYSIS

Prior to analysis, both socioeconomic status (SES) and student achievement (ACH) were converted to z-scores (standard normal distribution) and entered simultaneously into the equation. With an initial −2 log likelihood of 9967.24 and final −2LL of 8062.99, the model represented a significant improvement in fit ($\chi^2_{(2)}$ = 1904.52, p < .0001). As you can see in Table 8.3, both SES and ACH were significant unique predictors of graduation. Specifically, after controlling for all other variables in the analysis, as SES increased, the probability of graduation increased (odds ratio = 2.00 [95%CI = 1.87, 2.15]). Similarly, after controlling for all other variables in the analysis, increases in student achievement were associated with increased probability of graduation (odds ratio = 2.90 [95%CI = 2.66, 3.18]). Because these variables were standardized, each odds ratio represents the increase in odds of graduation for every increase of 1 standard deviation in either SES or ACH. (If you were summarizing this analysis, you would also talk about the nonsignificance of the interaction or you would be discussing the significant interaction in more detail.) To put these effects into perspective, students who come from families two standard deviations below the mean have an 84.93% percent chance of graduating high school, while students who come from families that are two standard deviations above the mean have a 98.91% chance of graduating (assuming average achievement, held constant). Likewise, holding SES constant at the mean, a student with achievement scores two standard deviations below the mean would have a 72.85% chance of graduation, whereas a student with achievement scores of two standard deviations above the mean would have a 99.48% chance of graduation.

DIFFERENT METHODS OF ENTRY ♦

There are several methods of entering variables into the equation, depending on your goals for the analysis. In general, the methods fall into two groups: analyst-controlled and software-controlled. I will start off this section by telling you that some fields have strong biases against software controlled entry (which includes procedures like stepwise, forward, or backward entry). All forms of entry were developed to address specific needs, and software-controlled entry procedures were developed with legitimate goals in mind.

User-Controlled Methods of Entry

The most widely used and most widely accepted is simultaneous or forced entry. In this entry method, the analyst tells the software what variables to enter, they are all entered at once (simultaneously), and that is the end of it. This is one of the most common and most accepted methods of entry because it is often theory driven—meaning that the analysis is proceeding based on prior theory or research, and as such is supposedly more defensible. That is the method of entry I use most often.

Hierarchical Entry

A variant of the user-controlled simultaneous entry is hierarchical (forced order) entry, where the user specifies which variables enter the equation in which order. Each variable represents a unique step, and each time a variable is entered into the equation. In OLS regression, we can compare the increment in R and R^2 that is attributable to that particular variable, in addition to examining how the individual effects of other variables already in the equation change as a result of entry of that variable. This often allows us to draw conclusions that are theoretically important, such as whether a particular variable's effect is spurious or whether a particular variable adds any unique predictive effect over that of those variables already in the equation. Of course, in logistic regression we do not look at R and R^2 (nor do I advocate the use of their *pseudo*-variants) but rather can look at overall model fit in −2 log likelihood increments. One thing I do not like about the labeling of this procedure as "hierarchical" entry is the potential for confusion with *hierarchical linear modeling* (HLM), which is a completely different procedure with completely different goals, methods, and so on and will be discussed in Chapter 13.

Blockwise Entry

A variant of hierarchical entry, this entry method allows us to enter blocks of variables in groups, rather than individually, assessing change in model fit and individual variable effects after each *group* of variables are entered. For example, we could have a group of variables that represent covariates (variables we need to have in the equation but are not substantively interested in), a group of variables that represent a theoretically coherent group, and another group of variables that represents another coherent group. To illustrate this example, let's refer to Figure 8.1, which I adapted from a recent article with my colleague Brett Jones (Osborne & Jones, 2011). As you can see in Figure 8.1, we hypothesize a rather complicated model to explain motivation and academic outcomes for students.

In a blockwise entry scheme, we could enter all antecedent variables (e.g., race, sex, family environment, etc.) as one group of variables; we could then enter identification with academics, goals, beliefs, and on as a group. After entering that second block, we could look at change in model fit and so forth as a function of the entire block of variables in addition to the individual variables. We could then enter a third block of variables representing the choices group of variables labeled choices, persistence, and effort, and again assess the contribution of this group of variables to the overall model.

This is particularly useful when you have dummy or effects coded variables but want to assess them as a single effect. As we covered previously, three dummy coded variables that represent smoking status are not

Figure 8.1 Precursors and consequences of identification with an academic domain

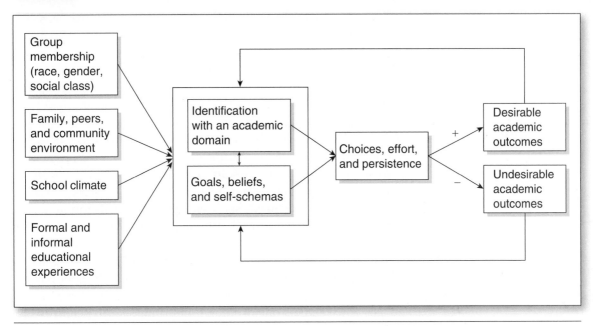

Source: Adapted from Osborne, J. W., & Jones, B. D. (2011). Identification with academics and motivation to achieve in school: how the structure of the self influences academic outcomes. *Educational Psychology Review, 23*(1), 131–158. doi: 10.1007/s10648-011-9151-1. Used with kind permission from Springer Science and Business Media.

three separate variables, but rather three terms that collectively account for one variable. Using blockwise entry, we could enter the three dummy coded variables representing smoking on a single block, assessing the overall effect of the variable in the individual model.

One important thing to keep in mind is that it does not matter how a variable gets into a regression equation. Once a particular set of variables are in the equation, their parameters are all estimated simultaneously controlling for all other variables in the equation, and thus the results are identical regardless of the order in which they were entered, whether they were entered all at once or one at a time or in groups or blocks. What will be different is the information you get in looking at incremental change in the model.

Software-Controlled Entry

Stepwise entry is an innocuous-sounding method of entry that has been part of statistical modeling for a long while. Stepwise methods were developed to let researchers automatically comb through large data sets to empirically select an optimal set of variables that best predict an outcome. For example, if you are analyzing a database (such as our NCES database examining dropout/graduation) with many thousands of data points and more than 2,000 variables, *and* if you do not have a theoretical basis for choosing variables, then you could imagine stepwise regression methods might be valuable to help you identify important predictor variables. I also suspect that stepwise methods can help identify *unexpected* results, which are often more interesting than expected results.[4] So if I were only interested in best predicting who will drop out or graduate from among the hundreds of variables available to me, I can run a stepwise regression analysis, and the software will identify variables with the largest predictive effects and enter them for you into the equation. I might discover variables that make sense are the best predictors (e.g., indicators of academic achievement), but it might be the case that something unusual is a strong predictor (e.g., shoe size). If you only care about creating the best prediction equation, this might be a good path for you. An unexpected result such as shoe size predicting dropout risk could also lead to new discoveries about the nature of the phenomenon (it it could get you laughed out of your profession; see Fleischmann, Pons, & Hawkins, 1989).

There are probably important applications for stepwise methods in many fields from medicine and business to the social sciences, and particularly in the "big-data" movement that has recently emerged. But you should know that in the academic literature, there has been significant pushback against these methods in recent decades (e.g., Cohen et al., 2002; Thompson, 1995), particularly within the social sciences. Specifically, many authors argue that atheoretical analyses lead to less valuable analyses than theory-driven analyses (although I might disagree, depending in particular on the application). One of the biggest criticisms of this approach is that stepwise techniques will capitalize on chance quirks in your data, which may lead to nonreproducable results (but see my article on prediction equations and cross-validation of regression analyses for a method to test reproducibility; Osborne, 2000, 2008). Thompson (1995) outlines some other serious challenges to the use of these methods, including issues with incorrect degrees of freedom and inability to identify a best variable set of a given size. However, Cohen et al. (2002) do concede that stepwise

---

[4]Unless you are analyzing your dissertation data. In this case, you definitely want only your expected results, or more precisely, the results expected by your dissertation chair and committee.

methods are less problematic when (a) the research goal is entirely predictive, as discussed above, (b) sample size is very large (to reduce odds of spurious results due to capitalization on chance), (c) number of variables is reasonable (they suggest a ratio of 40:1 for sample size to variable number), and (d) results are cross-validated (as I discuss in my papers). The easy availability of resampling techniques (which we will discuss in later chapters) also makes this potentially less of an issue, as researchers can test whether a particular solution is routine and generalizable.

There are two basic approaches to stepwise regression: forward entry and backward elimination, and often a "hybrid" version that leverages both forward entry and backward elimination. In forward entry, we start with a blank slate, and all variables are assessed for their potential predictive power. The variable with the single greatest relationship is entered into the equation, and then all remaining variables are assessed as to whether they add significant predictive power to the equation above that variable in the equation. The next strongest predictor is added, and the process continues until no variable rises above a particular threshold. In backward elimination, all variables are put in the equation and the non-significant ones are removed from the equation one at a time based on criteria similar to that used in forward entry. Once all variables in the equation are above the threshold for elimination, the equation is finalized. Depending on software used, there might be various hybrid techniques available. For example, if forward entry is used, it is possible that a variable entered early in the process has become a nonsignificant predictor once other variables are in the equation. In some procedures, those variables could be dropped from the analysis and reassessed. Likewise, in backward elimination, it is possible that a variable eliminated from the equation early on would be significant at a later point after other variables are removed. Hybrid processes can handle these situations, but again have benefits and drawbacks.

One significant objection I have to these processes is that they cannot take into account nonlinear relationships (curvilinear relationships) or interactions. We have already seen examples of curvilinear effects that would not enter an equation. Later in this chapter, we will see interaction terms that are important and not modeled in these methods. Finally, data cleaning is not straightforward in these situations. It is entirely possible that a variable has a strong effect but that without data cleaning the variable is not recognized as important. Because stepwise methods cannot easily handle these issues, which eliminates many important effects from being examined, I do not endorse it except as an exploratory technique.

◆ COLLINEARITY ISSUES

Collinearity issues can happen when predictor variables are highly correlated with each other. This has been discussed in previous chapters but is a particular issue when introducing multiple independent variables—thus, we will revisit it briefly here. While highly correlated variables are problematic, linearly dependent variables are particularly devastating to an analysis.

Linearly dependent variables are those that are either identical, inverses, or sums of other variables. For example, if I had three subscales (SUB1, SUB2, and SUB3) and a total score that was the sum of those three subscales, entering all three subscales *and* the total score can result in failure of the model to converge or in the failure of one or more of the variables to enter the equation. Another example of this sort of issue is entering a variable and then a transformation of that same variable (e.g., SES and zSES). When I attempted this in SPSS, I received the following error message:

Warnings

> Due to redundancies, degrees of freedom have been reduced for one or more variables.

This linear dependency is usually simple to modify. In this case SPSS refused to enter both variables, and I can choose which version I want and perform the analysis again.

But when variables are closely correlated odd things can happen. For example, I transformed zSES so that zSES_v2 is correlated at

Table 8.5 Example of High Collinearity Among Two Predictors

		Score	df	Sig.
Step 0	Variables zSES	1167.513	1	.000
	zSES_v2	1112.529	1	.000
	Overall Statistics	1321.861	2	.000

Omnibus Tests of Model Coefficients		Chi-square	df	Sig.
	Step	1247.025	2	.000
Step 1	Block	1247.025	2	.000
	Model	1247.025	2	.000

Variables in the Equation		B	SE	Wald	df	Sig.	Exp(B)	95% CI for Exp(B)	
								Lower	Upper
	zSES	−1.407	.568	6.126	1	.013	.245	.080	.746
Step 1[a]	zSES_v2	.130	.030	18.473	1	.000	1.139	1.074	1.209
	Constant	−10.356	3.044	11.571	1	.001	.000		

Data Source: NELS88, National Center for Educational Statistics, U.S. Department of Education.

0.99 with zSES. This allows both variables to enter the equation, but because they are highly correlated, they are evaluated controlling for each other.

As you can see in Table 8.5, both versions of SES individually account for substantial improvement in model fit ($X^2_{(1)}$ = 1167.51 and 1112.53, respectively). However, when both are entered, they improve model fit by only 1247.03 collectively. This is a significant clue that high collinearity is present. Further, we know that zSES should have an odds ratio of around 2.0, but these odds ratios are far from 2.00, and further the 95%CIs do not include that value. zSES has an odds ratio of 0.245, which is strong and in the opposite direction it should be, and zSES_v2 has a much weaker odds ratio than expected. This is because each is evaluated taking into account the other.

Collinearity issues also occur when interactions are entered into the model, as we will discuss later. Interaction terms are necessarily collinear with the simple effects, and thus can cause distortion of those simple effects once interactions are in the model. I generally suggest you do not interpret any simple effect of a variable when a complex effect (quadratic/cubic or interaction term) is in the model.

◆ ASSESSING THE OVERALL MODEL—WHY THERE IS NO R^2 FOR LOGISTIC REGRESSION

Those of you used to OLS regression are used to exploring overall model statistics. In OLS regression, we get an F statistic that tests whether the proposed model explains an amount of variance that is significantly different than 0. We also get an effect size, R (and R^2) that tell us the proportion of variance in the dependent variable might be explained from our model.[5] In this way, we get our first look at the goodness of our model—a significance test and an effect size. In simple regression R^2 is the square of the simple correlation between the two variables, and when there are multiple independent variables, it is the sum of the squared semipartial correlations (the unique correlations controlling for all other variables in the equation). When predictors are entered on more than one step, you can ask for (or calculate) the change in R (and R^2) and get a significance test of ΔR (which is also the test for ΔR^2).

It seems as though it should be simple to design analogous indicators for logistic regression. And indeed we do have some similar pieces of information. Some of this was already covered in previous chapters, and as such I will briefly review the basics. The overall summary for a logistic regression analysis has a −2 log likelihood statistic, which tests that all predictors' coefficients are 0.00. We also get a model chi-square. This is the difference between the −2 log likelihood for the initial *independence* model (no predictors in the equation) and the model being evaluated (which may be an intermediate step in the analysis or the final analysis), with degrees of freedom equal to the number of predictors added to the equation. If this chi-square statistic is significant, we can conclude that the model has improved significantly over either the independence model (no predictors) or the previous model. This is conceptually analogous to the F test in OLS regression. The difference is that there is no direct measure of effect size. Of course larger chi-square changes are better than smaller changes, but it is

---

[5] R^2 is easily calculated. We can calculate the total sum of squares (SST) as the sum of all squared differences between each individual score on the dependent variable (Y_i) and the mean of the dependent variable, $\hat{Y}$. The sum of squares for the error term (SSE) is the sum of the squared differences between each predicted value ($\hat{Y}_i$) and the actual score on the dependent variable (Y_i). The regression sum of squares is merely the difference between SST and SSE, and R^2 is SSR/SST (conceptually and literally, the amount of variance accounted for by the independent variables divided by the total possible variance in the dependent variable).

not measured on an absolute scale, and as such, it is difficult to compare non-nested models, whereas in OLS regression we can directly compare non-nested models: an $R^2 = .25$ is better than $R^2 = .10$ and is substantively interpretable. In the former analysis, we are explaining 15% more variance in the outcome than the second. But because the actual values of −2 log likelihoods vary widely from analysis to analysis, is a change from −2 log likelihood = 17000 to 16000 (chi-square of 1000) equal in magnitude and change in prediction as a change from −2 log likelihood = 5000 to 4000 or from −2 log likelihood= 1500 to 500? Probably not.

It is definitely legitimate to compare nested models, and lower −2 log likelihood indicates better fit within that particular set of nested models, but it is not legitimate to compare −2 log likelihood across non-nested models (different samples, or different dependent variable within the same sample, for example).

Those of us with roots in OLS regression yearn to know the answer to the questions "How much variance am I accounting for?" or "How good is my model?" Unfortunately, these are questions that are more challenging to answer in logistic regression. Conceptually, the difference between the −2 log likelihood for the independence model and the saturated model (which is perfect fit) is analogous to the SST—the goodness or lack of fit in the model. This is also sometimes referred to as *deviance*. Once predictor variables are entered into the model, the −2 log likelihood is a reduced amount of lack of fit and is now conceptually similar to SSE. The difference between the two can be thought of as SS_R—the amount of the model goodness of fit or deviance that is reduced by the independent variables. So it should be simple to construct an R^2 analogue, by dividing SSR/SST (model chi-square by deviance [0 minus the −2 log likelihood for the independence model]). This is essentially the approach taken in calculating the Nagelkerke R^2.

Other variants (e.g., Cox & Snell R^2, the contingency coefficient R^2, the Wald R^2, the Brier index, to name merely a few of the proposed options) have been proposed, but none seem to be universally accepted and to be without serious conceptual or mathematical problems. Menard (2010, pp. 45–57) has an extensive and thorough examination of the options, and DeMaris (2002) also reviews many of the common options through Monte Carlo study. Based on several studies, conceptual ambiguities, and personal experience, my conclusion is that none of them should be used as they tend to be contradictory and problematic. For example, in one analysis, I performed for another purpose produced the following information from SPSS:

Table 8.6 Model Summary

Step	−2 Log likelihood	Cox & Snell R Square	Nagelkerke R Square
1	507.465	.050	.438

Data source: Author data.

These statistics (which are not altered in any way from the SPSS output I saw) encapsulate, in an extreme way, the issue with these statistics in logistic regression. Which of the two R^2 analogues do I report? The one I *want* to report is the Nagelkerke R^2 = .44, rather than the Cox & Snell R^2 = .05, but there is no clear way for me to determine which is most accurate. And in fact, throughout my writing of this book, I routinely saw these two differ, often substantially, and not always in predictable ways.

More to the point, I don't think we need this statistic at all. In structural equation modeling, we have a similar issue, and seemingly endless possible indicators of goodness of fit (AIC, NFI, CFI, RMSEA, chi-square, etc.). That literature has not come to consensus as to what model fit statistics to report and how to evaluate them after several decades of development. Thus, I recommend against focusing on one specific index of overall model fit, and either report many (as I often do in structural equation modeling analyses) or report only the basic −2 log likelihoods and chi-square change statistics. The reality is that we have quantitative indicators of model goodness, but we also have qualitative indicators as well, such as the classification tables. Depending on your goal, it might be more important to have good classification than strong R^2 analogues.

◆ INTERACTIONS

Aiken and West (1991, pp. 4–5) note that although procedures for examining nonadditive models (i.e., interactions, curvilinearity) in regression have been in the literature since the 1960s, most published research involving multiple regression ignores both interaction and curvilinear effects. This is a shame, as complex effects such as interactions and curvilinear effects are often more interesting or important than simple effects. For example, what if our SES and Achievement variables interacted in predicting graduation such that family SES only mattered when students were low-performing and that high-performing students tended to have the same probability of graduating regardless of family SES?

What Is an Interaction?

As mentioned in Chapter 4, we assume that models are correctly specified. When one creates a regression equation, researchers are making an explicit statement (although they may not realize it). In this type of analysis, we assert the relationship of each predictor to the outcome of interest is modeled by a line that represents slope of the regression line. By not modeling an interaction, we are asserting that the slope of X_1 (SES) is constant regardless of where a person is on the other variable (i.e., achievement). Let's look at a regression equation containing an interaction term (X_1 multiplied by X_2):

$$\text{Logit}(\hat{Y}) = b_0 + b_1 X_1 + b_2 X_2 + b_3 X_1 X_2$$

In analysis of variance–type analyses, interactions are routinely checked because most statistical software packages model them by default. In most regression applications I am aware of, regression interactions must be created by the researcher and entered manually. If you as a researcher do not enter this term, you are asserting that the coefficient b_3 is 0: that there is no interaction or that the slope b_1 is constant across the range of b_2. While this is sometimes true, it is impossible to know whether it is true unless we actually test whether b_3 is different from 0.

Procedural Issues in Testing for Interactions Between Continuous Variables

Interactions are tested by entering the cross-product of two other variables (e.g., X_1 and X_2). When we are dealing with continuous variables, those variables should already be centered at 0 by virtue of conversion to z-scores as a best practice.

Because the interaction term and the individual variables are collinear (often highly so), it is good practice to enter cross-products on a separate step so that we can first assess the unique direct (simple) effects of the variables and then the effects of their cross-products. Once the cross-products are in the equation, it is not wise to interpret the effects of the variables as the collinearity will distort those effects. Indeed, if there are significant interactions between two variables, you should not substantively interpret their simple effects, as those simple effects are modified by the interaction term.[6]

Dichotomous predictors are routinely coded as 0 and 1, and as such can be directly multiplied with continuous variables. Categorical (polytomous) variables that are unordered are more complex, and must first be converted to dummy coded variables before multiplying each dummy variable by the other continuous variable.

When you enter groups of variables, your statistical software will give you statistics on how the model changed. For example, with sex, zSES, and zACH in the equation, the model −2 log likelihood was 8062.12, which was significant as mentioned earlier. Although sex was not significant as a predictor at that stage, it is sometimes the case that nonsignificant variables can have interaction effects. Thus, it was retained and I tested for three two-way interactions: sex *zACH, sex*zSES, and zACH *zSES.

When these three terms are entered on a second step in a blockwise fashion, the −2 log likelihood dropped to 8043.75. The test for whether this block of variables accounted for a significant improvement in the model is ($\chi^2_{(3)} = 18.37$, $p < .0001$). Although small, the effect is significant, and because interactions are usually collinear with their main effects, it is not necessarily an indication of a lack of importance. This is because much of the overlapping variance is already accounted for by the simple (main) effects of the variables.

As you can see in Table 8.7, sex of student does not have any significant interaction effect with either zSES or zACH, and as such could be entirely dropped from the model (unless you are going to test for three-way[7] interactions such as sex*zACH*zSES). However, you can also see that there is a significant interaction between SES and achievement. I find it not terribly useful to attempt direct interpretation of the effects at this point. Instead, my bias is to graph the interaction to make interpretation easier for both researcher and reader.

Graphing interactions is a source of contention among statisticians. I will not review all the controversies here but rather will focus on a few general principles: (a) you should graph interaction effects within reasonable,

---

[6]Again, this is like asserting that Drug X will cure you, or Drug Y will cure you, but taking both drugs simultaneously will kill you. The simple effect of either Drug X or Y is immaterial when both are present in the equation. Feel free to substitute your own random romantic relationship analogy here if you desire (i.e., if only girlfriend X is present in the room life is wonderful, and if only girlfriend Y is present life is fabulous, but if both were to be present in the same room at the same time . . .).

[7]Feel free to insert routine statistical double entendre here. I am not going to.

Table 8.7 Variables and Interactions in the Equation

	B	SE	Wald	df	Sig.	Exp(B)	95% CI for Exp(B)	
							Lower	Upper
zSES	.884	.067	175.666	1	.000	2.421	2.125	2.760
zACH	1.197	.073	272.162	1	.000	3.312	2.872	3.818
sex	−.124	.102	1.492	1	.222	.883	.723	1.078
zACH x zSES	.212	.052	16.903	1	.000	1.236	1.117	1.368
zACH by sex	−.034	.092	.135	1	.714	.967	.807	1.158
zSES by sex	−.054	.071	.570	1	.450	.948	.825	1.089
Constant	3.240	.078	1741.313	1	.000	25.529		

Data Source: NELS88, National Center for Educational Statistics, U.S. Department of Education.

realistic boundaries; (b) you should focus the graph so that it communicates the effect to the reader in the clearest possible way; and (c) you should interpret the effect for the reader, including both nature and implications of the effect as well as magnitude of the effect.

When I graph interactions using ± 2 *SD* (*z*-score of −2 and +2 representing "low" and "high"), I am representing some relatively extreme scores, but they are clearly within the bounds of the observed data. That is most defensible, as projecting beyond the observed data is risky. However, regression lines were made for prediction, and thus prediction of scores outside the observed data is defensible, if done carefully and with good data to support it. I would suggest that effects be graphed only within reasonable ranges, however. While graphing an interaction with age might produce spectacularly impressive effects if you use 1 and 99 years of age, if you are dealing with the adult population, you should probably stick to reasonable adult ages, such as 18–80. Following these simple rules helps keep you out of trouble on the X axis.

There is great controversy over the Y axis. Some statisticians believe you should always represent the 0 (origin) so that readers can get a realistic picture of where the interaction falls in relation to that 0 point. And while this might make sense, there are cases where this is not ideal. Let us take a fictitious example of a simple crossover interaction that involves annual income. As you can see in Figure 8.2, this represents a nice, strong effect. And if we are dealing with professionals in this income range, an income of 0 is not realistic or interesting. But some authors argue that 0 must be included in the graph or that the entire theoretical range of the variable should be graphed. As you can see in Figure 8.3, this obfuscates[8] the nature of the effect when the point of graphical representation is to clarify communication. Thus, I would argue that it is acceptable to focus the Y axis on the observed range of the variable so as to communicate the nature of the effect clearly. It is not defensible to artificially restrict the range of the interaction to make it appear to be larger or more important than it should be. Thus, we have a decision rule for the Y axis.

Figure 8.2 Fictitious Interaction Graphed Without the Origin

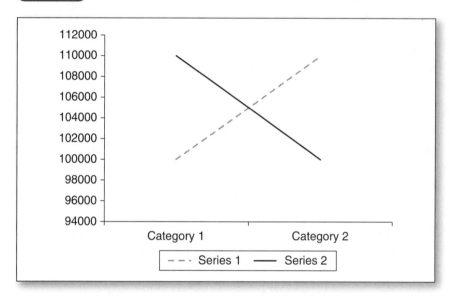

Interpreting the effect for the reader is probably the trickiest part of all. We can look at magnitude of $\Delta \chi^2$, but since interactions are highly collinear with the simple effects of each variable, the $\Delta \chi^2$ is often small for interactions, which may or may not appropriately capture the importance of the effect. There is no way to make an objective decision rule here. You, as researcher, much guide the reader on the implications of your interaction. This is helped by graphing in predicted probabilities, in my opinion, as readers can intuitively understand them.

---

[8]I have been a fan of National Public Radio's *Car Talk* program for longer than I care to admit. I am not sure if they invented this word or merely popularized it.

| Figure 8.3 | Fictitious Interaction Graphed With the Origin and Expanded Range |

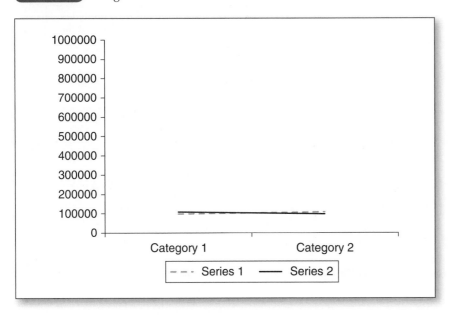

Procedural Issues With Graphing

It is important to center continuous variables by converting to *z*-scores prior to creating interaction terms (Aiken & West, 1991). This simplifies interpretation *and graphing,* as we have already seen in the last chapter. The first thing we need to do is remove effects that are irrelevant to the interaction (i.e., sex) by entering 0 for them (we will hold sex constant at 0, which removes it from the equation). This gives us a regression line equation of:

$$\text{Logit}(\hat{Y}) = 3.24 + 0.884(\text{zSES}) + 1.197(\text{zACH}) + 0.212(\text{zSES*zACH})$$

The next step is to create predicted values that will allow us to represent the interaction. To do this, I will estimate six points that I will use to graph the three groups that will illustrate the interaction:[9]

---

[9]Because these are linear effects, two points for each line are sufficient to model each line. For curvilinear interactions, we will want to model more points for each effect.

Table 8.8 Graphing an Interaction Effect With Two Continuous Variables

	zSES	zACH	zSESxzACH	Predicted Logit	Predicted Probability
low-low	−2	−2	4	−0.074	0.482
low-avg.	−2	0	0	1.472	0.813
low-high	−2	2	−4	3.018	0.953
high-low	2	−2	−4	1.766	0.854
high-avg.	2	0	0	5.008	0.993
high-high	2	2	4	8.25	0.999

Data Source: NELS88, National Center for Educational Statistics, U.S. Department of Education.

Because I have converted continuous variables to z-scores, we can use −2 to represent LOW regardless of the variable and +2 to represent HIGH

Figure 8.4 Interaction of SES and Achievement Predicting Graduation

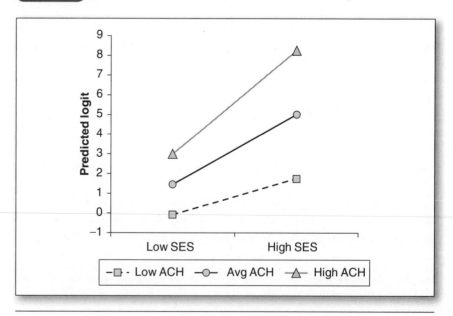

Data Source: NELS88, National Center for Educational Statistics, U.S. Department of Education.

(following the same logic). Zero is also fine to use as an "average" group if you desire that.

In early chapters in this book, I argued that converting predicted logits back to predicted conditional probabilities provided readers with more easily interpretable results (and more accurate results). I will again illustrate this point through this example. In graphing predicted logits, it becomes clear that as SES increases, the rate of graduation increases. It also is clear that this effect is more pronounced for high-ACH individuals. In other words, student achievement matters in predicting graduation, but the effect of student achievement depends upon the nature of that student's family SES. But due to the nature of logarithmic transformations, this graph does not accurately reflect the actual probabilities of graduation, which is why we must convert logits to conditional probabilities, as discussed earlier.

The actual graduation rates are presented below in Figure 8.5.

Figure 8.5 Observed Probabilities for Three Groups; Groups With *N* < 10 Are Not Represented

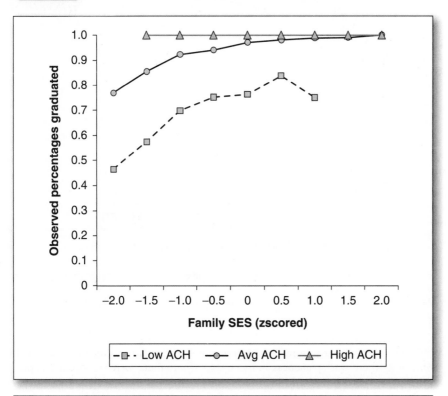

Data Source: NELS88, National Center for Educational Statistics, U.S. Department of Education.

As you can see from the actual observed probabilities, the interaction graphed in logits is misleading—it leads researchers to conclude the biggest gap between high- and low-achieving students is found in high-SES students when in fact the actual probabilities reflect the opposite—that at the higher SES ranges, there is a much smaller gap than at the low SES range.[10]

As you can see in Figure 8.6, when these predicted logits are converted to predicted probabilities, we see a very different (and more accurate) picture of graduation than that of Figure 8.4. As this final graph indicates, students with high achievement are highly likely to be retained regardless of family SES, whereas SES is much more influential on those with low achievement.

Figure 8.6 Interaction of SES and Achievement Graphed as Probabilities

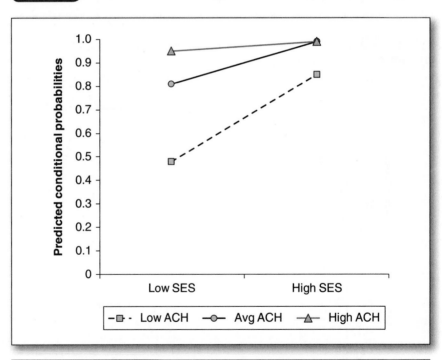

Data Source: NELS88, National Center for Educational Statistics, U.S. Department of Education.

[10]This graph is adapted from the dropout graph presented in Chapter 4. You will remember there was sparseness in those data where there were no students representing the very low-SES and high-ACH groups. This is found here as well.

You may still note that this is not a strong representation of the actual probabilities. But it is a more accurate representation of the observed probabilities than the graph of the interaction in logits. That is because the relationships are nonlinear, but the logistic regression equation does not account for that nonlinearity. Nonlinear interactions are complex creatures, and we will explore their applications a bit later in the chapter.

EXAMPLE SUMMARY OF INTERACTION ANALYSIS ♦

The previous summary of SES and ACH seems to be modified by a significant interaction. In this case, the direct effects should be downplayed because they are modified by the interaction. I will start the write-up below as though I already described the main effects (which I have).

> Following creation of the cross-product terms for ACH, SES, and sex, all three interaction terms were entered together on a separate block following entry of the main effects. Addition of these variables significantly improved the model fit ($\chi^2_{(3)}$ = 18.37, $p < .0001$). As you can see from TABLE X (*which would be an extension of the previous summary table you created to include the information in Table 8.7*), only one interaction was significant: the interaction of ACH and SES. To explore the nature of the interaction more fully, we graphed the regression line equation assigning a value of −2 for "low," 0 for "average," and +2 for "high." All values were converted from logits to conditional probabilities and graphed in FIGURE X (*where you would have something similar to Figure 8.6 in this chapter*). As you can see in FIGURE X, which graduation probabilities tend to increase as family SES increases, the effect is much stronger for low-achieving students. The effect of SES appears to be much less dramatic for average students, and almost nonexistent for high-achieving students. Thus, the effect of either achievement or SES must be considered in the context of the other variable.

INTERACTIONS BETWEEN CATEGORICAL AND ♦ CONTINUOUS VARIABLES

We have seen in previous chapters how it is possible to represent categorical variables such as race or smoking status through appropriate coding schemes like dummy coding. Using the same NELS88 graduation data, we will now explore whether and how race and eighth-grade family SES interact in predicting graduation status. In this data set, we will use race as a four-category variable, with Asian/Pacific Islander coded 1 ($N = 1,527$), Latino/Hispanic coded 2 ($N = 3,171$), Black/African American coded 3 ($N = 3,009$), and White/Caucasian coded 4 ($N = 16,317$).[11] In the United Sates in 1988, Caucasian was the largest group of students and commonly the comparison group for research. Thus, we will assign Caucasian to be the reference group in the dummy variable coding scheme as follows:

Table 8.9 Dummy Coded Race Variables

Race[12] category:	Original value	DUM1	DUM2	DUM3
Asian/Pacific Islander	1	1	0	0
Hispanic/Latino	2	0	1	0
Black/African American	3	0	0	1
White/Caucasian	4	0	0	0

On the first block, I entered all three dummy coded variables, which accounted for a significant increment in model fit improvement (original $-2LL$ = 10155.27, final $-2LL$ = 9909.57, $\Delta\chi^2_{(3)}$ = 245.70, significant at $p < .0001$). Thus, race accounts for a small but significant amount of variance in graduation. As you can see from the variable summary, all three racial groups are significantly different from Caucasian. Dum1 is significant, with an OR= 1.82, indicating that the odds of Asian/Pacific Islander students graduating are 1.82

---

[11]There were not enough students classified as "Native American/Inuit," and "multiracial" was not an available classification when these data were gathered. These, along with those students who had multiple answers or were missing an answer were removed from these analyses. Combined with those missing data on the outcome variable and SES, this left 16,895 in the analysis.

[12]I have been doing research on "race" and "ethnicity" since the early 1990s. I am sensitive to the fact that race/ethnicity variables are at best gross approximations of categories that are largely socially constructed, and as such find myself conflicted whenever I present an example including this variable. Anyone thinking seriously about race or ethnicity as a variable must acknowledge that it is necessarily imprecise. Yet at the same time, within many cultures, the social construction of race and/or ethnicity is a powerful influence on daily life. Thus I present examples involving race and/or ethnicity only as examples of the methodological process, not as an endorsement for the way this variable is conceptualized or coded in the data I use to generate these examples.

that of Caucasian students. Dum2 is significant, indicating that the odds of Hispanic/Latino students graduating are 0.41 that of Caucasian students, and Dum3 is significant, indicating that the odds of Black/African American students graduating are 0.47 that of Caucasian students. Not desirable, but not surprising given what we know of the educational environment from the late 1980s and early 1990s in the United States.

Entering zSES on the second step produced an expected improvement in model fit (original $-2LL = 10155.27$, $-2LL$ for block 1 = 9909.57, $-2LL$ for block 2 = 8874.16, $\Delta \chi^2_{(1)} = 1035.41$, significant at $p < .0001$), indicating that zSES accounts for a significant model improvement above that of race. As you can see in Table 8.10, as zSES increases 1 standard deviation, the odds of graduation are 2.785 that of a student with zSES one *SD* lower. Interestingly, when zSES is added to the model, two of the dummy variables (the Hispanic/Latino vs. Caucasian and Black/African American vs. Caucasian contrasts) become nonsignificant, while the first dummy variable remains significant (and actually strengthens a bit). Further, zSES is significant after controlling for race. This suggests that zSES is at least partially mediating, or explaining, the racial effects of graduation. In other words, once we control for family zSES, there are no differences in graduation rates between Caucasian students and either Black/African American or Hispanic/Latino students. Asian/Pacific Islander students are much more likely to graduate than Caucasian students, even after controlling for zSES.

In order to test for the interaction of family zSES and race, we must compute interaction terms for zSES and each dummy coded variable: zSES*DUM1, zSES*DUM2, and zSES*DUM3. These then get entered as a block on the third step in the analysis. For this step, the final $-2LL$ was 8811.51 ($\Delta \chi^2_{(3)} = 62.65$, significant at $p < .0001$). I do not find it helpful to attempt to interpret odds ratios or logits for complex terms like quadratic or interaction terms, so at this point we will construct our regression equation and attempt to graph the results. The final estimates from this block are at the bottom of Table 8.10 (see page 270). The regression line equation we are going to graph, derived from the final step of the analysis in Table 8.10, is:

$$\text{Logit}(\hat{Y}) = 2.7976 + 0.3688(\text{DUM1}) - 0.6027(\text{DUM2}) - 0.4788(\text{DUM3}) + 1.2479(\text{zSES}) - 0.5738(\text{DUM1* zSES}) - 0.5870(\text{DUM2* zSES}) - 0.4997(\text{DUM3* zSES}).$$

Because the dummy variables are all either 0 or 1, most of the terms will drop out when we graph lines by race. For example, if we graph a RACE × SES line for Caucasian students, we will substitute 0 for all DUM1–3

Table 8.10 Predicting Graduation From Dummy Coded Race Variables

Analysis of Maximum Likelihood Estimates						
Parameter	df	Estimate	Standard Error	Wald Chi-Square	Pr > ChiSq	Exp(Est)
Intercept	1	2.5432	0.0351	5259.0101	<.0001	12.721
dum1	1	0.6001	0.1579	14.4347	0.0001	1.822
dum2	1	−0.9019	0.0689	171.0145	<.0001	0.406
dum3	1	−0.7603	0.0772	98.0016	<.0001	0.468
Block 2						
Intercept	1	2.6854	0.0394	4636.4290	<.0001	14.664
dum1	1	0.6674	0.1635	16.6662	<.0001	1.949
dum2	1	−0.0980	0.0760	1.6649	0.1969	0.907
dum3	1	−0.0941	0.0836	1.2674	0.2603	0.910
zSES	1	1.0243	0.0347	871.4525	<.0001	2.785
Block 3						
Intercept	1	2.7976	0.0448	3892.9264	<.0001	16.405
dum1	1	0.3688	0.1715	4.6251	0.0315	1.446
dum2	1	−0.6027	0.1057	32.5110	<.0001	0.547
dum3	1	−0.4788	0.1139	17.6847	<.0001	0.620
zSES	1	1.2479	0.0464	722.9487	<.0001	3.483
dum1*zSES	1	−0.5738	0.1531	14.0391	0.0002	0.563
dum2*zSES	1	−0.5870	0.0870	45.5306	<.0001	0.556
dum3*zSES	1	−0.4997	0.0953	27.5178	<.0001	0.607

Data Source: NELS88, National Center for Educational Statistics, U.S. Department of Education.

terms, leaving just the intercept and zSES. When we graph a line for African American students, all terms with a DUM1 or DUM2 will drop out as those students have 0 for those variables. We will make a simple graph with just low and high SES for each group (substituting −2 or 2 for zSES).

Table 8.11 Calculations for Interaction of RACE × SES

	Dum1	Dum2	Dum3	zSES	zSES *DUM1	zSES *DUM2	zSES *DUM3	LOGIT	exp	prob
Low SES										
Caucasian	0	0	0	−2	0	0	0	0.3018	1.352291	0.574882
Asian	1	0	0	−2	−2	0	0	1.8182	6.160759	0.86035
Latino	0	1	0	−2	0	−2	0	0.8731	2.394322	0.70539
African American	0	0	1	−2	0	0	−2	0.8224	2.275956	0.694746
Hi SES										
Caucasian	0	0	0	2	0	0	0	5.2934	199.0189	0.995
Asian	1	0	0	2	2	0	0	4.5146	91.34102	0.989171
Latino	0	1	0	2	0	2	0	3.5167	33.67312	0.971159
African American	0	0	1	2	0	0	2	3.8152	45.38583	0.978442

Data Source: NELS88, National Center for Educational Statistics, U.S. Department of Education.

As you can see in Table 8.11 and Figure 8.7, we have an interesting interaction between family SES and race. When I am attempting to explain an interaction effect, I usually start with the simple effect I put on the X axis. Thus, I would explain this as: in general, the probability of graduation increases as family SES increases. However, you can see that the effect of family SES differs across groups. For example, SES seems to have the most profound effect on Caucasian students, while Asian students appear to be least affected by family SES.

INTERACTIONS AND DATA CLEANING ◆

As with our discussion in Chapter 7 concerning curvilinear trends, interaction terms are equally susceptible to influence from influential cases, and as such it is appropriate to examine your interaction analyses for potentially problematic cases. In this analysis, for example, DIFCHISQ ranged from 0.0001 to more than 190, with the 99th percentile being 19.88 and the 95th percentile being 4.74. I will use a very conservative cut score of 15, which

Figure 8.7 Interaction of RACE and SES

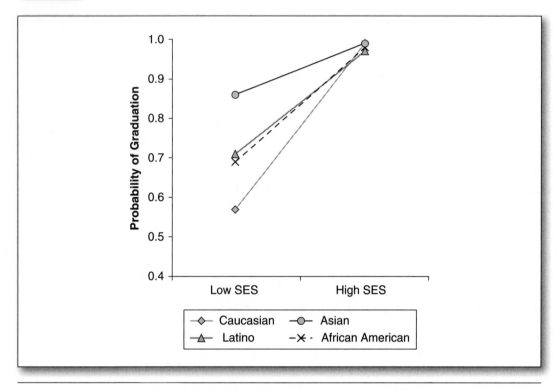

Data Source: NELS88, National Center for Educational Statistics, U.S. Department of Education.

left us with an *N* of 16,649—a loss of 246 cases. However, the change in −2LL from initial model to final was 1986.53 as compared with 1343.76 prior to data cleaning. Even though these are not directly comparable models as they have different sample sizes, the dramatically stronger change in model fit is notable. The results are presented in Table 8.12.

Other notable things include the nonsignificant interaction term DUM1*zSES. You have to keep in mind that this term is but one part of the interaction. Thus, while this particular aspect does not show a $p < .05$, the other two aspects do, and combined they account for a significant change in model fit (−2LL for model without interaction terms is 7118.59, with the terms it is 6940.33; $\Delta \chi^2_{(3)} = 178.26$ significant at $p < .0001$). Thus we need to model the entire interaction. The results are not strikingly different from those prior to data cleaning, except showing a stronger effect. Using the new regression line equation and the same type of table as above, the interaction is presented in Figure 8.8.

Table 8.12   Interaction of RACE and SES After Cleaning Data With DIFCHISQ < 15

Analysis of Maximum Likelihood Estimates						
Parameter	df	Estimate	Standard Error	Wald Chi-Square	Pr > ChiSq	Exp(Est)
Intercept	1	3.5982	0.0701	2634.0339	<.0001	36.533
dum1	1	1.1690	0.4037	8.3843	0.0038	3.219
dum2	1	−1.3558	0.1205	126.6011	<.0001	0.258
dum3	1	−1.0936	0.1347	65.9037	<.0001	0.335
zSES	1	1.9242	0.0650	875.1451	<.0001	6.849
dum1*zSES	1	−0.4235	0.2786	2.3102	0.1285	0.655
dum2*zSES	1	−1.2269	0.0992	153.0721	<.0001	0.293
dum3*zSES	1	−1.0345	0.1102	88.1258	<.0001	0.355

Data Source: NELS88, National Center for Educational Statistics, U.S. Department of Education.

Figure 8.8   Race and SES Interaction After Data Cleaning

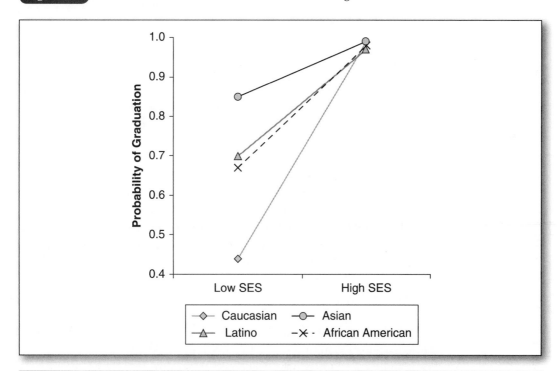

Data Source: NELS88, National Center for Educational Statistics, U.S. Department of Education.

◆ CURVILINEAR INTERACTIONS

To this point in the book, we have explored both curvilinear effects and interactions. It is not beyond the realm of possibility that there could be curvilinear interactions—that different groups could have different curves, or that interactions could have curves rather than lines. Aiken and West (1991) have an excellent chapter on how complex terms can be incorporated into equations such as this. The complexity comes into the varieties of combinations of linear and curvilinear components we can have. Following Aiken and West's lead, and for simplicity here, let us refer to the outcome as Y, the first predictor as X, and the second predictor as Z. Let us assume that there is curvilinearity in X only, and that X and Z interact. If we create the quadratic term X^2 by squaring the z-scored version of X, then we could constitute a simple curvilinear logistic regression equation as:

$$\text{Logit}(\hat{Y}) = b_0 + b_1 X + b_2 X^2$$

Remember, X and X^2 are the same variable—they are just different aspects of the same variable (the linear and the curvilinear). Now we can add the second variable, Z, to the equation:

$$\text{Logit}(\hat{Y}) = b_0 + b_1 X + b_2 X^2 + b_3 Z$$

This is where the fun begins. If there is an interaction between X and Z, we represent the interaction as the cross-product of X and Z. But now that there is a curvilinear component to X, we must cross Z with both aspects of X to fully explore the interaction:

$$\text{Logit}(\hat{Y}) = b_0 + b_1 X + b_2 X^2 + b_3 Z + b_4 XZ + b_5 X^2 Z$$

And now that we are into it, there is no reason to assume that only one variable would have a curvilinear component (if both variables are continuous—binary variables cannot by definition have curvilinear effects). So let us add the Z^2 term to the equation:

$$\text{Logit}(\hat{Y}) = b_0 + b_1 X + b_2 X^2 + b_3 Z + b_4 Z^2 + b_5 XZ + b_6 X^2 Z + b_7 XZ^2 + b_8 X^2 Z^2$$

This final regression equation shows both linear and curvilinear effects, the linear interaction, the linear by curvilinear interactions, and the curvilinear interaction. Of course, we could generalize this "basic" curvilinear equation to more complex forms, including cubic terms, third variables and so forth. But I would suspect that if you can master this particular example you could methodically explore other variations on this theme. To add a cubic effect of only X, the equation would be expanded as X^3 is crossed with every term:

$$\text{Logit}(\hat{Y}) = b_0 + b_1X + b_2X^2 + b_3X^3 + b_4Z + b_5XZ + b_6X^2Z + b_7X^3Z$$

and to add a curvilinear component of Z to this equation that included Z^2 and Z^3, we simply cross those terms with the others already in the equation:

$$\text{Logit}(\hat{Y}) = b_0 + b_1X + b_2X^2 + b_3X^3 + b_4Z + b_5Z^2 + b_6Z^3 + b_7XZ + b_8X^2Z+$$
$$b_9XZ^2 + b_{10}X^2Z^2 + b_{11}X^3Z + b_{12}X^3Z^2 + b_{13}XZ^3 + b_{14}X^2Z^3 + b_{15}X^3Z^3$$

Exploring interactions of any type, but especially curvilinear interactions, is an exercise in managing complexity. Thus, in order to keep track of effects and ensure you are appropriately crossing all effects, I recommend using a table such as the one I used to construct the above equation, wherein I delineate every term needed to fully express the interaction:

Thus, as you can see above, there should be 15 terms in an equation such as this (in addition to the intercept) to fully express just the curvilinear interaction with squared and cubed terms. You can see how complexity grows rapidly as one moves from linear interactions (3 terms needed) to quadratic interactions (8 terms needed) to cubic interactions (15 terms needed). Of course, if you had more than two independent variables, you would need to do this for every combination of independent variables you wished to test.

Let us continue our example of student achievement and SES predicting student retention in high school from earlier in the chapter to give concreteness to this concept. My personal recommendation for tackling this sort of complex analysis is to take each step at a time, carefully and methodically.

Table 8.13   Composing All Cross-Products for a Curvilinear Interaction Equation

	X	X^2	X^3
Z	XZ	X^2Z	X^3Z
Z^2	XZ^2	X^2Z^2	X^3Z^2
Z^3	XZ^3	X^2Z^3	X^3Z^3

Step 1: Create the Terms Prior to Analysis

Statistical packages vary in how easy they are to use in their two most common modes (graphical user interface or programming/syntax interface). In some programs, you can create squared and interaction terms "on the fly" while programming the analysis, and in others it is less simple.[13] Therefore, I simply avoid the issue and create the squared and interaction terms prior to analysis. Remember to always create these interaction and quadratic terms from the variables that were converted to z-scores. Then we want to create the following terms to fully explore the model:

- ACH^2
- SES^2
- $ACH * SES$
- $ACH * SES^2$
- $ACH^2 * SES$
- $ACH^2 * SES^2$

Step 2: Build Your Equation Slowly

One of the first mentors I had in regression (Harry Reis, from University of Rochester) always encouraged us to seek parsimony where possible. He would argue, I think, that we want to value the simplest model that best explains the data. Using this principle, we want to enter the simplest effects first, and the most complex effects last. Of course, we also have mathematical considerations. We have to enter simpler terms (linear effects of each variable) before the more complex (curvilinear or interaction) effects.

I would start the investigation of this analysis by entering ACH and SES on the first block of variables, and ACH^2 and SES^2 on the second block to see which of the variables have curvilinear effects, as described in previous chapters when we were looking at curvilinearity. If either does not have a significant curvilinear component, that substantially simplifies the situation. Recall from earlier in this chapter that both SES and ACH have significant unique effects, as we see again from the first block of the model summarized in Table 8.14.

---

[13]In both SAS and SPSS, if you are using syntax you can merely specify X, Z, and $X*Z$ in the model statement without first creating the $X*Z$ term in the data. Interestingly, in SPSS, this capacity is not present in OLS regression modeling.

Table 8.14 Summary of Curvilinear Interaction Model Before Data Cleaning

Model	−2LL	Δ −2LL	$p <$ for Δ −2LL
Intercept only	9967.24	—	—
Step 1: zSES, zACH	8062.99	1904.25	.0001
Step 2: zSES², zACH²	8051.86	11.13	.004
Step 3: zSES by zACH	8031.78	20.08	.0001
Step 4: zSES² by zACH, zSES by zACH², zSES² by zACH²	8029.03	2.75	not significant

Data Source: NELS88, National Center for Educational Statistics, U.S. Department of Education.

Table 8.15 Variables in the Equation

		B	SE	Wald	df	Sig.	Exp(B)	95% CI for Exp(B)	
								Lower	Upper
Step 1	zSES	.695	.036	381.240	1	.000	2.004	1.869	2.149
	zACH	1.066	.046	543.383	1	.000	2.904	2.655	3.176
	Constant	3.119	.048	4145.332	1	.000	22.613		
Step 2	zSES	.810	.056	208.151	1	.000	2.248	2.014	2.509
	zACH	.975	.057	292.324	1	.000	2.652	2.371	2.966
	zACH²	−.097	.044	4.851	1	.028	.907	.832	.989
	zSES²	.086	.032	7.329	1	.007	1.090	1.024	1.159
	Constant	3.129	.053	3457.709	1	.000	22.859		
Step 3	zSES	.937	.064	215.232	1	.000	2.552	2.252	2.892
	zACH	1.047	.060	304.965	1	.000	2.848	2.532	3.203
	zACH2	−.163	.045	13.049	1	.000	.849	.777	.928
	zSES2	.042	.033	1.626	1	.202	1.042	.978	1.111
	zACH by zSES	.239	.052	20.767	1	.000	1.269	1.146	1.407
	Constant	3.237	.060	2924.655	1	.000	25.447		

Data Source: NELS88, National Center for Educational Statistics, U.S. Department of Education.

When the quadratic components are entered, we see a small but significant increment in model fit and two significant curvilinear effects. Adding the linear interaction term (SES*ACH), we see another significant increment in goodness of fit for the model. At this point, I will add all remaining terms to the model on the fourth and final step. Unfortunately, this step did not significantly improve model fit above what was included in the first three blocks of variables, with a $\Delta{-}2LL$ of 2.75, $p < 0.43$.

However, there were indicators of tremendously influential data points. Standardized residuals (Figure 8.9) ranged from 1.22 to -25.87 (and DfBetas, not shown here, were equally dramatic). As you can see in Figure 8.9, these were mostly contained to the nongraduated group. When dealing with these complex interactions, I think it is best to be very cautious in cleaning the data. You do not want tremendously influential cases, creating a false effect or masking one. In this case, we have no effect, and I suspect that the influential

Figure 8.9 Standardized Residuals From Curvilinear Interaction Example

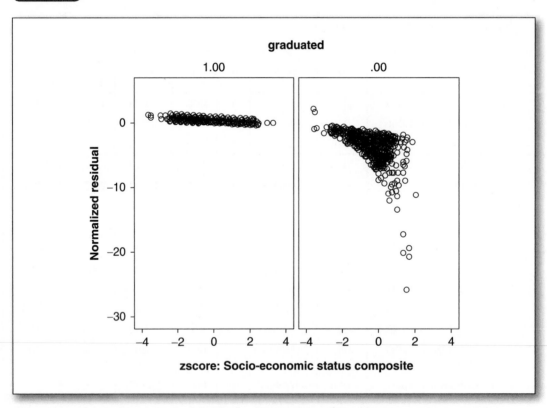

Data Source: NELS88, National Center for Educational Statistics, U.S. Department of Education.

cases are masking one that is there. But if I am too aggressive, I might eliminate the effect rather than reveal it. Thus, I will use $z = -5$ as a cutoff initially. This removes just less than 100 cases, shrinking our sample size from 16608 to 16511. Doing so reveals our significant curvilinear interaction.

As you can see in Tables 8.16 and 8.17, the final block of terms representing the fully expressed curvilinear interaction is significant. The final summary of the variable effects is:

Table 8.16 Summary of Curvilinear Interaction Model After Data Cleaning

Model	−2LL	Δ−2LL	$p <$ for Δ−2LL
Intercept only	9486.68	—	—
zSES, zACH	7256.97	2229.71	.0001
zSES by zACH	7163.50	93.47	.0001
zSES², zACH²	7153.59	9.92	.007
zSES² by zACH, zSES by zACH², zSES² by zACH²	7097.97	55.62	.0001

Data Source: NELS88, National Center for Educational Statistics, U.S. Department of Education.

Table 8.17 Final Step of Curvilinear Interaction Analysis After Data Cleaning zRE < 5

	B	SE	Wald	df	Sig.	Exp(B)	95% CI for Exp(B)	
							Lower	Upper
zACH	2.704	.251	115.612	1	.000	14.933	9.123	24.444
zSES	2.451	.226	117.926	1	.000	11.603	7.455	18.060
zACH by zSES	2.709	.435	38.778	1	.000	15.012	6.400	35.215
zACH²	.633	.148	18.236	1	.000	1.883	1.408	2.517
zSES²	.685	.111	37.860	1	.000	1.984	1.595	2.468
zACH by zSES²	.851	.195	19.160	1	.000	2.343	1.600	3.431
zSES by zACH²	.913	.235	15.104	1	.000	2.493	1.573	3.952
zSES² by zACH²	.229	.108	4.539	1	.033	1.258	1.019	1.553
Constant	3.882	.121	1029.937	1	.000	48.520		

Data Source: NELS88, National Center for Educational Statistics, U.S. Department of Education.

This leaves us with a final logistic regression equation of:

$$\text{Logit}(\hat{Y}) = 3.882 + 2.704(zACH) + 2.451(zSES) + 2.709(zACH*zSES)$$
$$+0.633(zACH^2) + 0.685(zSES^2) + 0.851(zACH * zSES^2) +$$
$$0.913(zSES * zACH^2) + 0.229 (zSES^2 * zACH^2)$$

When figuring curvilinear effects, more than two points per line are required, so we will use values ranging from −2 to 2 (by 0.5 increments) for SES and −2 (low) and 2 (high) and 0 (average) for ACH to attempt to replicate the observed probabilities in Figure 8.10 and represent the nature of the interaction across a reasonable range of the variables without complicating the graph unnecessarily.

A "simple" linear interaction indicates that the slopes of a regression line are different for different values of another variable. A curvilinear interaction indicates that the shape of the curves is different for different values of

Figure 8.10 Curvilinear Interaction Between Achievement and SES After Data Cleaning

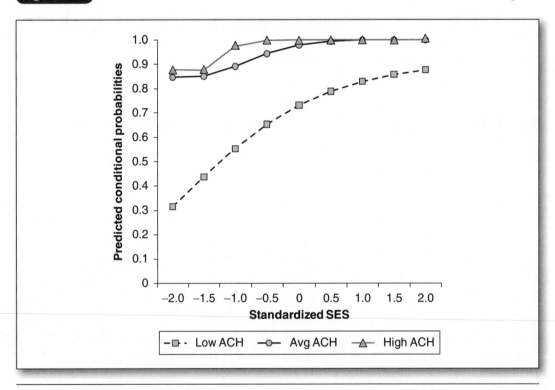

Data Source: NELS88, National Center for Educational Statistics, U.S. Department of Education.

another variable. In this case, we see a clear quadratic curve for relatively low-achieving students, indicating that the probability of graduation increases as SES increases, asymptoting slightly as SES tends toward relatively high values. For students with average or high achievement, the effect of SES is much less pronounced. The probabilities of graduation are higher and quickly asymptote toward 1.0 as SES increases.

CURVILINEAR INTERACTIONS WITH ♦ CATEGORICAL VARIABLES

The mechanics of this interaction are similar to the previous categorical interaction we explored, RACE by zSES. In this case, we only can explore curvilinear effects with continuous variables like zSES. The dummy variables merely remain themselves and are not raised to powers. Thus, our table of cross-products looks like this:

Table 8.18 Composing All Cross-Products for a Curvilinear Interaction Equation

	X	X^2	X^3
Dum1	X Dum1	X^2 Dum1	X^3 Dum1
Dum2	X Dum2	X^2 Dum2	X^3 Dum2
Dum3	X Dum3	X^2 Dum3	X^3 Dum3

Following the same blockwise entry scheme as before, I would enter the 3 dummy variables in a block, then zSES, then the linear interaction terms, then the quadratic interaction terms, then the cubic interaction terms. Doing this on the same DIFCHISQ cleaned data ($N = 16649$) as before yields the significant improvements in model fit at every step except the last, as summarized in Table 8.19 (see page 282). Although the last step was close to significance, we will eliminate that step as not significantly improving the model and focus on the quadratic interactions.

In Table 8.20 (see page 282), I present the last significant step of the model for the sake of saving some space. Since the last block had significant improvement to model fit, the prior blocks are not necessarily worth interpreting. Note how the odds ratios for certain terms get surprisingly

Table 8.19 Summary of Curvilinear Interaction Model After Data Cleaning

Model	−2LL	Δ−2LL	$p <$ for Δ−2LL
Intercept only	8926.86	—	—
Dum1, Dum2, Dum3	8540.81	386.05	.0001
zSES, zSES^2, zSES^3	6950.01	1590.80	.0001
zSES×DUM1, zSES×DUM2, zSES×DUM3	6835.11	114.90	.0001
zSES^2×DUM1, zSES^2×DUM2, zSES^2×DUM3	6780.46	54.65	.0001
zSES^3×DUM1, zSES^3×DUM2, zSES^3×DUM3	6774.65	5.81	.12

Data Source: NELS88, National Center for Educational Statistics, U.S. Department of Education.

large—this is due to collinearity issues that frequently arise when interactions are in the equation. These should not be interpreted substantively (as I have cautioned before) and we should rather perform interpretation subsequent to the graphing of the results.

Table 8.20 Summary of Last Significant Step in Model

	B	SE	Wald	df	Sig.	Exp(B)	95% CI for Exp(B)	
							Lower	Upper
dum1	4.916	2.080	5.583	1	.018	136.399	2.312	8046.207
dum2	−1.868	.161	134.484	1	.000	.154	.113	.212
dum3	−1.556	.177	76.988	1	.000	.211	.149	.299
zSES	3.907	.250	245.122	1	.000	49.764	30.513	81.161
zSES^2	1.522	.190	64.447	1	.000	4.582	3.160	6.643
zSES^3	.202	.049	16.653	1	.000	1.223	1.110	1.348
zSES by dum1	5.872	3.300	3.166	1	.075	355.094	.551	228788.970

	B	SE	Wald	df	Sig.	Exp(B)	95% CI for Exp(B)	
							Lower	Upper
zSES by dum2	−2.730	.288	89.795	1	.000	.065	.037	.115
zSES by dum3	−2.410	.327	54.305	1	.000	.090	.047	.170
zSES² by dum1	2.165	1.268	2.917	1	.088	8.718	.726	104.635
zSES² by dum2	−.793	.134	35.020	1	.000	.453	.348	.588
zSES² by dum3	−.738	.152	23.496	1	.000	.478	.355	.644
Constant	3.954	.111	1267.285	1	.000	52.121		

Data Source: NELS88, National Center for Educational Statistics, U.S. Department of Education.

Figure 8.11 Curvilinear Interaction Between RACE (Dummy Coded) and Family SES

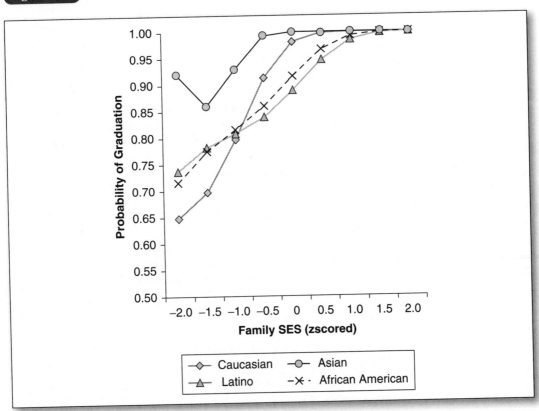

Data Source: NELS88, National Center for Educational Statistics, U.S. Department of Education.

If you compare this graph to Figure 8.8 (the linear version of this interaction), you will see that the substantive conclusions are not terribly different—SES seems to affect Caucasian students more and Asian students least. However, this graph gives a bit more nuance to the story. For example, at about mean SES, Asian and Caucasian students are roughly equal in probability of graduation, while the traditionally disadvantaged minority students lag behind until about one standard deviation above the mean. Likewise, the disadvantaged minority groups have higher probability of graduation at low SES levels than Caucasian students, but this graph shows that effect crosses over around one standard deviation below the mean. Thus, for the majority of the distribution (−1 to 1 SD, which covers about 68% of a normally distributed population), Latino and African American students have lower graduation probabilities than the other two groups. These interesting nuances cannot be gleaned from the linear interaction alone. And of course, let me once more remind you that these data have not been weighted appropriately to take into account sampling, so these results are merely for our statistical amusement, not for substantive discussion.

SUMMARY

In this chapter, we covered several topics related to logistic regression with multiple predictors. First, we covered methods of entry (and highlighted the potential drawbacks of computer-controlled entry). Next, we covered interpretation of variables with other variables in the equation. Specifically, once more than one variable is in the equation, all variables are estimated as unique effects controlling for all other variables in the equation. Thus, when SES and student achievement are both in the equation, they are unique effects controlling for the other variable.

We also covered problematic aspects of multiple variables, such as multicollinearity, and we reviewed (briefly) why summary statistics like pseudo-R^2 statistics are probably best avoided. Finally, we reviewed procedural and conceptual issues around testing for interaction effects between independent variables (both categorical and continuous). For those of you with an appetite for statistical adventure, I include a brief discussion of curvilinear interaction terms and how to test them and graph them—which is little more than a generalization of the previous chapter and this chapter to a special case.

The issues we covered in this chapter relate to two important concepts in advanced statistical modeling—mediation and moderation. In mediation, you covary potential mediators to see whether a specified relationship (i.e., relationship between race and graduation) is partially or fully explained by another variable (e.g., SES). If the original relationship is substantially reduced or eliminated, you can propose that partial mediation has occurred. Baron and Kenny and others (Baron & Kenny, 1986; Hayes, 2009; Zhao, Lynch, & Chen, 2010) have written detailed and thorough explanations and evaluations of methodology for assessing mediation. I encourage you to refer to them—I do!

Moderation is the concept that one variable moderates, or affects, another relationship. In other words, the regression slope of one variable predicting another (e.g., the relationship between SES and graduation) might be different for different groups or different levels of another variable (e.g., race). Interaction effects are classic examples of moderator effects, and Baron and Kenny (1986) and others have talked at length about evaluating this type of effect as well.

We are now on our way to a thorough mastery of the basic (and some highly advanced) aspects of logistic regression. Congratulations, and enjoy working through the challenging enrichment examples below.

ENRICHMENT

1. Download data from the book website (www.sagepub.com/osbornebplr) and replicate the analyses presented in the chapter.

2. Download National Health Interview Survey (NHIS) data set for this chapter from the book website and:

   a. Examine whether the effect of smoking status (similar to dummy coded variables we performed in Chapter 6) is reduced or eliminated once you enter BMI (z-scored) as a covariate.

      i. Be sure to examine the analysis for influence/leverage and clean appropriately.

   b. Explore whether BMI (z-scored) interacts with smoking status in predicting diabetes status. If so, graph the interaction and explain the effect so that a nontechnical audience could understand the interaction.

   c. Explore whether BMI has a curvilinear effect after smoking status has been covaried.

   d. Explore whether BMI (standardized) has a curvilinear interaction with smoking status. In this case, entering $BMI^2 \times DUM1$,

BMI^2 × DUM2, and BMI^2 × DUM3, will serve as there is no such thing as a curvilinear effect with a dummy coded variable.

e. In addition to testing for whether there is a quadratic curvilinear interaction, see if there is a cubic curvilinear interaction.

3. Using the same data set as #2, see if age and BMI interact in predicting diabetes.

a. Is there a simple interaction?

b. Is there a curvilinear interaction?

4. Using your own (or an advisor's) data, explore whether your variables interact (simple or curvilinear). Be particularly careful to watch for inappropriately influential data points while doing so!

ANSWER KEY

Enrichment #2

Enrichment Table 8.1 Variables in the Equation

		B	SE	Wald	df	Sig.	Exp(B)	95% CI for Exp(B) Lower	95% CI for Exp(B) Upper
Step 1	dum1	.607	.047	165.336	1	.000	1.834	1.672	2.012
	dum2	−.088	.109	.661	1	.416	.915	.740	1.133
	dum3	.026	.062	.170	1	.680	1.026	.908	1.160
	Constant	−2.393	.029	6749.127	1	.000	.091		
Step 2	dum1	.565	.048	135.790	1	.000	1.760	1.600	1.935
	dum2	−.078	.110	.504	1	.478	.925	.745	1.148
	dum3	.051	.064	.644	1	.422	1.053	.929	1.193
	zBMI	.559	.018	975.266	1	.000	1.748	1.688	1.811
	Constant	−2.521	.031	6611.931	1	.000	.080		
Step 3	dum1	.573	.052	120.199	1	.000	1.773	1.600	1.964
	dum2	−.058	.117	.242	1	.623	.944	.750	1.188
	dum3	.046	.068	.445	1	.505	1.047	.916	1.196
	zBMI	.563	.024	537.673	1	.000	1.756	1.674	1.841
	zBMI by dum1	−.016	.041	.152	1	.697	.984	.907	1.067

	B	SE	Wald	df	Sig.	Exp(B)	95% CI for Exp(B)	
							Lower	Upper
zBMI by dum2	−.048	.099	.233	1	.629	.953	.785	1.158
zBMI by dum3	.014	.054	.064	1	.800	1.014	.913	1.126
Constant	−2.523	.032	6213.823	1	.000	.080		

Initial analyses show the expected effect of being a former smoker and show a significant effect of BMI on diabetes, all of which we have covered in previous chapters. It does not appear that BMI substantially alters the effect of smoking status. There also does not appear to be any significant interaction between zBMI and smoking status. However, there appear to be undesirably large standardized residuals in the Diabetic group, as well as large DfBetas. Simple cleaning those below the 1st percentile or above the 99th percentile in DfBeta for the intercept provides a very different result:

Enrichment Figure 8.1

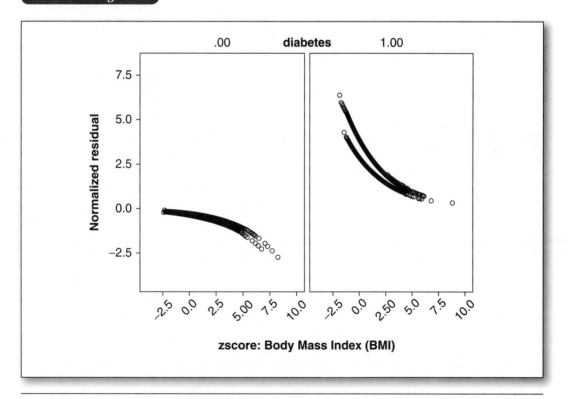

Data source: NHIS2010, Centers for Disease Control and Prevention.

Enrichment Figure 8.2

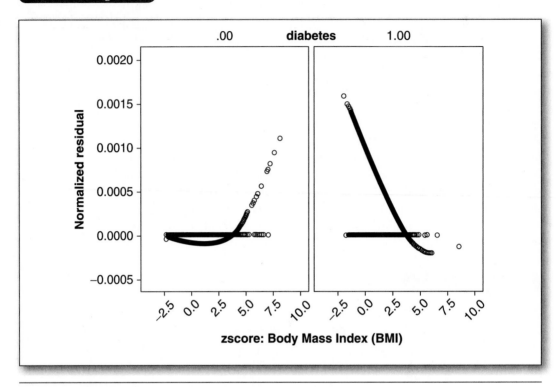

Data source: NHIS2010, Centers for Disease Control and Prevention.

Enrichment Table 8.2 Smoking by zBMI Interaction After Data Cleaning

		B	SE	Wald	df	Sig.	Exp(B)	95% CI for Exp(B)	
								Lower	Upper
Step 3	dum1	1.112	.059	354.033	1	.000	3.041	2.708	3.415
	dum2	.482	.121	15.936	1	.000	1.619	1.278	2.051
	dum3	.585	.074	63.080	1	.000	1.795	1.554	2.074
	zBMI	.842	.029	859.225	1	.000	2.322	2.195	2.457
	zBMI by dum1	−.296	.044	44.661	1	.000	.744	.682	.811
	zBMI by dum2	−.328	.100	10.635	1	.001	.721	.592	.878
	zBMI by dum3	−.266	.056	22.813	1	.000	.766	.687	.855
	Constant	−3.063	.042	5238.991	1	.000	.047		

a. Variable(s) entered on step 1: zBMI * dum1 , zBMI * dum2 , zBMI * dum3.

Data source: NHIS2010, Centers for Disease Control and Prevention.

Enrichment Table 8.3   Predicted Probabilities for Smoking × BMI Interaction

	Dum1	Dum2	Dum3	BMI	int1	int2	int3	logit	exp	prob
LOW BMI										
nonsmoker	0	0	0	−2	0	0	0	−4.7470000	0.008678	0.008603
former	1	0	0	−2	−2	0	0	−3.0430000	0.047692	0.045521
occasional	0	1	0	−2	0	−2	0	−3.6090000	0.027079	0.026365
daily	0	0	1	−2	0	0	−2	−3.6300000	0.026516	0.025831
high BMI										
nonsmoker	0	0	0	2	0	0	0	−1.3790000	0.25183	0.20117
former	1	0	0	2	2	0	0	−0.8590000	0.423585	0.297548
occasional	0	1	0	2	0	2	0	−1.5530000	0.211612	0.174653
daily	0	0	1	2	0	0	2	−1.3260000	0.265537	0.209822

Data source: NHIS2010, Centers for Disease Control and Prevention.

Enrichment Figure 8.3   Smoking by BMI Interaction

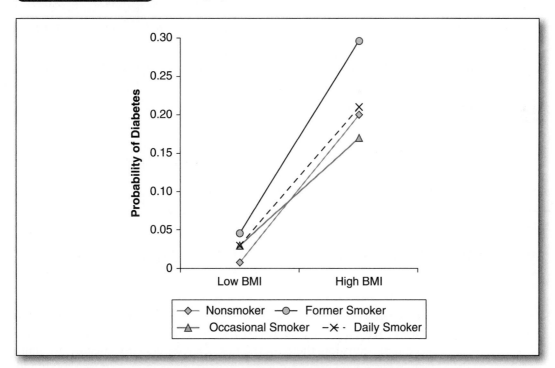

Data source: NHIS2010, Centers for Disease Control and Prevention.

As you can see in Enrichment Figures 8.3 and 8.4, BMI affects each group a bit differently. In general, as BMI increases, the probability of diagnosis increases. However, for former smokers the increase is most dramatic, whereas for occasional or daily smokers the effect of increased BMI is less dramatic.

Cleaning the first five DfBetas (intercept plus four main effects of the dummy variables and zBMI) at ± 6 SD (convert to z-scores for convenience) produced a bit stronger result for the interaction ($X^2_{(3)} = 94.42$, $p < .0001$) and produced the following results:

Enrichment Table 8.4 Variables in the Equation

		B	SE	Wald	df	Sig.	Exp(B)	95% CI for Exp(B)	
								Lower	Upper
Step 1[a]	dum1	.636	.057	124.837	1	.000	1.888	1.689	2.111
	dum2	−5.237	1.196	19.183	1	.000	.005	.001	.055
	dum3	−1.534	.151	102.625	1	.000	.216	.160	.290
	zBMI	.669	.030	509.568	1	.000	1.952	1.842	2.069
	zBMI by dum1	−.018	.046	.153	1	.696	.982	.897	1.075
	zBMI by dum2	1.518	.423	12.874	1	.000	4.564	1.992	10.460
	zBMI by dum3	.644	.085	57.823	1	.000	1.904	1.613	2.248
	Constant	−2.730	.036	5858.461	1	.000	.065		

a. Variable(s) entered on step 1: zBMI * dum1 , zBMI * dum2 , zBMI * dum3

Data source: NHIS2010, Centers for Disease Control and Prevention.

♦ CURVILINEAR EFFECTS WITH BMI AND SMOKING

Using the same (dfbeta0–4) cleaned data as the analysis above, and the same analysis as before, I added BMI^2 after entering the interaction terms, which produced a Δ−2LL of 404.30, $p <$.0001. Even after all interaction terms were in the equation, there is evidence of significant curvilinearity. We must then explore whether there is a curvilinear interaction between zBMI and smoking status. Adding the cross-product of $zBMI^2$ and each dummy variable on a final step produced a reasonable $\Delta-2LL$ of 80.23, $p < .0001$. Adding the cubic term $zBMI^3$ produced a significant $\Delta-2LL$ of 61.36, $p < .0001$, and adding the cubic cross-products produced a significant $\Delta-2LL$ of 22.53, $p < .0001$

Enrichment Table 8.5   Cubic Interaction Terms in Equation

		B	SE	Wald	df	Sig.	Exp(B)	95% CI for Exp(B)	
								Lower	Upper
	dum1	.479	.065	54.944	1	.000	1.614	1.422	1.832
	dum2	−46.265	37.875	1.492	1	.222	.000	.000	1400972103246.492
	dum3	−4.584	.608	56.809	1	.000	.010	.003	.034
	zBMI	1.583	.073	474.539	1	.000	4.868	4.222	5.613
	zBMI by dum1	−.312	.108	8.334	1	.004	.732	.592	.905
	zBMI by dum2	42.327	39.652	1.139	1	.286	2411452848058018800.000	.000	1.363E+052
	zBMI by dum3	5.219	.929	31.589	1	.000	184.840	29.944	1140.982
Step 1[a]	zBMI2	−.740	.052	200.811	1	.000	.477	.430	.528
	zBMI2 by dum1	.360	.076	22.341	1	.000	1.434	1.235	1.665
	zBMI2 by dum2	−12.549	13.581	.854	1	.355	.000	.000	1287482.810
	zBMI2 by dum3	−1.608	.423	14.433	1	.000	.200	.087	.459
	zBMI3	.073	.008	81.491	1	.000	1.075	1.058	1.092
	zBMI3 by dum1	−.037	.012	9.418	1	.002	.964	.941	.987
	zBMI3 by dum2	1.252	1.522	.676	1	.411	3.496	.177	69.016
	zBMI3 by dum3	.178	.057	9.808	1	.002	1.195	1.069	1.336
	Constant	−2.497	.041	3732.706	1	.000	.082		

a. Variable(s) entered on step 1: zBMI3 * dum1 , zBMI3 * dum2 , zBMI3 * dum3.

Data source: NHIS2010, Centers for Disease Control and Prevention.

Enrichment Table 8.6 Calculations for Cubic Interaction

	BMI	BMI2	BMI3	Dum1	Dum2	Dum3	logit	exp	prob
Nonsmoker	−2	4	−8	0	0	0	−9.207	0.00010033	0.0001003
	−1.5	2.25	−3.375	0	0	0	−6.782875	0.00113301	0.0011317
	−1	1	−1	0	0	0	−4.893	0.00749889	0.0074431
	−0.5	0.25	−0.125	0	0	0	−3.482625	0.03072665	0.0298107
	0	0	0	0	0	0	−2.497	0.08233162	0.0760688
	0.5	0.25	0.125	0	0	0	−1.881375	0.15238044	0.1322310
	1	1	1	0	0	0	−1.581	0.20576923	0.1706539
	1.5	2.25	3.375	0	0	0	−1.541125	0.21414006	0.1763718
	2	4	8	0	0	0	−1.707	0.1814092	0.1535532
Former	−2	4	−8	1	0	0	−6.368	0.00171559	0.0017126
	−1.5	2.25	−3.375	1	0	0	−4.901	0.00743914	0.0073842
	−1	1	−1	1	0	0	−3.705	0.02460022	0.0240096
	−0.5	0.25	−0.125	1	0	0	−2.753	0.06373637	0.0599174
	0	0	0	1	0	0	−2.018	0.13292104	0.1173260
	0.5	0.25	0.125	1	0	0	−1.473	0.22923674	0.1864871
	1	1	1	1	0	0	−1.091	0.33588045	0.2514300
	1.5	2.25	3.375	1	0	0	−0.845	0.42955736	0.3004828
	2	4	8	1	0	0	−0.708	0.49262847	0.3300409
Occasional	−2	4	−8	0	1	0	−200.338	9.8699E-88	0.0000000
	−1.5	2.25	−3.375	0	1	0	−148.999125	1.9521E-65	0.0000000
	−1	1	−1	0	1	0	−107.286	2.5485E-47	0.0000000
	−0.5	0.25	−0.125	0	1	0	−74.204875	5.9324E-33	0.0000000
	0	0	0	0	1	0	−48.762	6.6517E-22	0.0000000
	0.5	0.25	0.125	0	1	0	−29.963625	9.7043E-14	0.0000000
	1	1	1	0	1	0	−16.816	4.9763E-08	0.0000000
	1.5	2.25	3.375	0	1	0	−8.325375	0.00024229	0.0002422
	2	4	8	0	1	0	−3.498	0.03025784	0.0293692
Daily	−2	4	−8	0	0	1	−32.085	1.1632E-14	0.0000000
	−1.5	2.25	−3.375	0	0	1	−23.414125	6.7823E-11	0.0000000
	−1	1	−1	0	0	1	−16.482	6.9496E-08	0.0000001
	−0.5	0.25	−0.125	0	0	1	−11.100375	1.5107E-05	0.0000151

	BMI	BMI2	BMI3	Dum1	Dum2	Dum3	logit	exp	prob
	0	0	0	0	0	1	−7.081	0.00084093	0.0008402
	0.5	0.25	0.125	0	0	1	−4.235625	0.01447076	0.0142643
	1	1	1	0	0	1	−2.376	0.09292152	0.0850212
	1.5	2.25	3.375	0	0	1	−1.313875	0.26877653	0.2118391
	2	4	8	0	0	1	−0.861	0.42273913	0.2971305

Data source: NHIS2010, Centers for Disease Control and Prevention.

This regression equation produces the following data, which shows very different curves for each group. Let's start with just the quadratic effects:

Enrichment Figure 8.4 Quadratic interaction with data cleaned on first five dfbetas

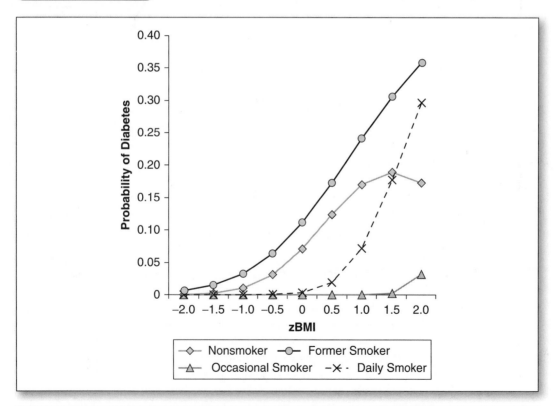

Data source: NHIS2010, Centers for Disease Control and Prevention.

Enrichment Figure 8.5 Cubic interaction with data cleaned on first five dfbetas

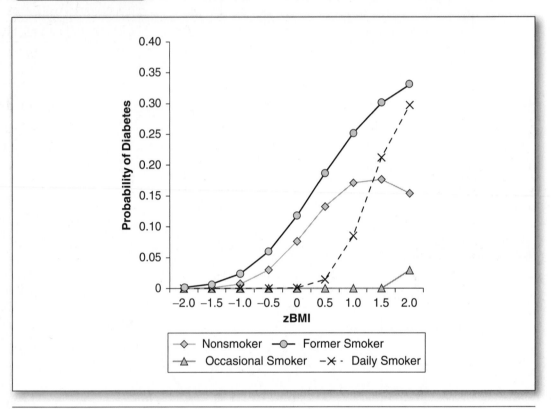

Data source: NHIS2010, Centers for Disease Control and Prevention.

REFERENCES

Aiken, L. S., & West, S. (1991). *Multiple regression: Testing and interpreting interactions*. Thousand Oaks, CA: Sage.

Baron, R. M., & Kenny, D. A. (1986). The moderator–mediator variable distinction in social psychological research: Conceptual, strategic, and statistical considerations. *Journal of Personality and Social Psychology, 51*(6), 1173.

Cohen, J., Cohen, P., West, S., & Aiken, L. S. (2002). *Applied multiple regression/correlation analysis for the behavioral sciences*. Mahwah, NJ: Lawrence Erlbaum.

DeMaris, A. (2002). Explained variance in logistic regression a Monte Carlo study of proposed measures. *Sociological Methods & Research, 31*(1), 27–74.

Fleischmann, M., Pons, S., & Hawkins, M. (1989). Electrochemically induced nuclear fusion of deuterium. *Journal of Electroanalytical Chemistry, 261*(2), 301–308.

Hayes, A. F. (2009). Beyond Baron and Kenny: Statistical mediation analysis in the new millennium. *Communication Monographs, 76*(4), 408–420.

Menard, S. W. (2010). Logistic regression: From introductory concepts to advanced concepts and applications. Thousand Oaks, CA: Sage.

Osborne, J. W. (2000). Prediction in multiple regression. *Practical Assessment, Research & Evaluation, 7*(2).

Osborne, J. W. (2008). Creating valid prediction equations in multiple regression: Shrinkage, double cross-validation, and confidence intervals around prediction. In J. W. Osborne (Ed.), *Best practices in quantitative methods* (pp. 299–305). Thousand Oaks, CA: Sage.

Osborne, J. W., & Jones, B. D. (2011). Identification with academics and motivation to achieve in school: How the structure of the self influences academic outcomes. *Educational Psychology Review,* 1–28.

Pedhazur, E. J. (1997). Multiple regression in behavioral research: Explanation and prediction. Fort Worth, TX: Harcourt Brace College Publishers.

Thompson, B. (1995). Stepwise regression and stepwise discriminant analysis need not apply here: A guidelines editorial. *Educational and Psychological Measurement, 55*(4), 525–534.

Zhao, X., Lynch, J. G., & Chen, Q. (2010). Reconsidering Baron and Kenny: Myths and truths about mediation analysis. *Journal of Consumer Research, 37*(2), 197–206.

9

A BRIEF OVERVIEW OF PROBIT REGRESSION

"To probit or to logit . . . that is the question. 'Tis better to use a logit or probit link function than to inappropriately use ordinary least squares regression with binary or categorical dependent variables . . ."

—attributed to Warren Shakespeare,
William's younger statistician brother

Y ou may have encountered this creature called "probit" regression, which sounds a bit like the topic of our book—logistic regression. Indeed, if you come across it in the literature, it looks to be dealing with a similar issue, binary dependent variables, in a similar way to logistic regression. Indeed, probit does handle similar issues in a very similar manner—with a link function that appropriately addresses the issues raised by these types of outcome variables.

It was developed in a separate tradition from logistic regression but shares many surface, procedural, and mathematical similarities to logistic regression. In this chapter, we will briefly explore the mathematical underpinnings of probit regression, contrast it with what you now know of logistic regression, and discuss pros and cons of this interesting technique.

◆ WHAT IS A PROBIT?

My research indicates that probit[1] was originally presented in the form we know today by Bliss (Bliss, 1934a, 1934b) as a method of dealing with an important nonlinear relationship in economic entomology—the relationship between pesticide toxicity and kill percentage.[2] In particular, Bliss (and others who preceded him) was trying to find a way of transforming the very nonlinear relationship between dosage and the percent of pests the pesticide would kill (which asymptotes at and low high dosages) to something that would be linear if plotted against each other. This was important as many scientific fields used cross section paper that made calculations simple if a line were straight. As with the logistic curve, introduced in previous chapters, you can imagine that at very low dosages (or concentrations) of a pesticide, there is very little effect (or a very low percentage of pests that is killed). Then, at some point, with increasing concentrations, the kill percentage increases markedly and continues increasing until some later point where effectiveness will asymptote and increased concentrations or dosages beyond this point may be less effective.

Bliss's and others' great contribution to practical toxicology was to convert this nonlinear relationship to something easily understood—the z-score of the probability or percentage killed—which then has a linear relationship with dosage or concentration and then could be used with the common tools of the time: linear graph paper of various types. Thus, this was a great practical breakthrough in fields from toxicology that was adapted to mental measurement (Finney, 1944), and is still in wide use today in diverse fields such as finance (Malkiel & Saha, 2005), medicine (Krentz, Auld, & Gill, 2004), and genetics (Zhou, Wang, & Dougherty, 2004). In fact, probit and logit analyses were so valuable that the U.S. Department of Agriculture supported the development of POLO, a program specifically designed to analyze data obtained from insecticide bioassays that was made available to anyone who requested a magnetic tape and had a Univac 1100

---

[1]The word "probit" is short for "probability unit."

[2]Yes, a morbid topic, but without this groundbreaking work, we would not have the current food security that many of us enjoy—and let's not forget that modern epidemiology got the odds ratio and framework for logistic regression from studying poor sewer sanitation in London (Snow, 1855)—although Brands (2010) reports that Benjamin Franklin may have been one of the earliest epidemiologists, systematically exploring the link between professions that provide exposure to lead and other metal toxins and maladies now known to be related to exposure to these substances.

series computer or equivalent "large" scientific computer (Robertson, Russel, & Savin, 1980).[3] Indeed, because both logistic and probit regression are all link functions in the same general linear model as ordinary least squares (OLS) regression, almost anything one can do with OLS linear regression can be done with logistic or probit regression. This chapter is but a brief introduction to probit regression, written with the understanding that everything else covered relating to logistic regression (curvilinear effects, interactions, complex curvilinear interactions, data cleaning, missing data, etc.) can be done with probit. As we will see in later chapters, multi-level modeling applied to the logit and probit link is possible, as is multi-variate analyses, nonlinear regression, random-effects models, and so on.

As the words "logit" and "probit" imply, if a logit is an attempt at quantifying a relationship between a dichotomous variable and a predictor variable in terms of log odds (in other words, working in a metric of log odds), probit works in a metric of probability. Thus we would consider probit regression a version of general linear modeling with a "probit link" connecting the predicted variable to the linear part of the regression equation (just as logistic regression use a "logit link" to connect the predicted variable to the linear part of the regression equation.

Recall that the "link function" for logistic regression is

$$\text{Logit} = \text{natural}\log\left(\frac{\pi}{1-\pi}\right)$$

Thus, the regression equation we calculate is:

$$\text{Logit}(\hat{Y}) = b_0 + b_1 X_1 \ldots b_k X_k$$

We also showed how by using exponentiation we can compute the odds ratio from the logit by

$$\text{Odds ratio} = \exp(\text{logit}(y))$$

And we can also directly convert a *predicted* logit back to a predicted conditional probability through

$$\text{Conditional probability} = \left(\frac{e^{\text{logit}(y)}}{1 + e^{\text{logit}(y)}}\right) \text{ or } \left(\frac{\exp(\text{logit}(y))}{1 + \exp(\text{logit}(y))}\right)$$

---

[3]Of course, the cell phone in your pocket today probably has exponentially more processing power than the room-sized computers scientists used to run these programs. And back in the old days of UNIVAC, you were required to walk uphill both ways in the snow in order to use the machine.

◆ THE PROBIT LINK

The probit link assumes that the observed binary outcome variable results from an underlying latent normally distributed random variable with a threshold that triggers a 0 turning into a 1.0. This is not dissimilar to what we do with high-stakes testing in the U.S. educational system, where we have high-stakes test scores that vary, often along a more or less normal distribution, and we set a particular cut score to signify whether the student has "passed" the test or not. The difference is that in the case of probit, the underlying normally distributed variable is not available to us.

Probit regression uses the standard normal cumulative distribution function (area under the curve less than Z—which is the boundary). If you are familiar with a z-score and the z-table associated with it, you are familiar with the basics of probit regression. Essentially, a probit regression is fitting a model to find the z-score such that area under the curve less than Z is equal to the observed probability.

So instead of looking at the data in Table 9.1 in terms of odds and logits, as logistic regression does, let's look at it in terms of the cumulative normal distribution. Look up the z-score of both of the conditional probabilities in any z-table (or use the =NORMSINV(X) command in Excel). The baseline conditional probability of dropping out if a student is not from a poor family (0.029) corresponds to a z-score of −1.896, and the conditional probability for those students coming from a poor family (0.145) corresponds to a z-score of −1.058. In essence, this view means that the threshold for dropout is much higher (in other words, easier to exceed) if a student is from a poor family than not from a poor family.

Furthermore, we can calculate the slope, or the change, in this threshold from one group to another by subtracting the two expected probits (−1.058 − [−1.896]), giving us a slope of 0.838. This slope is the difference

Table 9.1 Cross-Tabulation of Family Income and Dropout (Adapted From Chapter 2)

		Dropout		Total	Conditional Probabilities	z-Scores for Conditional Probabilities	Slope	Predicted Probits
		.00	1.00					
poor	Yes (1)	7312	1244	8556	0.145	−1.058	0.84	−1.057
	No (0)	7821	233	8054	0.029	−1.896		−1.897
Total		15133	1477	16610				

Data source: National Education Longitudinal Study of 1988 (NELS88), National Center for Educational Statistics, U.S. Department of Education.

Figure 9.1 Visual Representation of Probit Thresholds

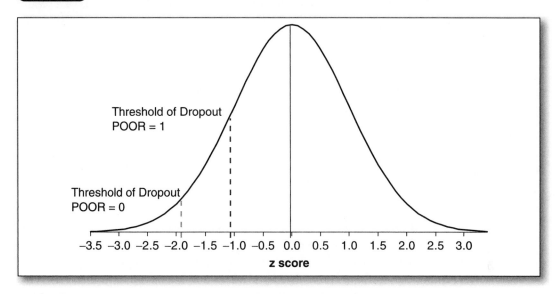

in the two thresholds. In this case, the threshold for the POOR = 0 group is 0.838 z units higher.

One interesting thing to note about the cumulative frequency distribution is that it is not a uniform, linear effect. The probabilities associated with a $z = 1.0$ change depend on the location of the initial threshold. If the first threshold is −3.0 and we increase by an increment of 1.0, the difference between $z = -3.0$ and −2.0 is the difference between probabilities of 0.00135 and 0.0228, or a difference in probability of 0.0214. However, if the initial threshold is −0.50 and we increase by an increment of 1.0, the corresponding probabilities are 0.31 and 0.69, or a change in probability of about 0.39. So, in probit regression as in real estate, location matters.

Using the same data as the previous example, and the same variables, we get the following output from SPSS.

Table 9.2 Probit Results of POOR and DROPOUT Data

		Estimate	Std. Error	Wald	df	Sig.	95% Confidence Interval	
							Lower Bound	Upper Bound
Threshold	[dropout = .00]	1.897	.028	4495.722	1	.000	1.841	1.952
Location	poor	.840	.033	654.647	1	.000	.776	.905

Link function: Probit.

Data source: NELS88, National Center for Educational Statistics, U.S. Department of Education.

One interesting thing to note is that the probit routine presents the intercept as positive, but it is in reality a negative number. Thus, we would write the probit regression line equation as:

$$\text{Probit}_{(dropout)} = -1.897 + 0.840 \text{ (Poor)}$$

Which gives us the same predicted zs and probabilities as we hand-calculated:

$$\text{Probit}_{(Poor=0)} = -1.897$$

$$\text{Probit}_{(Poor=1)} = -1.897 + 0.840(1)$$

$$= -1.057$$

Converting these predicted probits backward from z-scores to conditional probabilities,[4] we get predicted probabilities of 0.029 and 0.145, which are not only identical to our hand-calculated predicted probabilities but also identical to the results obtained from logistic regression. This is a good outcome, as we don't want different mathematical manipulations of the same data to return different results (beyond reasonable rounding errors).

Just as we did above with the confidence intervals for logistic regression, we could similarly convert the 95%CIs for the probits to 95%CIs for the predicted conditional probabilities. By calculating the predicted probits as

$$95\%CI = -1.897 \pm 1.96*SE_{(probit)}$$

we calculate the bounds as −1.12 and −0.99, which convert to 0.131 and 0.161, very close to what we calculated from the logistic regression above.

Of course, the results of logistic and probit regressions look very different if you examine the regression line equations, but as with logits and odds ratios and probabilities (and probits, or z-scores of probabilities), this is all the same information, and as such, will lead to the same conclusion if interpreted correctly.

◆ WHY ARE THERE TWO DIFFERENT PROCEDURES IF THEY PRODUCE THE SAME RESULTS?

As with many things in statistics, the different procedures evolved in parallel within different disciplines. Consider the simple case of analysis of variance

---

[4] Using Excel, we can use the NORMSDIST(Z) function.

(ANOVA) and OLS regression—for so many decades of our history, they were talked about as though radically different because they developed within different groups of researchers. Today, in the 21st century, we acknowledge the general linear model, of which OLS regression and ANOVA are two examples (as are logistic and probit regression). Mathematically, one can get identical data to produce identical results regardless of which method is used to analyze the data. This is another case of the same situation.

Because both probit and logistic regression use essentially the same information to come to the same conclusions (although each uses a different transformation of the information), in one sense it really does not matter which routine you use. Properly interpreted, you will come to largely the same conclusion.

The example I will use to demonstrate the concordance of probit and logistic regression is a simple example from National Health Interview Survey of 2010 (NHIS2010; http://www.cdc.gov/nchs/nhis.htm) from the U.S. Centers for Disease Control and Prevention, which we have used previously throughout the book. In this particular example, we will focus on 27,731 individuals who had complete data on three variables: Whether the individual had ever been told they had diabetes (DIABETES, recoded to 0 = no, 1 = yes), AGE (which ranged from 18 to 85+), and body mass index (BMI, which ranged from 12 to 79).[5] In this example, both AGE and BMI were used as continuous variables. Contrary to my own advice in earlier chapters regarding continuous variables, I chose NOT to standardize the two variables by converting to *z*-scores because these variables' scores have specific, interpretable meaning, particularly to a researcher in this field.

As you can see from Table 9.3 (see page 304), the model overall is significantly improved in model fit from the intercept-only (no predictor) model, with a $\chi^2_{(3)} = 2723.12$, $p < .0001$. As in logistic regression, many statistical packages provide several pseudo-R^2 estimates for probit analyses. These probit models have the same drawbacks with pseudo-R^2 estimates as logistic regression, as discussed in previous chapters As you can see, estimates vary widely (in this case, from .097 to .205 percent variance accounted for), and as such are not given much credence.

---

[5]A brief note on interpretation: I am using this public data for demonstration purposes only. I intentionally did not weight the data or do any of the methodologically important steps necessary to appropriately use data from this type of complex multistage sample for drawing substantive conclusions. Therefore, you should not draw any substantive conclusions about dropout and family income based on these data. They are for illustrative purposes only. For more on the importance of weighting complex samples such as this, I will refer you to my paper on the topic: http://pareonline.net/pdf/v16n12.pdf (Osborne, 2011).

Table 9.3 Model Fitting Information

Model	−2 Log Likelihood	Chi-Square	df	Sig.
Intercept Only	15457.530			
Final	12734.416	2723.115	3	.000

Link function: Probit.

Pseudo R-Square	
Cox and Snell	.097
Nagelkerke	.205
McFadden	.160

Link function: Probit.

Summary of Multiple Probit Regression Analysis							
		Estimate	Std. Error	Wald	df	Sig.	95% Confidence Interval	
							Lower Bound	Upper Bound
Threshold	[diabetes = .00]	3.452	.172	404.030	1	.000	3.115	3.788
Location	AGE	.008929	.003	8.412	1	.004	.003	.015
	BMI	.024209	.006	17.838	1	.000	.013	.035
	ageBMI	.000635	.000	36.236	1	.000	.000	.001

Link function: Probit.

Data Source: NHIS2010, National Centers for Disease Control and Prevention.

In Table 9.3, you can see the threshold intercept is −3.452 (again, remember that when we report these results from SPSS, we need to take the negative of the intercept). This is the z of the probability of someone at age 0 and BMI of 0 having been diagnosed with diabetes, which is obviously absurd and therefore rightly a very small probability (0.000278). Thus, in this analysis, the intercept is merely a theoretical starting point that has little meaning.

By solving the regression equation:

Probit($\hat{Y}$) = −3.452 + 0.008929(age) + 0.024209(BMI) + 0.000635(age*BMI)

we get the predicted probits in Table 9.4, which can then be converted to predicted conditional probabilities. In Table 9.4, I also provide the identical logistic regression analysis outcomes—the predicted logits and conditional probabilities corresponding to those predicted logits, as discussed in previous chapters. As you can see, the probabilities are very close, leading us to the conclusion that both probit and logistic regression, properly executed and converted to conditional probabilities, produce virtually identical results. The graphical results of these predicted conditional probabilities are presented in Figure 9.2.

Figure 9.2 Comparison of Logit and Probit Regression on the Same Analysis

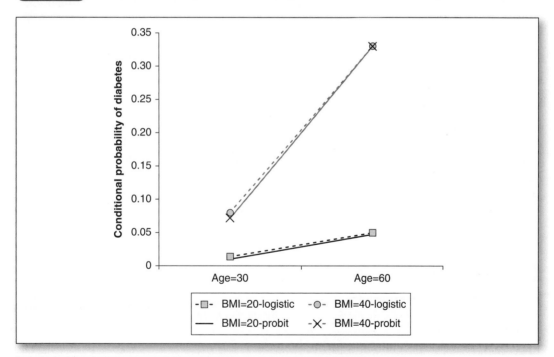

Data Source: NHIS2010, National Centers for Disease Control and Prevention.

Note that in producing these estimates and converting them to conditional probabilities, I initially achieved somewhat different results, primarily in the "high age, high BMI" group. This is because in these calculations, having precision to many decimals is important, and SPSS by default only gives 3. I edited the table in SPSS to more decimal points, converting the original interaction coefficient from 0.001 to the more accurate 0.000635. When I did the same with the logistic regression output, the conversion resulted in only minor differences. The moral of the story is that precision to more decimals is desirable, even if American Psychological Association style recommends we report fewer in routine practice.

◆ THE VALUE OF HAVING A SENSIBLE INTERCEPT

As mentioned earlier, the intercept in this analysis is meaningless. There are no children at age = 0 with BMI = 0. And although most researchers don't sweat this, it seems like a wasted opportunity. My recommendation to standardize most variables, repeated several times to this point gives us a meaningful interpretation—it is the expected score for those on the mean of all variables. But these variables are in a meaningful metric, so we center them at the mean for each variable, or at another interesting point, such as age of 20 and BMI of 20 (in other words, at a relatively young, healthy person within the actual range of our data). Conversely, we could center the data at a relatively older, unhealthy individual (age = 60, BMI = 40) if that were of interest. As we get into multilevel modeling in later chapters, this choice of intercept becomes more important as it becomes an outcome that is predicted from other explanatory variables. More on that later. For now, let's see what happens with this probit regression when we place the intercept at a more sensible point—the young, healthy individual (age = 20, BMI = 20).

The results of this interaction are very similar, as one might expect. In fact, the overall model fit statistics are identical, as Tables 9.4 and 9.5 show.

Table 9.4 Interaction Between Age and BMI

Age	BMI	int	Probit Regression		Logistic Regression		Probit With Age and BMI Centered at 20	
			probit	conditional probabilities	logit	conditional probabilities	probit	conditional probabilities
30	20	600	−2.31895	0.010199	−4.257	0.013967	−2.31881	0.010203
30	40	1200	−1.463	0.071734	−2.502	0.075718	−1.45381	0.072999
60	20	1200	−1.676	0.046869	−2.922	0.051077	−1.67024	0.047436
60	40	2400	−0.434	0.332144	−0.672	0.338049	−0.42424	0.335695

Data Source: NHIS2010, National Centers for Disease Control and Prevention.

Table 9.5 Model Fitting Information When Variables Centered at 20

Model	−2 Log Likelihood	Chi-Square	df	Sig.
Intercept Only	15457.530			
Final	12734.416	2723.115	3	.000

Link function: Probit.

Pseudo *R*-Square with variables centered at 20	
Cox and Snell	.097
Nagelkerke	.205
McFadden	.160

Link function: Probit.

Parameter Estimates With Age and BMI Centered at 20							
Parameter Estimates							
		Estimate	Std. Error	Wald	df	Sig.	95% Confidence Interval
							Lower Bound
Threshold	[diabetes = .00]	2.535	.045	3119.168	1	.000	2.446
Location	age_20	.021619	.001	365.461	1	.000	.019
	BMI_20	.036900	.004	95.562	1	.000	.030
	INT_20	.000635	.000	36.236	1	.000	.000

Upper Bound
2.624
.024
.044
.001

Link function: Probit.

Data Source: NHIS2010, National Centers for Disease Control and Prevention.

In the case of the individual estimates, the probit regression line equation is somewhat altered:

$$\text{Probit}(Y) = -2.535 + 0.021619(\text{Age} - 20) + 0.036900(\text{BMI} - 20) + 0.000635(\text{Age} - 20 * \text{BMI} - 20).$$

As you can see in Table 9.6, the intercept is slightly altered: −2.535, which is now the meaningful z of the probability of a 20-year-old individual with a BMI of 20 being diagnosed with diabetes (0.005622). You may also notice that the slopes are generally stronger, which is the effect of moving the intercept to within the observed data.

As you can see in Table 9.7, when centered at the median, the intercept is now the Z of the probability of a person of age 47 and

Table 9.6 Interaction Between Age and BMI, Comparing Regressions Centered at Age/BMI = 20 or Median

			Probit Regression		Probit With Age and BMI Centered at 20*		Probit With Age and BMI Centered at the Median	
Age	BMI	int	probit	conditional probabilities	probit	conditional probabilities	probit	conditional probabilities
30	20	600	−2.31895	0.010199	−2.31881	0.010203	−2.34023	0.009636
30	40	1200	−1.463	0.071734	−1.45381	0.072999	−1.48819	0.06835
60	20	1200	−1.676	0.046869	−1.67024	0.047436	−1.69178	0.045344
60	40	2400	−0.434	0.332144	−0.42424	0.335695	−0.45874	0.323209

Data Source: NHIS2010, National Centers for Disease Control and Prevention.

*Note that when you create values for the predicted equation where you have placed the intercept at something other than 0, you must subtract the same amount from your values being entered into the equation—so instead of age = 30 for my equation, when Age is centered at 20, I enter 10 (30−20). When age is centered at the median (47), that same value would be −17 (30−47). The same rules apply for BMI and the interaction between the two.

Table 9.7 Parameter Estimates When Age and BMI Are Centered at Median (47 and 27, Respectively)

		Estimate	Std. Error	Wald	df	Sig.	95% Confidence Interval	
							Lower Bound	Upper Bound
Threshold	[diabetes = .00]	1.599	.015	11502.992	1	.000	1.570	1.628
	age_m	.026060	.001	1333.792	1	.000	.025	.027
Location	BMI_m	.053397	.002	852.214	1	.000	.050	.057
	INT_m	.000635	.000	36.236	1	.000	.000	.001

Link function: Probit.

Data Source: NHIS2010, National Centers for Disease Control and Prevention.

BMI 27 being diagnosed with diabetes (0.05491), again a much more sensible intercept for these data than the original. Note that across all these models, the overall fit statistics have remained the same, and the significance and direction of the effects have remained similar. Further, if we compute predicted probits and conditional probabilities from Table 9.6, you can see the probabilities and conclusions are all the same (within rounding error).

One significant benefit one gets from placing the intercept in a sensible, meaningful location is that we get valuable information, such as the standard error of the estimate (*SE*; in this case, when variables are centered at the median, the *SE* is 0.015, telling us there is a good point estimate for these individuals). In addition, we get more meaningful confidence intervals. In this case, individuals at the median for age and BMI have a probit of −1.599 (95%CI = −1.570, −1.628), which converts to probability of diagnosis of 0.055, with a 95%CI of 0.052, 0.058. When we leave the intercept at AGE and BMI = 0, we get a *SE* and confidence interval, but as those people don't exist, the SE and 95%CIs are rather large—about 12 times larger than these.

SOME NICE FEATURES OF PROBIT ◆

As I have discussed in previous chapters, the logit (and logarithms in general) is difficult for people to interpret accurately, even if they are mathematically trained, as the log can exaggerate very small differences and can minimize very large differences once converted to logarithms. The metric for probit, *z*-scores, is more familiar, and exaggerates effects less dramatically. Again, remember that this is all the same information as presented in logistic regression, just presented in different form. Despite this, some authors express preferences for one over the other, such as Berkson (1951), who admitted that there is little functional difference between the results the two provide.

ASSUMPTIONS OF PROBIT REGRESSION ◆

Interestingly (or perhaps not . . .), probit uses maximum likelihood estimation, and as such, follows the same basic assumptions as logistic regression. Thus, this is one of the shortest discussions of assumptions I have ever written.

SUMMARY AND CONCLUSION

I think I have shown that probit regression is a simple mathematical transformation of logistic regression. And as it uses the same maximum likelihood estimation, it produces virtually identical results to logistic regression when best practices are followed and results are interpreted in light of predicted conditional probabilities. Thus the decision to use logistic versus probit regression is one of style and preference. In some fields, it is the preferred method; in others, logistic is the preferred method.

One factor might be the strength of the implementation of the two procedures in the software you use. In SPSS, which I use quite a bit, I find the logistic implementation to be more fun and versatile, but the probit is certainly adequate.

ENRICHMENT

Since we have many good examples of these types of analyses throughout the preceding chapters, my challenge for you is to choose a few binary logistic regression analyses, perform them via probit regression, and compare the results. My expectation is that you should come to identical conclusions.

SYNTAX EXAMPLES

For those of you using SPSS, there is a simple way to perform probit regression via syntax, which is not easily available via point-and-click. This is the syntax I used in the first example for this chapter before centering the intercept at locations other than 0.

```
plum diabetes with age BMI ageBMI
/link=probit
/print= PARAMETER SUMMARY.
```

REFERENCES

Berkson, J. (1951). Why I prefer logits to probits. *Biometrics, 7*(4), 327–339.

Bliss, C. I. (1934a). The method of probits. *Science, 79*(2037), 38–39. doi: 10.1126/science.79.2037.38

Bliss, C. I. (1934b). The method of probits—A correction. *Science, 79*(2053), 409.

Brands, H. W. (2010). *The first American: The life and times of Benjamin Franklin.* New York, NY: Anchor.

Finney, D. (1944). The application of probit analysis to the results of mental tests. *Psychometrika, 9*(1), 31–39.

Krentz, H., Auld, M., & Gill, M. (2004). The high cost of medical care for patients who present late (CD4< 200 cells/μL) with HIV infection. *HIV Medicine, 5*(2), 93–98.

Malkiel, B. G., & Saha, A. (2005). Hedge funds: risk and return. *Financial Analysts Journal,* 80–88.

Osborne, J. W. (2011). Best practices in using large, complex samples: The importance of using appropriate weights and design effect compensation. *Practical Assessment Research & Evaluation, 16*(12), 1–7.

Robertson, J. L., Russel, R. M., & Savin, N. (1980). *A user's guide to probit or logit analysis.* Pacific Southwest Forest and Range Experiment Station.

Snow, J. (1855). *On the mode of communication of cholera.* London: John Churchill.

Zhou, X., Wang, X., & Dougherty, E. R. (2004). Gene prediction using multinomial probit regression with Bayesian gene selection. *EURASIP Journal on Applied Signal Processing, 2004,* 115–124.

10

REPLICATION AND GENERALIZABILITY IN LOGISTIC REGRESSION

What is the goal of research? In my mind, the goal is to enable us to say something meaningful (and/or useful) about a given population at a given time. The purpose of research ought not to be the self-aggrandizement of the researcher, or awards of tenure or degrees. Those are important personal milestones but should be won in the pursuit of research; they should not be the sole purpose of performing the research. One of the principles of science is the principle of replication—that another scientist, performing similar tasks on similar subject matter, should see similar results. Another principle is objectivity—that anyone, seeing the same phenomena, would draw the same conclusions. Yet replication and objectivity seem in short supply in many areas of science today. One of the purposes of writing my last book on data cleaning and testing of assumptions was to demonstrate that performing these tasks usually makes research both more generalizable and more replicable (contrary to some of the mythology surrounding outliers prevalent in many fields). In presenting examples of data cleaning in parts of this book, I have attempted to encourage you as statistician and researcher to consider these issues. It does nobody any good if the data you analyze are biased or flawed to such extent that the results fail to generalize to the population you sought to understand, or if others (perhaps with cleaner or better data) fail to replicate your results. Too many "controversies" in the sciences seem to arise from poor data, or perhaps, poor power (e.g., Tressoldi, 2012).

The goal of this chapter is to focus on the goals many of us start research careers with: contributing constructively to a body of knowledge.

313

The most common question I get asked as a statistician is "How many participants do I need in my sample?" Sample size is a difficult and contentious issue in research methods, and it is no less an issue in logistic regression. We have decades of "wisdom," and rules of thumb concerning adequate sample sizes, such as the advice that you should have a sample of at least $N = 100$, or a minimum of $N = 10$ per group or per independent variable. We also know that larger samples help reduce standard errors (narrowing confidence intervals), improve power, reduce volatility, and improve generalizability. There is some guidance in terms of adequate sample size in logistic regression, and there are complex calculations available to estimate *a priori* power. Bootstrap resampling can be a more specific and direct method of estimating power, particularly with complex analysis designs, and I will provide a gentle introduction to this novel (and fun) technique toward the end of the chapter. But the answer to the most-asked question is usually "More than you wanted to have to gather."

◆ SAMPLE SIZE, POWER, AND VOLATILITY IN LOGISTIC REGRESSION

In this chapter, we will explore the effects of smaller and larger samples on volatility and generalizability of parameter estimates in logistic regression. Since sample size is a continuous variable, there is no magic cutoff point: $N = 499$ is not inadequate and $N = 501$ is not perfectly adequate. The honest advice you will glean from this chapter is that larger, representative (cleaned) samples are better than smaller or biased samples,[1] but also that there are several important best practices for minimizing potential volatility at a given sample size (which is not always under the researchers' control): removal of inappropriately influential scores, reporting confidence intervals in addition to point estimates, aggregation over independent samples, and bootstrap analysis.

◆ WHAT IS STATISTICAL POWER, AND WHY SHOULD YOU CARE ABOUT IT?

Statistical power is the ability to correctly reject a false null hypothesis (in other words, to detect effects when indeed there are effects present) and is calculated based on a particular effect size, alpha level, sample size, and in

---

[1]This epiphany wins the award for "most obvious piece of advice that nobody wants" because it is simultaneously obvious and self-evident while being maximally unhelpful in planning a study.

the context of a particular analytic strategy. Authors have been discussing the issue of power more for more than 60 years (see, e.g., Deemer [1947]). Jacob Cohen (e.g., 1962, 1988, 1992) spent many years encouraging the use of power analysis in planning research, reporting research, and in interpreting results (particularly where null hypotheses are not rejected). Although it is unclear how many researchers actually calculate power and sample size *before* conducting a study, few *report* having calculated power, and a relatively low percentage of studies meet Cohen's criterion for "acceptable" power— only 29% of randomized experimental studies and only 44% of nonexperimental (or quasi-experimental) studies in prominent psychology journals met the criterion of having calculated power of 0.80 or higher (Osborne, 2008; Osborne, Kocher, & Tillman, 2012). By the way, I personally find the "common wisdom" that power of 0.80 is adequate to be wholly *inadequate*. I doubt few of us would find it acceptable to choose to fail at something important 20% of the time when failure might be avoidable. Few of us would find it acceptable to have medical doctors incorrectly diagnosing our loved ones 20% of the time or for structural engineers to build bridges that stay up only 80% of the time. In the modern era of research, it seems to me we can do better, and it often doesn't take a great deal of extra effort to do so.

HOW NULL HYPOTHESIS ♦ STATISTICAL TESTING RELATES TO POWER

Null hypothesis statistical testing (NHST) has been reviled in modern literature by many as counterproductive and misunderstood (for an excellent overview of the issues, see Fidler & Cumming, 2008; Killeen, 2008; Schmidt, 1996). Many authors have acknowledged the significant issues with NHST, and some (Killeen, 2008; Schmidt, 1996) have proposed alternatives such as the probability of replication (p_{rep}) as a more interesting or useful replacement. NHST has roots in the very earliest aspects of statistical practice, where it was a source of bitter debate and disagreement. Despite this, it has become the *de facto* norm in most of quantitative methods, and we must simultaneously work with it and seek to augment it in the best way possible.

In NHST, a scientist proposes two hypotheses. The first, a null hypothesis (H_o) is generally a hypothesis that there is no effect (no relationship, no difference between groups, etc.) and can be stated in very simple forms for zero order correlation or simple logistic regression (respectively) as:

$$H_o: r_{xy} = 0; \text{ or}$$

$$H_o: \log (P_{(Y=1)} / (1 - P_{(Y=1)}) = 1.0$$

Conversely, alternative hypotheses are generally what the researcher expects or hopes to find and are often stated as there is a "significant effect" (i.e., a relationship between two or more variables, a significant odds ratio, etc.).

$$H_o: r_{xy} \neq 0; \text{ or}$$

$$H_o: \log (P_{(Y=1)} / (1 - P_{(Y=1)}) \neq 1.0$$

One common criticism of NHST is that in an absolute sense, the null hypothesis is almost always wrong. Almost no correlation will ever be exactly $0.0000000\overline{0}$, and few odds ratios are exactly $1.00\overline{0}$, so in an absolute sense, it is almost always the case that null hypotheses are false if taken to enough decimal places (Cohen, 1988). In other words, odds ratios of 1.00001 or 0.99998 are not equal to 1.00000 in the strictest mathematical sense,[2] but for practical purposes, they are functionally equal (not statistically different or practically different). Conversely, it is possible to have an odds ratio that looks very different from 1.00000 (e.g., OR = 2.00), yet one could imagine a scenario where low power yields this odds ratio not significant at $p < .05$—where the null hypothesis is not rejected.

Thus, while it is often informative to look descriptively at what the data tells us, examples like this should make it clear that we need a better way of making decisions about our data. Inferential tests such as NHST were developed to *guide* researchers in determining whether they could conclude that there was a significant effect or not (Fisher, 1925), but they are not sufficient by themselves (Wilkinson, 1999).

♦ WHAT DO STATISTICAL TESTS TELL US?

Statistical tests tell us the probability of obtaining the observed results (e.g., the observed correlation coefficient, F, odds ratio) if the null hypothesis were true in the population. This concept is a little confusing at first, as we are often told that the p value is the probability of obtaining the results "by chance" or some similar, but technically inaccurate, interpretation.

Thus, we establish two different possible decisions we can make regarding our hypotheses and two different (yet unknowable) states of

---

[2]As Steven Strogatz (2012) points out in his excellent book *The Joy of X,* the original examples I was going to use ($0.9999\overline{9}$ taken to an infinite number of decimal places, and $1.0000\overline{0}$ taken to an infinite number of decimal places) are mathematically identical.

"reality." Take, for example, a simple odds ratio. It is possible that the conditional probability of an event is either identical (not significantly different) or different across two groups. It is also possible that I, as a researcher, can draw one of two different conclusions about those groups based on data I collect: that the conditional probability of an event is or is not significantly different across groups. As Table 10.1 shows, this gives us four possible outcomes, two of which are potential errors:

Table 10.1 Hypothesis Testing and Errors of Inference

		Population or unknowable "reality"	
		Probabilities are not different	Probabilities are different
Decision based on data gathered	Probabilities are not different	Correct decision	Type II error
	Probabilities are different	Type I error	Correct decision

Thus, we hope that our data lead to a correct decision, but it is possible that we make either a Type I (concluding there is a significant effect when there is none in the population) or Type II error (failing to conclude there is a significant effect when there is in fact an effect in the population). As quantitative methods evolved early in the 20th century, a primary focus was on minimizing the probability of making a Type I error (i.e., concluding there are group differences when in fact there are not). For example, if I am testing a new drug on patients and comparing them with placebo/ control groups, I want to be very sure that new drug is actually producing significant differences before recommending doctors prescribe that drug. Likewise, we want to be relatively certain that a psychological or educational intervention will produce the desired differences over existing interventions prior to recommending implementation. In the earlier decades of the 20th century this decision rule ($\alpha = .05$) was more flexible (which is why you can still find reference to "setting alpha" in many statistics texts), although at this point it is routinely assumed that we fix alpha at 0.05, meaning that we give ourselves only a 5% chance of making a Type I error in our decision making.

Thus, when performing statistical tests that give us probabilities (p values), we accepted the rule that if $p < .05$ (in other words, that there is less than a 5% chance that we would get the observed data from a population where the null hypothesis was true), then we reject the null hypothesis and conclude that there are significant differences between groups. Why, might you ask, are we happy to institutionalize a 5% chance of making such an important error? Why not set the bar at 1% or 0.01% so that we are very certain of not making an error of this type? We could do that (and historically, many scholars have), but in doing so, we would drastically increase the odds of making the other type of error, a Type II error. Thus, the community of statistical practice, for better or worse, settled on 5% as small enough to avoid significant harm to the body of knowledge but large enough to avoid causing a high rate of the other type of error.

Significance tests *do not* tell us several critical things about our results. First, p values do not tell us the probability that the results would be replicated in a subsequent sample or study. In fact, it is power that gives us insight into the probability of replication given identical circumstances (Schmidt, 1996). Second, and most importantly, significance tests *do not* tell us the importance of a particular effect. We often see researchers use terms like "marginally significant," "significant," and "highly significant" to indicate ever smaller p values. Yet p values are determined by multiple factors, including sample size, alpha, and effect size. Thus, a very small effect in a very large sample can have a very small p value but be practically unimportant. Likewise, a large effect in a small sample may have a relatively large p value (i.e., $p > .05$). And in neither case do we know anything about the probability of replicating the result unless we know the power of each test. Finally, p values do not tell us anything about the probability of making a Type II error (failing to reject a null hypothesis when there is a significant effect in the population). Only power can tell us the probability of making this type of error.

◆ SO WHAT DOES FAILURE TO REJECT THE NULL HYPOTHESIS MEAN?

We must distinguish between *failure to reject the null hypothesis* and *acceptance of the null hypothesis*. This might seem like semantic tomfoolery, but the difference is conceptually critical. If you fail to reject the null hypothesis (i.e., if you do not get a p value of less than .05 when performing NHST), two different possibilities exist: (a) that you have no clear information about the nature of the effect (failure to reject the null hypothesis), or (b) that you have sufficient information about the nature of the effect, and you can conclude that the null is accurate (acceptance of the null hypothesis). It is very different to state that we cannot draw any conclusions or to state we know there is no relationship. Unfortunately, these two statements often become conflated in NHST. It is not clear that in the seminal works by Fisher (e.g., Fisher, 1925) he intended that failure to reject the null hypothesis to mean the *acceptance* of the null (Schmidt, 1996).

This is an important distinction. Imagine the situation where you are evaluating two educational interventions, one that is very simple, traditional, and inexpensive, and one that uses expensive instructional technology in an attempt to improve student outcomes. Failure to reject the null could mean that you have insufficient information to draw any inferences, or it could mean that the two interventions are not producing significantly different outcomes. The ability to make a strong statement that two interventions produce the same effect is important from a policy (and in this case, financial) perspective. It means school districts could save millions of dollars every year by implementing the "traditional" intervention in lieu of the high-technology intervention, as outcomes are identical. In contrast, not having enough information means just that: there is no conclusion possible.

The difference between being unable to draw no conclusions and being able to conclude the null hypothesis is valid is related to the power of the study. If the study had sufficient power to detect appropriate-sized effects and we did not detect any effect, we can be more confident in concluding the null is supported. If the study did not have sufficient power to reliably detect appropriate-sized effects, then no conclusion is possible. This is a common misconception in the scientific literature (Schmidt, 1996), and yet another reason to ensure you have the appropriate power in your research.

SO WHAT IS POWER AND HOW ♦ DOES IT RELATE TO ERROR RATES?

Power comes into play in this discussion in two different ways. First, power is the power to reject a false null hypothesis. In other words, if there really are differences between two groups in the unknowable "reality," a study with greater power will be more likely to reject the null hypothesis, leading the researcher to the correct conclusion—that there are differences between two groups (when, in fact, there are differences between the groups) or that there is a relationship between two variables (when, in fact, there is a relationship between the variables). So following our examples thus far, if you are testing a new drug and the drug is really having a beneficial effect on patients, power is the probability you will detect that effect and correctly reject the null hypothesis. Theoretically, if your power is 0.80, you will correctly reject the null hypothesis on average 80% of the time (given a particular effect size, sample size, and alpha level). Conversely, even in situations where there is a real effect in the population, and there are real group differences, with a power level of .80, 20% of the time you will *fail to detect that effect*. In other words, you may have a wonderfully effective drug that can save people from misery, disease, and death, but under this hypothetical scenario, 20% of the time you will not realize it. This is a Type II error—the failure to reject a null hypothesis when in the unknowable "reality" there is an effect.

As you can imagine, this is an undesirable outcome. While we want to be sure to avoid Type I errors (e.g., asserting an intervention is effective when in fact it is not), it seems to me equally troubling to fail to see effects when they are present. Fortunately, there is a simple way to minimize the probability of Type II errors—ensure you have sufficient *a priori* power to detect the expected effects. Researchers who fail to do *a priori* power analyses risk gathering too much little or too much data to test their hypotheses. If a power analysis indicates that $N = 100$ subjects would be sufficient to reliably detect a particular effect, gathering a sample of $N = 400$ is a substantial waste of resources. Likewise, if $N = 1,000$ is required to reliably detect an effect, a sample of $N = 400$ is woefully inadequate and an equal waste of effort.

Second, *a posteriori* analyses of power are useful in order to shed light on null results. For example, if a study that fails to reject the null hypothesis had power of .90 to detect anticipated or reasonable effect sizes, one can be more confident that failing to reject the null was the correct decision and more confident in asserting that the null hypothesis is an accurate description of the population effect. However, in the context of poor power, failure to detect a null hypothesis gives little information about whether a Type II error has occurred or not.

Power in Logistic Regression

Power in simple binary logistic regression is a bit more complicated than for simple analyses such as correlation, simple regression, or analysis of variance. The same basic ingredients are there: sample size, criterion for significance (α), and effect size (anticipated odds ratio, in this case). In all regression models we have to take the number of predictors into account, and in logistic regression, power calculations also take into account the relative proportions of individuals that fall into each group in the dependent variable.[3] Because of this complexity, general rules of thumb are almost always inadequate. For example, Harlow (2005; see also Aldrich & Nelson, 1984) recommended using $N = 50$ participants per independent variable, but this advice might be overkill or might yield an inadequate sample size depending on anticipated effect size and the proportion of the population in each group.

Figure 10.1 presents three examples of the relationship between power and sample size in a simple binary logistic regression analysis with one predictor, where we anticipate various effect sizes (OR = 1.5, 2.0, and 3.0) but holding the proportion of the population constant at 80%/20% (it does not matter which is $Y = 1$ or $Y = 0$). As you can see from Figure 10.1, with a population odds ratio of 2.0 and these parameters, an $N = 40$ gives power of about 35%—in other words, 65% of the time the analysis will not find an

Figure 10.1 *A Priori* Power as a Function of Total Sample Size

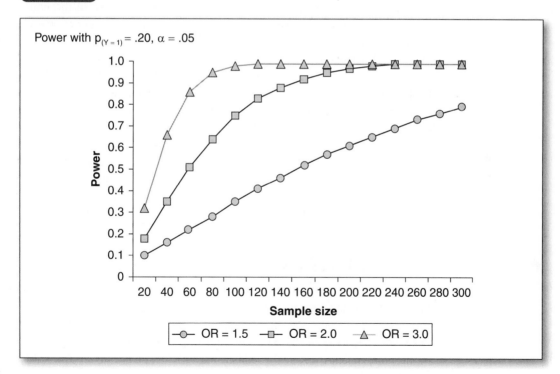

Power with $p_{(Y=1)} = .20$, $\alpha = .05$

³Power and sample size in multinomial logistic regression is a bit more complicated still.

effect that is, in fact, real. In this case, failure to reject the null is probably not strong evidence for equality between groups because there is a relatively small chance that we would have seen the effect if it were there. With an expected odds ratio of 1.5 the situation becomes more dire. With $N =$ 40, power is less than .20, and even with an expected odds ratio of 3.0, power is less than .70.

There are some general lessons we can learn from this figure. First, as one would expect, as effect size increases, power at any given sample size increases. Secondly, despite an odds ratio of 1.50 being a reasonable effect size, a sample size of $N = 300$ is required to attain power approaching .80, whereas a sample of approximately $N = 120$ accomplishes the same goal for an odds ratio of 2.0, and an odds ratio of 3.0 surpasses power of .90 with that sample size (again, keeping in mind the other parameters—20% of the population in one category and only one predictor in the equation).

Obviously, sample size is one of the factors in power that is easily controlled or manipulated by the researcher. As we see in Figure 10.2 (see page 323), the distribution of the population across the outcome variable groups also has a substantial effect on power. With only one predictor in the equation, power tends to increase as the proportion of the population in each group becomes more equal, and power is lowest when dealing with rare outcomes. But larger effect sizes and sample sizes ameliorate this issue. For example, when we expect an odds ratio of 2.0 and have $N = 250$ in our sample, any population with at least 10% in the outcome group has power over .90; in comparison, a smaller expected OR of 1.50 and sample size of $N = 100$ does not have power exceeding .50, even if the distribution of the population is 50%/50% across the two outcome groups.[4] Conversely, with the same OR = 1.50 and a sample of $N = 250$, your power reaches .80 if about 30% of the population is in the $Y = 1$ group. With larger effect sizes (OR = 2.0), smaller sample sizes ($N = 100$) allow us to reach power of .80 with 25% of the population in $Y = 1$, and with $N = 250$ at less than 10% of the population.

◆ SUMMARY OF POINTS THUS FAR

The complexities of logistic regression prohibit the effective formulation of simple, universal rules of thumb regarding sample size for even simple logistic regression analyses. Although our understanding of adequate sample size in logistic regression is still emerging, small samples are probably

---

[4]Note that these curves are symmetrical, so that power with a proportion of .60 is equal to that of .40, .90 is equal to that of .10, and so on.

Figure 10.2   How the Proportion in Y = 1 Affects Power

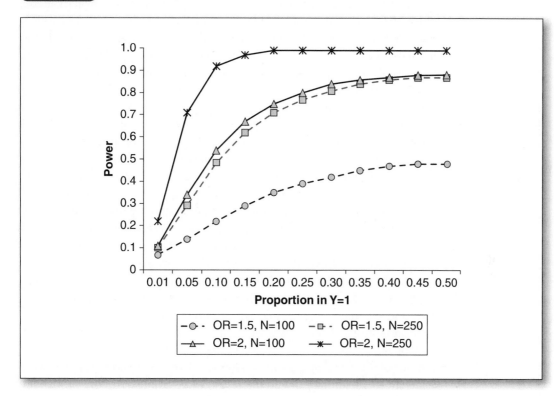

not replicable nor useful. Additional complexity is added to power analysis equations when phenomena being studied are relatively rare. However, as we will see below, power to reject the null hypothesis does not guarantee the ability to accurately or precisely estimate the population parameters, which is a primary goal of logistic regression.

WHO CARES AS LONG AS $p < .05$? VOLATILITY ♦ IN LOGISTIC REGRESSION ANALYSES

In this section, we are going to explore how volatile logistic regression analyses can be, even when analyses have adequate power. To demonstrate this, we utilized 16,610 participants in the National Education Longitudinal Study of 1988[5] who had complete data on variables of interest. For all analyses that

---

[5]For information on NELS88, visit http://nces.ed.gov/surveys/nels88/.

follow, our dependent variable is GRADUATE, whether a student in the initial eighth-grade sample was retained through graduation in 12th grade, which was coded 0 if the student did not graduate and 1 if the student graduated high school. In this sample, 1,477 out of 16,610 (8.9%) failed to graduate, and 91.1% were retained. In the examples that follow, we are going to explore the volatility of two different analyses. In the first, we will use the continuous variable socioeconomic status (SES; relatively normally distributed continuous variable converted to z-scores). In the full sample of $N = 16,610$, which we will refer to as the known "population," SES has an odds ratio of 2.83, which we will use as the population estimate for comparison to other analyses. As a point of comparison, *a priori* power analyses for these upcoming examples should be 0.52 for $N = 50$, 0.85 for $N = 100$, and 0.999 for $N = 250$ and $N = 500$.

The second example is a randomly generated variable (RND) with a standard normal distribution. As expected of a randomly generated variable, the odds ratio for the entire sample was about 1.00 (1.008), which was not significant despite the massive power of a sample this large. For analyses involving RND, there should be no findings of significant effects.

In the analyses that follow, we repeatedly selected samples of various sizes and examined how stable and accurate the parameter estimates for these variables are. In all cases we sampled with replacement, meaning any individuals selected from a previous sample were returned to the "population" prior to selecting the next sample. Given that most samples were relatively small compared with the size of the "population," the probability that a single individual influenced more than a single analysis was relatively small, even in the $N = 500$ condition. Thus, the samples are plausibly considered independent. This procedure simulates how real scientists pull samples from real populations, and inform us about how accurate we can expect our analyses to be. The advantage we have that real scientists don't have is that we have the "population" parameters to which we can compare our results.

SES Analyses

$N = 50$

The results of this first set of analyses are presented in Table 10.2 (see pages 326 and 327) and Figure 10.3. Because of the relatively small sample size, these results were expected to be the most volatile and least likely to accurately predict the known result. Twenty-one of the 50 analyses produced a significant result, with point estimates of the odds ratios ranging from 0.43 to 13.32. Not surprisingly, the 95% confidence intervals for these analyses were often very large and are truncated at 15 to make the graph more readable (the upper bounds for some 95% CIs ranged up to 135). Table 10.2 accurately reports the full 95%CIs.

Figure 10.3 Volatility in Odds Ratios With *N* = 50 Samples

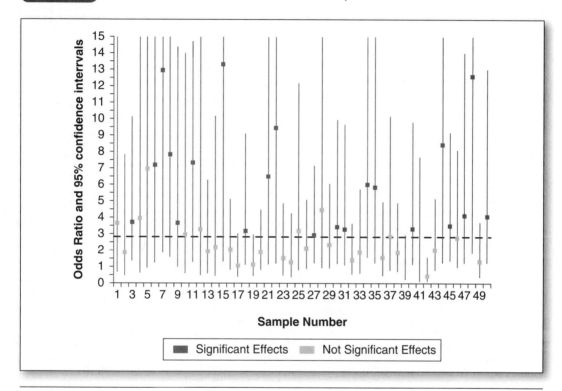

Data Source: National Education Longitudinal Study of 1988 (NELS88), National Center for Educational Statistics, U.S. Department of Education.

Expected power for this analysis was .52, and our results suggest this is reasonable—42% of our 50 samples in this group yielded significant results. What is noteworthy is the imprecision in estimating the population odds ratio—indicated by the dashed black line on the graph. Although many analyses estimated the odds ratio relatively accurately, those were often not statistically significant (dark markers indicate odds ratios significant at $p < .05$), and thus would constitute Type II errors. Eleven of the 21 significant odds ratios were in excess of 6.0, a serious misestimation of effect size. What is comforting (if anything in these analyses can be comforting) is that 49 of the 50 analyses had 95% confidence intervals that included the population odds ratio.

Table 10.2 Predicting the Odds of High School Graduation by Family SES When $N = 50$

Sample	B	SE	Wald	df	Sig.	Exp (B)	95% CI Lower	95% CI Upper
"Population"	1.041	.033				2.831	2.656	3.018
1	1.296	.861	2.264	1	.132	3.653	.676	19.745
2	.627	.730	.738	1	.390	1.872	.448	7.827
3	1.312	.512	6.554	1	.010*	3.713	1.360	10.137
4	1.374	.941	2.219	1	.145	3.950	.624	24.996
5	1.942	1.031	3.545	1	.060	6.973	.924	52.652
6	1.974	.895	4.864	1	.027*	7.202	1.246	41.635
7	2.562	.975	6.090	1	.009*	12.958	1.919	87.520
8	2.059	.813	6.412	1	.011*	7.837	1.592	38.572
9	1.300	.674	3.725	1	.054*	3.670	.980	13.745
10	1.084	.794	1.864	1	.172	2.956	.624	14.014
11	1.994	.890	5.017	1	.025*	7.343	1.283	42.027
12	1.188	.985	1.454	1	.228	3.281	.476	22.621
13	.657	.603	1.190	1	.275	1.930	.592	6.288
14	.778	.787	.977	1	.323	2.177	.466	10.183
15	2.590	1.182	4.803	1	.028*	13.324	1.315	135.039
16	.712	.471	2.289	1	.130	2.039	.810	5.131
17	.074	.529	.020	1	.889	1.077	.382	3.038
18	1.157	.537	4.639	1	.031*	3.179	1.110	9.109
19	.130	.490	.070	1	.791	1.138	.435	2.976
20	.644	.436	2.177	1	.140	1.903	.810	4.475
21	1.872	.887	4.458	1	.035*	6.501	1.144	36.948
22	2.246	1.051	4.570	1	.033*	9.452	1.205	74.115
23	.424	.593	.511	1	.475	1.529	.478	4.890
24	.247	.610	.164	1	.685	1.281	.387	4.232
25	1.160	.684	2.877	1	.090	3.188	.835	12.175
26	.745	.450	2.745	1	.098	2.107	.872	5.090
27	1.078	.454	5.623	1	.018*	2.938	1.206	7.160
28	1.499	.806	3.457	1	.063	4.476	.922	21.724
29	.848	.486	3.044	1	.081	2.336	.901	6.058
30	1.234	.543	5.157	1	.023*	3.434	1.184	9.960
31	1.191	.550	4.686	1	.030*	3.290	1.119	9.672

Sample	B	SE	Wald	df	Sig.	Exp (B)	95% CI Lower	95% CI Upper
32	.347	.483	.517	1	.472	1.416	.549	3.648
33	.636	.566	1.263	1	.261	1.890	.623	5.734
34	1.794	.686	6.841	1	.009*	6.011	1.568	23.052
35	1.765	.796	4.917	1	.027*	5.842	1.227	27.810
36	.449	.587	.585	1	.444	1.567	.496	4.951
37	1.046	.650	2.590	1	.108	2.845	.796	10.164
38	.629	.491	1.639	1	.200	1.875	.716	4.910
39	−.087	.597	.021	1	.884	.917	.284	2.953
40	1.198	.553	4.686	1	.030*	3.314	1.120	9.804
41	−.092	1.088	.007	1	.933	.912	.108	7.694
42	−.833	.660	1.593	1	.207	.435	.119	1.585
43	.702	.480	2.137	1	.144	2.018	.787	5.170
44	2.133	.954	4.994	1	.025*	8.437	1.300	54.761
45	1.253	.491	6.509	1	.011*	3.502	1.337	9.173
46	1.018	.544	3.503	1	.061	2.767	.953	8.033
47	1.416	.624	5.156	1	.023*	4.121	1.214	13.993
48	2.534	.986	6.605	1	.010*	12.604	1.825	87.052
49	.281	.527	.285	1	.594	1.324	.472	3.717
50	1.403	.593	5.598	1	.018*	4.069	1.272	13.013
AVERAGE	1.11					3.04		

Data Source: NELS88, National Center for Educational Statistics, U.S. Department of Education.

N = 100

The results of this second set of analyses are presented in Table 10.3 and Figure 10.4 (see page 328). These results were expected to be less volatile than the $N = 50$ samples but still relatively unstable. This sample size represents a minimum sample size according to many scholars (e.g., Long, 1997). Indeed, the parameter estimates were less inaccurate in these samples than in the previous group of analyses, but still contained startling inaccuracies. For example, odds ratios ranged from 1.59 to 11.28 (where the population OR = 2.83, again included as a dashed black line on the graph). Confidence intervals for these analyses were smaller, but many were still truncated on the graph at 14.0 (although accurately reported in the table) as upper bounds ranged up to 213.51. All confidence intervals in these analyses contained the population OR, and 40 of the 50 analyses (80%) found the odds ratio to be significant, which was in line with our *a priori* power estimate of .85.

Figure 10.4 Volatility in Odds Ratios With Sample Size *N* = 100

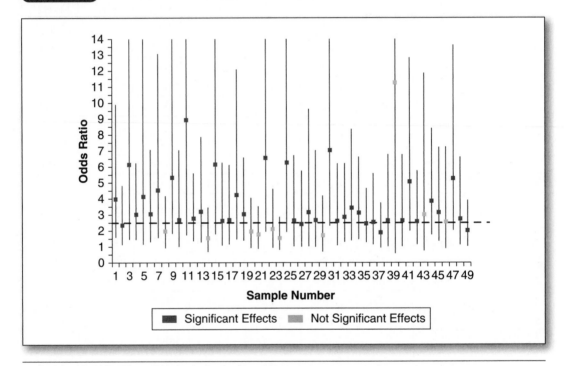

Data Source: NELS88, National Center for Educational Statistics, U.S. Department of Education.

Table 10.3 Predicting the Odds of High School Graduation by Family SES When *N* = 100

							95% CI	
Sample	*B*	*SE*	Wald	*df*	Sig.	Exp (*B*)	Lower	Upper
"Population"	1.041	.033				2.831	2.656	3.018
1	1.383	.464	8.870	1	.003*	3.986	1.605	9.904
2	.855	.365	5.473	1	.019*	2.351	1.149	4.813
3	1.816	.728	6.223	1	.013*	6.149	1.476	25.621
4	1.107	.369	8.976	1	.003*	3.024	1.466	6.238
5	1.421	.645	4.851	1	.028*	4.140	1.169	14.657
6	1.116	.429	6.785	1	.009*	3.053	1.318	7.072
7	1.513	.539	7.864	1	.005*	4.540	1.577	13.070

Sample	B	SE	Wald	df	Sig.	Exp (B)	95% CI Lower	95% CI Upper
8	.681	.380	3.206	1	.073	1.976	.938	4.163
9	1.675	.544	9.481	1	.002*	5.337	1.838	15.499
10	.986	.493	4.009	1	.045*	2.682	1.021	7.043
11	2.190	.835	6.886	1	.009*	8.940	1.741	45.906
12	1.020	.358	8.131	1	.004*	2.774	1.376	5.593
13	1.164	.458	6.448	1	.011*	3.202	1.304	7.862
14	.435	.409	1.128	1	.288	1.545	.692	3.447
15	1.817	.627	8.406	1	.004*	6.156	1.802	21.031
16	.964	.444	4.722	1	.030*	2.623	1.099	6.259
17	.984	.422	5.436	1	.020*	2.674	1.170	6.114
18	1.444	.535	7.279	1	.007*	4.236	1.484	12.091
19	1.111	.394	7.943	1	.005*	3.038	1.403	6.578
20	.670	.371	3.252	1	.071	1.954	.944	4.045
21	.569	.352	2.623	1	.105	1.767	.887	3.519
22	1.882	.616	9.318	1	.002*	6.565	1.961	21.979
23	.741	.401	3.408	1	.065	2.098	.955	4.608
24	.429	.317	1.836	1	.175	1.536	.826	2.858
25	1.826	.599	9.404	1	.002*	6.272	1.940	20.278
26	.971	.476	4.152	1	.042*	2.639	1.038	6.714
27	.883	.441	4.000	1	.045*	2.418	1.018	5.744
28	1.150	.568	4.102	1	.043*	3.159	1.038	9.619
29	.978	.496	3.899	1	.048*	2.660	1.007	7.026
30	.541	.454	1.417	1	.234	1.718	.705	4.184
31	1.952	.566	11.908	1	.001*	7.042	2.324	21.336
32	.961	.441	4.741	1	.029*	2.614	1.101	6.207
33	1.051	.396	7.046	1	.008*	2.860	1.316	6.214
34	1.234	.454	7.399	1	.007*	3.435	1.412	8.359
35	1.140	.383	8.880	1	.003*	3.126	1.477	6.617
36	.897	.326	7.591	1	.006*	2.452	1.295	4.641
37	.931	.402	5.366	1	.021*	2.538	1.154	5.582
38	.635	.349	3.301	1	.069*	1.887	.951	3.743
39	.972	.480	4.091	1	.043*	2.642	1.031	6.773
40	2.423	1.501	2.607	1	.106	11.276	.596	213.505
41	.971	.480	4.095	1	.043*	2.641	1.031	6.765

(Continued)

Table 10.3 (Continued)

Sample	B	SE	Wald	df	Sig.	Exp (B)	95% CI Lower	95% CI Upper
42	1.624	.473	11.787	1	.001*	5.075	2.008	12.827
43	.949	.409	5.378	1	.020*	2.583	1.158	5.759
44	1.105	.698	2.504	1	.114	3.019	.768	11.863
45	1.349	.398	11.476	1	.001*	3.852	1.765	8.404
46	1.146	.424	7.303	1	.007*	3.146	1.370	7.223
47	.941	.530	3.150	1	.076	2.563	.907	7.244
48	1.663	.484	11.801	1	.001*	5.275	2.043	13.625
49	1.008	.449	5.032	1	.025*	2.740	1.136	6.609
50	.701	.336	4.338	1	.037*	2.015	1.042	3.896
Average	1.16					3.19		

Data Source: NELS88, National Center for Educational Statistics, U.S. Department of Education.

$N = 250$

Given the relatively large sample size, these analyses were expected to be relatively stable. Indeed, the parameter estimates and confidence intervals were more reasonable and accurate than the analyses with smaller samples, but again logistic regression shows its volatility. The results of these 50 analyses, presented in Table 10.4 and Figure 10.5 (see pages 331 and 332), show odds ratios that range from 1.51 to 5.52. All but three (47 out of 50, or 94%) were significant at $p < .05$, a result that was in line with the .999 *a priori* power estimate. Surprisingly, one confidence interval failed to contain the population odds ratio. Of note is the fact that fully 11 of these analyses had odds ratios that were misestimated by 1.0 or more. Even at this size sample, although odds of a Type II error are low, odds of substantial misestimation of the point estimate is still rather high (~22%).

$N = 500$

The results of these analyses are presented in Figure 10.6 and Table 10.5. (see pages 333 to 335). All 50 of these analyses concluded, correctly, that the odds ratio is significant, and there was much less volatility within the parameter estimates—odds ratios ranged from 2.06 to 4.47. All confidence intervals included the population odds ratio. It is worthwhile noting that despite the relatively large sample sizes, most confidence intervals for this relatively simple analysis were still surprisingly large.

Figure 10.5 Volatility in Odds Ratios With $N = 250$

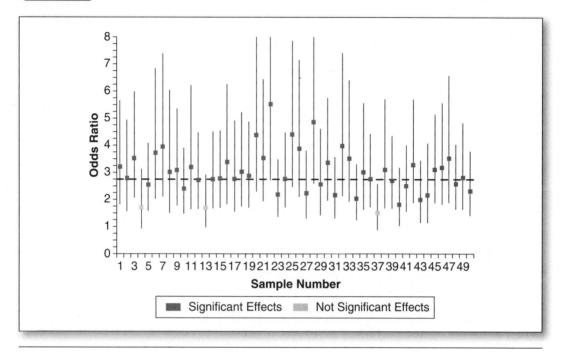

Data Source: NELS88, National Center for Educational Statistics, U.S. Department of Education.

Table 10.4 Predicting the Odds of High School Graduation by Family SES When $N = 250$

Sample	B	SE	Wald	df	Sig.	Exp (B)	95% CI Lower	95% CI Upper
"Population"	1.041	.033				2.831	2.656	3.018
1	1.166	.288	16.406	1	.0001*	3.210	1.826	5.644
2	1.026	.291	12.409	1	.0001*	2.790	1.576	4.937
3	1.259	.270	21.743	1	.0001*	3.522	2.075	5.979
4	.534	.309	2.993	1	.084	1.706	.931	3.124
5	.935	.240	15.122	1	.0001*	2.546	1.590	4.079
6	1.315	.309	18.042	1	.0001*	3.723	2.030	6.828
7	1.373	.319	18.510	1	.0001*	3.947	2.112	7.378
8	1.103	.353	9.748	1	.002*	3.015	1.508	6.027
9	1.128	.280	16.167	1	.0001*	3.088	1.782	5.350
10	.876	.246	12.656	1	.0001*	2.402	1.482	3.894
11	1.163	.339	11.790	1	.001*	3.199	1.647	6.212

(Continued)

Table 10.4 (Continued)

Sample	B	SE	Wald	df	Sig.	Exp (B)	95% CI Lower	95% CI Upper
12	1.002	.252	15.764	1	.0001*	2.722	1.661	4.463
13	.528	.276	3.671	1	.055	1.696	.988	2.911
14	1.012	.251	16.196	1	.0001*	2.751	1.681	4.503
15	1.022	.250	16.652	1	.0001*	2.778	1.700	4.537
16	1.220	.313	15.218	1	.0001*	3.386	1.835	6.250
17	1.017	.292	12.132	1	.0001*	2.765	1.560	4.900
18	1.107	.278	15.850	1	.0001*	3.027	1.755	5.221
19	1.058	.267	15.675	1	.0001*	2.881	1.706	4.866
20	1.477	.329	20.190	1	.0001*	4.380	2.300	8.341
21	1.263	.305	17.093	1	.0001*	3.535	1.943	6.433
22	1.708	.360	22.538	1	.0001*	5.521	2.727	11.177
23	.782	.237	10.882	1	.001*	2.185	1.373	3.477
24	1.018	.244	17.463	1	.0001*	2.767	1.717	4.460
25	1.482	.296	25.115	1	.0001*	4.401	2.465	7.857
26	1.356	.311	19.018	1	.0001*	3.881	2.110	7.140
27	.804	.271	8.785	1	.003*	2.234	1.313	3.802
28	1.581	.318	24.714	1	.0001*	4.859	2.605	9.061
29	.942	.298	9.958	1	.002*	2.565	1.429	4.604
30	1.213	.273	19.755	1	.001*	3.365	1.971	5.746
31	.773	.254	9.269	1	.002*	2.166	1.317	3.563
32	1.381	.317	19.038	1	.0001*	3.979	2.140	7.399
33	1.258	.305	16.985	1	.0001*	3.518	1.934	6.399
34	.711	.246	8.345	1	.004*	2.037	1.257	3.300
35	1.104	.312	12.527	1	.0001*	3.016	1.637	5.558
36	1.017	.239	18.107	1	.0001*	2.764	1.731	4.415
37	.413	.271	2.323	1	.127	1.511	.889	2.568
38	1.133	.310	13.400	1	.0001*	3.106	1.693	5.699
39	.994	.242	16.843	1	.0001*	2.702	1.681	4.345
40	.598	.285	4.390	1	.036*	1.818	1.039	3.180
41	.918	.238	14.898	1	.0001*	2.505	1.572	3.994
42	1.1890	.281	17.963	1	.0001*	3.285	1.895	5.694
43	.691	.278	6.194	1	.013*	1.996	1.158	3.439
44	.772	.322	5.751	1	.016*	2.165	1.152	4.070
45	1.136	.256	19.667	1	.0001*	3.114	1.885	5.143
46	1.159	.284	16.710	1	.0001*	3.187	1.828	5.556
47	1.261	.317	15.798	1	.0001*	3.528	1.895	6.569
48	.948	.227	17.368	1	.0001*	2.580	1.652	4.028
49	1.036	.274	14.312	1	.0001*	2.818	1.648	4.821
50	.840	.250	11.318	1	.001*	2.317	1.420	3.780
Average	1.06					2.87		

Data Source: NELS88, National Center for Educational Statistics, U.S. Department of Education.

Figure 10.6 Volatility in Odds Ratios With *N* = 500

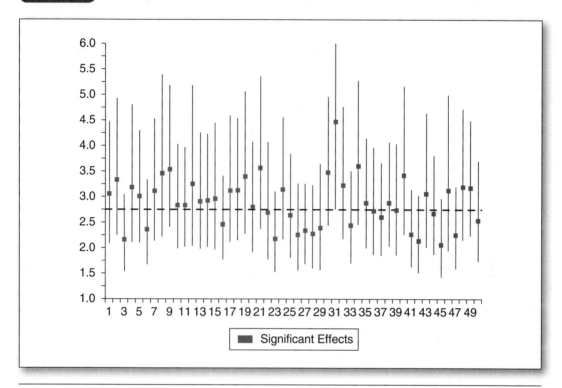

Data Source: NELS88, National Center for Educational Statistics, U.S. Department of Education.

Table 10.5 Predicting the Odds of High School Graduation by Family SES When *N* = 500

Sample	*B*	*SE*	Wald	*df*	Sig.	Exp (*B*)	95% CI Lower	95% CI Upper
"Population"	1.041	.033				2.831	2.656	3.018
1	1.117	.194	33.152	1	.0001*	3.056	2.090	4.471
2	1.204	.199	36.475	1	.0001*	3.332	2.255	4.924
3	.771	.173	19.895	1	.0001*	2.163	1.541	3.036
4	1.158	.210	30.554	1	.0001*	3.185	2.112	4.803
5	1.102	.182	36.824	1	.0001*	3.009	2.108	4.295
6	.860	.176	23.987	1	.0001*	2.363	1.675	3.334
7	1.136	.191	35.517	1	.0001*	3.115	2.144	4.525

(Continued)

Table 10.5 (Continued)

Sample	B	SE	Wald	df	Sig.	Exp (B)	95% CI Lower	95% CI Upper
8	1.241	.226	30.173	1	.0001*	3.460	2.222	5.388
9	1.263	.195	42.151	1	.0001*	3.537	2.416	5.179
10	1.042	.179	33.703	1	.0001*	2.834	1.994	4.028
11	1.042	.171	37.097	1	.0001*	2.834	2.027	3.962
12	1.180	.237	24.755	1	.0001*	3.254	2.044	5.179
13	1.068	.194	30.306	1	.0001*	2.909	1.989	4.254
14	1.073	.188	32.754	1	.0001*	2.925	2.025	4.224
15	1.085	.207	27.492	1	.0001*	2.961	1.973	4.443
16	.901	.166	29.348	1	.0001*	2.461	1.777	3.409
17	1.138	.197	33.401	1	.0001*	3.121	2.121	4.591
18	1.140	.190	36.091	1	.0001*	3.127	2.156	4.536
19	1.223	.203	36.305	1	.0001*	3.399	2.283	5.060
20	1.030	.191	29.105	1	.0001*	2.801	1.926	4.071
21	1.271	.207	37.644	1	.0001*	3.566	2.376	5.353
22	.990	.211	22.010	1	.0001*	2.691	1.780	4.070
23	.779	.180	18.827	1	.0001*	2.180	1.533	3.100
24	1.146	.189	36.881	1	.0001*	3.145	2.173	4.553
25	.971	.192	25.669	1	.0001*	2.640	1.813	3.843
26	.815	.187	18.914	1	.0001*	2.258	1.564	3.260
27	.851	.168	25.770	1	.0001*	2.343	1.687	3.255
28	.824	.178	21.385	1	.0001*	2.279	1.607	3.231
29	.873	.214	16.686	1	.0001*	2.394	1.575	3.639
30	1.247	.180	47.809	1	.0001*	3.480	2.444	4.956
31	1.497	.245	37.292	1	.0001*	4.470	2.765	7.229
32	1.171	.199	34.713	1	.0001*	3.226	2.185	4.762
33	.893	.184	23.617	1	.0001*	2.443	1.704	3.502
34	1.282	.194	43.460	1	.0001*	3.602	2.461	5.273
35	1.058	.185	32.688	1	.0001*	2.880	2.004	4.140

Sample	B	SE	Wald	df	Sig.	Exp (B)	95% CI	
							Lower	Upper
36	1.002	.191	27.618	1	.0001*	2.724	1.874	3.957
37	.957	.174	30.382	1	.0001*	2.603	1.853	3.659
38	1.058	.176	36.194	1	.0001*	2.880	2.040	4.065
39	1.008	.197	26.182	1	.0001*	2.740	1.862	4.031
40	1.230	.210	34.486	1	.0001*	3.423	2.270	5.161
41	.818	.166	24.332	1	.0001*	2.267	1.637	3.137
42	.762	.176	18.795	1	.0001*	2.142	1.518	3.023
43	1.118	.212	27.853	1	.0001*	3.060	2.020	4.636
44	.984	.180	29.846	1	.0001*	2.674	1.879	3.805
45	.724	.184	15.485	1	.0001*	2.063	1.438	2.960
46	1.139	.239	22.663	1	.0001*	3.124	1.954	4.992
47	.814	.177	21.077	1	.0001*	2.256	1.594	3.193
48	1.161	.199	33.951	1	.0001*	3.193	2.161	4.718
49	1.155	.176	42.877	1	.0001*	3.175	2.247	4.487
50	.932	.192	23.532	1	.0001*	2.538	1.742	3.698
Average	1.05					2.85		

Data Source: NELS88, National Center for Educational Statistics, U.S. Department of Education.

Random Variable Analysis

We randomly selected 50 samples of $N = 100$ each for this analysis (other analyses with smaller and larger samples produced similar results). As expected, most samples produced results (presented in Figure 10.7) that did not reject the null hypothesis, although four did, which is not substantially different than what we would expect via random chance (8% vs. expected alpha of 5%). It is noteworthy that 9 (18%) of the samples produced odds ratios over 2.0 or near 0.50[6] despite the completely random nature of the variable. Again, this is a cautionary note concerning using relatively small samples in logistic regression.

---

[6]Which is similar in magnitude to 2.0 but in the opposite direction.

Figure 10.7 Volatility of Odds Ratios With a Random Variable as Predictor

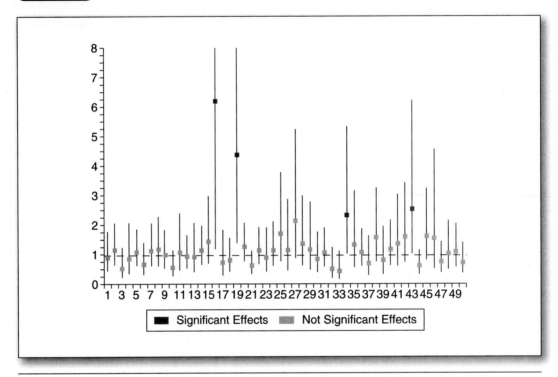

Data Source: NELS88, National Center for Educational Statistics, U.S. Department of Education.

Summary

These analyses highlight the importance of reporting confidence intervals routinely and of having very large samples, particularly when the probability of an event occurring ($Y = 1$ or the smallest group) is relatively low, as in these examples (< 10%). Even in relatively large samples, serious misestimation of odds ratios was common. Confidence intervals, although very large, usually included the population odds ratio. Our observed power, albeit based on a relatively small number of samples, still suggests that in practice *a priori* power might be lower than calculated by programs such as SAS or GPOWER, and as such, researchers should be looking to those sample-size calculations as lower bounds guides only.

Other variables have been shown to influence the accuracy and error rates of logistic regression beyond these, including Events Per Variable (EPV; Peduzzi, Concato, Kemper, Holford, & Feinstein, 1996). Events per variable refers to the number of individuals who experience the event that is the dependent variable ($Y = 1$), wherein the authors argue that researchers should have at least 10 events per independent variable at a minimum for valid logistic regression equations. This makes good sense, in that having extremely low numbers in one category leaves little information for the equations to work with. Further, small samples in either category leaves logistic regression vulnerable to spurious results or misestimation of effects. Ideally, there are strong, representative samples in both groups.

Despite the relatively gloomy results reported earlier, there is good news: averaging effects across multiple samples tends to lead to a reasonably accurate estimate of the population effect. Thus, meta-analysis can be a valuable tool in estimating population effects even if individual studies are inadequate in terms of power and precision.

CROSS-VALIDATION AND REPLICATION ♦ OF LOGISTIC REGRESSION ANALYSES

In light of these results, it might be desirable to suggest some sort of replicability or stability analysis for users of logistic regression. It is obvious that logistic regression analyses tend to be somewhat volatile even when samples include $N = 500$. Consumers of research involving logistic regression should have some indicator of the likelihood of replicability of the results in order to fully understand the usefulness of a particular analysis. For example, two researchers studying the effects of SES on retention in high school might draw radically different conclusions depending on which two samples they happened to get in their studies. Looking at Figure 10.6 (or Table 10.5), one researcher could conclude that the odds ratio for SES is 2.0, while another could conclude that it is almost 4.5. This seems all the more critical if the logistic regression equation is to be used not just for explanatory purposes, but rather for prediction purposes. In other words, if practitioners or researchers are intending to use the resulting logistic regression equation to predict outcomes for individuals, stability and accuracy are critical to usability.

Prediction and Explanation Using Regression

There are two general applications of general linear modeling, regardless of whether we are discussing ordinary least squares (OLS) regression or logistic regression. Explanatory applications seek to understand relationships between variables for the purpose of theory-building or validation.

Generally, relationships are discussed in relation to one or more groups of individuals. Applications of regression equations for predictive purposes generally use a previously generated regression equation to predict outcomes for individuals. An example of explanatory research involving logistic regression might be to understand the predictors of success in high school in order to build theory, understand phenomena, or design interventions (e.g., DeGroot, 1969; Kaplan, 1964, 1998; Osborne, 2000; Pedhazur, 1997, pp. 195–198). As we have explored in this chapter, SES is obviously a significant predictor of one type of success in high school (that of remaining in and completing), and others could be added to the analysis, such as parent education, prior achievement test scores, motivation and future plans, peer-group dynamics, and so forth. An example of prediction would be taking a previously developed (and validated) logistic regression equation that specifies specific effects of family SES, prior achievement test scores, and future goals in an attempt to predict which students are most or least likely to graduate high school. These predictions could theoretically be used to recruit students into various programs to help at-risk students or to enrich students on the fast track to good universities. Obviously this second application has higher stakes and requires higher standards for the results of regression analyses. It would not be acceptable to put a student in an intervention inappropriately, and likewise it would be unwise to accelerate a student who was more likely to drop out of high school than go to university.

In 2000, Osborne outlined and demonstrated some basic steps in evaluating (cross-validating) prediction equations in OLS regression. Briefly, when validating a prediction equation in OLS regression, one gathers a large, representative sample from the population to which we desire to generalize. Using half the sample, we first perform the appropriate regression analysis, recording overall model statistics and regression equation. We then create predicted scores in the second half of the sample using that regression equation and correlate the prediction of outcomes with actual outcomes. The square of this correlation is compared with the R^2 from the first half sample analysis, and the difference, termed "shrinkage" is evaluated. Minimal shrinkage indicates that the regression equation is similar in both samples, and thus has a reasonable expectation for generalizing to other individuals in this population. The final step in this case is that the two samples are combined and a final prediction equation is computed.

There are plentiful examples of this application across scientific disciplines. For example, prediction has been used to predict such diverse events as the incidence of postoperative nausea and vomiting (Toner et al., 1996), bankruptcy (Laitinen & Laitinen, 2001), macrobenthic species responses to estuary ecosystem conditions (Ysebaert, Meire, Herman, & Verbeek, 2002), six-month survival after serious head trauma (Lang, Pitts, Damron, & Rutledge, 1997), construction contractor performance (Wong, 2004), and wildfire ignition in Portugal (de Vasconcelos, Silva, Tome, Alvim, & Pereira, 2001).

However, the problem in calculating shrinkage in logistic regression is that pseudo-R^2 estimates can be volatile and as such do not provide reliable benchmarks for comparison, despite the recommendation of some authors.

Neural networks versus logistic regression

There has been a debate in the literature whether neural network analysis does a better job in predicting binary outcomes than logistic regression. In many recent studies, the difference in effectiveness between the two approaches is negligible, and thus logistic regression remains a viable method of predicting outcomes if well-validated prediction equations are used (for a summary, see Dreiseitl & Ohno-Machado, 2002).[7]

Internal versus external validation

Internal validation refers to validating a prediction equation on the same or very similar population as the sample that was used to develop the original equation. External validation refers to validating the equation on a population that may have substantial differences than the development sample. An example of external validation might be developing an equation predicting suicide attempt in a sample of individuals diagnosed as depressed and validating it on a nonclinical sample. Another example might be developing an equation predicting high school retention in an affluent suburban school system and validating it in a high-poverty urban environment. I will focus on internal validation for now as external validation seems of limited usefulness.

Cross-validation versus bootstrap

There is a large literature on cross-validation and bootstrap procedures to evaluate the robustness of a prediction model in logistic regression. Bootstrap procedures are automated procedures where samples are

---

[7]This is a relief to me, as I just wrote a whole book on applications of logistic regression!

"resampled" with replacement to create a large number of derivative samples, perform analyses on all these (often 1,000 or more) samples, and empirically devise point estimates and confidence intervals, for example. They work well when normal parametric assumptions are not viable or not known.

Some authors, such as Steyerberg et al. (2001) argue that bootstrap is preferable to cross-validation in logistic regression as it is more efficient. However, many of these same authors find cross-validation to be low bias and low variability, and as such reasonable, particularly when samples are not small (see also Shtatland, Kleinman, & Cain, 2004).

If one performs cross-validation and the prediction equation is found to be reasonable, then there are some proposed methods of correcting the equation for shrinkage (the overfitting of an equation to a particular sample) so that it can be used with more confidence such as adjusting of regression coefficients via AIC (see, e.g., Shtatland et al., 2004). If the equation is found to be not reasonable (i.e., not strong in cross-validation) the researcher is left with few options but to start over, acknowledging the failure.

However, recalling that the goal is a maximally generalizable prediction, Breiman (1996) suggested bootstrap aggregation, or BAGGING, in order to produce a more robust and generalizable prediction equation (Shtatland et al., 2004). In particular, Shtatland et al. suggest that averaging regression coefficients over multiple data sets would produce desirable outcomes for logistic prediction equations that are superior to AIC adjusted prediction equations. Indeed, aggregation is a powerful ally, and even using our original 50 "independent" samples at varying N presented above, we demonstrate that aggregation of *independent samples* can produce prediction equations that are very close to the population prediction equation.[8] As presented in Tables 10.2–5, the average of all the unstandardized regression coefficients in the $N = 50$ samples was 1.11 (odds ratio =3.04), in the $N = 100$ samples it was 1.16 (OR=3.19), in the $N = 250$ samples it was 1.06 (OR=2.87), and in the $N = 500$ samples it was 1.05 (OR=2.85). With a population regression coefficient of 1.041 and a population odds ratio of 2.831, it is plain to see that aggregating coefficients over multiple independent samples, even samples that are individually woefully inadequate, leads to a much more robust (and accurate) estimate of the true population parameters.

---

[8]This is similar to meta-analysis in logic, that aggregation and analysis of independent samples produces a much more replicable and accurate estimate of the population than any single independent sample.

Comparing Internal
Validation Models in Logistic Regression

As mentioned earlier, in OLS regression it is relatively straightforward to quantify validation analyses through R^2 and correlations between actual and predicted outcomes. It is slightly more complex to compare the replicability of logistic regression equations, but some authors have recommended some relatively simple guidelines. First, it is important to compare the similarity of regression equations. Let us take three new data sets representing the $N = 250$ SES analyses (similar to that represented in Table 10.4, above). The equations are:

$$\text{Sample 1: Logit}(\hat{Y}) = 2.851 + 1.178(\text{zSES})$$

$$\text{Sample 2: Logit}(\hat{Y}) = 2.958 + 1.220(\text{zSES})$$

$$\text{Sample 3: Logit}(\hat{Y}) = 2.301 + 0.695(\text{zSES})$$

These equations seem reasonably close at first glance. Let's examine our intuition by calculating predicted probabilities of graduation for four hypothetical students who have family zSES of −2, −1, 1, and 2 to see how replicable the predictions are:

Table 10.6   Predicted Outcomes From Internal Replication Equations

zSES:	Logits			Probabilities		
	Sample 1	Sample 2	Sample 3	Sample 1	Sample 2	Sample 3
−2	0.495	0.518	0.911	0.621	0.627	0.713
−1	1.673	1.738	1.606	0.842	0.850	0.833
1	4.029	4.178	2.996	0.983	0.985	0.952
2	5.207	5.398	3.691	0.995	0.995	0.976

Data Source: NELS88, National Center for Educational Statistics, U.S. Department of Education.

The first two replications seem to be reasonably close in this basic test of cross-validation, as one might expect from the similarity of equations. The equation from sample 3 seems to produce substantially different results, particularly in the logits. This might suggest that the findings do not replicate well given these parameters, particularly for low SES individuals.

◆ IN-DEPTH WITH BOOTSTRAP

Bootstrap analysis is a "resampling" methodology that is becoming more available as computers become more powerful and statistical computing software becomes more able to perform these types of analyses. In general, bootstrapping takes a particular group of cases and makes a large number of related samples from that single initial sample. It does this by sampling *with replacement,* meaning that any given case can be selected 0, 1, or more times into each new sample. Thus, by using this simple concept, proponents of this methodology argue that researchers can essentially "pull oneself up by their own bootstraps" and make more effective use of what might be an inadequate sample. In theory, if you use bootstrapping to create a large enough number of related samples, and then analyze all those samples, bootstrapping should be able to give a more robust estimate of the population parameters, as well as potentially eliminate the influence of highly influential outliers or data points. This is because, in theory, if a relatively small number of cases are highly influential, resampling the same data set thousands of times should yield a large number of samples where these cases are *not* influential, and thus are more accurate estimates of the population. Other authors have pointed to the use in bootstrapping to estimate the replicability of a result, as you can theoretically examine thousands of potential permutations of a data set. What you *cannot* do with bootstrapping is get estimates from data that are not in your data set (obviously). Thus, bootstrapping is probably not a substitute for a good, large, representative, unbiased original sample (or a second sample to test whether results replicate), but bootstrapping in the context of a good sample can be fun and informative.

The challenge presented next is whether nonindependent samples, such as that produced by bootstrap or jackknife methodology, can rescue a strongly biased or underpowered sample. For those wishing to experiment with bootstrap analysis in SPSS, I have appended macro syntax that can perform this type of analysis and extract the results of the analyses into data file format. Similar command syntax for SAS examples are also easily obtained online.

Biased Sample #1 ($N = 100$, $b = 0.361$, OR = 1.435)

The first example of bootstrap analysis involved a small ($N = 100$) highly biased sample taken from the same original large population ($b = 1.041$,

OR = 2.831). One weakness of this sample is the low number of events in the $Y = 0$ group ($N = 7$). Thus, in resampling the $Y = 0$ group can be volatile. Bootstrap analysis of 1,000 resampled data sets constructed with replacement produced an average regression coefficient of 0.375 (average OR = 1.57; median $b = 0.349$, median OR = 1.42). As you can see in Figure 10.8, the resampling produced some extreme results, resulting in a highly skewed distribution thanks to a small percentage of outliers. The median parameter estimate was largely unchanged from the original sample. Further, expectations of replication and cross-validation are not good, as the standard deviation of the sampling distribution (the standard error) was 0.37 for the regression coefficient and 0.95 for the odds ratio. The 95% CI for the regression coefficient (−0.28, 1.11) and odds ratio (0.75, 3.05) included the population parameters of 1.041 and 2.831, but just barely. One thing the highly skewed distribution does tell us is that there

Figure 10.8 Distribution of Odds Ratios From a Bootstrap Analysis

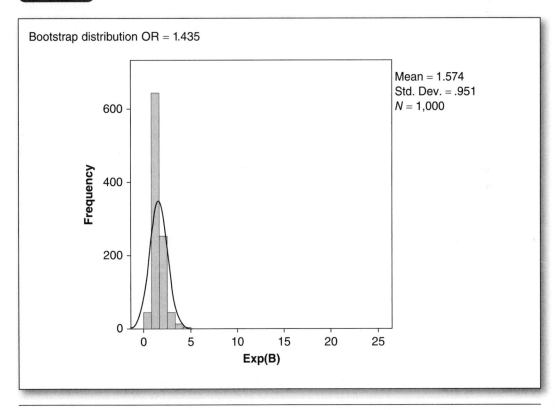

Data Source: NELS88, National Center for Educational Statistics, U.S. Department of Education.

might be some highly influential cases in this sample, as the majority of the samples produced OR estimates that ranged in reasonable fashion around the population OR.

Biased Sample #2 ($N = 100$, $b = 1.619$, OR = 5.051)

The second example of bootstrap analysis involved a small ($N = 100$) highly biased sample taken from the original population. In this case, the sample was biased toward severe overestimation of the parameter estimates. In this sample there were $N = 13$ in the $Y = 0$ group. Bootstrap analysis of 1,000 resampled data sets produced an average regression coefficient of 1.82 (average OR = 9.34, median $b = 1.69$, median OR = 5.42). As you can see in Figure 10.9, these analyses produced some surprisingly overestimated examples, as the maximum OR was 650.82. As with the previous example, bootstrapping did not produce a better prediction of the population parameters, and in this case, the bootstrap results were farther from the population than the simple analysis of the sample. In addition, the standard deviation of the sampling distribution for b was 0.67, and for the OR was 26.26. This yielded broad 95%CIs for both the regression coefficient (0.91, 3.48) and the odds ratio (2.49, 32.56). Again, the CIs contained the population parameter but were so ridiculously large as to be all but useless, and it is likely that there were some highly influential cases in this sample given the strong skew of the distribution.

Indeed, there is no reason to expect resampling to repair a seriously biased sample. Authors (Rodgers, 1999; Yu, 2003) have argued that resampling a biased sample should reproduce and perhaps amplify that bias.

Relatively Unbiased Sample #3

Thus far, bootstrap analysis does not seem to help produce better estimates of the population parameters when the initial sample itself is relatively small and strongly biased. A third example is a sample of $N = 250$ that was selected to be closer to the population parameters ($b = 0.77$, OR = 2.16, 95%CI for OR 1.29, 3.62) to investigate whether bootstrap analysis can help a more reasonable sample produce a more accurate population estimate. In this sample, the $Y = 0$ group had $N = 22$, proportionally in line with the previous samples. As with the previous two examples, bootstrap analysis did not appreciably improve estimation of the population beyond that of simply analysis of the sample itself. The average b was 0.793, the average OR = 2.29, and the medians were similar. As you can see in Figure 10.10, the larger sample size produced a sampling distribution free of ridiculously

Figure 10.9 Results of Bootstrap Analysis

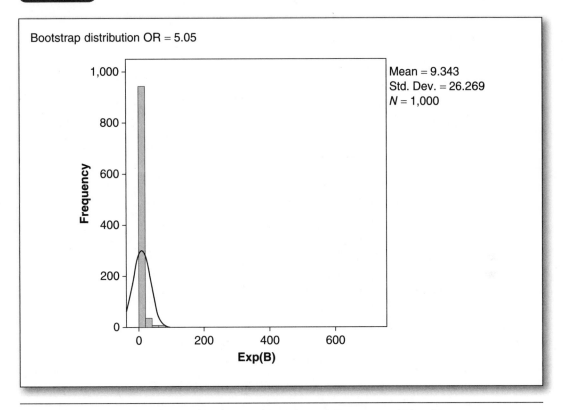

Bootstrap distribution OR = 5.05

Mean = 9.343
Std. Dev. = 26.269
$N = 1,000$

Data Source: NELS88, National Center for Educational Statistics, U.S. Department of Education.

inaccurate estimates. The standard deviations of the sampling distribution were 0.268 for *b* and 0.628 for OR, yielding 95%CIs of (0.26, 1.31) and (1.30, 3.72), respectively. These are much closer estimates, again including the desired population parameters. However, averaging the 1,000 bootstrap samples yielded only marginally more accurate population estimates and a not significantly different confidence interval. The regression coefficient in the sample was 0.77, with the average of the bootstrap estimates being 0.79, likewise the OR in the sample of 2.16 becoming slightly more accurate, averaging 1,000 bootstrap estimates to yield 2.29.

Can Data Cleaning Help?

One of the reasons why small samples can be volatile is the undue influence of extreme scores (outliers), which is a topic that has come up

Figure 10.10 Results of Bootstrap Analysis

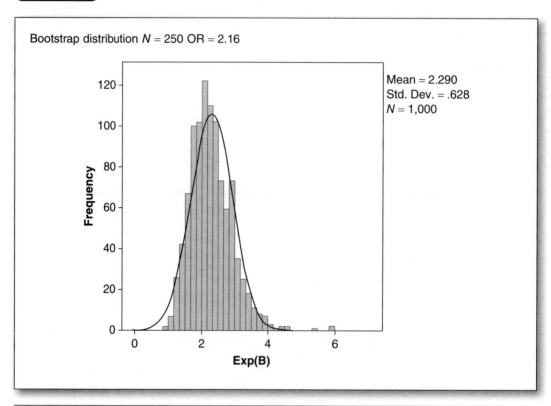

Bootstrap distribution N = 250 OR = 2.16

Mean = 2.290
Std. Dev. = .628
N = 1,000

Data Source: NELS88, National Center for Educational Statistics, U.S. Department of Education.

time and again in this book. Theoretically, bootstrap analyses should be able to help overcome the influence of extreme scores as they should be resampled relatively infrequently. One problem with identifying outliers in logistic regression is that the relatively small group (in this case, $Y = 0$) can have large standardized residuals compared with the larger group. Thus, care must be used when examining cases for unusual influence, particularly in relatively small samples, and particularly in the smaller group in the outcome variable. Returning to the previous example ($N = 250$, $b = 0.77$, $SE_b = .264$, OR = 2.16, 95%CI [1.288, 3.620]), where bootstrap analysis did not improve the accuracy (or replicability) of the analysis, analysis of standardized residuals revealed three cases in the ($Y = 0$) group (out of 22) that had standardized residuals in excess of −3.50: −7.76, −4.56, and −3.51. There were several between −3.0 and −3.50, but out of an abundance of caution, I chose to remove only the two most extreme cases from the analysis. Upon doing so, the accuracy of the estimates improved dramatically: $b = 1.067$, $SE_b = 0.299$, OR = 2.906, 95%CI [1.617, 5.223]. You may note that while the point estimates improved, the CI widened dramatically from the previous analysis with the extreme scores included. This is directly related to losing two of 22 in the $Y = 0$ sample.

Bootstrap analysis with cleaned data

Taking this new $N = 248$, OR=2.906 data set, we have a more accurate point estimate of the population, yet the confidence interval is relatively large. A simple bootstrap analysis with 1,000 samples (summarized in Figure 10.11) taken from this cleaned sample of $N = 248$ provides a mean $b = 1.089$, $SE_b = 0.216$, OR=3.04, 95%CI [2.03, 4.78]. While these point estimates remain good estimates of the "population" parameters, the bootstrap CIs are substantially narrower and more precise compared to the cleaned sample only.

Figure 10.11 Bootstrap Analysis After Data Cleaning

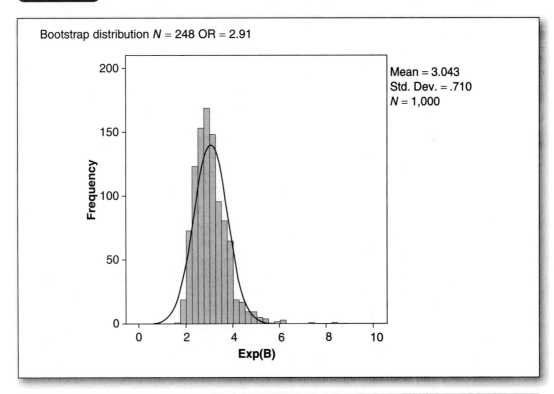

Data Source: NELS88, National Center for Educational Statistics, U.S. Department of Education.

Unfortunately, cleaning the smaller $N = 100$ examples discussed earlier yielded mixed results.

Cleaning two cases with the most extreme standardized residuals in the first example ($N = 100$, $b = 0.361$, $SE_b = 0.359$, OR = 1.435, 95%CI [0.710, 2.903]) improved the accuracy of the point estimate: ($N = 98$, $b = 0.724$, $SE_b = 0.437$, OR = 2.06, 95%CI [0.876, 4.857]) although the $Y = 0$ group decreased from $N = 7$ to $N = 5$. In addition, bootstrap analysis of this inadequately small sample *improved the population estimates:* average $b = 0.791$, $SE_b = 0.403$, OR = 2.43, 95%CI [1.13, 5.790], although Figure 10.12 still shows a good deal of misestimation across the various resampling trials. One other important piece of information from this bootstrap analysis is that, contrary to the original analysis of these data, this bootstrap analysis did not include 1.0. Because the original analyses included 1.0 in the 95% confidence interval, we would produce a Type II error (incorrectly concluding no effect when

Figure 10.12

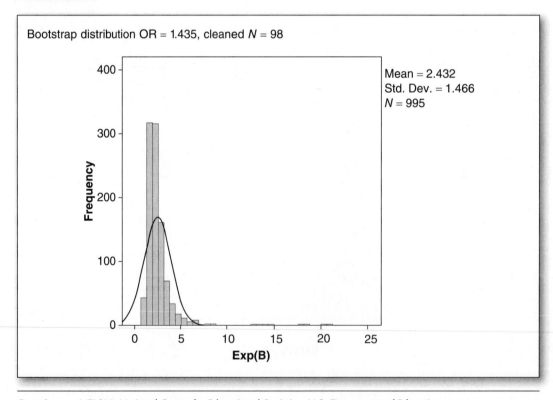

Data Source: NELS88, National Center for Educational Statistics, U.S. Department of Education.

in the population there is an effect). Through bootstrap analyses, we might (in this example) avoid a Type II error.

Unfortunately, the other $N = 100$ sample that produced OR = 5.05 was so hopelessly biased it was not helped by any measure of data cleaning. Both standardized residuals and DfBetas were analyzed, and removal of extreme scores only produced a more severely biased estimate (with odds ratios ranging up toward 16.00!). Thus, in some cases data cleaning can help relatively small samples, but it is not a panacea in hopelessly biased samples.

SUMMARY AND CONCLUSIONS

This chapter covered a number of related topics. The first, and important, point is that logistic regression requires relatively large samples in order to produce accurate, replicable population parameter estimates. Small samples (in this case, anything less than 500 cases seems to be small, particularly if the outcome of interest is not common) produce substantial and surprising volatility in parameter estimates. This can lead to confusion in the literature, as simply sampling the same population with inadequately sized samples can lead to strongly conflicting results.

Note also that these examples in this chapter are very simple examples with relatively robust effect sizes. Smaller effect sizes and more complex analyses (i.e., curvilinear or interaction effects) should be expected to be both harder to replicate and more likely to be misestimated in the absence of appropriately large, unbiased samples.

While this may seem esoteric, it is my contention that replication of results is the essential test of good science. It is the *sine qua non* of research in all fields, or it should be. Without the expectation of our results generalizing beyond our samples, why should anyone care about our results? Having good power is an excellent start on the path to replicable, generalizable results.

Authors have lauded bootstrap methodology as a panacea for many ills: small samples, influential cases, biased samples, etc. As I showed in the latter parts of this chapter, bootstrapping an inappropriately small, biased sample does not save your results. It can make them marginally better, but it can only overcome these obstacles to a certain extent.

Although I did not start out this book with the goal of repeatedly presenting the reader with examples of how important judicious data cleaning is, this chapter again reinforces the point that having a sample that contains inappropriately influential cases leads to misestimation of parameter estimates. What is interesting is that combining the powerful idea of boot-strapping with very conservative but appropriate data cleaning tended to be a powerful combination. In these limited examples, the results were much more accurate than with either bootstrapping or data cleaning alone.

ENRICHMENT

1. One of my recent students did a study on students from disadvantaged minority groups choices of attending two-year versus four-year postsecondary institutions. She had a sample of 250, of which 75 were in the two-year and 175 were in the four-year groups. Using G*power software (or using similar resources), calculate:

   a. She anticipated an effect size (odds ratio) of about 1.80 for one variable. What level of power would she have for this test (assuming this was the only variable in the equation)?

   b. How large of an odds ratio would she have to have to get power of .90 given this sample? What about power of .80 (which I rarely recommend but is the standard in the literature)?

   c. How large of a sample would she have needed to have power of .90 given this effect size? What about power = .80?

2. Find a study in one of your field's journals that used logistic regression, a study you might propose, or one of your colleague's or advisor's studies, and calculate power for that study. Was it adequate, too low, or so strong that the sample could have been smaller?

3. Choose an example of an interesting analyses we performed in previous chapters (such as DIABETES being predicted from smoking status and zBMI and the interaction). You know what the expected outcomes are in the context of a very large sample, but what if we had only had the resources for a more modest sample of $N = 300$, for example? Randomly select two small samples from those data (not from the cleaned data, but from the original data) and perform parallel analyses as though it were your study and those were your only samples available.

   a. After doing appropriate data cleaning and testing of assumptions (if relevant), compare the results of the analyses from the small samples to that of the original full sample.

   b. Do you replicate the results, or would your conclusions be very different?

c. Take one of your samples, clean the data appropriately, and subject it to bootstrap analysis. Look at the distribution of the various statistics (i.e., regression coefficient, odds ratios). If you take the median or mean of the odds ratio, does it come closer to an accurate representation of the large sample analysis?

ANSWER KEY

1a. Two-tailed power for this analysis was .98, according to my calculations. She had excellent power to detect this effect.

1b. According to my calculations, she had 90% power to detect an effect as low as an OR = 1.59, and at 80% power would have detected an OR =1.49.

1c. Given an effect size of 1.80 (and this distribution of individuals in each group), she would have needed 123 subjects for a power of .80, and $N = 161$ for power of .90.

APPENDIX A. SOFTWARE FOR CALCULATING POWER IN LOGISTIC REGRESSION

Online Power Calculation Methods

Several websites offer formulas for calculating power. The most popular website, http://www.dartmouth.edu/~eugened/power-samplesize.php, uses an algorithm created by Demidenko in 2007, which computes power, sample size, and minimal detectable odds ratios using the Wald test.

Researchers at UCLA, http://www.ats.ucla.edu/stat/stata/dae/logit_power.htm, detailed a simple method of computing power and sample size using Stata, but these estimates should be considered lower bounds.

Faul, Erdfelder, Buchner, and Lang (2009) also provide examples and a detailed breakdown of power analysis in logistic regression using the freely available G*Power software. Users of G*Power have two options for power analysis: the first uses an enumeration procedure which runs simulations to approximate sample size, and the second is based on Demidenko's and Whittmore's power formulas that use large-sample sizes to estimate power via the Wald statistic. G*Power 3.1 is available at http://www.psycho.uni-duesseldorf.de/abteilungen/aap/gpower3/.

SAS software has PROC POWER that is extremely versatile in specifying not only traditional aspects of power (alpha, *N*, effect size) but also the distributions of predictors, covariates, and the odds ratios of covariates. An overview of this procedure is available online from SAS at http://support.sas .com/documentation/cdl/en/statug/63347/HTML/default/viewer.htm#statug_ power_a0000001016.htm.

Syntax for Logistic Regression Bootstrapping in SPSS

This is a macro and syntax modified from the IBM macro for bootstrapping OLS regression found at: http://publib.boulder.ibm.com/infocenter/ spssstat/v20r0m0/index.jsp?topic=%2Fcom.ibm.spss.statistics.help%2Foms_ sav_examples_bootstrapping3.htm.

You can copy and paste this into a SPSS syntax window and alter the last lines to customize the following:

- Data set—you must enter the address for the data set here (e.g., c:\ data.sav).
- You can change the number of samples you want to analyze (currently set to 1000).
- Change DEPVAR to the name of the dependent variable you want to analyze.
- Change INDVARS to the name (or names of the independent variables) you want as predictors in the model. In this case, if you are examining two variables and the interaction, you could put: VAR1 VAR2 INT (but only if those variables and the interaction were already in the data set!).

```
DEFINE logistic_bootstrap (samples=!TOKENS(1)
/depvar=!TOKENS(1)
/indvars=!CMDEND)
COMPUTE dummyvar=1.
AGGREGATE
/OUTFILE=* MODE=ADDVARIABLES
/BREAK=dummyvar
/filesize=N.
!DO !other=1 !TO !samples
SET SEED RANDOM.
WEIGHT OFF.
FILTER OFF.
DO IF $casenum=1.
```

```
- COMPUTE #samplesize=filesize.
- COMPUTE #filesize=filesize.
END IF.
DO IF (#samplesize>0 and #filesize>0).
- COMPUTE sampleWeight=rv.binom(#samplesize, 1/#filesize).
- COMPUTE #samplesize=#samplesize-sampleWeight.
- COMPUTE #filesize=#filesize-1.
ELSE.
- COMPUTE sampleWeight=0.
END IF.
WEIGHT BY sampleWeight.
FILTER BY sampleWeight.
LOGISTIC REGRESSION VARIABLES !depvar with !indvars.
!DOEND
!ENDDEFINE.
GET FILE='<enter file location here>'.
logistic_bootstrap
samples=1000
depvar= graduate
indvars=zbyses.
```

REFERENCES

Afifi, A., May, S., & Clark, V. A. (2012). *Practical multivariate analysis* (5th ed.). Boca Raton, FL: Taylor & Francis.

Breiman, L. (1996). Bagging predictors. *Machine Learning, 24*(2), 123–140.

Cohen, J. (1962). The statistical power of abnormal-social psychological research: A review. *Journal of Abnormal and Social Psychology, 65,* 145–153.

Cohen, J. (1988). *Statistical power analysis for the behavioral sciences* (2nd ed.). Hillsdale, NJ: Lawrence Erlbaum.

Cohen, J. (1992). A power primer. *Psychological Bulletin, 122*(1), 155–159.

de Vasconcelos, M. J. P., Silva, S., Tome, M., Alvim, M., & Pereira, J. M. C. (2001). Spatial prediction of fire ignition probabilities: Comparing logistic regression and neural networks. *Photogrammetric Engineering and Remote Sensing, 67*(1), 73–81.

Deemer, W. L. (1947). The power of the *t* test and the estimation of required sample size. *Journal of Educational Psychology, 38,* 329–342.

DeGroot, A. D. (1969). *Methodology: Foundations of inference and research in the behavioral sciences.* Hague: Mouton.

Demidenko, E. (2007). Sample size determination for logistic regression revisited. *Statistics in Medicine, 26,* 3385–3397. doi: 10.1002/sim.2771

Dreiseitl, S., & Ohno-Machado, L. (2002). Logistic regression and artificial neural network classification models: a methodology review. *Journal of Biomedical Informatics, 35*(5), 352–359.

Faul, F., Erdfelder, E., Buchner, A., & Lang, A. G. (2009). Statistical power analyses using G*Power 3.1: Tests for correlation and regression analyses. *Behavioral Research Methods, 41*(4), 1149–1160. doi: 10.3758/BRM.41.4.1149

Fidler, F., & Cumming, G. (2008). The new stats: Attitudes for the 21st century. In J. W. Osborne (Ed.), *Best practices in quantitative methods* (pp. 1–14). Thousand Oaks, CA: Sage.

Fisher, R. A. (1925). *Statistical methods for research workers.* Edinburgh: Oliver & Boyd.

Harlow, L. L. (2005). *The essence of multivariate thinking: Basic themes and methods.* Mahwah: NJ: Lawrence Erlbaum.

Kaplan, A. (1964). *The conduct of inquiry: Methodology for behavioral science.* San Francisco, CA: Chandler.

Kaplan, A. (1998). *The conduct of inquiry: Methodology for behavioral science.* Piscataway, NJ: Transaction Publishers.

Killeen, P. R. (2008). Replication statistics. In J. W. Osborne (Ed.), *Best practices in quantitative methods* (pp. 103–124). Thousand Oaks CA: Sage.

Laitinen, E. K., & Laitinen, T. (2001). Bankruptcy prediction: Application of the Taylor's expansion in logistic regression. *International Review of Financial Analysis, 9*(4), 327–349.

Lang, E. W., Pitts, L. H., Damron, S. L., & Rutledge, R. (1997). Outcome after severe head injury: An analysis of prediction based upon comparison of neural network versus logistic regression analysis. *Neurological Research, 19*(3), 274.

Long, J. S. (1997). *Regression models for categorical and limited dependent variables* (Vol. 7): Thousand Oaks, CA: Sage.

Murphy, K. R., Myors, B., & Wolach, A. (2009). *Statistical power analysis: A simple and general model for traditional and modern hypothesis tests* (3rd ed.). New York, NY: Taylor & Francis.

Osborne, J. W. (2000). Prediction in multiple regression. *Practical Assessment, Research & Evaluation, 7,* 2.

Osborne, J. W. (2008). Sweating the small stuff in educational psychology: How effect size and power reporting failed to change from 1969 to 1999, and what that means for the future of changing practices. *Educational Psychology, 28*(2), 1–10.

Osborne, J. W., Kocher, B., & Tillman, D. (2012). *Sweating the small stuff: Do authors in APA journals clean data or test assumptions (and should anyone care if they do).* Paper presented at the annual meeting of the Eastern Education Research Association, Hilton Head, SC.

Pedhazur, E. J. (1997). *Multiple regression in behavioral research: Explanation and prediction.* Fort Worth, TX: Harcourt Brace College.

Peduzzi, P., Concato, J., Kemper, E., Holford, T. R., & Feinstein, A. R. (1996). A simulation study of the number of events per variable in logistic regression analysis. *Journal of Clinical Epidemiology, 49*(12), 1373–1379.

Rodgers, J. L. (1999). The bootstrap, the jackknife, and the randomization test: A sampling taxonomy. *Multivariate Behavioral Research, 34*(4), 441–456.

Schmidt, F. (1996). Statistical significance testing and cumulative knowledge in psychology: Implications for training of researchers. *Psychological Methods, 1*(2), 115.

Shtatland, E. S., Kleinman, K., & Cain, E. M. (2004). *A new strategy of model building in PROC LOGISTIC with automatic variable selection, validation, shrinkage and model averaging.* Paper presented at the SUGI.

Steyerberg, E. W., Harrell Jr, F. E., Borsboom, G. J. J. M., Eijkemans, M., Vergouwe, Y., & Habbema, J. D. F. (2001). Internal validation of predictive models: Efficiency of some procedures for logistic regression analysis. *Journal of Clinical Epidemiology, 54*(8), 774–781.

Strogatz, S. (2012). *The joy of X: A guided tour of math, from one to infinity.* New York, NY: Houghton Mifflin Harcourt.

Toner, C., Broomhead, C., Littlejohn, I., Samra, G., Powney, J., Palazzo, M., . . . Strunin, L. (1996). Prediction of postoperative nausea and vomiting using a logistic regression model. *British Journal of Anaesthesia, 76*(3), 347–351.

Tressoldi, P. E. (2012). Replication unreliability in psychology: Elusive phenomena or "elusive" statistical power? *Frontiers in Psychology, 3.*

Wilkinson, L. (1999). Task Force on Statistical Inference, APA Board of Scientific Affairs (1999). Statistical methods in psychology journals: guidelines and explanations. *American Psychologist, 54*(8), 594–604.

Wong, C. H. (2004). Contractor performance prediction model for the United Kingdom construction contractor: Study of logistic regression approach. *Journal of Construction Engineering and Management, 130*(5), 691–698.

Ysebaert, T., Meire, P., Herman, P. M. J., & Verbeek, H. (2002). Macrobenthic species response surfaces along estuarine gradients: Prediction by logistic regression. *Marine Ecology Progress Series, 225.*

Yu, C. H. (2003). Resampling methods: Concepts, applications, and justification. *Practical Assessment, Research & Evaluation, 8*(19), 1–23.

11

MODERN AND EFFECTIVE METHODS OF DEALING WITH MISSING DATA

I s emptiness meaningless? Modern researchers seem to view missing data as empty, useless, a void that should have been filled with information, a thing without pattern, meaning, or value. Yet the ancient Greeks saw emptiness as potential, much as a painter sees a blank canvas. The Greek goddess Chaos (Khaos) represented unfilled space (initially the unfilled space between the earth and the heavens in their creation mythology), and ancient Olmec, Indian, and Arabic mathematicians saw usefulness in the mathematical quantification of nothing, what we now call zero (Colebrooke, 1817; Diehl, 2004).

The modern computer era is built upon use of 0s and 1s as indicators of important states, both meaningful and critical to the functioning of devices that are now ubiquitous. In this chapter, we will explore important issues relating to missing data, how to effectively deal with missing data, and how your decisions concerning missing data can either improve or potentially doom your logistic regression analyses. Of course, missing data is also related to the topic from the last chapter—sample size, in that more missing data can mean fewer cases to analyze unless they are handled properly.

◆ DEALING WITH MISSING OR INCOMPLETE DATA IN LOGISTIC REGRESSION

Every study has the potential for incomplete or missing data. Missing data—the absence of an answer or response where one was expected—can occur for many reasons: participants can fail to respond to questions (legitimately or illegitimately—more on that later), equipment and data collecting or recording mechanisms can malfunction, subjects can withdraw from studies before they are completed, and data entry errors can occur. Data cleaning can also create missingness, as data points that are deemed outside the bounds of reasonable range (or inappropriately influential) can be deleted.

The issue with missingness is that nearly all classic and modern statistical techniques (including the various types of logistic regression we are discussing in this book) require complete data, and most common statistical computing packages default to some of the least desirable options for dealing with missing data: deletion of the case from the analysis. This approach is also called "complete case analysis" and has been the standard response to missing data for most researchers across most fields. In my chapter on missing data in my book on data cleaning (Osborne, 2012), I made the argument that complete case analysis can be a suboptimal choice in the modern age of statistical computing where we have ready access to more desirable methods for dealing with missing data, such as single and multiple imputation. The poorest option is what was at one time considered progressive—mean substitution.[1] The evidence regarding mean substitution and complete case analysis is compelling.

Vach and Blettner (1995) present compelling examples of complete case analysis introducing significant bias into the analysis when individuals with complete cases are a biased subsample of all possible or present participants. And as Greenland and Finkle (1995) point out, even when complete cases are a representative subsample of the overall sample, the loss of participants can cause increases in variance/standard errors, leading to misestimation or Type II errors. Logistic regression is a bit of a fickle process, and loss of power (sample size) due to missing data can dramatically harm power to detect effects. No modern author writing on missing data is a proponent of mean substitution, which can cause significant misestimation and

---

[1] Sadly, this appears to still be the case. In a survey of recent top-tier journals, authors seemed to ignore missingness (defaulting to complete case analysis) most of the time, but when they deviated from this, it was almost always to use mean substitution.

errors of inference as it leads to substantially reduced standard errors and underestimated variance. In simulations using real data from my book on data cleaning, I demonstrated empirically that mean substitution is just not acceptable as a best practice in the 21st century.

Modern researchers point to advanced techniques like imputation (using present data and a multiple regression framework to estimate what the missing values are likely to be) and multiple imputation (where multiple copies of the data set are generated with varying values inserted for the missing data, and then all data sets are analyzed and likely estimates of the parameters are produced) as valuable tools in the analyst's toolbox. While imputation is relatively simple, multiple imputation is not implemented in all statistical software packages (or is only available via costly add-ons; for example, SAS implements multiple imputation nicely, but in SPSS researchers are required to purchase an expensive missing data module).

Obviously, the ideal situation is to minimize exposure to the problem by attempting to reduce the opportunity for missing data. Where that fails, my argument here is that all researchers should examine their data for missingness, and researchers wanting the best (i.e., the most replicable and generalizable) results from their research need to be prepared to deal with missing data in the most appropriate and productive way possible. Of course, our focus in this book is on logistic regression, but many of the lessons from this chapter apply to other quantitative analyses as well. Through the course of this chapter, we will use data from the National Education Longitudinal Study of 1988 (NELS88), predicting variables such as SMOKING (whether a student has ever smoked cigarettes or other tobacco products). Using a sample of 5,550 students with complete data on all variables (the known "population"), we have a dependent variable with 367 (6.6%) who admit to smoking and 5,183 (93.4%) who do not. Our simple smoking example will use z-scored standardized achievement score tests that in this "population" has an odds ratio of 1.37 ($p < .0001$), with a 95%CI of 1.23 and 1.54. This represents a moderate effect, wherein the odds of smoking are 1.37 for every standard deviation increase in student achievement (which frankly, I found surprising). As I describe later, we will use this benchmark to assess various types of common problems researchers may encounter—data missing completely at random, and data missing not at random. By working with a population with known effects, we can use that as a benchmark to see the effects of missingness on parameter estimates and inference (Type I and Type II errors), and then see how well various methods of dealing with missing data recaptures the original population parameters.

Before launching into the chapter, I will warn readers of my other book that logistic regression is a bit quirky, and that while the general principles of missing data apply, because logistic regression is nonparametric, and because of the estimation algorithms used, effects can be a bit less predictable than in more common parametric analyses such as analysis of variance or regression. Logistic regression analyses are impacted by many factors, including the relative number of cases in each category on the dependent variable. This smoking dependent variable is not well-balanced, in that less than 7% of cases are in one group. But this is also not an uncommon percentage, and logistic regression is designed to handle much less equitably distributed dependent variables. Thus, this chapter will be a brief introduction to some of the issues, but it cannot cover every possible issue or combination of factors.

Further, there are several types of variables that we need to be concerned with: dependent variables, independent variables, and covariates. We will start with the simplest issue, the issue of missing values in the independent variable. But first, a brief overview of the issue at hand: why missing data matters.

Not All Missing Data Are the Same

The issue before us is whether we have complete data from all research participants on all variables (at all possible time points, if a repeated-measures design). If any data on any variable from any participant (at any time point) is not present, the researcher is dealing with missing or incomplete data. In many types of research, it is the case that there can be *legitimate missing data*. This can come in many forms, for many reasons. Most commonly, legitimate missing data is an absence of data when it is appropriate for there to be an absence. Imagine you are filling out a survey that asks you whether you are in a committed romantic relationship, and if so, how long you have been in this particular committed relationship. If you answer "no" to the first question (indicating you are not currently in a committed romantic relationship), it is legitimate for you to skip the follow-up question on how long you have been in that relationship. If a survey asks you whether you voted in the last election, and if so, what party the candidate was from, it is legitimate to skip the second part if you did not vote in the last election. If a survey asks if you are a smoker, and you answer no, it is legitimate for you to skip the next questions on whether you smoke cigarettes, pipe, cigar, or hookah, and how often. In a long-term study of people receiving a particular type of treatment, if you are no longer receiving treatment because you are cured, that might be a legitimate form of missing data. Or perhaps you are following employee satisfaction at a company. If an employee leaves the company (and thus is no longer an employee) it seems to me legitimate that person should no longer be responding to employee satisfaction questionnaires.

Large data sets, especially government data sets or large survey studies with complex skip patterns, are full of legitimately missing data, and researchers need to be thoughtful about handling this issue appropriately. But note too that even in the case of legitimate missingness, missingness is meaningful. Missingness in this context informs and reinforces the status of a particular individual—and can even provide an opportunity for checking the validity of an individual's responses. In cleaning the data from a survey on adolescent health risk behaviors many years ago, I came across some individuals who indicated on one question that they had never used illegal drugs, but later in the questionnaire, when asked how many times they had used marijuana, they answered that question indicating a number greater than 0. Thus, what should have been a question that was legitimately skipped was answered with an unexpected number. What could this mean? One possibility is that the respondent was not paying attention to the questions and answered carelessly or in error. Another possibility is that the initial answer (have you ever used illegal drugs) was answered inaccurately. Finally, it is possible that some subset of the population did not include marijuana in the category of "illegal drugs"—an interesting finding in itself and one way in which researchers can use data cleaning to improve their subsequent research or at least raise interesting questions.

There are different ways to deal with legitimate missing data. Survival analysis is particularly good at dealing with some types of missing data.[2] Another (perhaps more common) method of dealing with this sort of legitimate missing data is adjusting the denominator. Again taking the example of the relationship survey, we could eliminate those not in relationships from the particular analysis looking at length of relationship (in this case, the question is appropriate only to those with complete data on that item) but would leave all respondents in the analysis when looking at issues relating to being in a relationship or not. Thus, instead of asking a slightly silly question of the data: "How long, on average, do all people, even people not in a relationship, stay in a relationship?" we can ask two more refined questions: "What are the predictors of whether someone is currently

---

[2]Which can deal with issues like participants leaving the study (right-censored or truncated data) or entering the study at a particular point (left-censored or truncated data).

in a committed relationship?" and "Of those who are currently in a committed relationship, how long on average have they been in that relationship?" In this case, it makes no sense to include those not in a relationship when asking questions about how long someone has been in a relationship.

This example of dealing with legitimately missing data is relatively straightforward and mostly follows common sense. The best practice here is to make sure the denominator (the sample or subsample) is appropriate for the analysis. Make sure to report having selected certain parts of your sample for specific analyses when doing so.

Illegitimately missing data is relatively common in all types of research. Sensors fail or become miscalibrated, leaving researchers without data until that sensor is replaced or recalibrated. Research participants choose to skip questions on surveys that the researchers expect everyone to answer. Participants drop out of studies before they are complete. And at times, sampling frames purposefully administer select items to subsamples to help control length of interviews or for other purposes. Few authors seem to

Figure 11.1 Percent of Articles in Top Journals Reporting Any Handling of Missing Data

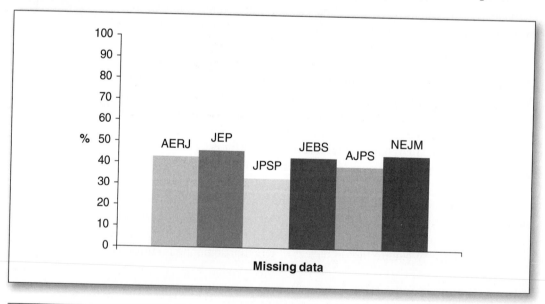

Source: Osborne, J. W., Kocher, B., & Tillman, D. (2012, February). *Many authors in top journals don't report testing assumptions: Why you should care and what we can do about it.* Paper presented at the annual meeting of the Eastern Educational Research Association, Hilton Head, SC.

appropriately deal with the issue of illegitimately missing data, despite its obvious potential to substantially skew the results (Cole, 2008). For example, in a recent survey my students and I performed in highly regarded journals (Osborne, Kocher, & Tillman, 2012; *American Education Research Journal, Journal of Educational Psychology, Journal of Personality and Social Psychology, Journal of Educational and Behavioral Statistics, American Journal of Political Science,* and the *New England Journal of Medicine*) we found that 30–50% of papers discussed the issue of missing data with surprisingly little variation across fields (as shown in Figure 11.1). For those half (or more) of studies that fail to report anything relating to missing data: (a) have complete data (rare in the social sciences, but possible), (b) have complete data because they removed all subjects with any missing data (i.e., performed complete case analysis, which is undesirable, and can potentially bias the results, as we will discuss later), (c) deal effectively with the missing data and fail to report it (less likely, but possible), or (d) allow the statistical software to treat the missing data however through whatever the default method is, which most often leads to the same result as (b), the deletion of subjects with missing data? If our survey is representative of researchers across the sciences, we have cause for concern. Our survey of the literature again found that of those researchers who did report something to do with missing data, most reported having used the classic but anachronistic methods of listwise deletion (complete case analysis) or mean substitution, neither of which are particularly effective practices (Schafer & Graham, 2002). In only a few cases did researchers report doing anything constructive with the missing data, such as imputation. And in no case did we find that researchers analyze the missingness to determine whether it was missing completely at random (MCAR), missing at random (MAR), or missing not at random (MNAR). As I suggested in my book on data cleaning, this suggests to me that there is a mythology in quantitative research that (a) individuals with incomplete data cannot contribute to the analyses and that (b) removing them from the analyses is an innocuous action. I hope to convince you that neither of these points is supported in the literature or by empirical evidence and that it is relatively simple to make your logistic regression analysis more methodologically sound by appropriately dealing with missing data.

Categories of Missingness: Why Do We Care If Data Are Missing Completely at Random or Not?

When exploring missing data, it is important to come to a conclusion about the *mechanism of missingness*—in other words, the hypothesized reason for why data are missing. This can range from arbitrary or random influences to purposeful patterns of nonresponse (e.g., most women in a study refuse to answer a question that is offensive or sensitive to women but that does not affect men in the same way).

If we can infer the data are missing at random (MCAR/MAR), then the nonresponse is deemed *ignorable*. In other words, random missingness can be problematic from a power perspective (in that it often reduces sample size or degrees of freedom for an analysis), but it does not potentially bias the results. However, data missing NOT at random (MNAR) could potentially be a strong biasing influence (Osborne, 2012; Rubin, 1976).

Let us take an example of an employee satisfaction survey given to schoolteachers in a local district as an example of MCAR, MAR, and MNAR. Imagine that in September (near the beginning of the traditional school year in the United States) all teachers are surveyed (X), and then in January teachers are surveyed again (Y). *Missing Completely at Random* (MCAR) would mean that missingness in January is completely unrelated to any variable, including September satisfaction level, age, years of teaching, satisfaction level at follow-up, and so on. At times, missingness of this type is a function of the study design. For example, due to lack of resources, the survey designers could have decided that only 50% of all respondents from September would be randomly sampled to respond to the survey again in January, with all potential respondents completing surveys at both time points. In this case, having data for Y present or absent is completely explained by random selection (if all selected respond to the survey). In other words, missingness has no systematic relation to any variable present or unmeasured (such as age, sex, race, level of satisfaction, years teaching, etc.) and is thus ignorable. You as a researcher can simply select cases with data at both time points without worry that your data are biased—*if* all other important conditions are met (namely a 100% response rate at all-time points) and if you can afford to lose the power associated with all those lost cases.

Now imagine that this surveying was part of the school district's initiative to keep teachers from leaving, and they wanted to focus on teachers with low satisfaction in September, perhaps with an intervention to help raise satisfaction of these low-satisfaction teachers. In this case, the missingness depends solely and completely on X, the initial score. Because the goal of the survey is to explore how these particular teachers fared, rather than all teachers in general, missingness is still considered *ignorable and Missing at Random (MAR)*.[3] If, on the other hand, other

[3]As with many things in statistics, the implications of MAR missingness being *ignorable* has been misapplied. MAR missingness is a very particular type of missingness and is only ignorable for certain types of analyses (e.g., Heitjan & Basu, 1996). I think that most researchers are best served by not ignoring any type of missingness, even MCAR.

factors aside from initial satisfaction level were responsible (or partly responsible for missingness), such that perhaps only teachers whose satisfaction had improved responded (the teachers who continued to be substantially dissatisfied may be less likely to return the survey), then the data are considered *Missing Not at Random (MNAR)* and are *not ignorable* (Rubin, 1976; Schafer & Graham, 2002) because they may substantially bias the results. In the case of MNAR, the average satisfaction of the follow-up group would be expected to be inflated if those who were most dissatisfied had stopped responding. If missingness were related to another external factor, such as if those teachers who were most dissatisfied were the most junior teachers (the teachers with least time in the profession), that would also qualify the missing data as MNAR.

In other words, it is only legitimate to assume that your observed data are representative of the intended population if data are convincingly missing at random or missing completely at random.[4] For simplicity, I will proceed through the rest of the chapter, focusing on MCAR versus MNAR. MAR (ignorable missingness) is probably more common than MCAR, but MNAR is probably most common, and thus, MCAR is merely presented as a comparison point. In truth, best practices in handling missing data appears to be equally effective regardless of whether the data are MCAR, MAR, or MNAR.

HOW DO YOU KNOW IF YOUR ♦ DATA ARE MCAR, MAR, OR MNAR?

It is important that a researcher investigate why missing data are present when they are not expected. There are many methods suggested in the literature, but one of my favorite methods is to use binary logistic regression for the purpose of this investigation (regardless of what type of analysis I am ultimately going to perform for my hypothesis testing). One of the methods for testing whether missingness is MCAR, MAR, or MNAR is testing whether missingness is related to other variables.

Quantifying missingness is relatively easy. In most modern statistical programs, there is a system missing value that appears in analyses as nothing

---

[4]Once again, let us be clear that values that are "out of scope" or legitimately missing, such as non-smokers who skip the question concerning how many cigarettes are smoked a day, are not considered "missing" and are not an issue (Schafer & Graham, 2002). In this example, let us imagine that non-classroom teachers (e.g., guidance counselors, teacher assistants, or other personnel) who took the initial survey were not included in the follow-up because they are not the population of interest, classroom teachers. This would be legitimate missing data.

but can be manipulated. For example, in SPSS we can recode system missing values into real values. Using our NHIS data as an example, we have 952 cases out of 27,731 who have missing values on the BMI variable we have been using throughout the book. If I want to explore missingness on this variable, I can create a dummy variable that represents whether each case has missing data or complete data on that variable:

```
Recode BMI (sysmis=1) (else =0) into MISSING_BMI.
Execute.
```

In SPSS, `sysmis` allows us to manipulate data that have system missing values. Using this simple recode command, I created a new variable called MISSING_BMI that is coded 1 if a case had a missing value on BMI, and 0 if a case did not.

In SAS, you can use statements such as

```
If BMI=. then do;
If missing(BMI) then do;
```

which allow for similar manipulation of missing values into useful dummy variables. Once I have a dummy variable that captures missingness on a particular variable, I can construct a logistic regression equation predicting missingness from other variables in the data set. My hope is that none are significantly related to missingness (strengthening my view that missingness might be random). The frequency distribution of MISSING_BMI confirms that my recode worked, as I have the expected number of cases with 1 and 0.

Once you have the missingness variable created, we need to test three different things: (a) that missingness is not related to the dependent variable

Table 11.1 Frequency Distribution of MISSING_BMI

		Frequency	Percent	Valid Percent	Cumulative Percent
Valid	.00	26779	96.6	96.6	96.6
	1.00	952	3.4	3.4	100.0
	Total	27731	100.0	100.0	

Data Source: National Health Interview Survey of 2010 (NHIS2010), Centers for Disease Control and Prevention.

of interest; (b) that missingness is not related to the independent variable(s) or any other important variable in the data set—even if it is not being used in this particular analysis; and (c) that when all variables are used to predict missingness, they collectively do not account for significant model fit improvement (as measured by Δ−2LL as we have done in previous chapters). If all three of these conditions are met, and it is reasonable to argue that you have measured all important variables that *could be related to missingness on this variable* then you can conclude missingness is completely at random. Furthermore, it must be reasonable that there was enough power to detect a significant effect if indeed it existed. Because we have more than 27,000 cases that is a reasonable assertion, and nonsignificance can be taken seriously. However, if we only had 75 cases in our data, establishing no relationship also requires looking at the odds ratios and regression coefficients and arguing they are small enough to be ignorable. A reasonably sized effect should have a reasonable probability of being detected for this type of analysis to matter.

The first test was conducted as a simple logistic regression analysis predicting MISSING_BMI from DIABETES, which was not significant. The other analyses can be combined into a single logistic regression equation, in which I include as many other variables with as little missing data as possible. Fortunately, in this case many of the other variables have few missing cases. I then created a logistic regression equation predicting MISS-ING_BMI from all other variables I could think of that had no missing data: AGE, DIABETES (0 = no, 1 = yes), currently MARRIED (0 = no, 1 = yes), SEX (1 = male, 2 = female), and the original RACE variable (coded into six categories).

Both the second and third condition were failed in this test. Unfortunately, the Δ−2LL was 217.05 (*p* < .0001) when all these variables were entered into the equation, causing me to conclude there are significant relationships between one or more of these variables and missingness on BMI. As you can see in Table 11.2 (see page 368), there is a slight trend with AGE, indicating that older respondents are more likely to be missing BMI than younger respondents. No other variable except SEX was significant, but the magnitude of the SEX effect is conclusive evidence that the data are not missing completely at random. The odds ratio indicates that women are *substantially less likely* to be missing BMI than males.

At times, these analyses can give insight into the reason data might be missing, but our primary motive is to establish whether the missingness mechanism can reasonably be considered random or not. Note that putting all variables in the logistic regression model simultaneously creates a higher standard as each variable must have a significant *unique* effect. Thus, if the

Table 11.2 Variables Predicting Missingness in BMI Variable

	B	SE	Wald	df	Sig.	Exp(B)
AGE	.004	.002	3.975	1	.046	1.004
diabetes	.116	.109	1.132	1	.287	1.123
married	−.013	.068	.038	1	.846	.987
SEX	−1.030	.079	171.160	1	.000	.357
RACE			8.919	5	.112	
RACE (1)	.062	.276	.051	1	.821	1.064
RACE (2)	−.103	.286	.130	1	.719	.902
RACE (3)	.327	.413	.628	1	.428	1.387
RACE (4)	−.313	.317	.976	1	.323	.731
RACE (5)	−.558	1.048	.283	1	.594	.572
Constant	−3.200	.287	124.744	1	.000	.041

Data Source: NHIS2010, Centers for Disease Control and Prevention.

overall model (Δ−2LL) is significant, that is sufficient to conclude nonrandom missingness. A more sensitive measure of each variable is to look at the *variables not in the equation* statistics that some software produces, as Table 11.3 shows:

Table 11.3 Variables Not in the Equation

			Score	df	Sig.
Step 0	Variables	AGE	8.848	1	.003
		diabetes	2.145	1	.143
		married	1.079	1	.299
		SEX	186.998	1	.000
		RACE	7.860	5	.164
		RACE (1)	3.793	1	.051
		RACE (2)	.778	1	.378
		RACE (3)	.808	1	.369
		RACE (4)	5.347	1	.021
		RACE (5)	.383	1	.536
	Overall Statistics		203.185	9	.000

Data Source: NHIS2010, Centers for Disease Control and Prevention.

This table summarizes whether each variable would be significant if it were the only variable entered into the equation (a zero-order effect) and thus is more sensitive. As you can see, two of the RACE dummy coded variables are significant in this table before other variable are entered into the model.

WHAT DO WE DO WITH MISSING DATA? ♦

In order to illustrate some of the effects of missing data handling on logistic regression, I used data from the National Education Longitudinal Study of 1988 (NELS88) from the National Center of Educational Statistics (Ingels, 1994) to provide an example. As mentioned earlier, the sample of 5,550 students who had complete data on the relevant variables (smoking, achievement test scores, and other variables we will introduce later on) were defined, for our purposes, as our population to which we will compare the results of our examples.[5]

DATA MISSING COMPLETELY AT RANDOM (MCAR) ♦

To simulate MCAR situations, I created a random yes/no variable for each student in order to randomly assign them 0 or 1. To do this, I used a Mersenne twister random number generator and a random variable Bernoulli probability generator with either a .25, .50, or .75 probability. This produced three dummy variables that identified 25%, 50%, or 75% of the sample for deletion from the analysis, thus simulating a situation no researcher wants to see—that a sizable portion of their sample has been potentially lost as missing data. As a confirmation of the randomness of the missingness, two analyses were performed. First, there was no relationship between the dependent variable and the missingness variable (similar to that created in the NHIS example above) in any of the three analyses case. Second, there was no correlation between the missingness variable and the independent variable or any other substantive variable in the data set. Finally, a logistic regression predicting missingness (0 = not, 1 = missing) from SMOKING, zACH, and other predictors we will introduce later was not significant overall. These types of analysis confirm to an inference of randomness or nonrandomness regarding the missing

---

[5]Note that this sample is not the complete NELS88 sample, but rather a subsample of those with complete data for purposes of this example.

Table 11.4 Comparison of "Population" to Sample That Lost 25–75% of Data Randomly Predicting Smoking Status From Student Achievement

		B	SE	Wald	df	Sig.	Exp(B)	95% CI for Exp(B)	
								Lower	Upper
Full sample N = 5550	zAch	.317	.058	30.150	1	.000	1.374	1.226	1.538
	Constant	−2.722	.058	2199.538	1	.000	.066		
25% missing N = 4116	zAch	.300	.066	20.387	1	.000	1.350	1.185	1.538
	Constant	−2.705	.067	1634.233	1	.000	.067		
50% missing N = 2853	zAch	.330	.084	15.333	1	.000	1.391	1.179	1.641
	Constant	−2.822	.085	1104.232	1	.000	.059		
75% missing N = 1387	zAch	.329	.112	8.560	1	.003	1.389	1.115	1.731
	Constant	−2.686	.114	553.251	1	.000	.068		
75% missing meansub	zAch	.330	.109	9.111	1	.003	1.390	1.123	1.722
	Constant	−2.690	.057	2237.091	1	.000	.068		
75% missing Strong imput.	zAch	.289	.066	18.946	1	.000	1.336	1.172	1.522
	Constant	−2.701	.057	2244.825	1	.000	.067		
75% missing Weak imput.	zAch	.336	.080	17.487	1	.000	1.400	1.196	1.638
	Constant	−2.704	.058	2201.363	1	.000	.067		
75% missing Multiple imputation	zAch	.306	.074	17.205	1	.000	1.358	1.175	1.569
	Constant	−2.698	.057	2248.827	1	.000	.067		

Data Source: NELS88, National Center for Educational Statistics, U.S. Department of Education.

data, which we already knew in this case because the missingness was designed to be random.

The assertion in the literature is that data missing completely at random (which this example attempted to simulate, albeit in an extreme way) should have no substantial effect on the results. Indeed, comparing the results in Table 11.4, this is confirmed. Loss of either 25% or 50% or even 75% of the sample in this random way resulted in no meaningful change in the results. Student achievement is significant at the same level, the coefficients are very similar, and the odds ratios are similar within decimal points. The standard errors predictably become larger as the percent of the sample that is missing increases, as larger samples have smaller standard errors, and correspondingly, the 95%CIs for the odds ratios become slightly wider as missingness increases. Wald statistics also scale with sample size, shrinking as the sample shrinks. I think one would be hard-pressed to claim that loss of even 75% of the sample in a completely random way influenced these results (except for a loss of power). Thus, in the case of data MCAR, it seems that complete case analysis does not substantially bias the results. But what if an enterprising researcher decided to attempt to recapture the missing data?

Mean Substitution

As mentioned earlier, this is a discredited method of dealing with missing data, as you will quickly see. In order to examine the effects of this method of dealing with missing data, the sample of 75% missing was recaptured by substituting the mean of the existing 25% for each missing value. This had the effect of very slightly altering the mean (from 0.10 in the original variable to 0.09 in the mean substituted variable) but more importantly, halved the standard deviation (from 0.98 in the original variable to 0.49 in the mean substituted variable). Interestingly, as you can see in Table 11.4, the problems introduced by the mean substitution do not substantially bias these results—indeed, the primary issue mean substitution introduces is creating a highly kurtotic variable. As logistic regression is nonparametric, this does not lead to substantial bias as in parametric procedures, as I showed in my book on data cleaning. Yet careful examination of this row in the table shows that the mean substitution did not give the analysis much in the way of power or precision over the 75% missing analysis. Indeed, comparing this with the 75% missing analysis and the 0% missing analysis, this mean-substituted analysis is almost identical to the 75% missing analysis than the full sample analysis—the 95%CIs, Wald statistics, and standard errors are all substantially different than the initial analysis with complete data. Thus we cannot conclude that mean substitution did anything positive for the analysis in the case of data missing completely at random. Further, remember that this is a best-case scenario in that the data are truly missing at random. This is not often the case, and in the case of nonrandom missingness, mean substitution can be less benign.

Strong and Weak Imputation

Many authors have argued that using imputation (predicting scores via multiple regression modeling) is superior to mean substitution or complete case analysis, particularly when data are missing not at random. In the case of these data, which are missing completely at random, we will still introduce these two possibilities, which will become more useful later in the chapter. In this case, we will impute the missing cases using *strong imputation*—in this case, a highly correlated variable—or *weak imputation*—in this case, two variables that are more weakly related to the variable with the missing data, eighth-grade student achievement. The strong imputation will be performed by utilizing 10th-grade student achievement, which is correlated $r = 0.82$ with eighth-grade achievement. The weak imputation will use two less closely related variables, socioeconomic status (SES; z-scored) and grades (1 = mostly Fs to 5 = mostly As). These latter two variables have a multiple correlation $R = .58$. Thus, in the strong imputation example, we are using a variable that shares 67.24% of the variance of the target variable, and in the weak imputation case, we have variables that share 33.70% of the variance. Still, my previous explorations of missing data suggest that even weak imputation is superior to complete case analysis when the missingness is highly biased.

Weak imputation

Using a simple multiple regression equation, predicting the zACH variable with 75% missing completely at random from zSES and eighth-grade grades produced a regression equation:

$$\hat{Y} = -2.954 + 0.264(\text{zSES}) + 0.719(\text{grades}).$$

I then used this equation to impute values for each of the 75% of cases with missing data. The results of this procedure were to produce a variable that is strongly correlated with the original variable ($r = .71$,

$p < .0001$.[6] As you can see in Table 11.4, weak imputation with 75% data missing at random (admittedly a relatively extreme case) produced results that were better than either complete case analysis or mean substitution—with point estimates, statistics, standard errors, and confidence intervals that were approximating or better than the 50% MCAR sample. In other words, the weak imputation did not completely recapture the results when all 5,550 students had complete data, but it essentially recaptured much of the situation that was lost—about one third (returning the analysis to that of the 50% missing analyses—or better—rather than 75% missing), which is about the amount of variance the weak imputation equation accounted for in the dependent variable.

Strong imputation

Using a simple multiple regression equation, predicting the zACH variable with 75% missing completely at random from 10th-grade achievement test scores produced a regression equation:

$$\hat{Y} = -5.118 + 0.092(\text{ACH10}).$$

I then used this equation to impute values for each of the 75% of cases with missing data. The result of this procedure was to produce a variable that is strongly correlated with the original variable ($r = .86$, $p < .0001$). As you can see in Table 11.4, strong imputation with 75% data missing at random (admittedly a relatively extreme case) produced results that were better than either complete case analysis or mean substitution or weak imputation—with point estimates, statistics, standard errors, and confidence intervals that were approximating the 25% MCAR sample. In other words, the strong imputation did not completely recapture the results when all 5,550 students had complete data, but it essentially recaptured much of the information that was lost—which is expected as the prediction equation accounted for a good deal of variance.

---

[6]Some authors have argued that this overfits the data, as only values on the regression line are estimated, whereas in real data, values vary around the regression line. Thus, some have suggested that adding a small random error to each prediction more closely simulates real-world data and prevents overfitting. However, how large an error to add is open to debate. It is not my experience that the data are overfit, and I do not add this slight modification to simple imputation although it is something that should be considered, particularly if the predictors are very strongly related to the variable being imputed.

Both of these imputation procedures had laudable outcomes but obviously would be more efficient with a lower percentage of data missing.

Multiple imputation (Bayesian)

Using AMOS software from IBM/SPSS (although many software packages, including SAS, can perform multiple imputation), I used Bayesian estimation to produce the recommended minimum of 20 parallel data sets using the *weak imputation* variables of eighth-grade grades and family SES. The workings of multiple imputation are explored elsewhere in detail, including in my book (Osborne, 2011) and are too lengthy to detail here. Briefly, multiple imputation creates multiple parallel data sets that impute different values for the missing values to give the researcher a theoretical range of outcomes, rather than a single outcome. This has certain benefits, including being able to estimate the stability or volatility of the results of imputation, as well as estimating a reasonable confidence interval within which the actual results should fall.

The results of this analysis, however, are illustrative. As Table 11.4 shows in the final row, multiple imputation even with relatively suboptimal prediction produced superior outcomes over single imputation with weak predictors. Most notably, the 95%CI for the multiple imputation analysis is closer to that of the full sample than either simple imputation with "weak" predictors or even (in this case) with a single strong predictor. The standard errors are better than the original weak imputation as well.

Summary

This first section explores a relatively rare situation—where data are truly missing at random. In this case, even large portions of missing data can produce relatively accurate point estimates, although handling the missing data through imputation or multiple imputation seems to produce better results. Admittedly, this is splitting hairs between pretty good and very good results from an extremely bad situation. In the next section, we will explore what happens more commonly—when data are *not* missing at random. In this case, I suspect you will see more profound benefits to dealing with missing data.

◆ DATA MISSING NOT AT RANDOM

To explore this more common issue of data missing *not* at random (MNAR), I created three types of nonrandom missingness: MNAR-low, MNAR-high, and MNAR-smoke. For the first two examples, I separated students into low achieving (scoring at or below the 25th percentile on the standardized eighth-grade composite, by2xcomp), average achieving (between the 25th and 75th percentiles), and high achieving (above the 75th percentile) and used a random Bernoulli generator to individually identify individuals within each of those groups as missing or not.[7] For MNAR-low (an imaginary scenario where low-achieving students were least likely to respond), I randomly assigned 95% of low-scoring students to be missing (40% for low-scoring smokers), 75% of the average-scoring students to be missing (40% for low-scoring smokers), and 1% of the high-scoring students to be missing. For MNAR-high (an imaginary scenario where high achieving students were least likely to respond), I randomly assigned 1% of low-scoring students to be missing, 75% of the average-scoring students to be missing (40% for low-scoring smokers), and 95% of the high-scoring students to be missing (40% for high-scoring smokers). This created highly skewed samples on achievement, representing perhaps a worst-case scenario, as the goal was to highlight the effect of MNAR missingness. For MNAR-smoke, (a scenario where the target of the study, smokers, are less likely to respond), I randomly assigned 66% of smokers to be missing (independent of achievement level), and 10% of nonsmokers were randomly assigned to be missing (again, irrespective of achievement). As a result of these schemes, about 59% of subjects were selected to be missing in the MNAR-low and MNAR-high conditions. In the MNAR-smoke condition, only 13% of the subjects were selected to be missing. Of course, there are infinite ways in which missingness can occur, and these are only intended to be examples, and rather extreme ones at that.

The Effects of Listwise Deletion (Complete Case Analysis)

We are examining the effects of different types of nonrandom missingness on the goodness of results that average researchers might see. As you can see in Table 11.5 (see page 376), the "population" odds ratio of achievement predicting smoking is 1.37, with a 95%CI of 1.23–1.54. As the default in most statistical packages, complete case analysis, or listwise deletion of data with missing values, leads to varying degrees of bias. You can also see in the subsequent three rows that two of the three MNAR scenarios I have imagined (low-performing students are more likely to be

---

[7]In the case of MNAR-low and MNAR-high, smokers were privileged with lower missingness rates as they were such a small portion of this fictitious population to begin with (6.6%).

Table 11.5 Effectiveness of Various Missing Data Handling Strategies When Data Are Missing Not at Random

		B	SE	Wald	df	Sig.	Exp(B)	95%CI for Exp(B)	
								Lower	Upper
Full sample N = 5550	zAch	.317	.058	30.150	1	.000	1.374	1.226	1.538
MNAR-low	zAch	-.307	.081	14.189	1	.000	.736	.627	.863
MNAR High	zAch	1.148	.088	168.749	1	.000	3.153	2.652	3.750
MNAR smoke	zAch	.353	.094	14.060	1	.000	1.423	1.183	1.711
Mean substitution									
MNAR-low	zAch	-.441	.094	22.098	1	.000	.643	.535	.773
MNAR High	zAch	1.113	.074	228.284	1	.000	3.045	2.635	3.518
MNAR smoke	zAch	.150	.060	6.280	1	.012	1.162	1.033	1.306
Weak imputation									
MNAR-low	zAch	-.009	.086	.012	1	.914	.991	.838	1.172
MNAR High	zAch	.860	.080	116.522	1	.000	2.364	2.022	2.763
MNAR smoke	zAch	.209	.060	12.350	1	.000	1.233	1.097	1.385
Strong imputation									
MNAR-low	zAch	.178	.067	6.981	1	.008	1.195	1.047	1.363
MNAR High	zAch	.635	.077	68.056	1	.000	1.887	1.623	2.194
MNAR smoke	zAch	.270	.059	21.115	1	.000	1.310	1.167	1.470
Multiple imputation with weak imputation variables									
MNAR-low	zAch	.039	.083	.223	1	.637	1.040	.883	1.225
MNAR High	zAch	.832	.078	113.145	1	.000	2.298	1.971	2.678
MNAR smoke	zAch	.208	.059	12.431	1	.000	1.231	1.097	1.382

Data Source: NELS88, National Center for Educational Statistics, U.S. Department of Education.

missing, high-performing students are more likely to be missing) produce odds ratios and 95%CIs that vary wildly from the population. In fact, MNAR-low inverts the population relationship from positive to negative.[8] This is not surprising but does give one pause when considering what these examples imply for the state of the results reported in our journals.

The MNAR-smoke example tended to be not substantially biased, probably because it was a random sample of each group. This is not ideal, but is not as biasing as samples that include nonrandomly missing data.

However, the goal of this exercise is not to show that missing data can bias results, but rather that there are ways that even extremely unfortunate missing data situations can be made better through effective use of best practices, and of course, that using the default of complete case analysis may not be the best choice if your goal is to generalize your findings to the population of interest.

The MNAR-low scenario produced an odds ratio of 0.74, $p < .0001$, with 95%CIs of 0.63, 0.86. Not only is this a significant finding in the incorrect direction (leading an unsuspecting researcher to an error of inference), but it is so wildly inaccurate that the 95%CI *does not include the population odds ratio.* This is important, as when data were missing completely at random (MCAR) even massive missingness still kept the population odds ratio within the 95%CIs, thus somewhat protecting the researcher who correctly uses confidence intervals to avoid serious mistakes in inference. In this situation, where data are missing not at random, the researcher is now not protected in this case and is open to serious problems.

The same situation is true for the MNAR-high example. This scenario produced an odds ratio of 3.15, $p < .0001$, with 95%CIs of 2.65, 3.75. Again, the confidence interval does not come remotely close to the population value of 1.37. In this case, the researcher would be on moderately safer ground in that the conclusion that higher achievement is associated with higher odds of smoking, despite the effect size is wildly exaggerated. In the population, one standard deviation increase in achievement is roughly equal to a 37% increase in the odds of smoking. Under MNAR-high, that effect is approximately 8 times larger.

The final scenario, where our population of interest is most likely to be missing, resulted in a relatively close approximation of the population despite reducing that group by about 66%. Logistic regression tends to lose

---

[8] I think we should propose that this type of error of inference be called a Type III error. It is an error that involves correctly rejecting the null hypothesis but asserting the effect is in the exact opposite direction from the population. This type of error can lead to decades of debate in the literature and can be destructive.

power as groups become less evenly split on the dependent variable (as we saw in Chapter 10), but even after listwise deletion, the point estimate of 1.42 is very close to the population odds ratio of 1.37, and the 95%CIs clearly include the population odds ratio. You may note that the standard error is almost doubled in this scenario compared with the population, despite only losing about 13% of the sample. That is because this (relatively) small loss disproportionately influenced the smaller group, increasing the disparity in numbers between smokers and nonsmokers. Consequently, the 95%CIs are wider.

These examples show the risk of using complete case analysis when data are not missing completely at random (for more examples of this effect, see Shafer et al. [2002, Table 2]). The important thing to remember is that as a researcher, one does not generally have access to the true population values, and thus has no idea if missingness is leading to a serious error of inference (as in MNAR-low), a wild misestimation of effect size (as in MNAR-high) or is relatively accurately estimate of the population parameters (as in MNAR-smoke). Thus, I and many others have argued it is important to deal responsibly with missing data. As you will see in coming sections, there are possible courses of action that make it less likely that you will seriously misestimate the nature of the effect in the population.

Thus, case deletion is only an innocuous practice when (a) the number of cases with missing data is a small percentage of the overall sample, (b) the data are *demonstrably* missing at random, and (c) power in the remaining cases is sufficient to detect a reasonable range of effects.

The Detrimental Effects of Mean Substitution

I have seen two types of mean substitution. In one case, you have an observed variable (e.g., number of years of marriage) that is unreported. In this case, mean substitution means substituting the group or overall sample mean for each individual with missing data under the theory that in the absence of any other information, the mean is the best single estimate of any participant's score. The flaw in this theory is that if 20% of a sample is missing, even at random, substituting the identical score for a large portion of the sample artificially reduces the variance of the variable, and as the percentage of missing data increases, the effects of missing data become more profound. These effects have been known for many decades now (Cole, 2008; Haitovsky, 1968), yet many researchers still view mean substitution as a viable, or even progressive method, of dealing with missing data. As you see in Table 11.5, mean substitution can create more inaccurate population estimates than simple case deletion when data are not MCAR.

To explore the effects of mean substitution, missing values were replaced with the mean of the valid values for each scenario (means = 0.806, −0.60, and 0.095 for MNAR-low, high, and smoke, respectively). Note that because achievement was converted to z-scores, the mean is close to 0 ("population" mean = 0.10). Immediately, the practice of mean substitution becomes suspect, as in two of the three examples, the mean being substituted is over a half a standard deviation from the population mean.

As you can see in Table 11.5, in the section titled "mean substitution," this process did inflate the sample size back to the original value, but the information contained in those recaptured cases is suspect. Mean substitution was ineffective in eliminating the problems posed by missing data. In the case of MNAR-low, it exacerbated the problem, moving the point estimate for the odds ratio from 0.74 (complete case analysis) to 0.64, about a 15% increase in the magnitude of the misestimation of the effect. The results for MNAR-high remained largely unchanged unchanged, still strongly misestimated. Interestingly, mean substitution for MNAR-smoke, originally a relatively accurate estimate of effect under complete case analysis, is now attenuated to 1.16, and the 95%CI no longer includes the population odds ratio. Thus, in two of the three examples (most notably, the one example that was most accurately reproducing the population odds ratio), mean substitution was counterproductive and harmful to the analysis.

The Effects of Weak Imputation of Values

I will use the same variables I used in the previous section (SES and eighth-grade grades) to model a weak imputation situation, as above when discussing MCAR.

Prediction equation for POPULATION:

$$zACH = -2.94 + 0.255(zSES) + 0.718(grades) \ (R^2 = 0.34).$$

Prediction equation for MNAR-low sample:

$$zACH = -2.067 + 0.177(zSES) + 0.632(grades) \ (R^2 = 0.29).$$

Prediction equation for MNAR-high sample:

$$zACH = -2.87 + 0.249(zSES) + 0.583(grades) \ (R^2 = 0.29).$$

Prediction equation for MNAR-smoke sample:

$$zACH = -2.916 + 0.257(zSES) + 0.711(grades) \ (R^2 = 0.34).$$

It should not be surprising that the prediction equations are relatively dissimilar in the MNAR-low and -high samples, as the samples are strongly biased. Missing values were imputed using these prediction equations as a researcher with missing data would, in each sample. The results, in Table 11.5, show some benefits in correcting the bias in these samples.

Specifically, following imputation, MNAR-low is now not significant. This may not seem like an improvement, but from an inference perspective, it is better to miss an effect than to conclude the opposite effect. Thus, the odds ratio is now demonstrably closer to what it should be than what it was under either complete case analysis or mean substitution. In the MNAR-high data, the odds ratio is still misestimated, but the error is less egregious than previously: the odds ratio after weak imputation was 2.36 compared with 3.15 (complete case analysis) or 3.05 (mean substitution). Although never seriously biased, MNAR-smoke also became less so after weak imputation compared with mean substitution. The 95%CI once again includes the population odds ratio.

Overall, weak imputation was a better solution than either complete case analysis or mean substitution for the two most seriously biased samples, and for the third (MNAR-smoke) it performed better than mean substitution and compared well to complete case analysis. Once again, this emerges as one of the safer choices, even in this relatively weak example of imputation. With stronger imputation, the situation should improve further.

Strong Imputation

I will use the same variables I used in the previous section (10th-grade achievement test scores) to model a strong imputation situation, as earlier when discussing MCAR.

Prediction equation for POPULATION:

$$zACH = 0.105 + 0.802(zACH10) \ (R^2 = 0.66).$$

Prediction equation for MNAR-low sample:

$$zACH = 0.380 + 0.760(zACH10) \ (R^2 = 0.59).$$

Prediction equation for MNAR-high sample:

$$zACH = -0.183 + 0.700(zACH10) \ (R^2 = 0.61).$$

Prediction equation for MNAR-smoke sample:

$$zACH = 0.103 + 0.797(zACH10) \ (R^2 = 0.66).$$

As you can see in Table 11.5, strong imputation proved to be the best solution thus far for severely biased missing data. This is the only technique thus far that remedied the problematic inverted relationship present in MNAR-low sample. Indeed, following strong imputation, the relationship is now significant in the correct direction, rather than significant in the incorrect direction or not significant. Although it is still slightly under-estimated, the 95%CIs now are 0.011 away from containing the population odds ratio, and conclusions are much less problematic for a body of literature in this area. This is a much better situation than complete case analysis, mean substitution, or weak imputation could give us.

Likewise, with MNAR-high, although the odds ratio is still overestimated, it is overestimated by a factor of about 2, a much better situation than any other method of dealing with this example of missing data. Again, while the confidence intervals do not contain the population odds ratio, they are substantially closer.

Finally, in the case of the example of MNAR-smoke, this strong imputation provided very good estimation of the population parameters indeed. The odds ratio is 0.06 below the population odds ratio, and the 95%CI and standard errors are also close. While this example has generally not been as problematic as the others, note that the next best case for this example, that of complete case analysis, had standard errors much larger than with imputation. When one is working with smaller samples and more marginal power, those standard errors might make the difference between accurate results and a Type II error.

So Where Does That Leave Us?

Comparing these more classic methods of treating missing data, imputation appears to give the best results, particularly when there are variables that are strongly correlated with the variable with missing values. When done poorly, imputation can cause distortion of estimates and lead to errors of inference (Little & Rubin, 1987), just as complete case analysis can (Stuart, Azur, Frangakis, & Leaf, 2009). However, recent research has shown that taking the extra effort of using advanced, modern estimation procedures can have benefits for those researchers with relatively high rates of missingness, particularly if you are not fortunate enough to have variables that are strongly correlated to the variable with missingness in your data set.

◆ MULTIPLE IMPUTATION AS A MODERN METHOD OF MISSING DATA ESTIMATION

In my book on data cleaning, I go into more detail on how multiple imputation works and how it may be superior to simple imputation or other, anachronistic methods of dealing with missing data and give more examples of how appropriately dealing with missing data can protect researchers from making serious errors of inference or estimation. This example of multiple imputation again (as above, in the section on MCAR) uses the variables from the "weak imputation" model—zSES and eighth-grade grades—in a multiple imputation technique, primarily to explore whether researchers without the fortune of strongly correlated variables can benefit from this type of treatment over single imputation. I use Bayesian imputation, as above, and again produce 20 parallel data sets.

Ultimately, multiple imputation (and other modern missing value estimation techniques) is increasingly accessible to average statisticians and therefore represents an exciting frontier for improving data cleaning practice. As the results in Table 11.5 show and Figure 11.2 show, appropriately

Figure 11.2 Results of Treating Missingness

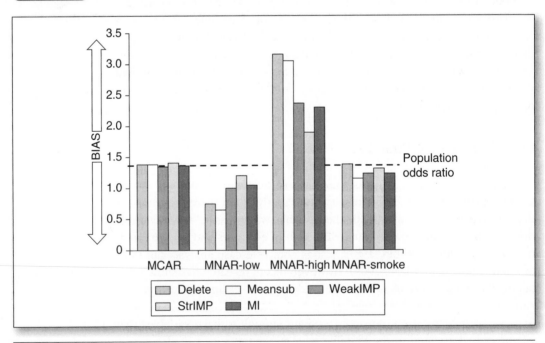

Data Source: NELS88, National Center for Educational Statistics, U.S. Department of Education.

handling missing data makes it less likely that you as a researcher will seriously misestimate a logistic regression analysis. In this analysis, the multiple imputation analyses fared little better than simple imputation and slightly worse than the strong imputation. I suspect it is due to several factors. First, with such severe levels of missing data, it is difficult to imagine any missing data procedure could do better than the results already achieved. Second, with better predictors, the procedures can do a better job of estimating the population parameters.

These examples represent extremely challenging missingness issues often not faced by average researchers, but it should be comforting to know that appropriately handling missing data even in extremely unfortunate cases can still produce desirable (accurate, reproducible) outcomes. Unfortunately, no technique can completely recapture the population parameters when there are such high rates of missingness, and in such a dramatically biased fashion. But these techniques would at least keep you, as a researcher, on safe ground concerning the goodness of inferences you would draw from the results.

HOW MISSINGNESS CAN BE AN ♦ INTERESTING VARIABLE IN AND OF ITSELF

Missing data are often viewed as lost, an unfilled gap, although as I have demonstrated in this chapter, they are not always completely lost, given the availability of other strongly correlated variables. Going one step farther, missingness can be considered an outcome itself and in some cases can be an interesting variable to explore. There is information in missingness. The act of refusing to respond or responding in and of itself might be of interest to researchers, just as quitting a job or remaining at a job can be an interesting variable. Aside from attempting to determine if the data are MCAR, MAR, or MNAR, these data could yield important information. Imagine two educational interventions designed to improve student achievement, and further imagine that in one condition there is much higher dropout than in the other condition, and further that the students dropping out are those with the poorest performance. Not only is that important information for interpreting the results (as the differential dropout would artificially bias the results), but it might give insight into the intervention itself. Is it possible that the intervention with a strong dropout rate among those most at risk indicates that the intervention is not supporting those students well enough? Is it possible that intervention is alienating the students in some way, or might be inappropriate for struggling students? All of this could be important information for researchers and policymakers, but many researchers discard this potentially important information. Remember, you (or someone) worked hard to obtain your data. Don't discard anything that might be useful!

◆ SUMMING UP: BENEFITS OF APPROPRIATELY HANDLING MISSING DATA

There are some very good books by some very smart people dealing solely with missing data (e.g., Little & Rubin, 1987; Schafer, 1997), and I had no wish to replicate that work here. The goal of this chapter was to convince you, the researcher, that this is a topic worthy of attention, that there are good, simple ways to deal with this issue, and that effectively dealing with the issue makes your logistic regression results better. Logistic regression is not immune from the effects of nonrandomly missing data that can bias your sample and results. Complete case analysis and mean substitution are not generally considered best practices. Simple or multiple imputation can minimize the damage missing data can do to inference and estimates of population parameters, and in the age of modern computing, neither is tremendously difficult to attempt.

Because we often gather multiple related variables, we often know (or can estimate) a good deal about the missing values. Aside from examining missingness as an outcome itself (which I strongly recommend), modern computing affords us the opportunity to fill in many of the gaps with high-quality data. This is not merely "making up data" as some fear, but rather is the act of utilizing the vast amount of data you do have. As these limited examples show, the act of estimating values and retaining cases in your analyses most often leads to more replicable findings as they are generally closer to the actual population values than analyses that discards those with missing data (or worse, substitutes means for the missing values). Thus, using best practices in handling missing data makes the results a better estimate of the population you are interested in. And it is surprisingly easy to do, once you know how.

Thus, it is my belief that best practices in handling missing data include the following:

- First, do no harm! Use best practices and careful methodology to minimize missingness. There is no substitute for complete data[9] and

---

[9]Except in certain specialized circumstances where researchers purposely administer selected questions to participants or use other advanced sampling techniques that have been advocated for in the researching of very sensitive topics.

some careful forethought and planning can often save a good deal of frustration in the data analysis phase of research.

- Be transparent! Report any incidences of missing data (rates, by variable, and reasons for missingness, if possible). This can be important information to reviewers and consumers of your research and is the first step in thinking about how to effectively deal with missingness in your analyses.

- Explicitly discuss if data are missing at random or not (i.e., if there are differences between individuals with incomplete and complete data). Using analyses similar to those I model in this chapter, you can give yourself and the reader a good sense of why data might be missing and whether it is at random or not. That allows you, and your audience, to think carefully about whether missingness may have introduced bias into the results. I would advocate that all authors report this information in the methods section of formal research reports.

- Discuss how you as a researcher dealt with the issue of incomplete data and the results of your intervention. A clear statement concerning this issue is simple to add to a manuscript and can be valuable for future consumers as they interpret your work. Be specific—if you used imputation, how was it done, and what were the results? If you deleted the data (complete case analysis) justify why.

If there are no missing data, state that clearly so consumers and reviewers have that important information as well!

ENRICHMENT

1. Download some of the missing data sets I discuss in this chapter, and see if you can replicate the results I achieved through various means. In particular, I would challenge you to attempt multiple imputation!

   a. The NHIS data used for analyzing the missingness in BMI is available on the book website (www.sagepub.com/osbornebplr).

   b. MNAR analyses (DV = smoking, IV = zACH) is available on the book website.

      i. Select cases using MNAR_low, MNAR_high, or MNAR_smoke dummy variables, where 0 = keep, 1 = delete

      ii. zACH = achievement test scores, z-scored

    iii. zACH10 = achievement test scores from 2 years later

    iv. zSES = SES at first time point

2. Choose a data set from a previous study you conducted (or your advisor did) that had some missing data in it. Review how missing data was handled originally (I also have another data set online that you can play with for this purpose).

    a. Conduct a missingness analysis to see if those who failed to respond were significantly different than those who responded.

    b. Use imputation or multiple imputation to deal with the missing data.

    c. Replicate the original analyses to see if the conclusions changed.

    d. If you found interesting results from effectively dealing with missingness, send me an e-mail letting me know! I'll gather your results (anonymously) on the book website and may include you in future projects.

REFERENCES

Cole, J. C. (2008). How to deal with missing data. In J. W. Osborne (Ed.), *Best Practices in quantitative methods*. Thousand Oaks, CA: Sage.

Colebrooke, H. (1817). *Algebra with arithmetic of Brahmagupta and Bhaskara*. London: John Murray.

Diehl, R. (2004). *The Olmecs: America's first civilization*. London: Thames & Hudson.

Greenland, S., & Finkle, W. D. (1995). A critical look at methods for handling missing covariates in epidemiologic regression analyses. *American Journal of Epidemiology, 142*(12), 1255–1264.

Haitovsky, Y. (1968). Missing data in regression analysis. *Journal of the Royal Statistical Society. Series B (Methodological), 30*(1), 67–82.

Heitjan, D. F., & Basu, S. (1996). Distinguishing "missing at random" and "missing completely at random." *The American Statistician, 50*(3), 207–213. doi: 10.2307/2684656

Ingels, S. (1994). *National Education Longitudinal Study of 1988: Second follow-up: Student component data file user's manual*. Washington, DC: U.S. Department of Education, Office of Educational Research and Improvement, National Center for Education Statistics.

Little, R., & Rubin, D. (1987). *Statistical analysis with missing data*. Hoboken, NY: Wiley.

Osborne, J. W. (2012). *Best Practices in data cleaning: A complete guide to everything you need to do before and after collecting your data*. Thousand Oaks, CA: Sage.

Osborne, J. W., Kocher, B., & Tillman, D. (2012). *Sweating the small stuff: Do authors in APA journals clean data or test assumptions (and should anyone care if they do)*. Paper presented at the annual meeting of the Eastern Education Research Association, Hilton Head, SC.

Rubin, D. (1976). Inference and missing data. *biometrika, 63*(3), 581.

Schafer, J. (1997). *Analysis of incomplete multivariate data*. Boca Raton, FL: Chapman & Hall/CRC.

Schafer, J., & Graham, J. (2002). Missing data: Our view of the state of the art. *Psychological Methods, 7*(2), 147–177.

Stuart, E. A., Azur, M., Frangakis, C., & Leaf, P. (2009). Multiple imputation with large data sets: A case study of the children's mental health initiative. *American Journal of Epidemiology, 169*(9), 1133–1139. doi: 10.1093/aje/kwp026

Vach, W., & Blettner, M. (1995). Logistic regression with incompletely observed categorical covariates—investigating the sensitivity against violation of the missing at random assumption. *Statistics in Medicine, 14*(12), 1315–1329.

12

MULTINOMIAL AND ORDINAL LOGISTIC REGRESSION

Not all outcomes are simple dichotomous variables. Graduation, for example, can be broken into more than two groups. Some students graduate, but not on time. Some students drop out of school and then come back. Smoking status, as we have seen in previous chapters, is rarely as simple as whether you ever smoked or not. There are different types of diabetes, as well—Type I (usually diagnosed in childhood) and Type II (more traditionally diagnosed in adulthood), which might have different risk factors and prognoses. Even marijuana use could be more subtly classified. Is it fair to group people who tried it once with people who are frequent users? In our previous analyses we did, comparing individuals who "never" tried marijuana to those who have "ever" tried it.

Multinomial logistic regression (also sometimes called polytomous logistic regression) allows us to leverage the power of binary logistic regression and generalize it to a categorical dependent variable with more than two categories. Similar to our discussion of categorical independent variables in Chapter 6, this more complex procedure will require comparisons between groups and will introduce complexity to the analysis. Specifically, if you have a dependent variable with M groups, multinomial logistic regression will estimate $M - 1$ equations. Each equation will compare a particular category with the reference group you chose.

Let's start with a simple example. If we return to our National Education Longitudinal Study of 1988 (NELS88) data from earlier in the book, and revisit the marijuana variable, we see it is originally coded as a four-category variable, as you see below in Table 12.1:

Table 12.1 In Lifetime, # of Times R Used Marijuana

Original category:	Label:
0	Tried marijuana 0 occasions
1	Tried marijuana 1–2 occasions
2	Tried marijuana 3–19 occasions
3	Tried marijuana 20 or more occasions

Data Source: NELS88, National Center for Educational Statistics, U.S. Department of Education.

By this point in the book, you know I dislike having continuous variables broken into categories, but the National Center for Education Statistics provided the data this way, and there is nothing else we can do about it. To treat it as a continuous variable would be to violate basic assumptions about interval data, but we can assume there was a good rationale for the survey designers to provide the data in this form and treat this variable as categorical.[1]

Since multinomial logistic regression can get complex, let's start with the raw data, as we did in Chapter 2. These data are summarized in Table 12.2:

Table 12.2 Sex * Marijuana Cross-Tabulation

		MJ				1 vs. 0	2 vs. 0	3 vs. 0
		0	1	2	3			
Sex	1 (Male)	5829	743	499	380	743 / (743 + 5829) = **0.1131**	499 / (499 + 5829) = **0.0789**	380 / (380 + 5829) = **0.0612**
	0 (Female)	6465	679	503	266	679 / (679 + 6465) = **0.0950**	503 / (503 + 6465) = **0.0722**	266 / (266 + 6465) = **0.0395**
		Relative Risk:				**1.189**	**1.092**	**1.549**

Data Source: NELS88, National Center for Educational Statistics, U.S. Department of Education.

---

[1]In other words, we will assume, for the moment, that each group is qualitatively different than the other. Later in the chapter we will examine this same variable as an *ordered ordinal* variable, which will allow us to get different information from it.

As you can see in Table 12.2, boys and girls do not have the same conditional probabilities of self-reported marijuana use across the four categories. For example, girls are more likely to report having never tried marijuana, and boys are more likely to report having tried marijuana 20 or more times. In setting up this multinomial logistic regression analysis, we have four categories in our dependent variable and thus will have three regression equations, each comparing the probabilities of being in one group versus being in a comparison group.

This is similar to setting up dummy variables—you want the comparison group to make sense and to not be extremely small relative to the other groups. In this case, it makes sense to me to have 0 (never tried marijuana) as the reference group and to compare all other groups with it. Thus, the first analysis would compare the probability of being in group 1 versus 0, the second analysis would compare the probability of being in group 2 versus 0, and the third analysis would compare the probability of being in group 3 versus 0. Similar to categorical independent variables, we do not get all possible comparisons (e.g., we do not get a test of the probabilities of being in group 2 vs. 3). Thus, we need to be thoughtful in how we set up our comparison group.

Referring back to Table 12.2, we can hand-calculate the expected conditional probabilities of each of these groups and then calculate relative risk ratios. As you can see, we expect boys to be about 19% more likely to admit to trying marijuana 1–2 times, we expect little sex difference in the 3–19 times category, and we expect boys to be about 55% more likely to admit to trying marijuana 20 or more times in their lives.

In performing this analysis using statistical software, we have $N = 15,364$ valid cases, the majority of which are in group 0. Sex produced a small but statistically significant effect ($\chi^2_{(3)} = 42.14$, $p < .0001$).[2] This procedure gets more complex when attempting to interpret the parameter estimates, presented in Table 12.3. As you can see, the output is presented in terms of three logistic regression equations, each with different intercepts and regression coefficients. The key to deciphering this output is to remember that each one is a comparison, just as a simple binary logistic regression is a comparison between two groups. What we have is essentially three separate binary logistic regression analyses. The first compares group 0 to 1 (never tried marijuana vs. tried once or twice). This comparison is significant, yielding a positive logit and odds ratio (OR) of 1.21, which is in line with our relative risk (RR) calculation of 1.19. Indeed, if we construct a regression equation

---

[2]Which is almost identical to the Pearson or likelihood ratio chi-square values that can be calculated from the contingency table.

and create predicted probabilities, the three regression equations would be:

$$\text{Eq. 1 (category 0 vs. 1) Logit}(\hat{Y}) = -2.254 + 0.194(\text{Sex})$$

$$\text{Eq. 2 (category 0 vs. 2) Logit}(\hat{Y}) = -2.554 + 0.096(\text{Sex})$$

$$\text{Eq. 3 (category 0 vs. 3) Logit}(\hat{Y}) = -3.191 + 0.460(\text{Sex})$$

Looking at the first equation, we calculate predicted logits of -2.254 and -2.06 for female and male, respectively. These convert to probabilities of 0.095 and 0.113. Girls have a 0.095 probability of trying marijuana 1–2 times in their life, while boys have a probability of 0.113, or about 19% higher probabilities (RR = 1.19), both of which match nicely with the observed probabilities.

Note that each equation has a different intercept, which might be unexpected for some readers. In this analysis, the intercept is interpreted as the probability of the event happening when all predictors are 0. Thus, the -2.254 (which converts to probability of 0.095) is the probability of trying marijuana 1–2 times in a student's life when all predictors (in this case, sex) are 0. In the next equation, the intercept is different because it is the log of the odds of trying marijuana 3–19 times (vs. 0) when all predictors are 0.

The second equation shows a nonsignificant effect for sex, with 95%CIs that include 1.00. If we perform the same predictions for the second

Table 12.3 Parameter Estimates

MJ[a]		B	Std. Error	Wald	df	Sig.	Exp(B)	95% CI for Exp(B)	
								Lower Bound	Upper Bound
0 vs.1	Intercept	−2.254	.040	3120.515	1	.000			
	sex	.194	.056	11.922	1	.001	1.214	1.087	1.355
0 vs.2	Intercept	−2.554	.046	3043.149	1	.000			
	sex	.096	.066	2.115	1	.146	1.100	.967	1.252
0 vs.3	Intercept	−3.191	.063	2600.951	1	.000			
	sex	.460	.082	31.533	1	.000	1.584	1.349	1.861

a. The reference category is: 0.

Data Source: NELS88, National Center for Educational Statistics, U.S. Department of Education.

comparison (comparing students who claim to have tried marijuana 3–19 times vs. 0 times in their lives), we get predicted probabilities of 0.072 and 0.079 for girls and boys, respectively, which gives us a RR = 1.09, identical to what we calculated in Table 12.2 from the observed probabilities. Finally, the third analysis, which compares the probability for girls and boys to have tried marijuana 20 or more times (vs. 0 times in their lives), we get a significant and relatively strong effect. Predicted probabilities are 0.040 and 0.061 for girls and boys, respectively, giving us RR = 1.55, again in line with what we calculated in Table 12.2.

These results indicate that there is a modest sex difference in the probability of trying marijuana, no significant sex difference in moderate users, and a strong sex difference in those students admitting to more extensive use of marijuana.

MULTINOMIAL LOGISTIC REGRESSION ◆ WITH A CONTINUOUS VARIABLE

As you can see in the first section of this chapter, multinomial logistic regression is a simple extension of binary logistic regression, and if each contrast is taken one at a time, is not much more complex to interpret, particularly when results are converted back to conditional probabilities. Let us look at the same analysis, but this time using z-scored student achievement scores (similar to the analysis we performed previously with the binary EVER_MJ variable). Simply entering the continuous, z-scored variable as a covariate[3] produces a similar analysis. In this case, the change in model fit is significant ($\chi^2_{(3)} =$ 129.49, $p < .0001$). The parameter estimates are presented in Table 12.4 (see page 394). As you can see, zACH is a significant predictor in each equation, although the magnitude of the effect varies a bit. In general, for all three comparisons, as student achievement increases, the probability of using marijuana decreases. In order to make this concept easier for your readers, let's calculate predicted probabilities for each comparison at ± 1 standard deviation.

Consistent with the odds ratios and expectations, higher student achievement is generally associated with lower probabilities of marijuana use, although the magnitude of the probabilities vary depending on the comparison. Students are more likely, overall, to try marijuana once or twice (first comparison) than more times (second and third comparison).

---

[3]Recall in logistic regression that "covariates" are merely continuous variables and "factors" are categorical. Having too many categorical variables can lead to sparse data and should be avoided.

Table 12.4 Parameter Estimates

	MJ[a]	B	Std. Error	Wald	df	Sig.	Exp(B)	95% CI for Exp(B)	
								Lower Bound	Upper Bound
1	Intercept	−2.150	.029	5625.854	1	.000			
	zACH	−.241	.030	65.496	1	.000	.786	.741	.833
2	Intercept	−2.502	.034	5535.874	1	.000			
	zACH	−.200	.035	33.272	1	.000	.818	.764	.876
3	Intercept	−2.949	.042	5040.454	1	.000			
	zACH	−.292	.044	44.839	1	.000	.747	.686	.813

a. The reference category is: 0.

Data Source: NELS88, National Center for Educational Statistics, U.S. Department of Education.

Figure 12.1 Predicted Probabilities of Marijuana Use Given Student Achievement

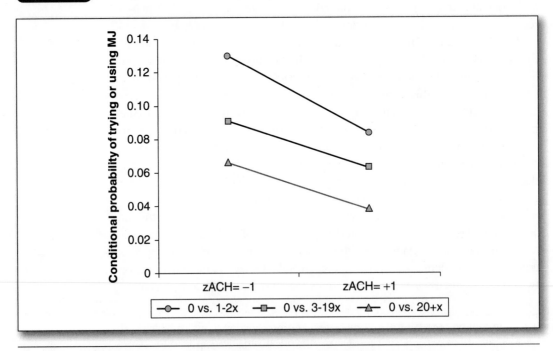

Data Source: NELS88, National Center for Educational Statistics, U.S. Department of Education.

MOVING BEYOND SIMPLE ♦
MULTINOMIAL LOGISTIC REGRESSION

If you have followed to this point, you should be wondering how much of the preceding chapters we can generalize to multinomial logistic regression. You have seen that with a dependent variable of more than two categories, things are more complex than with binary logistic regression. Thus, I would caution you against getting too complex with an already complex process. However, there is no reason that we cannot add dummy coded variables, interactions, curvilinear effects, and so forth. For example, let us add a quadratic term ($zACH^2$) to the equation already described earlier.

This yields a significant effect beyond the simple linear effect of student achievement (original $\chi^2_{(3)} = 129.49$, $p < .0001$, adding $zACH^2$ adds $\chi^2_{(3)} = 22.41$, $p < .0001$). The cubic effect did not add a significant improvement to model fit and was disregarded. As you can see in Table 12.5, there is no significant curvilinear effect for the first comparison (0 vs. 1–2 times), but the other comparisons do contain curvilinear effects. Thus, it makes sense to graph these results for the convenience of the reader.

Table 12.5 Parameter Estimates

	MJ[a]	B	Std. Error	Wald	df	Sig.	Exp(B)	95% CI for Exp(B)	
								Lower Bound	Upper Bound
1	Intercept	−2.104	.040	2813.651	1	.000			
	zACH	−.221	.032	48.273	1	.000	.801	.753	.853
	zACH²	−.049	.030	2.635	1	.105	.952	.897	1.010
2	Intercept	−2.404	.046	2736.645	1	.000			
	zACH	−.159	.038	17.068	1	.000	.853	.791	.920
	zACH²	−.110	.037	9.030	1	.003	.896	.834	.962
3	Intercept	−2.806	.057	2457.751	1	.000			
	zACH	−.247	.048	26.506	1	.000	.781	.711	.858
	zACH²	−.165	.048	12.033	1	.001	.848	.772	.931

a. The reference category is: 0.

Data Source: NELS88, National Center for Educational Statistics, U.S. Department of Education.

Figure 12.2 Curvilinear Effect of Student Achievement on Marijuana Use

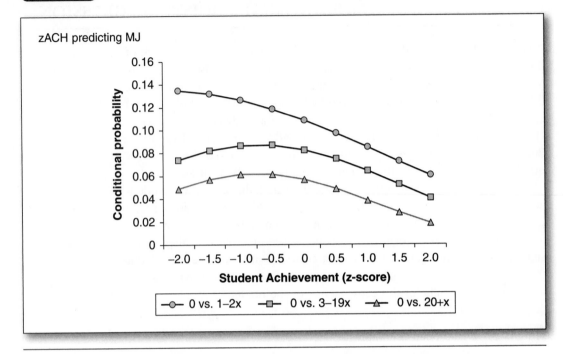

Data Source: NELS88, National Center for Educational Statistics, U.S. Department of Education.

◆ MORE COMPLEX TERMS IN MULTINOMIAL LOGISTIC REGRESSION

Technically, we can do everything in multinomial logistic regression that we could do in binary logistic regression, so interactions, curvilinear effects, and curvilinear interactions are all possible if you can manage the complexity of those tasks within the layer of added complexity that multinomial logistic regression brings. For example, let us explore whether student achievement (zACH) and family socioeconomic status (zSES) interact in predicting marijuana use. As in binary logistic regression, we would enter the simple z-scored effects first and then the interaction on a second step. The two variables account for a significant reduction in $-2LL$ (20795.29, $\chi^2_{(6)}$ = 131.76, $p < .0001$). Interestingly, family SES was not a significant predictor of marijuana use once achievement was in the equation. The interaction significantly improved model fit ($-2LL$ = 20773.47, $\chi^2_{(3)}$ = 21.82, $p < .0001$). The final parameter estimates are presented in Table 12.6.

Table 12.6   FINAL Parameter Estimates

MJ[a]		B	Std. Error	Wald	df	Sig.	Exp(B)	95% CI for Exp(B)	
								Lower Bound	Upper Bound
1	Intercept	−2.132	.032	4552.265	1	.000			
	zACH	−.216	.034	39.846	1	.000	.805	.753	.861
	zSES	−.034	.034	.998	1	.318	.967	.905	1.033
	INT	−.039	.031	1.554	1	.213	.962	.905	1.022
2	Intercept	−2.459	.036	4548.622	1	.000			
	zACH	−.163	.040	16.910	1	.000	.850	.786	.918
	zSES	−.037	.039	.879	1	.349	.964	.892	1.041
	INT	−.104	.037	7.741	1	.005	.902	.838	.970
3	Intercept	−2.881	.044	4232.367	1	.000			
	zACH	−.246	.049	25.498	1	.000	.782	.711	.860
	zSES	−.046	.048	.919	1	.338	.955	.869	1.050
	INT	−.179	.048	13.807	1	.000	.836	.761	.919

a. The reference category is: 0.

Data Source: NELS88, National Center for Educational Statistics, U.S. Department of Education.

As you can see, in the first equation, comparing group 0 to 1, the only significant effect is of zACH, while in the other equations, there are significant interactions between zACH and zSES. It becomes increasingly complicated to represent the entirety of these results in one graph, so it might be worthwhile to represent each equation in a different graph. I will skip graphing the first equation as there is no interaction: increasing achievement leads to decreasing odds of trying marijuana 1–2 times and this effect is not modified by family SES.

As you can see in Figure 12.3 (see page 398), an interesting interaction of achievement and family SES emerges when these effects are graphed. Looking at the graphs, it is now clear why there was no simple SES effect—if you average the two "high" SES probabilities, it is not that different from "low" SES until you account for student achievement. In this case, low-achieving students become more likely to use marijuana as family SES increases,

Figure 12.3 Interaction of zSES and zACH Predicting Marijuana Use

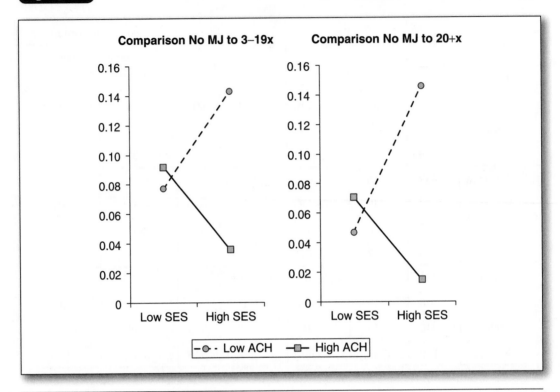

Data Source: NELS88, National Center for Educational Statistics, U.S. Department of Education.

and the opposite is true for high-achieving students. They become less likely to use marijuana as family SES increases. Of course, as we are analyzing *self-reported* data, this could merely be that high-achieving students become less willing to disclose their marijuana use as they come from more affluent families. Regardless, this is an interesting finding.

The patterns for both models are similar, but for the most part the second model has lower probabilities, which makes sense. Students are generally less likely to report using marijuana 20 or more times in their lives than 3–19 times. The exception is for low-achieving, high-SES students, who are about equally likely to report trying marijuana 3–19 and 20+ times (14.3% vs. 14.6% probability, according to my calculations).

Thus, you can see that while multinomial logistic regression gets more complex quickly as we get more complex with our analysis, the complexity is manageable if you take things one step at a time, graph out complex effects, and take great care to walk the reader through the analyses.

MULTINOMIAL LOGISTIC REGRESSION AS A SERIES ◆ OF BINARY LOGISTIC REGRESSION EQUATIONS

Multinomial logistic regression is *similar to* a series of binary logistic regressions comparing each level of the dependent variable to a chosen reference group. Multinomial logistic regression routines in popular software packages produce most results that are similar to performing all analyses separately. To demonstrate this point, I dummy coded the marijuana dependent variable with 0 (never tried MJ) as the reference group and each other group receiving a 1 on their separate dummy coded variable. Thus, I can perform individual binary logistic regressions to approximate the single multinomial logistic regression.

If you compare Tables 12.6 and 12.7 (see pages 397 and 400), you can see that the analyses are identical to several decimal places' rounding error. This is an important epiphany, as many software packages have very limited options in the multinomial logistic regression routine. For example, in SPSS you cannot request DfBetas or standardized residuals, and you cannot enter terms on separate steps (or in blocks) as you can within the binary logistic routine. Blockwise analyses must be performed manually, by running nested models.

Understanding this can free you as a statistician to perform more interesting and technically advanced analyses. For example, you can perform a series of binary logistic analyses, cleaning the data (I recommend a relatively conservative data cleaning strategy).

One downside to separate estimation of the models is that overall measures of goodness of fit are not applicable. Because the reference group is used three separate times in these analyses, one cannot merely sum the deviance or $-2LL$ to get an overall measure of model fit. Indeed, when I performed these three separate analyses, the final $-2LL$s were 8723.97, 6779.41, and 4846.57 for the three separate models (total = 20349 vs. 20773.47 for the multinomial model). Thus, it is probably most desirable and parsimonious for us to perform data cleaning using binary logistic regression models, and then retaining only those cases that are deemed to be appropriate in terms of influence or leverage, perform a final simultaneous multinomial logistic regression analysis.

| Table 12.7 | Replicating Multinomial Logistic Regression as a Series of Binary Logistic Regression Analyses |

| | | B | SE | Wald | df | Sig. | Exp(B) | 95% CI for Exp(B) | |
								Lower	Upper
MJ1: 0 vs. 1	zACH	−.214	.034	39.408	1	.000	.807	.755	.863
	zSES	−.035	.034	1.073	1	.300	.966	.904	1.031
	INT	−.040	.031	1.652	1	.199	.961	.904	1.021
	Constant	−2.132	.032	4556.957	1	.000	.119		
MJ2: 0 vs. 2	zACH	−.162	.039	16.847	1	.000	.851	.787	.919
	zSES	−.038	.039	.961	1	.327	.962	.891	1.039
	INT	−.104	.037	7.931	1	.005	.901	.838	.969
	Constant	−2.459	.036	4558.006	1	.000	.086		
MJ3: 0 vs. 3	zACH	−.244	.049	25.353	1	.000	.783	.712	.861
	zSES	−.049	.048	1.036	1	.309	.952	.866	1.046
	INT	−.179	.048	14.029	1	.000	.836	.762	.918
	Constant	−2.881	.044	4240.631	1	.000	.056		

Data Source: NELS88, National Center for Educational Statistics, U.S. Department of Education.

Data cleaning in this way has some complexities. First, you must model each contrast as a binary logistic regression, using *only those cases* in the reference group and in the comparison group. All other cases are eliminated from that particular analysis. This has the effect of leaving all cases not in a particular analysis with *missing data* on any diagnostic measure (such as DfBetas, standardized residuals, Cook's Distance, leverage, etc.). Thus, if you try to select only cases with valid standardized residuals between −5 and 5, for example, on each standardized residual variable from each of the analyses, you will end up with only those cases in the comparison group, as they were the only cases in all of the analyses. Thus, you must select cases that are either in the range you desire *or* that have missing values, or you must recode the missing values in some way to allow cases not part of other analyses to be retained. My preference is to evaluate the indicators of influence or leverage, and then after I have decided my cutoff scores for cleaning, to recode missing values to 0 (or some other value in the middle of the distribution) so that they are retained. Note that performing this recode prior to evaluating the indicators of influence or leverage will skew those results, and thus this should only be performed after evaluation.

EXAMPLE OF DATA CLEANING ◆
USING BINARY LOGISTIC REGRESSION

I already have created dummy variables that compare each group with the comparison group (0). Thus, using the analyses I just performed (summarized in Table 12.7), I can request leverage or influence statistics of my choice. In this case, I will choose DfBetas as I like their ability to detect inappropriate influence. Each analysis will produce four DfBetas (constant, zACH, zSES, and the interaction), for a total of 12. Although I usually examine 1st and 99th percentile cutoffs for these variables, I will convert them to z-scores for easy examination. Initial data cleaning using ± 5 as a cutoff eliminated 889 cases. Using ± 6 as a cutoff eliminated only $N = 525$ while eliminating the most egregiously influential cases, and thus this was used as a cutoff for data cleaning.[4]

The results of conservative data cleaning should not by now be surprising. The overall model change in −2LL was stronger. Specifically, the overall change in the model following entry of all three terms was $\chi^2_{(9)} = 303.03$, $p < .0001$, more than double that of the uncleaned data, and the interaction effect was more than twice as large (original $\chi^2_{(3)} = 21.82$, following data cleaning $\chi^2_{(3)} = 58.06$, $p < .0001$). The individual parameter estimates for this new analysis are presented in Table 12.9 (see page 403). As you can see, the interaction is now significant for all three comparisons, whereas before it was not significant for the first comparison.

As you can see in the graphs, all three comparisons follow a similar pattern: lower achieving students are more likely to try marijuana than higher achieving students. As family income for lower achieving students increases, the probability that they will try marijuana increases, while increasing family income leads to decreasing probability of trying marijuana for higher achieving students. This pattern holds for all three comparisons, although the absolute probabilities decrease as we move from trying marijuana 1–2 times to 3–19 times to more than 20 times (which makes sense

---

[4]The SPSS syntax for cleaning is included at the end of the chapter. Similar syntax can be used in SAS and other programs.

Table 12.8 DfBetas Before and After Data Cleaning

Before data cleaning		
	zDFB0_1	zDFB0_2	zDFB0_3
Minimum	−2.84729	−4.02533	−3.20960
Maximum	7.19233	9.80470	9.24314
	zDFB1_1	zDFB1_2	zDFB1_3
Minimum	−6.52244	−7.39790	−8.49555
Maximum	10.71997	13.93869	12.84328
	zDFB2_1	zDFB2_2	zDFB2_3
Minimum	−7.88210	−11.64026	−12.30524
Maximum	11.98710	9.80194	11.85334
	zDFB3_1	zDFB3_2	zDFB3_3
Minimum	−10.60939	−17.89822	−14.02430
Maximum	14.18976	19.55783	25.20774
After data cleaning		
	zDFB0_1	zDFB0_2	zDFB0_3
Minimum	1.04116	−1.12589	−1.12646
Maximum	4.91659	5.09480	5.82232
	zDFB1_1	zDFB1_2	zDFB1_3
Minimum	−5.63372	−5.96351	−5.99854
Maximum	5.99374	5.99384	5.89779
	zDFB2_1	zDFB2_2	zDFB2_3
Minimum	−5.94605	−5.91997	−5.99879
Maximum	5.98322	5.97017	5.93194
	zDFB3_1	zDFB3_2	zDFB3_3
Minimum	−5.26373	−4.96522	−4.71161
Maximum	5.97111	5.91025	5.61719

Data Source: NELS88, National Center for Educational Statistics, U.S. Department of Education.

Table 12.9   Marijuana Analysis After Data Cleaning

MJ[a]		B	Std. Error	Wald	df	Sig.	Exp(B)	95% CI for Exp(B)	
								Lower Bound	Upper Bound
1	Intercept	−2.212	.033	4502.330	1	.000			
	zACH	−.318	.037	73.965	1	.000	.728	.677	.783
	zSES	−.029	.036	.639	1	.424	.971	.904	1.043
	INT	−.133	.036	13.725	1	.000	.876	.816	.939
2	Intercept	−2.645	.040	4370.853	1	.000			
	zACH	−.318	.045	49.655	1	.000	.727	.666	.795
	zSES	−.015	.045	.113	1	.737	.985	.902	1.076
	INT	−.214	.046	21.983	1	.000	.807	.738	.883
3	Intercept	−3.259	.053	3725.651	1	.000			
	zACH	−.404	.061	43.624	1	.000	.668	.593	.753
	zSES	−.051	.061	.688	1	.407	.951	.844	1.071
	INT	−.328	.065	25.028	1	.000	.721	.634	.819

a. The reference category is: 0.

Data Source: NELS88, National Center for Educational Statistics, U.S. Department of Education.

given that fewer students admit to using it 20 or more times than trying it one or two times).

TESTING WHETHER GROUPS CAN BE COMBINED ♦

Those of you familiar with structural equation modeling and confirmatory factor analysis will easily relate to the logic of testing hypotheses via comparison of nested models in this section. For those of you without this background, remember that we can test quantitative hypotheses

Figure 12.4 Interaction of Student Achievement and Family SES Predicting Marijuana Use

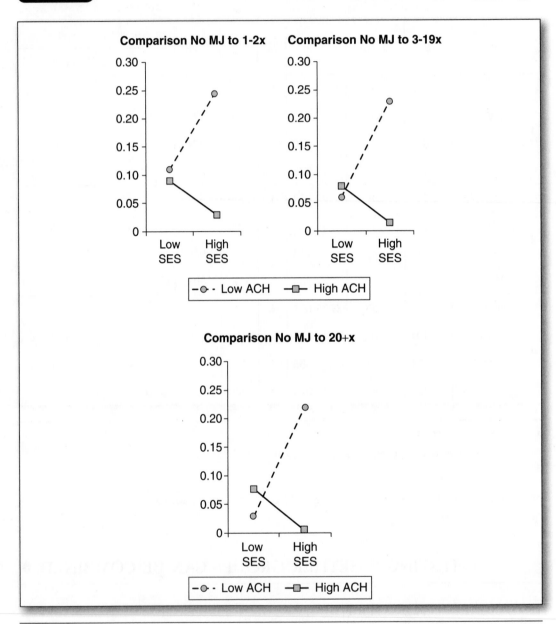

by examining change in −2LL. For example, we have tested the hypothesis that the coefficients for interaction terms are all zero by adding interaction terms on a block and examining the Δ−2LL. If the change in model fit is significant, we reject the hypothesis that all coefficients for those terms are zero and examine the parameter estimates.

This is an example of using nested models to test hypotheses, and we have many other examples throughout the book thus far. Testing whether groups can be combined is merely another example of this type of hypothesis testing using −2LL (model fit) as the decision rule.

Let us imagine that we want to test whether it is legitimate to keep our dependent variable, marijuana use, as the original four categories, or whether it is acceptable to combine the last two groups. There are many reasons one might want to do this: improving the simplicity of the model, combining two relatively small groups, or testing substantive hypotheses, such as whether keeping the groups separate improves the model fit.

Technically, to combine groups is to hypothesize that all regression coefficients for the two groups are equal. Thus, examining the regression equations for the last two groups:

$$\text{Logit}(\hat{Y}) = -2.459 - 0.163(\text{zACH}) - 0.037(\text{zSES}) - 0.104(\text{INT})$$

$$\text{Logit}(\hat{Y}) = -2.881 - 0.246(\text{zACH}) - 0.046(\text{zSES}) - 0.179(\text{INT})$$

Combining the last two groups would argue that the constants are equal ($b_{02} = b_{03}$), that the coefficients for zACH are equal ($b_{12} = b_{13}$), that the coefficients for zSES are equal ($b_{22} = b_{23}$), and that the coefficients for the interaction are equal ($b_{32} = b_{33}$). If any of these conditions are not tenable in the data, we will see a significant difference between overall model fit. In the language of structural equation modeling, we are constraining these parameters to be equal across groups. While these coefficients *seem* to be different, the question is whether they are *significantly* different. In our sample, we have tremendous power to detect small differences, and so I suspect that the result of this analysis will be a significant different in model fit. However, in smaller samples, small differences in coefficients will not be significantly different.

Setting up the analysis to test these hypotheses are relatively straightforward. These are nested models, with the constrained model nested within the nonconstrained model. So, first we make sure that neither of the two groups we are examining for combination are the reference group (in our example, 0 remains the reference group), and we perform an analysis with the groups not combined (not constrained to equality) and then with the groups combined, comparing the −2LL or deviance. If there is no significant change in goodness of fit between the nonconstrained and constrained models, we can plausibly conclude that the two groups are not significantly different (at least in terms of the variables modeled) and that it is defensible to combine them. If, on the other hand, model fit is harmed by this constraint (if −2LL for the constrained model is significantly higher than −2LL for the nonconstrained model), then the hypothesis that the coefficients are equal across groups is not tenable and is rejected. Continuing with our example, the −2LL for the model without constraints is 20773.47 with 9, and the constrained model is 18672.87 with 6 df. The difference is evaluated as a χ^2 with df equal to the number of predictors in the model ($\chi^2 = 2101.47$ with 3 df with is obviously significant at $p < .0001$). Other suggestions have included comparing deviance for the models, which tends to result in the same conclusions (in this case deviances were 20763.77 and 18663.17, respectively; when evaluated with 3 df that difference would still be significant).

An alternative method for testing whether two groups could be legitimately combined would be to select the two categories in question and perform a binary logistic regression, including all relevant independent variables. If there are significant effects of any of the independent variables in this context that implies that the two groups differ significantly and thus are not eligible for combination.

Note that one must have sufficient power to detect differences in order to perform any of these analyses and large enough groups to reasonably detect differences. If one has only two or three cases in each group, there is obviously not enough power to detect differences, and those groups should be removed from the analysis as inadequate rather than combining them.

Using this alternative methodology, recoding category 2 to 0 and category 3 to 1, and using the same independent variables (zACH, zSES, and interaction), there was no significant improvement in the model when the variables were entered into the analysis ($\chi^2_{(3)} = 4.72$, $p < .19$).[5] Using the cleaned data discussed prior in the chapter, this analysis is more ambiguous. With $N = 1188$ cases, the $\chi^2_{(3)} = 7.43$, $p < .06$. This alternative analysis, which I believe to be more specific to the question at hand (i.e., are there any significant differences between the two groups in question) gives some

---

[5]Note that this analysis included $N = 1573$ cases, more than sufficient to detect differences across groups if there are any.

support to the argument that the two groups are not significantly different and are thus defensibly combined.

As a comparison, I performed the same analysis testing whether groups 1 and 3 (least frequent users vs. the most frequent users) could legitimately be combined. This analysis produced a small but significant overall effect ($\chi^2_{(3)} = 7.67, p < .05; \chi^2_{(3)} = 16.21, p < .001$ following data cleaning), indicating it probably would not be legitimate to combine these two groups. As with everything, I believe the analysis must follow theory and common sense. If it makes theoretical, empirical, and common sense to combine groups, then it might be defensible to do so.

ORDERED LOGIT (PROPORTIONAL ODDS) MODEL ♦

Another extension of the binary logistic regression model is the ordered logit, or proportional odds model. This model is designed to deal with ordinal (ordered, ranked) variables such as the marijuana variable we have been exploring through the first part of this chapter. Multinomial logistic regression can handle this variable just fine, as you have seen, but it is most specifically designed for handling *nonordered* variables (e.g., what type of diet is one going to attempt, which method of birth control will an individual use, what college major will a student matriculate into). Although I made a passing argument that the marijuana classification may represent qualitatively different groups (nonusers, people who tried it but never used it, occasional user, frequent user), the multinomial analysis does not take advantage of the fact that in this variable, categories are ordered. This variable meets the definition of an ordinal variable, where there is rank ordering but no consistent intervals between groups.

In the social sciences, one of the most common applications of this model *should be* analysis of Likert-type scales, where responses are on a scale such as:

Table 12.10 Example Likert Scale

Value	Description
1	Strongly disagree
2	Disagree
3	Neutral
4	Agree
5	Strongly agree

Although these scales are often treated as ordinal variables, in reality we have no idea how much distance is between "strongly disagree" and "agree," and whether that is the same distance as between "neutral" and "agree." Another example of this type of scale is from the same National Health Interview Survey data we have been using for our diabetes analyses:

Table 12.11 In the Past 30 Days, How Often Have You Felt So Sad That Nothing Could Cheer You Up?

Value	Description
1	ALL the time
2	MOST of the time
3	SOME of the time
4	A LITTLE of the time
5	NONE of the time

There are several types of ordinal logit models, as discussed thoroughly in Menard (2010). Although there are interesting choices in the literature, it seems the most commonly implemented choice in the statistical software is the cumulative logit model. This ordinal logistic regression model essentially performs a series of cumulative binary logistic regressions comparing all groups below a particular threshold with all groups above a threshold. For example, with the marijuana variable, the first binary comparison would be group 0 versus all other groups (1, 2, 3). The next comparison would be groups 0 and 1 versus all other groups (2, 3). The third and final comparison would be groups 0, 1, and 2 versus 3. In this way, ordinal logistic regression provides three estimates for the effect that each independent variable has on the response. While this is interesting, because we are assuming that there is a continuous latent variable underlying the ordinal variable we are modeling, we would like to be able to summarize the model with a single set of parameter estimates that summarizes the effect of each predictor variable on the dependent variable. In order to do this, we must make two assumptions: that the dependent variable is *ordered* and that the relationship of each predictor is constant across all possible comparisons for the dependent variable.

Other options (e.g., the continuation ratio logit model, the adjacent category model) have slightly different assumptions about the nature of the data and answer slightly different questions. Because they are relatively rare compared to the cumulative logit model, I will focus on it in this chapter but encourage readers to explore other possibilities if their software supports those options.

ASSUMPTIONS OF THE ORDINAL OR ♦
PROPORTIONAL ODDS MODEL

One important assumption of this model is that the dependent variable is in order. In other words, like the marijuana example, increasing numbers indicate more of something. We do not know how much more of something, but it is more. If this basic assumption is not met, then multinomial (unordered) analyses are appropriate.

Another important assumption of this model is that of the "proportional odds" assumption, which states that the effects of any (and all) independent variables are the same regardless of what two groups are being compared. So, using our marijuana variable as a continuing example, the effect of student achievement on marijuana use should be the same when comparing groups 0 and 1 (nonusers vs. those who tried it 1–2 times) as when comparing groups 2 and 3 (used 3–19 times vs. used 20+), and when comparing groups 0 and 3. This assumption is important because, unlike multinomial logistic regression, the goal of ordinal logistic regression is to create a single estimate that predicts the probability of being in the next higher group as a function of a change in the independent variables (s) regardless of which group transition we are talking about. In essence, the ordinal logistic regression model is attempting to model the latent underlying continuous variable rather than a variable that has a series of groups or transitions.

Most statistical packages will test this assumption for you. In SAS, for example, this is called the "Score test for the proportional odds assumption" while in SPSS it is called the "test of parallel lines." Examples of these tests are presented in Table 12.12a and 12.12b. As you can see in Table 12.12a (see page 410), this test performed in SAS, predicting MJ from zACH and zSES (not the interaction) is not significant ($p < .14$), and thus we can conclude this analysis would meet the assumption. In Table 12.12b (see page 410), you can see that the SPSS test of parallel lines comes to a similar conclusion. One problem with this test is that it is very sensitive, especially in large samples where there are several predictors in the model. You have to be thoughtful, however. In Table 12.12c (see page 410), for example, is a significant test of parallel lines, but the chi-square is very small relative to the overall −2LL.

Is this a case where it is significant because of large sample size and power rather than it being an important deviation from parallel?

| Table 12.12a | Score Test for the Proportional Odds Assumption From SAS |

Chi-Square	df	Pr > ChiSq
3.4399	4	0.4871

Data Source: NELS88, National Center for Educational Statistics, U.S. Department of Education.

| Table 12.12b | Test of Parallel Lines from SPSS |

Model	−2 Log Likelihood	Chi-Square	df	Sig.
Null Hypothesis	20799.113			
General	20795.666	3.447	4	.486

The null hypothesis states that the location parameters (slope coefficients) are the same across response categories.

Data Source: NELS88, National Center for Educational Statistics, U.S. Department of Education.

| Table 12.12c | Test of Parallel Lines |

Model	−2 Log Likelihood	Chi-Square	df	Sig.
Null Hypothesis	17443.529			
General	17375.465	68.064	12	.000

The null hypothesis states that the location parameters (slope coefficients) are the same across response categories.

Data Source: NELS88, National Center for Educational Statistics, U.S. Department of Education.

The rest of the analysis is relatively straightforward if these assumptions are met. In this case, the effects of each binary comparison discussed earlier are averaged to provide a single parameter estimate for each independent variable.

INTERPRETING THE RESULTS OF THE ANALYSIS ♦

When these assumptions are met, we get the usual model fit statistics, tests of whether the added variables significantly improve model fit, and the parameter estimates. In this case, the −2LL is 20936.75 ($\chi^2_{(2)}$ = 127.93, $p <$ .0001). Thus, we know that the addition of zACH and zSES improves model fit (just as we saw in the multinomial analyses earlier in the chapter).

As you can see in Table 12.13, there are two pieces of information in the output: the intercepts for each increment and the averaged parameter estimates.[6] You can also see, as in previous analyses, zSES is not a significant predictor when zACH is in the model.

Table 12.13   Results of SAS Ordinal Logistic Regression Analysis

Analysis of Maximum Likelihood Estimates						
Parameter		df	Estimate	Standard Error	Wald Chi-Square	Pr > ChiSq
Intercept	4.00	1	−3.1312	0.0412	5772.0790	<.0001
Intercept	3.00	1	−2.1197	0.0267	6291.0865	<.0001
Intercept	2.00	1	−1.3825	0.0207	4467.3367	<.0001
zACH		1	−0.2184	0.0242	81.4431	<.0001
zSES		1	−0.0354	0.0241	2.1582	0.1418

Odds Ratio Estimates		
Effect	Point Estimate	95% Wald Confidence Limits
zACH	0.804	0.767	0.843
zSES	0.965	0.921	1.012

Data Source: NELS88, National Center for Educational Statistics, U.S. Department of Education.

---

[6] I routinely use the SAS command to analyze the data in "descending" order, as I have done throughout the book, which has the effect of giving estimates that are intuitive. Positive logits then mean increasing odds, and negative logits mean decreasing odds.

Interpreting the Intercepts

Keep in mind that in this analysis, the comparisons are not between one group and another group but rather between cumulative groups of groups. So, for example, the INTERCEPT for group 4 is the logit (log of the odds) for Marijuana = 20+ compared with all other groups when the predictors are estimated at 0 (in this case, because the continuous variables are z-scored, they are estimated at the mean). Converting the logits to probabilities, this particular logit corresponds to a probability of 0.042. This means that for a student with average achievement and coming from an average SES family, there is only a 4.2% chance that student would admit to using marijuana 20+ times over all other groups. Similarly, the Intercept for group 3 is the log of the odds of being in groups 3 or 4 versus 1 or 2 when all variables are 0. In this case, that equates to a 10.7% chance that a student who is average in achievement and SES will admit to trying marijuana either 3–19 or 20+ times compared with 0 or 1–2 times. Finally, the intercept for group 2 equates to a 20.1% chance that a student who is average in achievement and SES would admit to trying marijuana at all (1–2, 3–19, or 20+ times) versus never having tried it.

Interpreting the Parameter Estimates

Because zSES is not significant, we will not interpret those results at this point. However, the effect of zACH is −0.22, which means that as achievement increases one standard deviation, the probability that a student would be in the next higher group decreases (the odds ratio, estimated by SAS, is 0.804, which tells us the same information). In other words, as we saw in previous analyses, students with higher achievement test scores are less likely to be in the next highest level of marijuana use. Since the proportional odds assumption is met, this effect is uniform across all levels of the dependent variable. Using this information, we could convert these numbers to predicted conditional probabilities, as we have done with previous analyses, for the ease of the reader. Let us use the following equations to compare the predicted conditional probabilities for students at ± 1 standard deviation:

Contrast 1: Group 1 vs. 2, 3, 4 $\text{Logit}(\hat{Y}) = -1.3825 - 0.2184(\text{zACH})$

Contrast 2: Groups 1, 2 vs. 3, 4 $\text{Logit}(\hat{Y}) = -2.1197 - 0.2184(\text{zACH})$

Contrast 3: Groups 1, 2, 3 vs. 4 $\text{Logit}(\hat{Y}) = -3.1312 - 0.2184(\text{zACH})$

Figure 12.5 Ordinal Regression Results Graphed as Conditional Probabilities

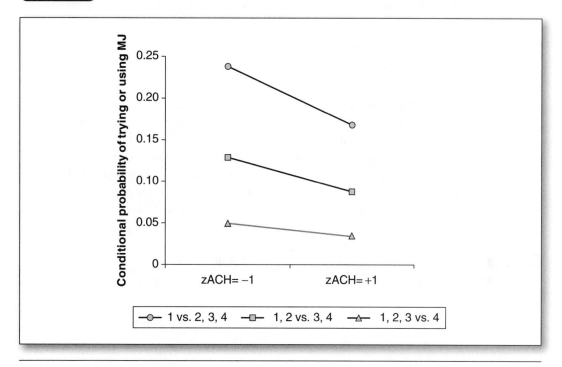

Data Source: NELS88, National Center for Educational Statistics, U.S. Department of Education.

Note that these results look similar to that of Figure 12.1, although the binary comparisons are different. In general, those with higher achievement have lower probabilities of trying marijuana, and students are more likely to admit to trying it at all than to having used it 20 or more times.

DATA CLEANING AND MORE ADVANCED ♦ MODELS IN ORDINAL LOGISTIC REGRESSION

As with multinomial logistic regression models, those desiring to perform data cleaning (and I hope by now that includes ALL of you) need to perform those data cleaning analyses by performing a series of binary logistic regression analyses, selecting the cases for analysis, and then performing the ordinal logistic regression analysis. In this case, you would constitute three models that compare the cumulative groups: 1 vs. 2, 3, and 4; 1 and

2 vs. 3 and 4; and 1, 2, and 3 vs. 4. Those cases that are inappropriately influential can be removed from the final analysis.

Why Not Just Use OLS Regression for This Type of Analysis?

If the latent variable underlying the dependent variable is truly continuous, why not use OLS regression predicting an imperfect outcome variable? The most obvious answer is that having data with nonequal intervals violates some of the most basic assumptions of OLS regression. Looking at the original data, we cannot assume that the difference between 0 and 1 is the same as between 1 and 2, or 2 and 3. Furthermore, the residuals are far from normally distributed, as you can see in Figure 12.6.

Figure 12.6 Residuals From an OLS Regression Predicting MJ From zACH and zSES

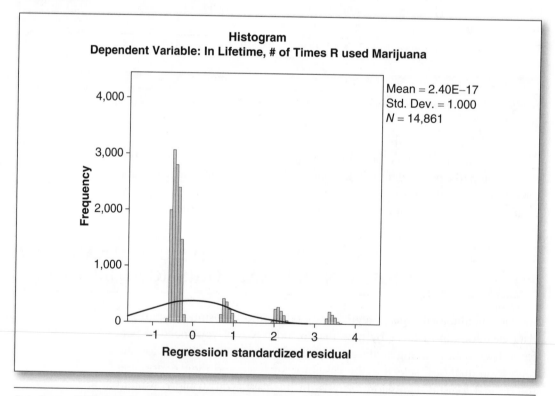

Data Source: NELS88, National Center for Educational Statistics, U.S. Department of Education.

SUMMARY AND CONCLUSIONS

Although less common than binary logistic regression, multinomial and ordinal logistic models are available in most commonly used statistical packages and are easily applied when appropriate. Further, they are more appropriate than models often used in the literature. For example, using OLS regression on Likert-type scales is questionable at best and unnecessary with the availability of ordinal logistic models. Further, simplistic analyses that some authors resort to (i.e., analysis of variance analyses rather than multinomial logistic regression) are limited, in that they have difficult assumptions to meet and cannot provide the same level of inference. They cannot, for example, easily compare several predictor variables and determine which is the most influential on the outcome, nor can they examine curvilinear or interaction effects on the outcome variable.

While I have explored simple interaction effects during the course of this chapter, as well as some simple curvilinear effects, there is no reason why you could not explore more complex effects, such as curvilinear interactions, in the context of either of these techniques. Performing the analyses and then disseminating the results is not substantially different than for binomial logistic regression; it merely requires a little more care and thought. Those of you who have mastered the material to this point are well-equipped to explore these types of effects within multinomial and ordinal models.

Note also that there are multinomial and ordinal probit models. Given mastery of Chapter 9, it is simple to generalize from multinomial or ordinal logit models to probit models.

ENRICHMENT

1. Download the NELS88 data used in the examples from the chapter and replicate the results.

2. Using the above NELS88 data, predict EDUCATIONAL PLANS (BYPSEPLN) from the same variables (zSES, zACH, zSES x zACH) to see if student achievement, family SES, and their interaction predict student educational plans.

   a. Educational plans is coded as follows:
      i. 1 = Won't finish high school
      ii. 2 = Will finish high school

iii. 3 = Vocational/trade school after high school

iv. 4 = Will attend college but may not finish

v. 5 = Will finish college

vi. 6 = Will seek higher degree college

b. Category 5, completion of college, is the largest group, and thus should be set as the reference group.

c. Graph the interactions for each group.

d. Test whether it is legitimate to combine the first two categories (won't finish high school and will finish high school) for this analysis.

e. Test whether this analysis would be appropriate for ordinal logistic regression (with just zSES and zACH in the model or with the two terms and the interaction). If so, perform an appropriate ordinal logistic regression analysis and interpret the results.

3. Using the following data subset from the book website—NHIS_SM in CH12 folder—predict the dependent variable SAD (in the past 30 days, how often have you been so sad that nothing could cheer you up) from SEX (0 = F, 1 = M), age, ER_use (number of emergency room visits last 12 months), and average hours of sleep a night.

a. Is an ordinal logistic regression analysis appropriate for these data? If so, interpret results.

b. If not, perform multinomial logistic regression analysis using the same independent variables and dependent variables.

ANSWER KEY

Enrichment #2: Multinomial Logistic Regression Without Data Cleaning

Without performing any data cleaning and setting category 5 as the comparison group, we get the following results: both zACH and zSES are significant, and the interaction accounts for a significant improvement in model fit once entered into the model (initial $-2LL = 69068.36$, $-2LL$ with only simple effects in the model $= 62378.27$, final $-2LL = 62048.72$, model fit improvement for addition of interaction is $\chi^2_{(5)} = 329.55$, $p < .0001$).

Enrichment Table 12.1	Parameter Estimates for Final Model Predicting Educational Plans From zACH, zSES, and Their Interaction

bypsepln[a]		B	Std. Error	Wald	df	Sig.	Exp(B)	95% CI for Exp(B)	
								Lower Bound	Upper Bound
1	Intercept	−4.472	.109	1685.909	1	.000			
	zACH	−1.388	.109	160.941	1	.000	.250	.201	.309
	zSES	−.396	.112	12.578	1	.000	.673	.540	.838
	INT	.451	.095	22.295	1	.000	1.569	1.301	1.892
2	Intercept	−2.165	.039	3058.425	1	.000			
	zACH	−1.067	.043	622.493	1	.000	.344	.316	.374
	zSES	−.919	.041	490.621	1	.000	.399	.368	.433
	INT	−.150	.043	12.341	1	.000	.861	.792	.936
3	Intercept	−1.832	.031	3554.738	1	.000			
	zACH	−.666	.035	365.162	1	.000	.514	.480	.550
	zSES	−.679	.034	393.467	1	.000	.507	.474	.542
	INT	−.172	.037	22.144	1	.000	.842	.783	.904
4	Intercept	−1.333	.024	3033.306	1	.000			
	zACH	−.567	.027	428.016	1	.000	.567	.538	.599
	zSES	−.443	.027	260.551	1	.000	.642	.609	.678
	INT	−.092	.029	9.952	1	.002	.913	.862	.966
6	Intercept	−.761	.019	1558.043	1	.000			
	zACH	.199	.021	93.132	1	.000	1.220	1.172	1.270
	zSES	.222	.021	111.569	1	.000	1.248	1.198	1.301
	INT	.278	.019	216.833	1	.000	1.321	1.273	1.370

a. The reference category is: 5.

In order to make sense of these analyses, I am going to graph each of the analyses. Calculations for each are presented in Enrichment Table 12.2 as they appeared in my spreadsheet:

Enrichment Table 12.2 Enrichment Interaction Between zACH and zSES

	zACH	zSES	int	y	exp	prob
< HS						
lo-lo	−2	−2	4	0.9	2.459603111	0.71095
lo-hi	−2	2	−4	−4.292	0.013677543	0.013493
hi-lo	2	−2	−4	−8.26	0.000258659	0.000259
hi-hi	2	2	4	−6.236	0.001957671	0.001954
HS						
lo-lo	−2	−2	4	1.207	3.343439274	0.769768
lo-hi	−2	2	−4	−1.269	0.281112594	0.219428
hi-lo	2	−2	−4	−1.861	0.155517036	0.134587
hi-hi	2	2	4	−6.737	0.0011862	0.001185
Voc/trade school						
lo-lo	−2	−2	4	0.17	1.185304851	0.542398
lo-hi	−2	2	−4	−1.17	0.310366941	0.236855
hi-lo	2	−2	−4	−1.118	0.326933007	0.246382
hi-hi	2	2	4	−5.21	0.005461674	0.005432
attend college						
lo-lo	−2	−2	4	0.322	1.379884776	0.579812
lo-hi	−2	2	−4	−0.714	0.489681549	0.328716
hi-lo	2	−2	−4	−1.21	0.298197279	0.229701
hi-hi	2	2	4	−3.718	0.024282484	0.023707
beyond college						
lo-lo	−2	−2	4	−0.491	0.612014074	0.379658
lo-hi	−2	2	−4	−1.827	0.160895531	0.138596
hi-lo	2	−2	−4	−1.919	0.146753642	0.127973
hi-hi	2	2	4	1.193	3.296957258	0.767277

Note that all graphs from this example have the same values on the X and Y axis so that readers can compare the graphs. Interpreting these

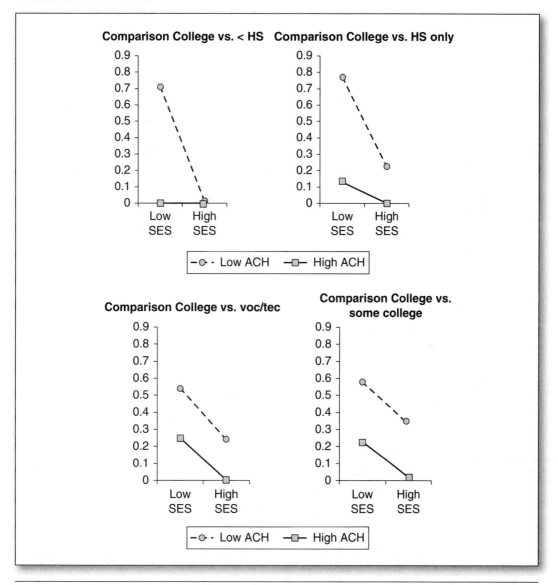

Enrichment Figure 12.1 Interaction of student achievement and family SES in predicting Educational Plans

(Continued)

Enrichment Figure 12.1 (Continued)

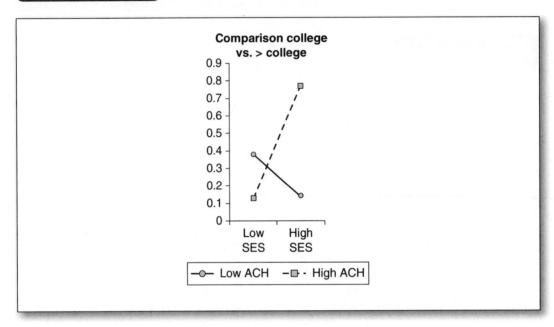

graphs and effects can be tricky, and care should be taken to walk the reader through each effect one step at a time. For example, let us take the first graph. In this graph, we are comparing the probability of planning to complete less than a high school education with the probability of planning to attend college. As you can see in the first graph, the probability of holding these educational aspirations is virtually nil except for those students who are both very low in achievement and very low in family SES. In the second graph, we see the probability of planning to complete only high school compared with aspiring to complete college. Again, for most groups the probabilities are relatively low except for those students who are both low in achievement and family SES. Those with either high achievement or high SES and low achievement are not likely to aspire to only complete high school.

The next two graphs are much weaker interactions. When examining plans to attend a vocational or technical school compared with aspiring to complete college, those with low achievement are more likely to plan on attending vocational or technical school than those with high achievement, and for both groups, increasing family income relates to decreasing probability of choosing vocational or technical school over college. A similar pattern is evident in the results comparing those planning to only attend (and not complete) college to those aspiring to complete college. Those with low achievement are more likely to have these plans than those with high achievement, and as family SES increases, the probability of holding these plans decreases (compared with those holding college aspirations).

Finally, examining the last graph that compares those with postcollege plans to those who have plans to complete college, we see effects of achievement are strongly influenced by family SES. Those students who are high achieving are much more likely to have these aspirations if they are from a relatively affluent family. Those high achieving students from relatively poor families have a very low probability of choosing to aspire to postcollege study compared with the probability of choosing to complete college. The converse is true for low-achieving students. Those who are low achieving and come from low-SES families are more likely to hold these aspirations than low-achieving students from high-SES families.

Data Cleaning

In order to examine whether there are inappropriately influential cases in these data, I performed five binary logistic regression analyses, comparing our reference group (5; complete college) with each of the other groups, requesting DfBetas. This produced four DfBetas for each analysis (constant, zACH, zSES, and interaction). To make interpretation easier, I converted all DfBetas to z-scores, and we can assume anything outside 3 standard deviations from the mean is suspect.

It would be space-prohibitive to present all 20 plots of the DfBetas, but some examples are given in Enrichment Figure 12.2.

As you can see, there are some inappropriately influential cases, although most tend to be in nonreference groups.

To clean these data, I used the following SPSS syntax. First, I recoded system missing values to 0, which allowed me to use relatively simple filters without worrying about cases being dropped because they were not part of a particular analysis.

```
recode ZDFB0_1 ZDFB0_2 ZDFB0_3 ZDFB0_4 ZDFB0_5
ZDFB1_1 ZDFB1_2 ZDFB1_3 ZDFB1_4 ZDFB1_5
ZDFB2_1 ZDFB2_2 ZDFB2_3 ZDFB2_4 ZDFB2_5 (sysmis=0).
EXECUTE.
```

Enrichment Figure 12.2 DfBetas for Constant

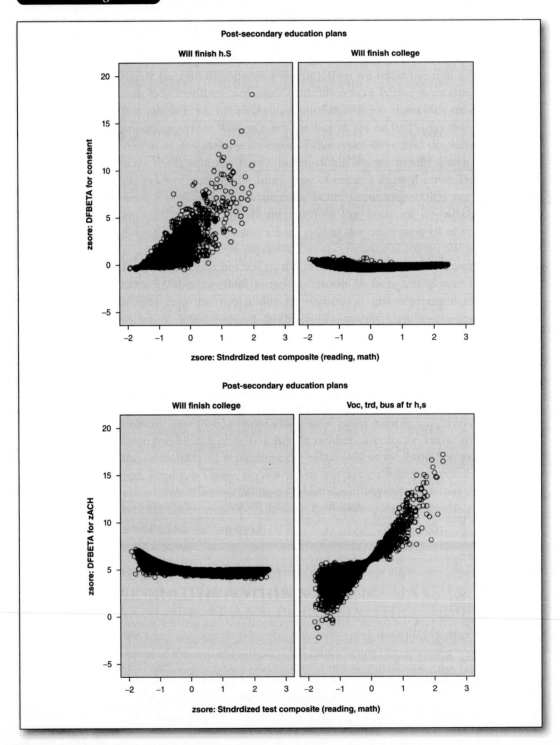

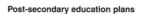

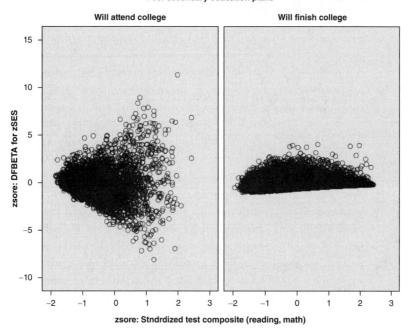

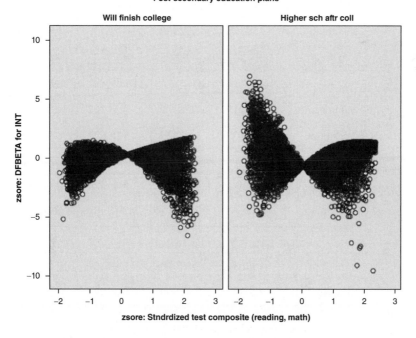

| Enrichment Table 12.3 | Summary of DfBetas for All Binary Logistic Regression Analyses |

	zDFB0_1	zDFB0_2	zDFB0_3	zDFB0_4	zDFB0_5
Minimum	−2.26627	−.52566	−1.22138	−1.81929	−1.04278
Maximum	25.85881	18.03237	7.40833	4.71656	5.14454
	zDFB1_1	zDFB1_2	zDFB1_3	zDFB1_4	zDFB1_5
Minimum	−15.14047	−7.14844	−7.27462	−5.59419	−3.66932
Maximum	30.46738	22.57966	12.00603	8.87391	8.68413
	zDFB2_1	zDFB2_2	zDFB2_3	zDFB2_4	zDFB2_5
Minimum	−21.68414	−9.33824	−11.19161	−8.05034	−5.59302
Maximum	39.24935	25.21509	13.16202	11.31604	5.11768
	zDFB3_1	zDFB3_2	zDFB3_3	zDFB3_4	zDFB3_5
Minimum	−15.00193	−10.88407	−12.61938	−8.76473	−9.46579
Maximum	44.76237	29.60064	15.60661	17.55145	6.93952

Following data cleaning

	zDFB0_1	zDFB0_2	zDFB0_3	zDFB0_4	zDFB0_5
Minimum	−2.26627	−.52566	−1.22138	−1.81929	−1.04278
Maximum	4.90123	4.97815	4.99787	4.50116	4.89982
	zDFB1_1	zDFB1_2	zDFB1_3	zDFB1_4	zDFB1_5
Minimum	−4.91711	−4.96779	−4.57702	−4.95869	−3.66932
Maximum	2.76112	5.07309	5.96691	8.53570	8.68413
	zDFB2_1	zDFB2_2	zDFB2_3	zDFB2_4	zDFB2_5
Minimum	−4.89493	−4.94571	−4.92617	−4.96836	−4.97576
Maximum	4.88741	6.27634	7.12755	4.99265	5.11768
	zDFB3_1	zDFB3_2	zDFB3_3	zDFB3_4	zDFB3_5
Minimum	−7.38803	−7.57060	−5.67781	−7.04069	−9.46579
Maximum	4.73032	5.41098	6.48680	6.36940	6.93952

Then, based on the data in Enrichment Table 12.3, I decided to be relatively conservative and filter all DfBetas that are 5 *SD* away from the mean. You can see, for example, in the first row of DfBetas that there are none below −5, but there are cases above 5, so there is no need to include syntax filtering out those cases below −5 as there are none. Taking this step tends to get rid of most cases with any DfBetas that are in the positive extreme of the distribution.

```
USE ALL.
COMPUTE filter_$=((ZDFB0_1 < 5 and ZDFB0_2 < 5 and
ZDFB0_3 < 5 and ZDFB0_4 <5 and ZDFB0_5< 5) and
(ZDFB1_1 > -5 and ZDFB1_2 > -5 and ZDFB1_3> -5 and
ZDFB1_4 >-5 and ZDFB1_5> -5) and
(ZDFB2_1 > -5 and ZDFB2_2 > -5 and ZDFB2_3> -5 and
ZDFB2_4 >-5 and zdfb2_4 < 5 and ZDFB2_5> -5)).
FILTER BY filter_$.
```

As you can see in Enrichment Table 12.3, performing this selective, conservative filtering eliminates most of the most egregiously influential cases without eliminating too many cases. In this example, only 450 cases were removed from the analysis. This judicious data cleaning has the effect of strengthening some of the effects observed prior to data cleaning. For example, entry of the interaction into the model previously improved model fit $\chi^2_{(5)} = 329.55$, $p < .0001$, whereas after data cleaning entry of the interaction is $\chi^2_{(5)} = 370.63$, $p < .0001$.

Further, parameter estimates seem a bit stronger, as Enrichment Table 12.4 shows:

Enrichment Table 12.4 Parameter Estimates Following Data Cleaning

bypsepln[a]	B	Std. Error	Wald	df	Sig.	Exp(B)	95% CI for Exp(B) Lower Bound	Upper Bound
Intercept	−6.527	.320	416.275	1	.000			
zACH	−2.626	.272	93.091	1	.000	.072	.042	.123
zSES	−.593	.285	4.336	1	.037	.553	.316	.966
INT	.478	.226	4.468	1	.035	1.613	1.035	2.514

(Continued)

Enrichment Table 12.4 (Continued)

bypsepln[a]		B	Std. Error	Wald	df	Sig.	Exp(B)	95% CI for Exp(B)	
								Lower Bound	Upper Bound
2	Intercept	−2.585	.053	2412.662	1	.000			
	zACH	−1.482	.055	725.552	1	.000	.227	.204	.253
	zSES	−1.149	.054	460.948	1	.000	.317	.285	.352
	INT	−.358	.054	44.029	1	.000	.699	.629	.777
3	Intercept	−1.999	.035	3353.148	1	.000			
	zACH	−.864	.040	478.370	1	.000	.421	.390	.455
	zSES	−.766	.039	379.706	1	.000	.465	.431	.502
	INT	−.261	.042	37.905	1	.000	.770	.709	.837
4	Intercept	−1.377	.025	3062.098	1	.000			
	zACH	−.632	.029	483.648	1	.000	.531	.502	.562
	zSES	−.489	.029	284.567	1	.000	.613	.579	.649
	INT	−.142	.031	20.659	1	.000	.867	.816	.922
6	Intercept	−.766	.019	1573.958	1	.000			
	zACH	.197	.021	88.725	1	.000	1.218	1.169	1.269
	zSES	.230	.021	117.149	1	.000	1.259	1.207	1.312
	INT	.283	.019	218.313	1	.000	1.328	1.279	1.378

a. The reference category is: 5.

The effects of this data cleaning, aside from strengthening some of the parameter estimates, are subtle. In large part, if you examine the graphs below, there are three main differences: the probability of low achieving, low income students not planning on graduating high school (compared with attending college) is higher, and the estimates for the low-achieving, high-SES students increased for some of the least ambitious outcomes (completing high school only, for example). It makes sense that very low-achieving students should be most likely to have these least ambitious aspirations, despite having relatively high family SES. Note that I have taken care to keep all graphs on the same Y axis range (0.00 to 0.90) so that graphs are visually comparable both before and after data cleaning.

| Enrichment Figure 12.3 | Interaction of student achievement and family SES in predicting Educational Plans |

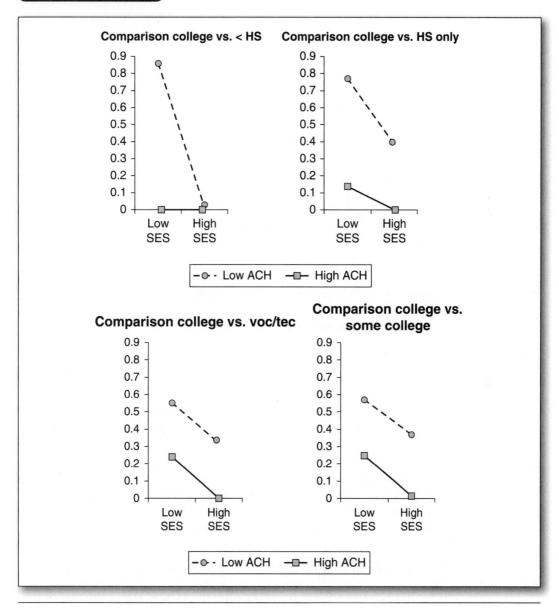

Enrichment Figure 12.3 (Continued)

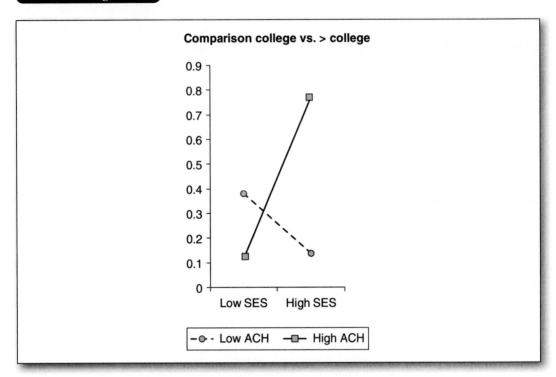

Can We Combine the First Two Categories?

Following the recommended procedure, I combined the first two categories, leaving College Completion (formerly category 5, now category 4) as the comparison group. Following data cleaning, the original analysis had $-2LL = 58526.38$ with 15 *df.* Using the same data except with the first two categories combined, the $-2LL = 57307.57$ with 12 *df.* This is a difference of $\chi^2_{(3)} = 1218.31$, $p < .0001$. This implies that it is not legitimate to combine these two categories.

The alternate analysis I suggested at the end of the chapter (performing binary logistic regression analyses comparing only the two categories) produced a significant result as well ($\chi^2_{(3)} = 173.92$, $p < .0001$). Thus, neither analysis supports combining these two groups.

Is Ordinal Logistic Regression Appropriate for These Data?

In both cases (with or without the interaction term), the test of parallel slopes (or proportional odds) yields a significant chi square, and thus it is not appropriate to model these variables using ordinal logistic regression.

Enrichment #3: Predicting SADNESS via Ordinal Regression

This analysis is a bit of a challenge just to decide whether the ordinal logit model is appropriate. Before any data cleaning, the test for parallel lines is significant, but relatively small (as alluded to earlier in the chapter):

Enrichment Table 12.5 Test of Parallel Lines[a]

Model	−2 Log Likelihood	Chi-Square	df	Sig.
Null Hypothesis	17443.529			
General	17375.465	68.064	12	.000

The null hypothesis states that the location parameters (slope coefficients) are the same across response categories.

a. Link function: Logit.

It is clearly significant, meaning the assumption of proportional odds or parallel slopes is violated. However, the violation is so minor compared to the overall model fit, one is left to wonder if this is merely a significant effect due to the large sample size. Cleaning the data does little to improve the situation. My efforts at using DfBetas or standardized residuals failed to lead to a nonsignificant test. If you are of the mind that this is a minor violation driven by sample size rather than truly non-parallel lines then the rest of the analysis is relatively straightforward:

Enrichment Table 12.6 Model Fitting Information

Model	−2 Log Likelihood	Chi-Square	df	Sig.
Intercept Only	18474.371			
Final	17443.529	1030.842	4	.000

Link function: Logit.

The change in −2LL is significant, as are all the predictors in the model. Specifically, as Age increases, there is a small increase in the odds of increasing sadness for every year of age, and a larger effect for every time an individual has visited the emergency room in the past 12 months. Males are less likely to report increased sadness, and individuals getting more sleep are less likely to report increased sadness. Note that because all those variables were measured on a meaningful metric, I left them in their original state, although it would have been acceptable to convert to z-scores. Note also that these results are presented without data cleaning:

Enrichment Table 12.7 Parameter Estimates

		Estimate	Std. Error	Wald	df	Sig.	95% CI	
							Lower Bound	Upper Bound
Threshold	[SAD = 1.00]	.335	.080	17.383	1	.000	.177	.492
	[SAD = 2.00]	1.274	.081	248.224	1	.000	1.116	1.433
	[SAD = 3.00]	2.676	.085	989.320	1	.000	2.509	2.843
	[SAD = 4.00]	3.933	.098	1613.627	1	.000	3.741	4.125
Location	Age	.002	.001	8.969	1	.003	.001	.004
	ER_use	.381	.014	726.961	1	.000	.353	.408
	SEX	−.381	.028	185.674	1	.000	−.436	−.326
	SLEEP	−.105	.010	109.742	1	.000	−.124	−.085

Link function: Logit.

If you are conservative and decide that the assumption of parallel lines or proportional odds is not met, then performing a multinomial logistic regression is appropriate. Without cleaning the data, the multinomial logistic regression (using "NONE" as the reference group) shows a similarly strong change in −2LL:

Enrichment Table 12.8 Model Fitting Information

Model	Model Fitting Criteria	Likelihood Ratio Tests		
	−2 Log Likelihood	Chi-Square	*df*	Sig.
Intercept Only	18474.371			
Final	17352.156	1122.216	16	.000

Enrichment Table 12.9 Parameter Estimates

SAD[a]		B	Std. Error	Wald	*df*	Sig.	Exp(B)	95% CI for Exp(B)	
								Lower Bound	Upper Bound
2.00 a little	Intercept	−1.039	.106	96.899	1	.000			
	Age	−.002	.001	3.100	1	.078	.998	.996	1.000
	ER_use	.259	.021	151.933	1	.000	1.295	1.243	1.350
	SEX	−.368	.036	102.091	1	.000	.692	.644	.743
	SLEEP	−.063	.013	23.302	1	.000	.939	.915	.963
3.00 some	Intercept	−1.578	.123	163.566	1	.000			
	Age	.003	.001	8.732	1	.003	1.003	1.001	1.006
	ER_use	.450	.021	478.475	1	.000	1.568	1.506	1.632
	SEX	−.417	.044	89.304	1	.000	.659	.604	.719
	SLEEP	−.092	.015	35.704	1	.000	.912	.885	.940
4.00 a lot	Intercept	−2.562	.218	137.554	1	.000			
	Age	.007	.002	11.758	1	.001	1.007	1.003	1.012
	ER_use	.530	.029	328.011	1	.000	1.699	1.605	1.800

(Continued)

Enrichment Table 12.9 (Continued)

SAD[a]		B	Std. Error	Wald	df	Sig.	Exp(B)	95% CI for Exp(B)	
								Lower Bound	Upper Bound
	SEX	−.447	.081	30.526	1	.000	.639	.546	.749
	SLEEP	−.169	.027	38.006	1	.000	.845	.801	.891
5.00 all the time	Intercept	−2.691	.328	67.212	1	.000			
	Age	.014	.003	19.186	1	.000	1.015	1.008	1.021
	ER_use	.558	.040	192.393	1	.000	1.747	1.615	1.890
	SEX	−.294	.122	5.869	1	.015	.745	.587	.945
	SLEEP	−.344	.042	67.592	1	.000	.709	.653	.770

a. The reference category is: 1.00 none.

These results mirror the ordinal results. Age is a weak predictor but gets slightly stronger as the contrast becomes more extreme (not significant for categories 1 vs. 2 but highly significant for 1 vs. 5). Similarly, ER use becomes stronger, as does SLEEP. Sex differences vary slightly across the different comparisons. So while the conclusions are largely the same (i.e., males have lower odds of being in higher categories of sadness, increasing age tends to lead to increases odds of being in higher categories, ER use also increases the odds of being in higher categories, and sleep tends to lead to lower odds of increased sadness), you can see why the assumption of parallel lines was difficult to meet.

SYNTAX EXAMPLES

SPSS Syntax From the Chapter for Filtering Out Influential Cases From the Results of Binary Logistic Regression

```
DESCRIPTIVES VARIABLES=DFB0_1 DFB0_2 DFB0_3 DFB1_1
DFB1_2 DFB1_3 DFB2_1 DFB2_2 DFB2_3 DFB3_1 DFB3_2 DFB3_3
 /SAVE
 /STATISTICS=MEAN STDDEV MIN MAX.
```

```
  recode ZDFB0_1 ZDFB0_2 ZDFB0_3 ZDFB1_1 ZDFB1_2 ZDFB1_3
ZDFB2_1 ZDFB2_2 ZDFB2_3 ZDFB3_1 ZDFB3_2 ZDFB3_3
  (sysmis=0).
  execute.
  USE ALL.
  COMPUTE filter_$=((ZDFB0_1 < 6 and ZDFB0_2 < 6 and
ZDFB0_3 < 6 ) and
  (ZDFB1_1 < 6 and ZDFB1_2 < 6 and ZDFB1_3 < 6 and
ZDFB1_1 >-6 and ZDFB1_2 >-6 and ZDFB1_3 >-6) and
  ( ZDFB2_1 < 6 and ZDFB2_2 < 6 and ZDFB2_3 < 6 and
ZDFB2_1 >-6 and ZDFB2_2 >-6 and ZDFB2_3 >-6) and
  ( ZDFB3_1 < 6 and ZDFB3_2 < 6 and ZDFB3_3 < 6)).
  FILTER BY filter_$.
```

SAS Syntax for Ordinal Logistic Regression[7]

```
proc logistic data = BOOK.ch12b descending;
model MJsas = zACH zSES ;
run;
```

REFERENCE

Menard, S. W. (2010). *Logistic regression: From introductory concepts to advanced concepts and applications*. Thousand Oaks, CA: Sage.

---

[7]For some reason, SAS did not like the original MJ variable coded 0–3 and misordered the variable when imported from SPSS data. Thus, I created MJSAS, recoding 0–3 to be 1–4.

13

MULTILEVEL MODELING WITH LOGISTIC REGRESSION

No Child Left Behind (NCLB) was an initiative within the United States to attempt to improve the educational system—particularly to ensure that lower performing students are brought up to standards that are considered at least minimally acceptable. Although there is great controversy over whether it was a good idea or a poor idea and whether it was helpful or harmful, one policy was to evaluate whether schools were being successful (and, by proxy, whether teachers were being successful) by evaluating student achievement. This has long been a central question and a central conflict within the culture and community of researchers—that is, how best to measure the effects of schools and teachers on students. It makes sense, from a simple, commonsense perspective, that teachers (and schools) matter. That is why many parents pay close attention to the schools in their area when choosing where to live—and why many are willing to pay thousands of dollars a year to send their child to private school when they deem the public schools lacking.

I will not attempt to answer the questions raised by NCLB (and the community of researchers and policymakers who think about it for a living). Instead, let us appreciate that the central questions asked are multilevel questions—does a teacher in a classroom have an effect on the students within the class (and if so, is it the same effect for every student)? Do schools really influence those within their walls in some way? While researchers have been attempting to answer these questions for decades, it is only recently, with the widespread use of multilevel modeling (also called hierarchical linear modeling [HLM]) that we can more appropriately test and answer these questions. In this chapter, we will briefly explore how logistic regression is adapted to HLM to examine binary (or multinomial) outcomes within a multilevel framework.

Multilevel modeling (often also called HLM) is gaining broad acceptance in the social sciences as a powerful tool. It is conceptually relatively straightforward to generalize ordinary least squares or logistic or probit regression questions to an HLM framework. The difference between OLS, logistic, or probit regression and HLM is that HLM appropriately models nested or multilevel data, whereas the other regression techniques generally do not without explicitly managing the complex nature of the data.

HLM also lets us ask more interesting questions. For example, if we track student growth over an academic year, or patient outcomes over a specific period of time, we can ask not only what teacher or physician characteristics generally produce the better outcome for which individuals (which is confounded with what sort of students or patients come through the door) but what teacher or physician characteristics are generally predictive of the *slope or rate of change,* since we can model slopes (growth curves too) for each group of students/patients. Since much of our data exists within organizational structures such as schools, hospitals, communities, or other types of organizations, and at different levels, HLM is often an appropriate choice for analysis. Importantly, if data are not nested, using HLM will provide accurate estimates of effects, leaving us with little disincentive to consider using this procedure. The generalization of HLM to binary logistic regression is also relatively straightforward. In this chapter, we will briefly explore what HLM is and how it can be an important tool in your statistical toolbox, and then we will explore how logistic regression works within HLM.[1]

♦ WHAT IS HLM?

What Is a Hierarchical Data Structure?

People (and most living creatures, for that matter) tend to exist within organizational structures, such as families, schools, business organizations, churches, towns, states, tribes, or geographic regions. In education, students exist within a hierarchical social structure that can include family, peer group, classroom, grade level, school, school district, state, and country. Workers exist within production or skill units, businesses, and sectors of the economy, as well as geographic regions. Health care workers and patients exist within households and families,

---

[1]Portions of this chapter are drawn from previously published works (Osborne, 2000, 2008).

medical practices and facilities (a doctor's practice, or hospital, e.g.), counties, states, and countries. Many other communities exhibit hierarchical data structures as well.

Raudenbush and Bryk (2002) also discuss two other types of data hierarchies that are less obvious but equally important and well-served by HLM: repeated-measures data and meta-analytic data. In this case, we can think of repeated measures as data that are nested or clustered within individuals, and meta-analytic data similarly involves clusters of data or subjects nested within studies.

Once one begins looking for hierarchies in data, it becomes obvious that data repeatedly gathered on an individual are hierarchical, as all the observations are nested within individuals. While there are ways of adequately dealing with nested and partially nested data in analysis of variance paradigms that have existed for decades, they are often not easily or effectively used. Further, the assumptions relating to them are challenging, whereas procedures relating to hierarchical modeling require fewer assumptions that are easily met. In fact, HLM uses maximum likelihood estimation, similar to logistic regression, and thus you are already familiar with many of the differences between OLS regression and HLM regression.

The Issue With Nested Data

Hierarchical, or nested, data present several problems for researchers wanting to use traditional analysis techniques (like logistic regression). First, individuals that exist within hierarchies tend to be more similar to each other than individuals randomly sampled from the entire population. For example, students in a particular third-grade classroom are more similar to each other than to students randomly sampled from the population of third graders as a whole. This is because (in many countries) students are not randomly assigned to classrooms from the population, but rather are assigned to schools based on geographic factors or other characteristics (e.g., aptitude). When assigned based on geography or proximity, students within a particular classroom tend to come from a community or community segment that is more homogeneous in terms of morals and values, family background, socioeconomic status, race or ethnicity, religion, and even educational preparation than a similar-sized group randomly sampled from the entire population as a whole. When assigned based on similarity in other characteristics, students are obviously more homogenous than a random sample of the entire population. Further, regardless of similarity or dissimilarity of background, students within a particular classroom share the experience of being in the same environment—the same teacher, physical environment, curriculum, and similar experiences, which may increase homogeneity over time.

The problem of independence of observations

This discussion could be applied to any level of nesting, such as the family, the school district, health care facilities, county, state, or even countries. Based on this discussion, we can assert that individuals who are drawn from a group, such as a classroom, school, business, town or city, or health care unit, will be more homogeneous than if individuals were randomly sampled from a larger population. This is often referred to as a *design effect*.

Because these individuals tend to share certain characteristics (environmental, background, experiential, demographic, or otherwise), observations based on these individuals are not fully independent, yet most statistical techniques require independence of observations as a primary assumption for the analysis. Because this assumption is often violated in the presence of hierarchical or nested data, most parametric statistical procedures produce standard errors that are too small (unless these so-called design effects are incorporated into the analysis). In turn, this leads to a misestimation of the statistical tests, which can lead to Type I errors.

The problem of how to deal with cross-level data

It is often the case in educational research that a researcher is interested in understanding how environmental variables (e.g., teaching style, teacher behaviors, class size, class composition, district policies or funding, or even state or national variables) affect individual outcomes (e.g., achievement, attitudes, retention). But given that outcomes are gathered at the individual level, and other variables at classroom, school, district, state, or nation level, the question arises as to what the unit of analysis should be and how to deal with the cross-level nature of the data.

One strategy (called disaggregation) has been to assign classroom or teacher (or other group-level) characteristics to all students (i.e., to bring the higher level variables down to the student level). The problem with this approach is that all students within a particular classroom assume identical scores on a variable, clearly violating assumptions of independence of observation.

Another way to deal with this issue (called aggregation) has been to aggregate data up to the level of the classroom, school, district, and so on. Thus, we could talk about the effect of teacher or classroom characteristics on average classroom/school/school district achievement. However, there are several drawbacks or problems with this approach, including that (a) much (up to 80–90%) of the individual variability on the outcome variable is lost, which can lead to dramatic under- or overestimation of observed relationships between variables (Raudenbush & Bryk, 2002) and (b) the outcome variable changes significantly and substantively from individual achievement to average classroom achievement (for more on this issue, and an example analysis comparing these two strategies with a true HLM analysis, see Osborne, 2000). Aggregation also prevents us from asking interesting questions such as "Which students benefit most from intervention X?"

Neither of these strategies constitutes a best practice, although they have been commonly found in many fields of research. A third approach, that of HLM, becomes necessary in this age of educational accountability and more sophisticated hypotheses.

How Do Hierarchical Models Work? A Brief Primer

The goal of this chapter is to introduce the concept of hierarchical modeling and explicate the need for the procedure. It cannot fully communicate the nuances and procedures needed to actually perform a hierarchical analysis. The reader is encouraged to refer to Raudenbush and Bryk (2002) and the other suggested readings for a full explanation of the conceptual and methodological details of HLM. To make this concrete, let us take an example from the NELS88 data (National Education Longitudinal Study of 1988, from the National Center for Educational Statistics; Ingels, 1994). In these data, a large national sample of eighth graders were followed longitudinally over time on hundreds of variables. We will explore predictors of whether a student drops out before completing their high school diploma (12th grade in the United States). Thus, our independent variable is DROPOUT (1 = yes, 0 = no). We will also select the following student variables: BYACH (eighth-grade composite achievement test score), BYSES (family socioeconomic status [SES]), and EVER_MJ (whether the student has ever admitted to trying marijuana). Because this is an HLM example, we will also include one school-level variable: %LUNCH (the percent of students in the school who are eligible for free or reduced-price lunch, an indicator of poverty in the United States). Thus, the question we can ask is whether school environment is a separate predictor of student dropout above that of student-level variables such as family SES, achievement, and so forth. Similar to simple logistic regression, when performing

HLM with a binary outcome, the dependent variable is the log of the odds of DROPOUT, denoted η_{ij}.

The basic concept behind HLM is similar to that of logistic regression as we have discussed it throughout the book to this point. On the base level (usually the individual level referred to here as level 1, the most granular level of your data), the analysis is familiar to anyone familiar with regression analyses: an outcome variable is predicted as a function of a linear combination of one or more level-1 variables, plus an intercept, as so:

$$Y_{ij} = \beta_{0j} + \beta_{1j}X_1 + \ldots + \beta_{kj}X_k + r_{ij}$$

where β_{0j} represents the intercept of group j, β_{1j} represents the slope of variable X_1 of group j, and r_{ij} represents the residual for individual i within group j. Adapting our equation to our example, our level-1 equation will look something like this:

$$\eta_{ij} = \beta_{0j} + \beta_{1j}*(zBYACH_{ij}) + \beta_{2j}*(zBYSES_{ij}) + \beta_{3j}*(EVER\_MJ_{ij}) + r_{ij}$$

Note that following best practices discussed earlier in the book, continuous predictor variables are converted to z-scores. The novelty of HLM becomes more evident in the next step. HLM then estimates a level-2 equation where we enter the higher level variables, which in this case is the school-level variable %LUNCH. In level-2 equations, the level-1 slope(s) and intercept become dependent variables being predicted from a certain number (*m)* of level-2 variables:

$$\beta_{0j} = \gamma_{00} + \gamma_{01} W_1 + \ldots + \gamma_{0m} W_m + u_{0j}$$
$$\beta_{1j} = \gamma_{10} + \gamma_{11} W_1 + \ldots + \gamma_{1m} W_m + u_{1j}$$

$$\ldots$$

$$\beta_{kj} = \gamma_{k0} + \gamma_{k1} W_1 + \ldots + \gamma_{km} W_m + u_{kj}$$

and so forth, where γ_{00}, γ_{10}, to γ_{k0} are intercepts, and γ_{01} and γ_{11} to γ_{1m} represent slopes predicting β_{0j} and β_{1j} to β_{kj}, respectively, from variable W_1 and from all other variables. Note that there will be a level-2 equation, as shown earlier, for each level-1 parameter estimated (intercept, slope of each predictor at level 1). Going back to our example, our level-2 equations would look like this:

$$\beta_{0j} = \gamma_{00} + \gamma_{01}*(z\%LUNCH_j) + u_{0j}$$
$$\beta_{1j} = \gamma_{10} + \gamma_{11}*(z\%LUNCH_j) + u_{1j}$$

$$\beta_{2j} = \gamma_{20} + \gamma_{21}*(z\%LUNCH_j) + u_{2j}$$

$$\beta_{3j} = \gamma_{30} + \gamma_{31}*(z\%LUNCH_j) + u_{3j}$$

These two sets of equations can then be combined to achieve the final single equation that will be estimated (u_{1j} to u_{3j} were left out of the equation for technical reasons beyond the scope of this chapter):

$$\eta_{ij} = \gamma_{00} + \gamma_{01}*z\%LUNCH_j + \gamma_{10}*zBYACH_{ij} + \gamma_{11}*z\%LUNCH_j*zBYACH_{ij} +$$
$$\gamma_{20}*zBYSES_{ij} + \gamma_{21}*z\%LUNCH_j*zBYSES_{ij} + \gamma_{30}*EVER\_MJ_{ij} +$$
$$\gamma_{31}*z\%LUNCH_j*EVER\_MJ_{ij} + u_{0j}$$

Through this process, we accurately model the effects of level-1 variables on the outcome and the effects of level-2 variables on the outcome. In addition, as we are predicting slopes as well as intercepts (means), we can model cross-level interactions, whereby we can attempt to understand what explains differences in the relationship between level-1 variables and the outcome.

We will follow this example through the rest of this chapter.

A Brief Note About HLM and Statistical Software

Modern statistical software is often capable of performing HLM-type analyses, and additionally there are standalone software packages that specialize in this type of analysis. SPSS, SAS, R, and other statistical packages have various strengths and weaknesses in performing HLM-type analyses. I personally use HLM software that was developed with Bryk and Raudenbush as collaborators, primarily because that is the software I learned to use back when HLM was being introduced before SPSS and SAS and other packages routinely made it accessible. It is relatively simple to use with the graphical user interface and easily imports and exports SPSS, SAS, STATA, and other types of data files. The analyses presented in this chapter should be possible in almost any HLM-capable software package, however. If you wish to explore HLM, there is a free "student" download available from Scientific Software International (http://www.ssicentral.com/hlm/student.html) that is capable of analyzing this example as well as the other examples at the end of the chapter.

Residuals in HLM

Those of you more mathematically inclined will also note that several different error terms (i.e., r and u terms) are computed in this process, rather than just a simple residual present in the types of analyses we have been familiar with. Each of these residuals is similar to the residuals we have seen in logistic regression. However, in this case we get two different types of residuals. In HLM we also get two different data files containing the residuals from each level. Of particular interest in the level-1 data file we get unstandardized level-1 residuals and other metrics of influence and leverage (depending on which software package you are using). If you are using HLM, you may want to refer to Raudenbush and Bryk (2002) and the HLM user manual for more detailed information about what each data file contains. In the example we are discussing, there were some hugely influential data points, one with a residual 12 standard deviations outside the normal range of residuals.

In HLM, the level-2 residual file presents Mahalanobis distance (MDIST) as a measure of influence for the residuals. MDIST is a common multivariate indicator of leverage or influence that ranges from 0 to ∞. Generally cases with MDIST over 4 may be considered suspect, with increasingly large MDIST values relating to increasingly suspect cases. I generally clean the level-1 data file of unacceptably influential data points and then re-run the analysis before looking at level-2 residuals. Of course, other indices of leverage/influence, when available, are also appropriate for this purpose.

Logits, Odds Ratios, Conditional Odds, Conditional Probabilities, and Relative Risk in HLM

Predicted values, odds ratios, and probabilities work the same way in HLM as they do in most other logistic regression analyses, and as we discussed in Chapter 2. You will get a logistic regression coefficient that represents the relationship to the dependent variable, significance tests, odds ratios, and 95% confidence intervals for the odds ratios.

As in logistic regression, the odds ratios are simply calculated as

$$\text{Odds ratio of } \eta_{ij} = \text{Exp}[\eta_{ij}]$$

One nice thing about logistic regression analyses in HLM is that, similar to single-level logistic regression analyses, you get output for the intercept, and this table is more likely to be published in its entirety in journal articles (at least in my observations) than non-HLM logistic regression. That means that, should you want, you can decompose the odds ratios to conditional odds, conditional probabilities, and then compute relative risk as we did in Chapter 2 if you chose to have fun with that sort of thing. Obviously, when the data are your own, this is less of an issue as you can always produce the numbers you need to do this. When the data are others', and published in journals, it is important to have the intercept included in the results for this to occur. Again, this is somewhat useful as relative risk tends to reduce the apparent exaggeration of effects that odds ratios tend to produce in certain circumstances.

Results of DROPOUT Analysis in HLM

Results of our HLM analyses are presented in Table 13.1.[2] As you can see in the following tables, the results are similar to the type of output you would see in a simple logistic regression analysis. The logistic regression coefficients are in the first column. In HLM, with all variables appropriately centered

Table 13.1 Results of DROPOUT Analyses in HLM

Fixed Effect	Coefficient	Standard error	t-ratio	Approx. df	p-value	Odds Ratio	Confidence Interval
For INTRCPT1, β_0							
INTRCPT2, γ_{00}	−5.483036	0.168747	−32.493	195	<0.001	0.004157	(0.003,0.006)
z%LUNCH, γ_{01}	1.630046	0.211962	7.690	195	<0.001	5.104110	(3.360,7.754)
For zBYACH slope, β_1							
INTRCPT2, γ_{10}	−1.776596	0.175515	−10.122	1968	<0.001	0.169213	(0.120,0.239)
z%LUNCH, γ_{11}	−0.016114	0.233401	−0.069	1968	0.945	0.984015	(0.622,1.556)
For zBYSES slope, β_2							
INTRCPT2, γ_{20}	−1.034264	0.129101	−8.011	1968	<0.001	0.355488	(0.276,0.458)
z%LUNCH, γ_{21}	0.504195	0.152356	3.309	1968	<0.001	1.655652	(1.228,2.232)
For EVER_MJ slope, β_3							
INTRCPT2, γ_{30}	0.726309	0.271777	2.672	1968	0.008	2.067436	(1.213,3.524)
z%LUNCH, γ_{31}	−0.135861	0.246234	−0.552	1968	0.581	0.872964	(0.538,1.415)

Data Source: NELS88, National Center for Educational Statistics, U.S. Department of Education.

[2]Note that these data are a random subsample of cases from the full NELS88 data and are not weighted appropriately to reflect the complex sampling. Thus, as with all other examples in this book, you should not interpret these results substantively, but rather use them *solely* as an example of binary logistic regression analysis in HLM.

(which allows us to interpret the intercept as the mean, since the mean is 0), we interpret γ_{00} as the overall intercept or grand mean. The second line is the effect of %LUNCH (z-scored) on dropout. As you can see from the coefficient, as %LUNCH increases, the odds of dropping out increases as well (coefficient = 1.63). The odds ratio for %LUNCH (exp [1.63]) is 5.10, as you can see in the Odds Ratio column, with a corresponding CI of 3.36–7.75. This is interpreted identically to a simple logistic regression odds ratio—that as you increase %LUNCH one standard deviation (increasing school level poverty), the odds of a student dropping are 5.10 times that of a student in a school one standard deviation lower in %LUNCH.

The next section of the output deals with zBYACH, the eighth-grade student achievement composite. The intercept (γ_{10}) represents the average effect of zBYACH—which is −1.78. In other words, the odds of dropping out decrease as student achievement increases. This is not surprising. The corresponding odds ratio (0.17, CI: 0.12–0.24) is interpreted similarly to that of %LUNCH. As a student increases one standard deviation in achievement test scores, the odds that student will drop out are .17 that of a student one standard deviation lower in achievement. The next line is the effect of %LUNCH on zBYACH—in other words, testing whether there is an interaction between achievement and school poverty. It is not significant, indicating there is no moderating effect of poverty on the effect of achievement.

Similarly, we can interpret the next sections relating to SES and marijuana use. The effect of zBYSES on DROPOUT (γ_{20}) is significant, and negative. This indicates that as family SES increases, the odds of a student dropping out decreases. Below that is the effect of %LUNCH on SES, and it is significant. Let us come back to this interaction after discussing the effect of EVER_MJ, marijuana use. The effect of marijuana use (γ_{30}) is significant, and positive, indicating that (after controlling for all other variables) students who admit to using marijuana are more likely to drop out than those not admitting to using. The odds ratio for this variable indicates that for those who admit to using marijuana, the odds of dropping out are approximately twice that of those who do not admit to having used marijuana. And there is no significant interaction with %LUNCH for this variable.

Note also that as with simple logistic regression, all effects in the model are unique, indicating that all other variables are controlled for, and the difference between this analysis and other analyses is that the school-level variable is appropriately modeled and the data nesting is accounted for.

Cross-Level Interactions in HLM Logistic Regression

Recall that there is a significant interaction between %LUNCH and zBYSES—between school environment and family environment. I prefer to graph out results such as this, as I have described and demonstrated in previous chapters. Because all continuous variables are converted to z-scores prior to analysis, we can form the regression equation from the coefficients in the output, substituting the mean (0) for variables that are not relevant to this interaction (zBYSES, z%LUNCH, and the interaction between the two).

For our analysis, we could constitute the equation to graph the interaction from the output, using the intercept (γ_{00}) and coefficients presented in Table 13.1. For this example, the equation becomes:

$$\hat{\eta}_{ij} = \gamma_{00} + \gamma_{01}*z\%LUNCH_j + \gamma_{20}*zBYSES_{ij} + \gamma_{21}*z\%LUNCH_j*zBYSES_{ij}$$

by substituting values for gammas, we get:

$$\hat{\eta}_{ij} = -5.95 + 1.76*z\%LUNCH_j + -1.13*zBYSES_{ij} + 0.55*z\%LUNCH_j*zBYSES_{ij}$$

Following the procedure I have suggested in previous chapters for graphing interactions, we would substitute a relatively low score

Figure 13.1 Interaction Between %Free or Reduced-Price Lunch and Family SES

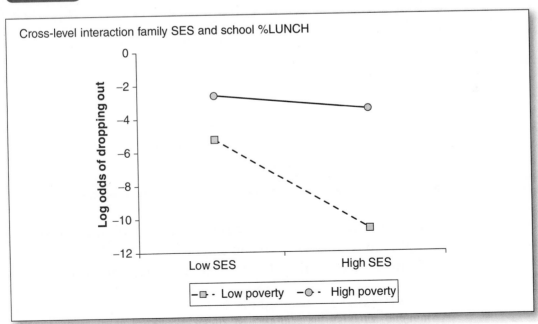

(−1.5, to keep the estimates conservative and reasonable) for percent free or reduced-price lunch (school poverty) and family SES. I used 1.5 to represent high scores on each variable as well.

As Figure 13.1 (see page 445) shows, when graphed in logits, those in high-poverty schools have higher odds of dropping out than lower poverty schools, and as family SES increases, odds of dropout decreases, but primarily for those in low-poverty schools. As you can see in Figure 13.2, however, the conclusion is largely the reverse when graphed as probabilities rather than logits. Specifically, controlling for all other variables in the equation, those in low-poverty schools tend to have a very low probability of dropping out regardless of family SES, while those in high-poverty schools are much more affected by family SES.

Figure 13.2 Interaction Between %LUNCH and Family SES Graphed in Probability

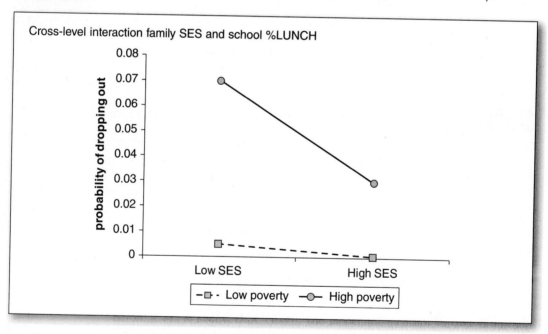

So What Would Have Happened If These Data Had Been Analyzed via Simple Logistic Regression Without Accounting for the Nested Data Structure?

In Table 13.2, I analyzed the data using the strategy of disaggregation, which is a common (although not recommended) practice when

Table 13.2 Inappropriately Disaggregated Analysis

	B	SE	Wald	df	Sig.	Exp(B)	95% CI for Exp(B)	
							Lower	Upper
ever_mj	.511	.505	1.021	1	.312	1.667	.619	4.489
zBYACH	−2.402	.417	33.229	1	.000	.090	.040	.205
zBYSES	−1.371	.316	18.877	1	.000	.254	.137	.471
z%LUNCH	2.273	.457	24.708	1	.000	9.706	3.961	23.780
zBYSES by z%LUNCH	.567	.242	5.501	1	.019	1.763	1.098	2.832
zBYACH by z%LUNCH	.039	.328	.014	1	.906	1.039	.547	1.975
ever_mj by z%LUNCH	.208	.406	.261	1	.609	1.231	.555	2.729
Constant	−7.291	.707	106.249	1	.000	.001		

Data Source: NELS88, National Center for Educational Statistics, U.S. Department of Education.

dealing with nested data. As you can see in Table 13.2, these results are not a complete departure from the appropriately modeled analysis (although I have seen some that are). However, there are some important differences. For example, the intercept itself is altered substantially from the appropriate HLM analysis. The interactions and effects are generally concordant whether they are significant or not, although the effect of EVER_MJ is misestimated—in this case it is not significant when it should be significant. Further, the effect of %LUNCH is misestimated—the correct odds ratio of 5.83 is inflated to 9.70, a 66% inflation of the effect because of the mishandling of the data. Similarly, the effect of zBYACH is overestimated—an odds ratio of 0.09 versus 0.14 in the appropriately modeled analysis. This may not sound like a large difference, but if you take the inverse of each, this analysis is the equivalent of an OR of 11.11 versus 6.94—again, a substantial overestimation. SES is similarly overestimated as well.

This is not intended to be representative of the effect of nesting and inappropriate disaggregation, but it does show the potential for disaggregation and inappropriately modeling nested data for causing serious misestimation of effects. As you can see from Figure 13.3 (see page 448), which represents the same interaction effect resulting from the disaggregated analysis, the interaction is less pronounced.

Figure 13.3 Same Interaction Resulting From the Inappropriate Analysis Where %LUNCH Was Disaggregated to the Student Level

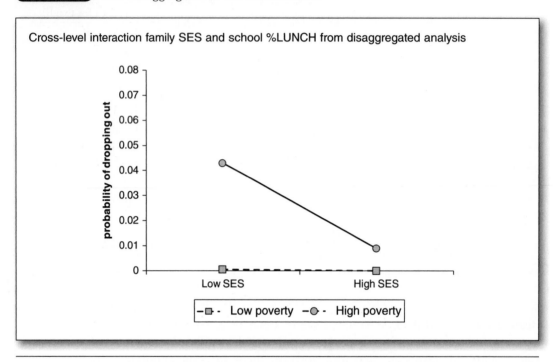

Cross-level interaction family SES and school %LUNCH from disaggregated analysis

Data Source: NELS88, National Center for Educational Statistics, U.S. Department of Education.

SUMMARY

This is a brief and altogether inadequate introduction to logistic regression via HLM if you have never performed an HLM analysis. It is likely that this could be expanded to an entire book on all the possibilities and quirks of this type of analysis, including curvilinear effects and interactions, multinomial outcomes, and so on. However, the goal of this chapter was to encourage those of you who are not yet trained in HLM to seek out that training so that you might take advantage of that beneficial methodology. Perhaps if the Fates smile on me, I will have an opportunity to expand this chapter in the next version of this book!

ENRICHMENT

1. Using the data downloaded from the book website (www.sagepub .com/osbornebplr), replicate the results presented above.

2. On the website, I have another example HLM analysis you can perform using the freely downloaded student HLM software or your own favorite statistical software.

REFERENCES

Ingels, S. (1994). *National Education Longitudinal Study of 1988: Second follow-up: Student component data file user's manual.* Washington, DC: U.S. Department of Education, Office of Educational Research and Improvement, National Center for Education Statistics.

Osborne, J. W. (2000). Advantages of hierarchical linear modeling. *Practical Assessment, Research & Evaluation, 7*(1).

Osborne, J. W. (2008). A brief introduction to hierarchical linear modeling. In J. W. Osborne (Ed.), *Best practices in quantitative methods* (pp. 445–450). Thousand Oaks, CA: Sage.

Author Index

Subject Index

⑤SAGE research**methods**

The essential online tool for researchers from the world's leading methods publisher

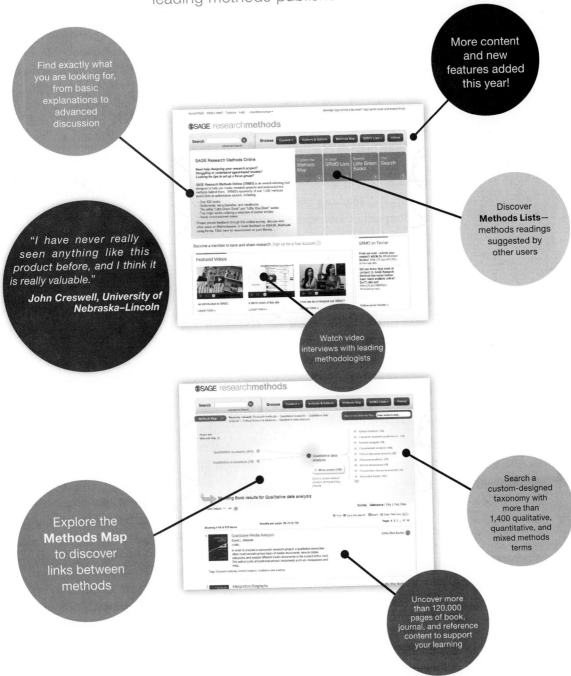

Find exactly what you are looking for, from basic explanations to advanced discussion

More content and new features added this year!

Discover **Methods Lists**— methods readings suggested by other users

"*I have never really seen anything like this product before, and I think it is really valuable.*"
John Creswell, University of Nebraska–Lincoln

Watch video interviews with leading methodologists

Explore the **Methods Map** to discover links between methods

Search a custom-designed taxonomy with more than 1,400 qualitative, quantitative, and mixed methods terms

Uncover more than 120,000 pages of book, journal, and reference content to support your learning

Find out more at
www.sageresearchmethods.com